D1528179

The Twilight of
British Ascendancy
in the Middle East

Also by Daniel Silverfarb

■ ■ ■

Britain's Informal Empire in the Middle East:
A Case Study of Iraq, 1929-1941

The Twilight of British Ascendancy in the Middle East

A Case Study of Iraq, 1941–1950

Daniel Silverfarb

ST. MARTIN'S PRESS
NEW YORK

First published in the United States of America 1994
Printed in the United States of America

ISBN 0-312-12090-7

The maps on pages xii and xiii are taken from Daniel Silverfarb's
*Britain's Informal Service in the Middle East: A Case Study of Iraq,
1929–1941* and are reproduced courtesy of Oxford University Press.

Library of Congress Cataloging-in-Publication Data

Silverfarb, Daniel, 1943-
    The twilight of British ascendancy in the Middle East : a case
study of Iraq, 1941-1950 / Daniel Silverfarb.
        p. cm.
      ISBN 0-312-12090-7
    1. Great Britain—Foreign relations—Iraq. 2. Iraq—History—
Hashemite Kingdom, 1921-1958. 3. Great Britian—Foreign
relations—1936-1945. 4. Great Britain—Foreign relations—1945-
5. Iraq—Foreign relations—Great Britain.
DA47.9.I72S56 1994
327.410567'09'044—dc20   93-49550
                                                              CIP

Interior design by Digital Type & Design

To my parents,
Louis and Dora Silverfarb

Contents

PREFACE

This work is an account of Anglo-Iraqi relations from Britain's reconquest of Iraq in 1941 until the end of the immediate post–Second World War period in 1950. In particular, it shows how Britain reasserted its dominant position in Iraq during the war and attempted to maintain this position after the conflict when, under the pressure of nationalist sentiment in Iraq and manpower and financial constraints at home, and in accordance with its treaty obligations, it had withdrawn all of its ground troops. It is thus a study of the possibilities and limitations of indirect rule. It is also a description of an important episode in the fairly rapid disintegration of British hegemony in the Middle East after the war. Finally, it is the story of how the ruling class of a recently independent Arab nation struggled to free itself from the lingering grip of a major European power while still preserving sufficiently close ties with that power to ensure its external security and internal control.

I stopped my account in 1950 before the new situation in the Middle East created by the growth of American interest in Iraq, the rise of Nasser in Egypt, the formation of the Baghdad Pact, and the Suez War. I hope to continue the story until the revolution of 1958 in another volume.

This work is based primarily on unpublished British documents located at the Public Record Office in London. The Foreign Office files were the most valuable, although for various chapters other collections were essential. For example, much of the material in chapter 2 on oil and other denial plans and operations is in War Office and Air Ministry files, and much of the material in chapter 4 on the Kurdish uprisings is in Baghdad embassy files. Supplementing the British material, State Department papers in the published *Foreign Relations of the United States* series and the unpublished collections at the National Archives in Washington were useful. Iraqi archives on this period are not open to researchers. Partially compensating for this loss, both the British and American archives contain a fair amount of official and unofficial Iraqi material.

All quotations from documents at the Public Record Office appear by permission of the Controller of Her Majesty's Stationary Office.

The two maps in this book are taken from my previous work entitled *Britain's Informal Empire in the Middle East: A Case Study of Iraq, 1929-1941* (New York: Oxford University Press, 1986) and are reprinted with the kind permission of Oxford University Press. The one entitled "Syria and Iraq Mid-1941" was originally adapted from a Crown copyright map held in the Public Record Office. The sketch map of Kuwait was originally drawn by Ms. Pat Kattenhorn of the India Office Library and Records, to whom I would like again to express my gratitude.

For reading my manuscript and offering useful suggestions I would like to thank Professor Robert Koehl of the University of Wisconsin, Professor Aviel Roshwald of Georgetown University, and Dr. Michael Van Vleck. Needless to say, any errors or shortcomings in this work are solely my own responsibility.

NOTE ON CURRENCY

During the period of this study the Iraqi dinar (ID) was linked to the British pound and had the same value. It could be freely exchanged for the pound.

Unlike the British pound, which was subdivided into twenty shillings and 240 pence, the Iraqi dinar was subdivided into 1,000 fils.

Both the British pound and the Iraqi dinar were worth $4.03. After devaluation in September 1949 their value became $2.80.

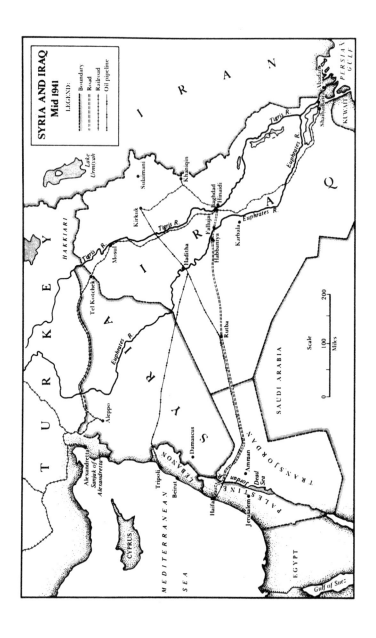

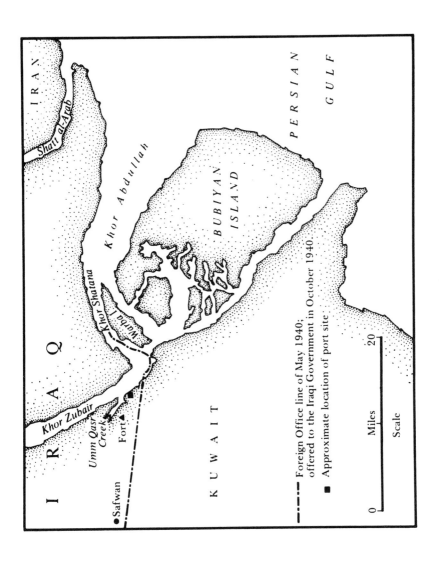

IRAN

Shatt al-Arab

Khor Abdullah

PERSIAN

GULF

BUBIYAN ISLAND

IRAQ

Khor Shatana

Wadi al Bat'ha

Khor Zubair

Umm Qasr Creek

Fort

Safwan

KUWAIT

- · — · Foreign Office line of May 1940;
  offered to the Iraqi Government in October 1940.

■ Approximate location of port site

0   Miles   20

Scale

Introduction

In 1941 Iraq had about 5 million inhabitants. The population was divided into various groups of which, roughly, Shiite Arabs constituted 51 percent; Sunni Arabs 20 percent; Kurds, nearly all of whom were Sunni, 19 percent; and Turks, Iranians, Christians, Jews, and Yazidis 10 percent. About one-third of the population lived in urban areas, primarily in Baghdad, Basra, and Mosul, the three largest cities.[1]

The Iraqi government was a constitutional monarchy with a two-house Parliament based on the British model. However, it was dominated by a small group of wealthy landowners and businessmen, primarily Sunni Arabs, who in rotation occupied the major cabinet positions and regularly rigged elections to maintain power.[2]

Iraq had been in the British sphere of influence since the First World War when Britain seized the area from the Ottoman Empire.[3] Initially Britain controlled Iraq under the terms of a League of Nations mandate. In 1932 Britain granted Iraq independence but kept a considerable degree of influence under the terms of a treaty between the two countries concluded in 1930.[4] Indicating the extent of this influence, the treaty permitted Britain to maintain two air bases in Iraq and move its military forces across the country. It also stipulated that Iraq would use British subjects whenever it needed foreign experts, employ the services of a British military mission, send its military personnel to British military academies whenever they needed further training, and purchase virtually all of its military equipment in Britain.

In addition to the provisions of the treaty, Britain's position in Iraq was secured by the fact that the regent, Prince Abd al-Ilah, who reigned in the stead of the boy king Faysal II, was strongly pro-British. Most of the leading politicians were also pro-British, or at least willing to accept the treaty and work closely with Britain.

Thus in the spring of 1941, at the beginning of our story, one and one-half years into the Second World War, Iraq appeared to be firmly in the British camp. However, in early April the Iraqi army, under the control of four colonels known collectively as the Golden Square, revolted and forced the regent to flee the country. They then installed Rashid Ali al-Gaylani, a leading politician of anti-British persuasion, as prime minister, though they retained the real authority.

Rashid Ali and the Golden Square were determined to side with Germany because they wanted to break Britain's hold on Iraq and assert their country's unfettered independence. They also believed that a German alliance would help them end British rule in Palestine and French rule in Syria, and unite the Arab lands of the Fertile Crescent into a single state under Iraqi leadership. In addition, they thought that Germany was going to win the war, and that it would be advisable to ingratiate themselves with the victor as soon as possible. In April 1941 their belief in the likelihood of German victory increased because during that month the Germans evicted the British from Libya (except for Tobruk) and Greece.

Aside from these German successes, Rashid Ali and the Golden Square were encouraged by the fact that, with the exception of 1,250 Iraqis whom the British had recruited into a military force known as the levies to guard their air bases, the British had only air force personnel stationed in Iraq and no ground troops. Iraq, by contrast, had 46,000 troops 12,000 police, and large numbers of former soldiers who were familiar with the use of firearms. Thus, apart from any help that Iraq might receive from Germany, the balance of power appeared to favor Iraq.

Against the background of these events, in early April 1941 British leaders decided to send a battalion of British troops by air from India to the British air base at Shaiba in southern Iraq, and three brigades of Indian troops by sea to the port of Basra. In large measure this decision was motivated by the desire to establish a secure base at Basra for assembling military aircraft shipped directly from the United States for the use of British forces in the Middle East. If enemy action forced the closure of the Suez Canal, the British could also use such a base to supply their forces in Egypt and Palestine, and the important neutral nation of Turkey. If Rashid Ali moved Iraq into the Axis camp, a base at Basra would serve the further purpose of helping Britain gain control of the rich oil field in northern Iraq and pipelines to the Mediterranean, or at least deny these assets to Germany. Finally, the British believed that a base at Basra would encourage pro-Allied sentiment in Iran, and if necessary enable them to defend the valuable oil fields and refinery in the southwestern part of that country.

For Britain Basra was a desirable location for all of these purposes because it had a large modern port that the British themselves had built during the First World War. The port was so spacious that seven ocean going vessels could unload simultaneously at its wharves, while at the same time five more big ships could unload in midstream onto smaller craft for which ample additional wharf space was available. From Basra a railway proceeded northward to Baghdad and then onward through Mosul to Syria and Turkey, while a branchline connected Baghdad with the oil fields around Kirkuk. For Britain Basra was a desirable location also because it had a modern civil airport and a British seaplane base with onshore maintenance facilities, while the British air base at Shaiba was only twelve miles away.

On 17 April 1941 the first elements of the British battalion arrived by air at Shaiba, and the following day the first of the Indian brigades docked at Basra. These developments alarmed Rashid Ali and the Golden Square because a large British force in southern Iraq could be used to threaten and possibly overthrow their government. Consequently, they now informed Sir Kinahan Cornwallis, the British ambassador, that the troops at Basra must immediately pass through Iraq to Palestine, that no more troops could land at Basra until the first lot had left Iraq, that at no time could there be more than one brigade of British or Imperial troops in Iraq, that all troop movements through Iraq must be in small contingents, and that in the future reasonable advance notice must be given before the arrival of troops.

Iraqi leaders believed that they were legally entitled to make these demands because the Treaty of 1930 did not explicitly state that Britain was permitted on its own initiative to station troops in Iraq even in wartime. In the opinion of Rashid Ali, the only possible justification for Britain's action was article 5 of the treaty, as modified by a letter from the British high commissioner in Iraq to the Iraqi prime minister on 15 July 1930, which allowed Britain, in an emergency and after prior consultation with the Iraqi government, to send troops temporarily to reinforce the British air bases. But Rashid Ali was convinced that article 5 did not apply in this case because the British government was now demanding the right to maintain troops at Basra in unlimited numbers for an unlimited period of time without prior consultation or permission.

The British would not accept any of the restrictions that Rashid Ali attempted to place on their use of Iraqi territory. They believed that their position at Basra was fully covered by article 4 of the treaty which stipulated that "should . . . either of the high contracting parties become engaged in war, the other high contracting party will . . . immediately come to his aid in the capacity of an ally," and which specified that "the aid of His Majesty the King of Iraq in the event of war or the imminent menace of war will consist in furnishing to His

Britannic Majesty on Iraq territory all facilities and assistance in his power, including the use of railways, rivers, ports, aerodromes and means of communication." In their opinion, the phrase "all facilities and assistance in his power" was especially relevant because it was certainly in Iraq's power to allow Britain to establish a base at Basra. They also laid particular emphasis on the word *including*, which they believed implied that the assistance that Iraq was obligated to provide did not consist merely or exclusively of "the use of railways, rivers, ports, aerodromes and means of communication." Finally, the British would not accept Rashid Ali's demand that reasonable advance notice should be given before the arrival of additional troops because they were unwilling to trust the Iraqi government, which they knew was hostile and in constant contact with the Axis powers, with vital information regarding the movement of British troopships.

Because the treaty was imprecise and open to divergent interpretations, honorable men could sincerely differ on the question of whether Britain was legally entitled to establish a base at Basra. However, neither Britain nor Iraq suggested recourse to arbitration or judicial settlement because the dispute between them was not primarily of a legal nature. For military reasons owing to the eastward extension of the war and the German victories in Libya and Greece, in April 1941 the British were determined to establish a base at Basra, by force if necessary, regardless of the treaty position. Similarly, Rashid Ali and the leading army officers were determined to prevent the establishment of such a base, regardless of the treaty position, because they considered it derogatory to national sovereignty, a threat to the existence of their government, and even a menace to their personal safety.

In spite of growing Iraqi anger and suspicion, the Indian brigade remained at Basra. Because of the strained atmosphere in Iraq and the general deterioration of Britain's strategic position in the eastern Mediterranean in April 1941 as a result of the German victories in Libya and Greece, British officials in Iraq became alarmed about the possibility of an attack by German paratroopers on the lightly defended British air base at Habbaniya, fifty-five miles west of Baghdad. In addition to fears for the safety of the garrison, they were concerned that if Habbaniya fell German planes based there or at Baghdad could bomb the British forces at Basra and Shaiba. Consequently, after giving notification one day in advance, on 24 April the British military authorities in Iraq began transporting the troops from the British battalion at Shaiba by air to Habbaniya. This move further angered Rashid Ali because the treaty stated that Britain could reinforce its air bases with ground troops only after consultation with the Iraqi government, and because British troops at Habbaniya would be well-situated to march rapidly on Baghdad.

On 28 April Cornwallis informed the Iraqi government that three troopships would soon arrive at Basra. These ships carried ancillary formations and various types of equipment for the Indian brigade already at Basra. Because none of the original contingent had passed through Iraq on the way to Palestine, Rashid Ali refused permission for the additional troops to land. If the British government proceeded anyway, he threatened to broadcast a denunciation of the action. In this tense situation, with the very real possibility of mob action against British civilians, Cornwallis ordered the immediate evacuation of all British women and children from Iraq.

On the following day, 29 April, the British troopships docked at Basra and began to disembark. Iraqi leaders may have feared that this move, which was taken against their express wishes and was coupled with the evacuation of British women and children, would be followed by bombing raids on Baghdad from the British air base at Habbaniya. Their apprehension in this regard was probably increased by a reconnaissance flight over Baghdad by a British plane based at Habbaniya. In any event, the Iraqi government now began to mass forces around Habbaniya that soon numbered about nine thousand troops and fifty artillery pieces, plus light tanks and armored cars.

Acting on instructions from Baghdad, on 30 April the commander of the Iraqi military forces at Habbaniya threatened to attack any aircraft, vehicle, or person that attempted to leave the base. Now, for the first time, war between the two countries became virtually inevitable. Probably the leading army officers, who dominated the government and controlled most of Rashid Ali's actions, had long believed that eventually they would have to challenge Britain in order to achieve their goal of eliminating British influence in Iraq and liberating Palestine and Syria from colonial rule. They chose this particular moment because they were angered and frightened by the continual buildup of British troops at Basra. Influenced by the recent German victories in Libya and Greece, and encouraged by Axis pledges of support, they thought that Germany would immediately come to their assistance in the event of hostilities. Iraqi leaders were probably also emboldened by an awareness of Habbaniya's weak defenses—aside from 1,300 air force personnel it had only 350 British ground troops recently flown up from Shaiba, 800 native levies, eighteen armored cars, two antiquated artillery pieces, no tanks, and no fortifications beyond a fence designed to keep out wild animals and marauding bedouin—and believed that they could score an impressive victory. At the least they thought that they could hold out until German help arrived.

The British authorities in Iraq immediately demanded that Rashid Ali withdraw his forces from the vicinity of Habbaniya. He refused but said that he would take no hostile action provided that Britain did likewise. This assurance was not good enough for British leaders. They feared that the Iraqi troops would soon begin to shell Habbaniya and thereby destroy or at least immobilize the British aircraft at the base. They were also concerned that given time Germany would send military forces through Turkey or Syria to aid Rashid Ali. In addition, British leaders, and especially Cornwallis, were resolved to seize the opportunity presented by this provocative action to overthrow Rashid Ali's regime, restore the regent to power, and place a friendly government in office in Baghdad. Consequently, without warning and without first issuing an ultimatum, on 2 May 1941 British aircraft from Habbaniya attacked the Iraqi troops surrounding the base. The Iraqi forces immediately retaliated by bombarding Habbaniya. In this manner Britain and Iraq went to war.

After four days of intensive fighting, on 6 May the British forces at Habbaniya compelled the Iraqi troops besieging the base to withdraw from the vicinity. Twelve days later the garrison at Habbaniya was reinforced by 2,000 British troops from Palestine and British-led Arab troops from Transjordan. In early May the garrison was also reinforced by several hundred Indian troops flown up from Shaiba. (The Iraqi artillery around Habbaniya was never able to prevent flight operations from the base.) This combined force then moved rapidly eastward, defeating the Iraqi army in several engagements. Simultaneously, the Royal Air Force rendered ineffectual the intervention of two squadrons of German aircraft flying from an Iraqi base at Mosul. On 30 May, only four weeks after the start of hostilities, two British columns totalling about 1,400 men approached the outskirts of Baghdad. This force had only eight field guns, ten armored cars, and no tanks, and its supply line was dependent upon vulnerable ferries crossing badly flooded terrain. (The Iraqis had opened the banks of the Euphrates in order to impede the advance of the British forces.) But at this point the most important Iraqi leaders fled to Iran, and the remaining ones sued for an armistice.

The British were now confronted with the task of reestablishing a compliant government in Iraq and defending the country against German attack. They also had to prepare Iraq's oil installations and transportation facilities for demolition in the event that they were compelled to withdraw from the area. And so it is to these matters that we must now direct our attention.

THE SECOND WORLD WAR
AND THE PERIOD OF
MAXIMUM BRITISH INFLUENCE
1941–45

.1.

The Defense of Iraq

We have observed that the British moved into Iraq in May 1941 largely because they perceived a serious German threat to that country and the Middle East generally. After 22 June 1941 this perception diminished somewhat because most of Germany's forces were now occupied in the Soviet Union. Nonetheless, the British were still concerned because until the end of 1942 they feared that the Soviet Union might collapse, and that Germany would then have significant strength for an attack on Iraq from the Caucasus in the northeast. During this period they also feared that by massing troops in Thrace Germany might be able to bludgeon Turkey into admitting German forces for an attack on Iraq from the northwest. Indicating the extent of the threat that they envisaged, in July 1941 British commanders believed that by September 1941 Germany could operate three armored divisions against Iraq.[1] In September 1941 they believed that by April 1942 they might be confronted with a simultaneous German attack by ten divisions from the Caucasus and nine divisions from Turkey.[2] In February 1942 they believed that by July 1942 they might be confronted with a simultaneous German attack from the Caucasus and Turkey supported by one thousand aircraft.[3] In September 1942 they believed that preparatory to an attack on Iraq German forces might enter northern Iran at any time after 15 November 1942.[4] And in October 1942 they believed that in the spring of 1943 they might be confronted with a German attack on Iraq by five divisions from the Caucasus.[5]

The British were determined to resist a German attack because Iraq's rich oil field at Kirkuk supplied vitally needed crude oil via a pipeline to Haifa in Palestine. All of this oil, amounting to about 800,000 tons per year, was treated at a refinery at Haifa, and most of it was then used to supply the British fleet in the Mediterranean.[6]

Control of Iraq also enabled Britain to defend the major oil field in southwestern Iran and the large refinery at Abadan. This field produced about 10 million tons of oil per year, all of which was treated at Abadan. For Britain Abadan was particularly significant because, unlike the refinery at Haifa, it produced large quantities of aviation spirit. Thus while Iraqi oil was important for the conduct of British military operations in the Middle East, Iranian oil was essential.[7]

Control of Iraq had the further advantage of providing Britain with air bases from which to bomb the Soviet oil fields near Baku in the event that Germany conquered that area. For the British this was an important consideration because they gave a high priority to denying Germany access to oil.[8]

Aside from oil, the British were determined to defend Iraq because it was a vital link in their Imperial communications. For example, Iraq enabled them rapidly to shift troops between Egypt and Iran to counter the most urgent threat. It also enabled them to move troops from India to Egypt without transitting the Suez Canal, an important consideration because that waterway might be blocked by enemy action. For the British Iraq had the further advantage of enabling them to supply their forces in Palestine in the event that they were compelled to withdraw from Egypt. And, of course, it occupied a key position on their air route to India and onward to the Far East.[9]

In addition to oil and communications, the British wanted to hold Iraq because it enabled them to send vitally needed supplies to the Soviet Union. Although most Allied supplies to the Soviet Union from the Middle East went entirely through Iran, the capacity of that country's ports, railways, and roads was severely limited. Consequently, in May 1942 the British began using Iraq as a supplementary route. These supplies landed at Basra and were then moved by rail, barge, and road to Baghdad. At that point they were moved by rail to Khanaqin near the Iranian border, and then by road to northern Iran where they were handed over to the Soviets.[10]

The importance of the Persian Gulf route as a whole is illustrated by the fact that in the summer of 1943 it carried 170,000 tons of supplies to the Soviet Union per month, and in the summer of 1944 this figure increased to 290,000 tons per month. And the importance of Basra in particular is illustrated by the fact that from May 1942 until May 1943 it was one of only four ports in the Persian Gulf used for this purpose, and after May 1943 it was one of only three.[11]

For Britain control of Iraq also provided an important and secure supply route to Turkey. Although Turkey was a neutral power and there-

:ore did not have the same high priority as the Soviet Union, the British wanted to provide assistance to dissuade it from joining the Axis camp.[12]

To oppose a German attack the British brought substantial forces to Iraq. For example, in September 1941 the combined British and Indian forces in Iraq totalled three divisions and one independent brigade.[13] And by December 1942 the combined British and Indian forces in Iraq and Iran totalled six divisions and one independent brigade, plus two Polish divisions operating under British command.[14]

As far as air strength was concerned, at the end of 1942 the British had a total of five squadrons in Iraq and Iran. Although this number was not large for the purpose, they had a rapid reinforcement capability because they had stockpiled spare parts, aviation fuel, and munitions for as many as thirty-two squadrons and for as long as six months of combat operations.[15]

Aside from bringing in troops and aircraft, to counteract the German threat British commanders gave a high priority to the construction of defenses. For example, in September 1941 they warned that "time is short and the construction of these defences will employ the whole of the divisions now in Iraq for the coming cold weather. It must be realised that facilities for training will suffer severely."[16] The following month they again stressed that "the utmost speed must be exercised in planning and execution of defensive works."[17] And in November 1941 they reiterated that "speed is truly vital. Every hour matters. Preparation of defences in the forward areas must be pressed on at maximum speed. Guards, duties, escorts, patrols, and games, and the training of other ranks must be cut down drastically."[18]

To enhance their ability to defend Iraq, the British also considerably improved the country's railway system. For example, they constructed 600 miles of new tracks, brought in nearly 9,000 locomotives and wagons, and allocated more than 2,000 of their military personnel to assist Iraq in operating the railways.[19]

To free as many of their own troops as possible for frontline duty in defending Iraq, the British substantially increased the number of levies. The levies were a British-officered and controlled military organization that Britain had long recruited in Iraq to defend its air bases in that country. But the number of British air bases in Iraq was now rising, and so between October 1941 and September 1942 the British increased the levies from 1,600 to more than 6,000. The British were confident about the loyalty of this force because it had performed well in combat against the Iraqi army in May 1941. Moreover, most of the members were either

Assyrians, a small, imperfectly assimilated Christian minority with a history of hostility toward the Iraqi state, or Arabs provided by pro-British tribal leaders in the southern part of the country.[20]

But the British were less confident about the loyalty of the 32,000-man Iraqi army because it had risen against them in May 1941, and in spite of subsequent purges was still permeated with anti-British sentiment. They were especially afraid that it might stab them in the back if the Germans approached the country, and to eliminate this danger they considered disbanding it. However, they rejected this alternative because they believed that it would violate the armistice agreement ending the conflict against Rashid Ali's forces that stipulated that the Iraqi army would be permitted to retain its arms. They rejected it also because they did not believe that Iraqi leaders would willingly accept such a blow to their country's amour propre, and to push the policy through they might have to increase British troop strength in Iraq and even assume administrative responsibility for the country. Still, to mitigate the risk they encouraged Iraqi leaders to reduce the army's size, and for the most part they refused to supply it with arms and equipment. In addition, they relegated it to protecting Britain's lengthy line of communications between Basra and Kirkuk, guarding some of the mountain passes in northeastern Iraq, and watching for mines in the Shatt al-Arab. In this manner they kept it weak and dispersed.[21]

In the event, Britain never had to defend Iraq because the Allied victories in the Soviet Union and North Africa at the end of 1942 eliminated the German threat to the Middle East. Consequently, in early 1943 British commanders began withdrawing their forces from Iraq and transferring them to other theaters where they could now be more usefully employed.[22] However, they did not remove all of their troops because some were needed to facilitate the movement of supplies to the Soviet Union, to guard the large quantities of military stores that Britain had accumulated in Iraq, and generally to bolster the regime and maintain British influence in the country. The incompleteness of the process is indicated by the fact that in September 1945, four months after the termination of hostilities in Europe, they still had eight battalions in Iraq.[23]

After their military triumph in Iraq in May 1941, the British rejected the option of direct rule because they feared that it would provoke widespread internal opposition and therefore require considerable numbers of military and administrative personnel who were badly needed elsewhere. It would also contradict the liberal ideals for which, at least ostensibly, they were fighting the war. In addition, it did not appear to be necessary because there were at hand a significant number of influential Iraqis who were willing to work closely with Britain in upholding Imperial interests in the Middle East.[24]

Consequently, the British chose a form of indirect rule through the monarchical regime that they had originally created in 1921. This regime was now headed by Prince Abd al-Ilah, the regent who since April 1939 had ruled in the stead of Faysal II, the boy king. The regent was the grandson of the Sharif Husayn of the Hijaz who in league with Britain had revolted against the Ottoman Empire in the First World War, and the nephew of Faysal I whom the British had selected to be the first king of Iraq. From Britain's perspective he was a good choice for head of state because his family had a history of close ties with Britain, he had been educated at a British school, had primarily British friends, and generally consulted British officials before making major decisions. Moreover, his fate was now intimately linked with that of Britain because he had returned to power on the back of the British army in a war against his own countrymen.[25]

Under the Iraqi constitution the regent had considerable power because he had the right to choose the prime minister. In 1943 his power was substantially increased when a change in the constitution also gave him the right to dismiss the prime minister. Although the regent officially did not have the right to choose the other ministers, in reality he usually collaborated with the prime minister in this task. During elections to the Chamber of Deputies, the lower house of Iraq's Parliament, he also usually collaborated with the prime minister and the minister of interior in choosing the government's list of candidates. This function was especially important because local government officials, who were dependent upon the central government for their positions, almost invariably insured that these men were voted into office. Finally, the regent had the power to appoint the members of the Senate, the upper house of Iraq's Parliament. Since senators served a lengthy term of eight years, politicians considered these seats particularly valuable.[26]

Together with the regent the regime was led by a small group of politicians, mainly Sunni Arabs, who sat in Parliament and in rotation occupied the key cabinet positions. Many of them were former Ottoman army officers of junior rank from humble backgrounds who came to Iraq with Faysal in 1921 and were now wealthy landowners and businessmen because they had employed the government's machinery to enhance their commercial interests. Others were from more well-established families, but nearly all were deeply conservative men who viewed political democracy and social reform as inimical to their interests. And usually they were willing to work closely with Britain because they believed that this policy was in Iraq's interests; because Britain was an upholder of the regime from which they derived so much political and personal advantage; and because, like the regent, they were now so closely identified with Britain that they could have only the dimmest prospects in the event of a German victory or a revolutionary upheaval.[27]

The extent of the cooperation that Britain received was demonstrated in June 1941 when Jamil al-Midfai, Iraq's first prime minister after the ouster of Rashid Ali, agreed that for the duration of the war Britain could station its ground and air forces anywhere in Iraq.[28] And the following August he gave all possible assistance to the British forces when they invaded Iran to establish a secure channel for supplies to the Soviet Union.[29]

In November 1941 Nuri al-Said, who had succeeded Midfai the previous month and remained in power until June 1944, pledged that Iraqi troops would assist in the defense of the country and would deploy anywhere in Iraq that British commanders thought advisable.[30] He also agreed that Britain could greatly increase the size of the levies.[31]

In the diplomatic sphere, in June 1941, immediately after the restoration of the old regime, the Iraqi government broke relations with Italy. (Iraq had broken relations with Germany at the outset of the war.) Two months later it withdrew cypher facilities from Vichy France and Japan, the only pro-German countries that still had legations in Baghdad. And the following November it broke relations with both Vichy France and Japan.[32]

In the area of propaganda and communications, Iraqi leaders instructed the press and radio to support Iraq's close association with Britain, vilify Germany and Rashid Ali, and emphasize Allied successes in the war. They also instituted postal and telegraphic censorship to root out opponents and prevent the leakage of sensitive information.[33]

In addition, Midfai and Nuri cooperated with Britain in purging the Iraqi army. For example, between June and December 1941 they discharged about 160 officers, some for inefficiency and personal reasons, but most on political grounds. As a further precaution against subversive activities, Iraqi leaders sent many of the discharged army officers, plus numerous civilians who had conspicuously sided with Rashid Ali, to internment camps. By January 1943 the number of these prisoners totalled 310. Finally, in May 1942 Iraqi leaders executed two of the four army officers who had placed Rashid Ali in power and dominated his government, and in 1944-45 they executed the remaining two.[34]

Midfai and Nuri also cooperated with Britain by continuing the prewar practice of employing the services of a British military mission to advise and inspect the Iraqi army. Of course, by gathering information about conditions and sentiment within the army the mission had the further purpose of helping to prevent fifth-column activity or another coup.[35]

In addition, and in a departure from prewar practice, Nuri gave British officials considerable administrative authority in the Ministry of Interior, which controlled the police. For example, he made one head of the Criminal Investigation Division and gave another a large say in all appointments and promotions.[36]

In several other departments too Nuri gave British officials administrative authority. For example, he made them head of the port of Basra, the railways, road and river transportation, foreign currency, imports, local produce, irrigation, and the veterinary service. By contrast, before the war British officials had only been head of the port and the railways.[37]

Aside from giving British officials administrative authority, in several ministries Nuri appointed them as advisers. In some of these ministries, such as Interior, this was a continuation of prewar practice. But in others, such as Education, it was a departure. Indeed, in Education there had not been a British adviser since 1930, two years before the termination of the mandate. Thus with Nuri's assistance, during the war the British strengthened their position within the Iraqi government.[38]

With the consent of the Iraqi government the British also strengthened their position in the provinces. Here their method was to appoint a small group of British officials to live in the outlying areas, travel extensively, and feed information about local conditions to the embassy. Most of these men were former employees of the Iraqi government or the Iraq Petroleum Company and had long resided in Iraq and spoke Arabic. Known as political advisers, their duties also involved transmitting the embassy's views downward to tribal leaders, urban notables, and local government officials. In this manner the embassy was able to maintain direct contact with, and to exert influence upon, an appreciable segment of the leading elements of society throughout the country.[39] Indeed, in this manner the embassy, in the words of an important and long-serving British official in Iraq, "pushed its tentacles into the internal administrative machine even more deeply than the High

Commission [the predecessor of the embassy, before Iraqi independence in 1932] in its later days."[40]

While the ambassador controlled the political advisory staff, the British military authorities in Iraq employed their own intelligence officers in the provinces. These men, known as area liaison officers, had functions similar to those of the embassy's political advisory staff.[41]

In addition to giving British embassy officials and military officers free rein of the country, in January 1943 Nuri cooperated by declaring war on the Axis powers. He was probably motivated more by a desire to pry military hardware out of Britain, further his pan-Arab schemes, and secure a seat for Iraq at the peace conference than to do much fighting. Nevertheless, Iraq's declaration, the first from an Arab state, was a propaganda triumph for Britain.[42]

In February 1943 Nuri followed up his declaration of war with an offer to place one brigade of the Iraqi army at the disposal of British military commanders for deployment in Turkey if that country became involved in the war, and a second brigade for deployment along Britain's lines of communication in Syria or Palestine.[43] And in September 1943 he again offered to send Iraqi troops to operate under British command in Syria.[44]

The British rejected Nuri's offers because they believed that the Iraqi army could be most profitably employed maintaining internal security and guarding Britain's lines of communication within Iraq. They also did not want to provide the arms and equipment that the Iraqi army would require for combat or movement abroad because they did not trust it, and in any case they preferred to allocate their limited quantities of surplus war matériel to countries like the Soviet Union and India that were making very substantial contributions to the Allied war effort. In addition, the British did not like the idea of placing Iraqi troops in Syria or Palestine because Iraq would then be well-placed to influence the political destinies of those countries. Finally, they rejected Nuri's offers because they feared that sending the Iraqi army abroad would be unpopular within Iraq and, since Britain was so closely linked to the regime, would result in a weakening of Britain's position in the country.[45]

Although Nuri's offers came to naught, they are another example of his willingness to cooperate with the Allied war effort. Indeed, in this case his willingness was so great as almost to constitute an embarrassment for Britain.

For British leaders the conquest of Iraq and the subsequent stationing of substantial British forces in the country, combined with the restoration of the old regime and the method of indirect rule, were dictated by strategic considerations resulting from the war with Germany. Given the importance of Iraq in their grand strategy and their information about Germany's capabilities and intentions, the policy was sound in conception and successful in implementation. Indeed, in the short run it led to a significant strengthening of their position in the country.

But in the long term Britain's wartime policy, however necessary, undermined Britain's position in Iraq because it did not have much support within the country. This fact is hardly surprising because for Iraqis Britain's policy meant the reestablishment of an undemocratic regime dominated by a small group of wealthy and repressive politicians who were unrepresentative of the country's ethnic or sectarian balance and who generally demonstrated considerably more concern for personal financial aggrandizement than for the welfare of the great bulk of the population. This regime then permitted or accepted the stationing of large numbers of British, Indian, and Polish troops in Iraq; the transformation of Iraq's military from a nationalist force to little more than an appendage of Britain's army; the placing of British officials in numerous important positions throughout Iraq's government; and, as we shall soon have occasion to discuss, a terrible inflation that enriched a small group of landowners and businessmen while impoverishing most of the rest of the population.

Thus for many Iraqis their country's leaders were now so closely identified with Britain that they could no longer be considered true nationalists. So, by insisting upon, and receiving, a large amount of collaboration, Britain weakened the regime that it wanted to strengthen. And, ominously, it was upon this regime, illegitimate and discredited in the eyes of many Iraqis, that Britain would have to depend for the maintenance of its dominant position in Iraq after the war when, in accordance with its treaty obligations, it withdrew all of its ground troops from the country.

.2.

The Destruction of Iraq

As we observed in the previous chapter, after May 1941 the British made a strong effort to hold Iraq. However, until the end of 1942 they were always conscious of the possibility that German pressure would compel them to withdraw from the country. In such an event, they were determined to use their residual strength to destroy Iraq's oil and other resources to prevent Germany from gaining control of them.

By September 1939, at the beginning of the Second World War, Iraq was producing about 4 million tons of oil per year from an extremely rich field located at Kirkuk in the northeastern part of the country. All of this oil flowed to the Mediterranean Sea through a pipeline system consisting of two parallel lines, each twelve inches in diameter, from Kirkuk to Haditha on the Euphrates River in northwestern Iraq. At that point one line extended through Transjordan to Haifa in Palestine (620 miles in all) and the other through Syria to Tripoli in Lebanon (532 miles in all). There were two pumping or boosting stations along the pipeline before the bifurcation at Haditha and a third one at Haditha. After the bifurcation, there were four stations along the Tripoli branch and five along the Haifa branch. In addition to the oil fields, at Kirkuk there was a power plant, a stabilizing plant that removed hydrogen sulphide (a colorless, inflammable, poisonous gas) from the oil, and a topping plant that produced a small quantity of refined products strictly for use at the field. This entire system of wells, pipelines, and pumping stations, together with the power, stabilizing, and topping plants, was operated by the Iraq Petroleum Company, a British-controlled international consortium.[1]

Through a subsidiary, the IPC also operated oil fields near Mosul at Ain Zala and Qayara, plus power and topping plants similar to those at Kirkuk. However, these fields only produced a small amount of inferior quality oil that the company had not yet begun to export.[2]

Besides these assets, Iraq's oil resources included a refinery at Alwand near Khanaqin, about 100 miles northeast of Baghdad near the Iranian border. This installation provided about 150,000 tons of refined products per year for use in Iraq. It drew on a relatively small oil field straddling the Iraqi-Iranian frontier in that area known as Naftkhana. Both the refinery and the oil field were operated by a subsidiary of the entirely British-owned Anglo-Iranian Oil Company.[3]

On 10 June 1940 Italy entered the war on the side of Germany and closed the central Mediterranean to Allied shipping (except for a few heavily protected convoys carrying urgently required munitions and supplies from Britain to Malta and Egypt). The following day the IPC, acting on instructions from the British government, closed the pipeline to Tripoli because there was no longer any convenient way to market this large quantity of crude oil. The company also reduced the flow of crude oil through the pipeline to Haifa from 2 million tons per year to 800,000 tons per year because this lower figure was the capacity of a refinery at Haifa that provided fuel for the British fleet in the Mediterranean.[4]

As we observed in the Introduction, on 2 April 1941 a militantly anti-British government came to power in Iraq under the leadership of Rashid Ali. Almost simultaneously, German forces in Libya began a major offensive, while other German troops attacked Greece. Both German attacks were successful, and by the end of April the British were compelled to withdraw from both Libya (except for Tobruk) and Greece. Encouraged by these developments, on 30 April the Iraqis placed a blockade around the British base at Habbaniya. To break the blockade, and also to oust the anti-British government in Iraq, on 2 May British troops and aircraft attacked Rashid Ali's forces. To aid Iraq in this battle, Germany sent two squadrons of aircraft from an Italian base on the island of Rhodes. Because of the considerable distance involved, these planes were obliged to land in Syria for refueling. They then proceeded to an Iraqi base at Mosul, and on 13 May began operations against the British forces in Iraq. Notwithstanding this assistance, after four weeks of fighting Britain defeated Rashid Ali's forces and reestablished a friendly government in Iraq. However, while this battle raged, Germany scored another victory by conquering the island of Crete.

As a result of these events, in April and May 1941 the British became alarmed that Germany, operating in collaboration with Rashid Ali's government and the Vichy French authorities in Syria, and possibly even with the hitherto neutral government in Turkey, might attempt to gain control of Iraq's valuable oil resources. Their concern in this regard was much affected by Germany's seizure intact of Romania's oil fields in September 1940. Consequently, for the first time in the war they began seriously to consider the idea of destroying Iraq's oil resources to prevent them from falling into German hands. Aside from denying Germany access to Iraq's oil, this step appealed to some British leaders, such as Prime Minister Winston Churchill and his adviser Professor F. A. Lindemann, because they believed that by destroying this oil they might simultaneously reduce Germany's motivation for seizing Iraq and increase its motivation for attacking the Soviet Union to gain control of the abundant oil resources of the Caucasus. Thus by destroying Iraq's oil they hoped to facilitate their objective of bringing the Soviet Union into the war against Germany.[5]

However, from Britain's perspective a major problem was the fact that the Royal Navy in the Mediterranean was heavily dependent upon Iraqi oil flowing through the pipeline from Kirkuk to Haifa. While Britain could have replaced this oil by drawing on more oil from Iran, the adjustment would have required at least seven additional tankers (and possibly as many as eleven) at a time when tankers were in short supply and in any case could not have reached the Persian Gulf for three months. Moreover, taking these tankers from other routes would have reduced the supply of oil to the United Kingdom by 300,000 tons per year.[6]

In an effort to implement significant oil denial measures without reducing the flow to Haifa or otherwise hindering British military operations, on 24 May 1941, at the height of the fighting in Iraq, the Chiefs of Staff instructed British military commanders in the Middle East that, barring any strong objections, they should immediately destroy the four pumping stations on the Tripoli branch of the pipeline and the refinery at Alwand. The Chiefs of Staff chose these pumping stations because the Tripoli branch of the pipeline had been shut down since June 1940 and so its pumping stations were of no use to Britain, but conceivably they might be of great use to Germany. And they chose the Alwand refinery because Britain could obtain refined products from the large refinery at Abadan in southwestern Iran, while Germany and its Iraqi allies did not have any other local source for these vital commodities.[7]

However, British military commanders in the Middle East did not carry out these orders because in late May 1941 they believed that they would soon triumph in the campaign in Iraq. Moreover, they feared that their efforts to gain Iraqi goodwill and set up a friendly government in that country would be jeopardized if they destroyed Iraq's oil wealth. Consequently, during the fighting in Iraq the British forces did not make any attacks on oil-related targets.[8]

After the success of British arms in Iraq on 31 May 1941, British leaders in London were still not confident about holding that country against an anticipated German attack through Syria or Turkey. Consequently, on 6 June they instructed British military commanders in the Middle East to make all necessary preparations for a prompt and thorough oil denial campaign in Iraq including the wells, stockpiled supplies of crude oil and refined products, drilling equipment, pipelines, pumping stations, Alwand refinery, and power, stabilizing, and topping plants.[9]

With the cooperation of the Iraq Petroleum Company and the Anglo-Iranian Oil Company, British military commanders now made extensive oil denial preparations in Iraq. Indicating the priority they gave to this task, in June 1941 they diverted to Iraq approximately 200 army engineers who had been employed on important projects in Palestine, Transjordan, and Egypt.[10] Further indicating their determination not to allow any of Iraq's oil resources to fall intact into German hands, in the same month they informed the demolition parties that, although normally required to await the orders of higher authority before starting destruction, in the event of a sudden threat they were to act immediately without awaiting orders.[11]

In an effort to prevent a German move into Iraq or Egypt from Syria, on 8 June 1941 Britain attacked the Vichy French administration in that country. After heavy fighting, on 10 July the British forces emerged triumphant, and Syria was now firmly in the Allied camp. During the campaign in Syria, on 22 June Germany launched a massive attack on the Soviet Union. Although Germany enjoyed substantial success in 1941 and 1942, the operation tied up most of its strength. This fact, coupled with the elimination of the Vichy French administration in Syria, meant that Germany's ability to attack Iraq was now considerably reduced. However, as we observed in the previous chapter, the British feared that the Soviet Union might soon collapse and thereby enable Germany to present a serious threat to Iraq from the Caucasus in the north. They were also still concerned about a German attack through Turkey, possibly with the connivance of the Turkish government; and a German attack from Palestine following a breakthrough in Egypt.

Consequently, the British pressed on with their oil denial preparations, and by late August 1941 they had made substantial progress. For example, at the Kirkuk field, which contained fifty-five wells and was the only major oil-producing field in Iraq, they had junked (that is, in various ways rendered inoperable for an extended and possibly indefinite period) forty-five wells. Since three of the remaining wells did not contain any oil, this left only six producing wells and one standby well. And even in these seven they had made extensive preparations for junking.[12]

The story at the other oil fields was similar. For example, by late August 1941 at Ain Zala they had junked all of the wells; at Qayara they had junked all of the wells except for one that was producing bitumen for the construction of British airfields in Iraq; and at Naftkhana they had junked all of the wells except for one that they needed to supply the Alwand refinery.[13]

While the British junked many oil wells in Iraq, they did not set fire to any of them or make any preparations to do so because they hoped to reconquer the area eventually and did not want to do irreparable damage to the fields. Moreover, as we shall observe presently, they were attempting to conceal their activities from the Iraqis and firing would have been conspicuous.[14]

In addition to their junking operations, in the second half of 1941 the British withdrew from all of the oil fields in Iraq large quantities of drilling and other equipment that was not essential for current production. In this manner they hoped to prevent it from falling into the hands of the Germans.[15]

In 1942 the British continued to give oil denial preparations in Iraq a high priority. For example, they carried out more thorough well-junking operations, and withdrew from the oil fields all remaining drilling and other equipment that was not essential for current production.[16] They decided that technical advisers and special troops allocated for the purpose of oil denial could not do any other work unless this could be accomplished without detriment to their primary job.[17] They made plans to forcibly evacuate—in other words, to kidnap—140 members of their skilled Iraqi labor force so that these men would not be available to assist the Germans in resuming production.[18] And they issued an order stating that "protective detachments will on no account be withdrawn until the work of the demolition parties has been finished, and will be prepared to fight to the last man and the last round to carry out this task."[19]

In view of the measures that they took and their preparations for additional steps, there is little doubt that if the British had been compelled to withdraw from Iraq they would have attempted utterly to demolish all of the country's oil facilities. Further evidence for this conclusion comes from the extensive oil-denial campaign that they conducted in Burma in March and April 1942 just before the Japanese conquest. In this operation they destroyed virtually all stockpiled oil and oil products, amounting in total to about 170 million gallons, plus all refineries and drilling equipment.[20]

Oil facilities were by no means the only installations in Iraq that the British were determined to destroy to prevent from falling intact into German hands. From their perspective railways were also very important, especially the bridges and tunnels that would cause a severance of communications for a substantial period. British military leaders remembered that their campaign in Syria in June-July 1941 would have been greatly impeded if the Vichy French had managed to blow up the Tel Shehab railway bridge at the head of the Yarmuk Gorge. They also realized that the railways in Iraq and elsewhere in the Middle East could not easily be dispensed with because most roads in the region were not designed to stand up to heavy and continuous use by motor transport. For example, after three weeks of use by British military vehicles during the Syrian campaign, the Dera-Damascus road, which was a major transportation link, was so cut up as to be almost unusable.[21]

As far as railway rolling stock was concerned, the British were resolved to evacuate as much as possible and to destroy the remainder.[22] While at first glance this appeared to be the obvious approach under the circumstances, there was, interestingly, a dissenting view. In August 1942 Brigadier-General Sir Frederick Carson, the director-general of transportation at the headquarters of Middle East Forces in Cairo, maintained that attempts at evacuation would lead to terrible chaos and serious impediments to the war effort. In reaching this conclusion, Carson was heavily influenced by Allied experience in the campaign in Belgium and France in the spring of 1940 when efforts to withdraw rolling stock had had just such a result. And as bad as that situation had been, he feared that it would be worse in Iraq because in Belgium and France double and quadruple railway lines usually existed, while in Iraq single tracks were the rule. Carson was also concerned that the rapid destruction of some 10,000 railway wagons in an emergency situation would be beyond the capability of the British forces in Iraq and would waste valuable time and explosives. Instead, he recommended that they concentrate their efforts on the destruction of the far fewer but much more precious locomotives and cranes.[23]

Besides the railways, the British planned to destroy other transportation and communication links like road bridges, trucks and busses (unless they could be evacuated), garages and workshops, tires, tools, spare parts for motor vehicles, airports, wharfs and their attendant cranes, inland water craft (unless they too could be evacuated), broadcasting stations, telegraph and telephone exchanges, and junctions of underground cables and overhead telephone lines. And, to impede German reconstruction efforts (of workshops, for example), they planned to destroy all electrical power and distributing stations.[24]

In addition, to impede a German advance from Palestine the British planned to destroy all four major sources of water in the desert west of the Euphrates River, plus all water pumping and drilling machinery in the area.[25] They also planned to open the barriers restraining the Euphrates and thereby cause widespread flooding.[26]

While the British were determined to do a thorough job of destroying Iraq's oil, transportation, communication, and power facilities and to dehydrate one section of the country and inundate another part, they did not plan to implement a total scorched-earth policy. For example, they intended to leave intact irrigation works and wells in the countryside and desert, water systems in the towns, flour mills, fuel oil for irrigation machinery, and kerosene supplies. As far as foodstuffs in warehouses and granaries were concerned, they planned, as far as possible, to distribute these items to the local population.[27]

The British restricted their demolition policy in this manner because they believed that any possible military advantage to be secured by the destruction of these installations and supplies would be outweighed by the disadvantage of alienating the Iraqi people and thereby creating a serious internal security problem. They also feared that widespread civilian demolitions in Iraq would have a detrimental effect on internal security in other places in the Middle East, such as Egypt, where Britain badly needed a friendly or at least acquiescent government and people. In this connection they recalled the enduring hatred that the Turks incurred in Lebanon in 1918 when, upon evacuating Beirut, they destroyed thousands of tons of wheat at a time when the local inhabitants were starving.[28]

It is important to note that all of Britain's denial measures were taken without informing the Iraqi government, much less obtaining its consent. On the contrary, the British made a strong effort to conceal their activities and plans because they feared, probably with justification, that the Iraqis would not willingly agree to, and might even attempt forcibly to prevent, the deliberate destruction of their own country.[29]

In the event that the Iraqis did attempt to interfere with Britain's denial efforts, the British military authorities were prepared to use force against them. Indeed, in July 1942 the commander of the Tenth Army, who was responsible for Iraq, emphasized this very point.[30]

In spite of Britain's efforts at concealment, Iraqi leaders undoubtedly learned about the denial measures and probably surmised that further steps were in the offing.[31] However, as far as I can determine they never mentioned the subject to the British, perhaps because they wanted to avoid quarrelling fruitlessly over this issue with their powerful and determined ally.

The British planned to implement extensive denial measures throughout the Middle East and not only in Iraq. As in the case of Iraq, in Lebanon, Syria, Iran, Saudi Arabia, Kuwait, Bahrain, and Qatar they kept these plans secret from the local governments. They even kept their Free French allies largely in the dark, informing them only about tactical demolitions.[32] In Egypt, however, they were more forthcoming, perhaps because the Egyptian government, unlike the other governments in the area, pressed them on the subject, imploring them to avoid destruction that would threaten the survival of the civilian population.[33]

In early 1943 the British ended work on all of their denial schemes in Iraq because serious German reverses in North Africa and the Soviet Union in late 1942 eliminated the German threat to the Middle East.[34] However, the episode illustrates the high-handed manner in which the British used their dominant position in Iraq during this period. Without informing the Iraqi government, they destroyed most of Iraq's oil wells and made serious preparations to destroy all remaining oil installations, plus transportation, communication, power, and water facilities. If they had implemented all of their plans the amount of destruction in Iraq would have been quite substantial, and the country's economic development would have been significantly set back. Probably there would also have been famine and pestilence because flooding would have hampered the growing of food, while the loss of transportation facilities would have impeded the distribution of food, medicine, and fuel oil for irrigation machinery and urban water systems. Of course, to be fair it is necessary to point out that the British took these measures at a time when they were locked in a life-and-death struggle with a powerful enemy whom they did not want in any way to strengthen. Moreover, they acted for the sake of the Allied war effort and not from any desire to harm Iraq. While Iraqi leaders certainly realized this, nonetheless it is difficult to imagine that they were pleased about the activity. On the contrary, for most of them the affair probably increased their desire to reduce Britain's influence in Iraq, and especially to eliminate the presence of British ground troops, so that they could finally become masters of their own house.

.3.

The Great Inflation

During the Second World War, and especially from 1941, Iraq experienced terrible inflation. Indicating its extent, the wholesale price index, which covered fifty-seven commodities including twenty-two foodstuffs, rose from 100 in August 1939 to 614 in January 1944. The rise in wholesale prices was, of course, generally passed on to the consumer.[1]

The major cause of the inflation in Iraq was British military expenditure. These outlays went for purposes such as the construction of railways, roads, ports, and fortifications; transportation; purchases of foodstuffs; wages for levies, laborers, and guards; and renting of accommodations. The quantities involved are indicated by the fact that between 1941 and 1943 British military expenditure in Iraq amounted to £61.5 million.[2]

(In Iraq the British actually spent dinars rather than pounds, although the two currencies had the same value. They obtained these dinars by depositing an equivalent amount of pounds with the British-managed Iraq Currency Board in London. The board then issued new dinar notes and gave them to the British government.)[3]

As British troops began to leave Iraq, in 1943 British military expenditure started to decline. However, British civilian authorities continued to purchase sizable quantities of Iraqi foodstuffs, like barley and dates, to feed other Middle Eastern countries, India, and Italy. In this manner they continued to inject large amounts of money into the economy.[4]

All of this British expenditure led to a great increase in the amount of currency in circulation. Thus in August 1939 there were ID 4.7 million in circulation, while in October 1944 this figure had increased nearly nine times to ID 40.3 million.[5]

The great increase in the amount of currency in circulation would not have caused such terrible inflation if it had been matched by a comparable increase in the amount of goods in circulation. However, rather than increase, the amount of goods available declined greatly because Britain, which before the war had supplied more than 30 percent of Iraq's imports, had converted nearly all of its industry to war work. American industry too was busy with war work; and trade with other industrial countries, like Germany, Japan, France, and Belgium, was impossible because they were enemies or enemy-occupied. Imports were also reduced because worldwide military activity had produced a severe shortage of shipping.[6]

The British tried to assist Iraq by providing supplies from India. Indeed, in 1942 India provided 51.5 percent of Iraq's imports, and in the first four months of 1943 this figure rose to 66.6 percent. By comparison, in 1938 India had only provided 6.5 percent of Iraq's imports. However, in several areas India's ability to help was limited because its industry was not highly developed, and in any event it too had to devote much of its productive capacity to war work or domestic needs.[7]

The effect of these factors on Iraq's supply situation is illustrated by the fact that during the 1942-45 period imports of textiles were only 56 percent in quantity of their prewar level, while imports of sugar, tea, and coffee were only 58 percent. In the area of capital goods the situation was even worse. For example, during the 1942-45 period of imports of iron, steel, cement, timber, machinery, electrical equipment, and vehicles were only 15 to 20 percent in quantity of their prewar level.[8]

One of the effects of the reduction in imports of capital goods was the decline in the construction of houses. This decline was accentuated by the fact that in 1942 and 1943 the British put pressure on the Iraqi government to halt all construction not essential to the war effort so that they would have unrestricted access to bricks and other locally made building materials. Combined with the large-scale demand by the British for rented accommodations, this led to a serious housing shortage with a consequent significant increase in rents.[9]

The Iraqis often complained to Britain about the shortage of supplies but the British, after doing what they could, sometimes became exasperated. In their view, all countries were suffering from wartime dislocations and Iraq at least, unlike Britain and many other countries, was not incurring any loss of life or material destruction. Illustrating this attitude, in June 1944 the British ambassador in Baghdad berated an Iraqi minister for

> making no attempt to face realities. The British people were
> fighting a life and death battle in France, in Italy, in Burma and

in the Far East; we all of us had relatives and friends risking their lives daily in the struggle and our thoughts were constantly with them. Iraqis, of course, could not have these personal feelings but they should at least realise that on the result of this struggle depended their own future.

It seemed to me that many Iraqis had grown rich and spoilt and I had no sympathy with those who complained of small inconveniences. They must realise that everything has to be subordinated to the needs of the war and that their own lot, compared with that of many countries, is to be envied.[10]

Even with the shortage of supplies, the great increase in the amount of currency in circulation would not have caused such terrible inflation if the Iraqi government had mopped up much of it through increased taxation. However, wealthy and influential elements in society, and especially the agricultural interests, strongly resisted increased taxation. The extent of their success in this endeavor is indicated by the fact that farmers were exempt from the income tax, and for others the rate was low. For example, in 1944 in Iraq a single man with an earned income of £1,500 per year (which was a very appreciable amount at this time) paid income tax at a rate of 10 percent, while in Britain he paid at a rate of 40 percent.[11]

Because of this resistance, and also for administrative reasons such as the shortage of competent and reliable assessors, the Iraqi government did not mop up much of the currency in circulation through increased taxation. For example, in 1943 it acquired only 19 percent of the combined total of its own expenditure and Allied military expenditure in the country. By contrast, in that year in Britain and the United States the comparable figures were 49 percent and 42 percent respectively, with the result that inflation in these two countries was much less severe than in Iraq. Still, in fairness we should note that several Middle Eastern countries actually did worse in this regard than Iraq. For example, in 1943 the comparable figures for Palestine, Syria, and Iran were 18 percent, 16 percent, and 13 percent respectively.[12]

As another means of mopping up some of the currency in circulation, Iraqi leaders considered internal loans. Initially, however, they were reluctant because they feared that the public would not subscribe to the loans and the government's prestige would then be damaged. But by January 1945 inflation had become so bad and other measures had proven so ineffectual that they issued two loans totalling ID 2 million. Although the public response was good and the bonds were quickly sold, they were issued too late and the total amount was too small to have a significant impact on the wartime inflation.[13]

While Iraqi leaders did not do much in the area of taxation or internal loans, they did attempt to hold down inflation by introducing price controls. Their efforts in this direction began in January 1942 and by June 1944 included a large number of items such as tea, coffee, sugar, bread, fruit, vegetables, wheat, barley, matches, most cotton textiles, footwear, certain steel building materials, certain medical supplies, paper, carbon paper, typewriter ribbons, electric light bulbs, heating and cooking stoves, mechanical appliances, engineering supplies, jute products, leather, whiskey, and locally manufactured cigarettes.[14]

To insure that everyone received a fair share of the basic essentials, Iraqi leaders also introduced rationing. Their efforts in this area began in March 1942 and by March 1944 extended to sugar, tea, coffee, and cotton textiles.[15]

The British strongly supported Iraq's price control and rationing schemes and even provided some trained personnel to help staff the appropriate offices.[16] But for various reasons these schemes were generally ineffective in holding down prices and insuring an equitable distribution of the available commodities.

To begin with, there was a certain lack of seriousness on the part of government leaders because in many cases the holding down of prices would adversely affect their personal interests. For example, landowners among them gained from high prices for domestically grown agricultural commodities, and industrialists among them gained from high prices for domestically manufactured products. Indicating the effect of this consideration on public policy, in December 1943 Tawfiq al-Suwaydi and Ali Mumtaz al-Daftari, who with others owned a cigarette-manufacturing factory, joined the cabinet; and the following month the government increased the controlled price for cigarettes.[17]

Another problem was that farmers and merchants did everything possible to thwart the government's efforts. For example, they hoarded supplies to create artificial shortages, sold controlled items on the black market at much higher prices, adulterated products, and smuggled goods abroad to take advantage of higher prices prevailing in neighboring countries.[18]

There was also considerable corruption as officials connived at or participated in illegal activity because they desperately needed more money to cope with the great rise in prices. But even without this factor, Iraq's administrative machinery was probably not sufficiently developed to cope with large-scale projects of this nature. This was especially true in rural areas, where the distribution of goods was impeded by distance and dispersion.[19]

Still another problem was that Nuri al-Said, the prime minister from October 1941 to June 1944, devoted a great deal of time and effort to the question of Arab unity and generally showed little interest in administrative matters. Moreover, he was extremely reluctant to incur unpopularity by offending the powerful vested interests that opposed effective measures to control prices.[20]

Not surprisingly, those on fixed incomes, such a civil servants, white collar employees, and pensioners were hit hardest by the inflation. Laborers generally did better because due to a shortage of workers their wages increased. However, laborers still suffered because their wages did not increase nearly as much as prices. Thus between 1939 and 1945 prices rose by a factor of six, while wages only rose by a factor of three.[21]

In other words, for most Iraqis the wartime inflation led to a significant decline in an already low standard of living. In July 1943 the British chargé d'affaires noted that "meat, fruit and vegetables are now dearer than ever and a large proportion of the working classes cannot afford to buy them."[22] A year later he cited a British intelligence report that observed that the "strain on the physical constitution of men is becoming more and more apparent as a result of undernourishment."[23] And in January 1945 another embassy official commented that "the poorer Iraqis are hard put to it to clothe themselves, and, in view of the inordinate price of many common food-stuffs, particularly meat, fruit and vegetables, their diet is ill-balanced and often inadequate."[24]

While inflation impoverished most of the population, landowners generally benefited from the steep rise in agricultural prices that resulted from large-scale British purchases. The extent of these rises is indicated by the fact that between August 1939 and the high point of 1943 (the exact date of which varied from commodity to commodity), a ton of wheat rose from ID 2.500 to ID 25 at the official price and ID 60 at the black market price; a ton of rice from ID 21.650 to ID 100; a ton of dates from ID 2.850 to ID 30; and twenty-five kilograms of ghee (butter) from ID 1.735 to ID 17.750.[25]

A few other elements in society also did well during this period, for example, contractors who provided services to the British as well as manufacturers, merchants, and landlords who were able to greatly increase prices for their goods and accommodations.[26]

During the war the British were concerned that the terrible impoverishment of most of the population combined with the enrichment of a relatively small number would discredit the regime and because they were so closely linked to it thereby weaken their position in the country. As a result, in November 1943 the British ambassador warned Nuri that "if everything were allowed to drift on as at present, the eventual departure of the British forces would inevitably give rise to grave internal dangers. . . . the old order might be very rudely disturbed at no very distant date."[27]

But there was not that much the British could do to ameliorate the situation. They had to spend a lot of money in Iraq to prepare for a German attack. They had to purchase large quantities of Iraqi foodstuffs to feed their military forces and the civilian population in neighboring countries. They could not easily increase Iraq's imports because of the shortage of supplies, urgent domestic needs, pressing demands from other countries, and shipping problems. And while they encouraged greater efforts in the areas of taxation, internal loans, price controls, and rationing, they did not rule Iraq and could only advise and cajole politicians who were tenacious in defense of their interests and expert at tergiversation.[28]

Britain's difficulty in effecting a reduction in prices is illustrated by a look at the area of vehicular transportation. Here we observe that by November 1942 the British army had leased 40 percent of the civilian trucks in Iraq, and many other trucks were leased by contractors working for the British army. Thus the number of trucks remaining for civilian needs was small and their price, and therefore the price of all of the products carried, rose considerably. But if the British had released these trucks their ability to defend Iraq against German attack, shuttle troops between Iran and Egypt, and deliver supplies to the Soviet Union would all have been reduced.[29]

Britain's difficulty in effecting a reduction in prices is further illustrated by a look at the question of barley purchases. Here we observe that in April 1944 Britain halted all purchases of barley in Iraq. As a result, the price of barley declined precipitously, thereby aiding the Iraqi consumer. However, at this point the Iraqi government, at the behest of the agricultural interests, put considerable pressure on Britain to resume purchases of barley and to pay a high price. In order to preserve amicable relations with the government, in August 1944 the British agreed, thereby obviating the anti-inflationary impact of their suspension of purchases.[30]

One step that the British did take to hold down prices was to offer substantial quantities of gold for sale in Iraq. In this manner they hoped to absorb some of the surplus purchasing power in the country and thereby reduce inflation. These sales began in August 1943, and by the following March totalled £2.2 million. Although the sales probably had some effect in holding down prices, given the powerful forces at work in creating the inflation they could only be regarded as a minor palliative.[31]

Another step which the British took to absorb some of the surplus funds in the country was to facilitate the purchase of British governmental and corporate securities. As a result, between November 1942 and March 1945 Iraqi residents bought £1.4 million of these securities. But given the amount of money that the British were pumping into the economy during this period, these purchases, like the gold sales, were on too small a scale to reduce inflation significantly.[32]

While neither the gold sales nor the purchases of securities had much effect on the internal price level, the considerable amounts of money involved in the transactions indicate the extent of the wealth that some elements in Iraqi society were accumulating. Because so many others were simultaneously being impoverished, during the war the gap between the rich and poor grew appreciably. Naturally this development provoked the discontent of the masses, and thus rendered the position of the ruling class more precarious.

The wartime inflation in Iraq was caused mainly by a great increase in British expenditure coupled with a great decline in imports. Under the prevailing circumstances, neither of these factors was particularly tractable. Nonetheless, in Iraq there was widespread belief that the government was responsible for the inflation because it was subservient to the wealthy agricultural and mercantile communities and would not take any measures inimical to their interests.[33] This belief was not entirely unjustified because the government could have done better in the areas of taxation, internal loans, price controls, and rationing. Probably more effective steps in these areas, while not dealing with the principal causes of inflation, would have ameliorated its effects. In Egypt and Palestine, for example, which suffered from similar conditions, more effective economic management resulted in price rises roughly half that of Iraq.[34] But regardless of the Iraqi government's degree of responsibility for the inflation, the fact remains that because Britain was so closely linked to the regime it too received much of the blame. Thus by alienating large sections of the population from their government, the inflation weakened Britain's position in Iraq. Indeed, as we shall observe in chapter 11, within three years of the end of the war public hostility, caused largely by economic hardship, nearly destroyed Britain's position entirely.

.4.

The Kurdish Uprisings

In the early 1940s Kurds constituted nearly 20 percent of the total population of Iraq.[1] They were congregated in the northeastern part of the country, primarily in the provinces of Mosul, Arbil, Sulaimaniya, and Kirkuk. Most of them lived in rural areas, and were under the sway of various *aghas* (tribal leaders). Although mainly a Sunni Muslim people, the Kurds spoke a language quite distinct from Arabic, and had many customs and traditions of their own.[2]

During this period the Kurds suffered from various forms of discrimination at the hands of the Arab-dominated government in Baghdad. For example, in the cabinet the two portfolios customarily reserved for Kurds (out of a total of ten) were generally given to members of a group of about six denationalized or arabized Kurds whose connections with Kurdistan were tenuous, often amounting to little more than their Kurdish names, and who did not really represent their community.[3] In the Senate, the upper house of Iraq's Parliament whose members were appointed by the regent, there was only one Kurd, and he a denationalized one, among the twenty members.[4] And in the Chamber of Deputies, the lower house of Iraq's Parliament, the government usually chose Kurdish representatives (for the members were only ostensibly elected by the people) who were docile and accommodating and not inclined forcefully to represent their area.[5]

In economic development too there was discrimination. For example, although the government completed numerous irrigation schemes, none of them were in the northeastern part of the country.[6]

There was also discrimination in the pricing of agricultural products. For example, tobacco was widely grown in Kurdistan, and by law the government purchased the entire crop. However, the government set a relatively low price for tobacco and then resold the crop at a much

higher price, thereby making a large profit. Simultaneously, it permitted
the price of rice, which was a staple of the Kurdish diet and was grown
primarily in the southern part of the country, to rise greatly. The extent
of the problem is indicated by the fact that in August 1939 the price of
a kilogram of tobacco was 116 fils, and in October 1943 it was 280 fils.
By contrast, during this period the price of a sack of rice rose from 900
fils to ID 10. In other words, the price of tobacco increased two and one-
half times, while the price of rice increased eleven times. Thus for the
Kurds the economic consequences of the great disparity in the prices of
agricultural products were very detrimental.[7]

In 1942 the government compounded this problem by delaying payment for the tobacco crop. For the Kurdish farmers this was very unfortunate because they depended upon prompt payment, at least by
October, to enable them to purchase grain and other necessities before
the winter snows closed roads and made movement difficult.[8]

In addition, there was discrimination in the allocation of rationed
supplies such as cloth, sugar, tea, and coffee. While the government distributed fewer supplies to the rural areas in general, this problem appears
to have been especially acute in the Kurdish regions.[9]

These factors often led to terrible poverty. Thus in 1942 W. A.
Lyon, one of Ambassador Cornwallis's political advisers, observed
that in many Kurdish areas "the economic state . . . is really tragic.
These unfortunate people have literally went to nothing between
them and starvation. . . . Everywhere one sees people lying about in
an emaciated condition. Their clothes spread out on the hedges to dry
show more holes than cloth. They have not even the wherewithal to
patch them."[10] In 1943 a British intelligence report pointed out that
"last winter was disastrous for the villagers and many people [in
Kurdistan] died of starvation."[11] In the same year Cornwallis noted that
"the people of Barzan, and indeed of many other northern districts,
were bordering on starvation and that the Government, although
their attention had been repeatedly drawn to the subject, had entirely
failed to give them adequate help."[12] In 1944 a British subject working for the Iraqi government commented that in Sulaimaniya "the
poverty is such as I have never seen. . . . the children are practically
naked and half starved."[13] And in 1945 an American official observed
that "conditions were particularly bad throughout the northern districts where it was reported that women were confined to their homes
because they lacked the most elementary material with which to clad
themselves."[14]

A great shortage of health care compounded the problem. Thus in 1944 Lyon reported that "there are vast and insalubrious areas [of Kurdistan] completely devoid of all medical services."[15]

In education too there was discrimination. For example, from 1922 to 1943 only 4.5 percent of the students sent abroad for further education were Kurds.[16] In 1944 this figure declined to 1.5 percent, and in that year not a single Kurd was admitted to the Medical, Higher Teachers Training, or Military Cadet colleges.[17] In 1949 only a total of three people from the Kurdish-inhabited provinces of Sulaimaniya and Arbil were admitted to the law college, while twelve people were admitted from the Shiite-inhabited province of Karbala.[18] (Both the provinces of Sulaimaniya and Arbil had larger populations than the province of Karbala.)[19] And in 1952 the provinces of Sulaimaniya and Arbil had three and four secondary schools respectively, while each of the Shiite-inhabited provinces had between five and eight secondary schools.[20]

Commenting on the education situation in the north, in 1941 Professor Hamley, a British expert who inspected schools all over Iraq, maintained that in Sulaimaniya education was the worst in the country, indeed almost nonexistent.[21] And in 1945 Stewart Perowne, the oriental counsellor at the British embassy, observed that "there is not a single new school in Mosul town or in Kirkuk, where the Secondary School is housed in little more than a ruin."[22]

In contrast to the dismal situation in the north, in 1944 K. J. Ritchie, a British subject in the Iraqi Ministry of Education, reported that the general condition of the boys' primary schools in the towns in the south was "not at all bad. I have seen several that, in their range of activities, in and out of school, compare by no means unfavourably with schools of similar type in England."[23]

A major explanation for the education problem was that the Sunni Arab elite that controlled the political system usually fobbed off the Shiite Arabs with Education and a few other ministries which were generally considered to be relatively unimportant. The Shiite ministers of education, and the Shiite aides whom they employed, then proceeded to allocate most of their department's money to the southern part of the country, which was inhabited primarily by Shiites, to the detriment of the Kurdish and, incidentally, Sunni Arab-inhabited districts in the north.[24]

In addition to discrimination in admissions and the allocation of financial resources, Shiite officials in the Ministry of Education engaged in petty harassment of the Kurds. For example, they did not permit

Kurdish children to wear their national clothes in school, which meant
that many, too poor to purchase other garments, could not go to school
at all.[25]

The question of national clothes, incidentally, affected more than just
school children. For example, in 1943 Lyon observed that "a Kurd may
still in his native costume, be jeered in the streets of the capital."[26]

Finally, the Kurds suffered from the fact that the government administrators in their areas were usually Arabs with little understanding of,
or sympathy for, the local inhabitants. Because they were urban and lit-
erate, and considered themselves modern and progressive, these administrators were often condescending toward their charges. They were
especially scornful of the *aghas*, whom they viewed as a feudal anachro-
nism, and frequently obstructed programs designed to benefit them or
their followers.[27]

In 1931-32, in the last months of the British mandate, there was a
revolt of Kurdish tribes near Barzan, a remote and mountainous district in the extreme northeastern part of Iraq. The uprising was led by
two prominent tribal and religious leaders, the brothers Mulla
Mustapha and Shaykh Ahmad. Essentially the uprising was caused by
the Barzanis' desire for local autonomy in the face of creeping government encroachment. However, it was crushed by the combined
forces of the Iraqi army and the Royal Air Force; and Mulla Mustapha,
Shaykh Ahmad, and a few other leaders were then exiled to Sulaimaniya,
120 miles south of Barzan.[28]

In July 1943 Mulla Mustapha escaped from Sulaimaniya and made his
way back to Barzan. After collecting a group of followers, he began negotiating with the government for a pardon and the release of his brother
and the other Barzanis from confinement. Obtaining no satisfaction, in
late September he began to apply pressure on the government, and to
obtain arms, by raiding police posts in his area. His raids were generally
successful and with each victory his prestige in the area, and the number of followers, grew.[29]

Responding to this threat to its authority, in October 1943 the Iraqi
government concentrated eight army and police battalions in the
affected region, plus armored cars and aircraft. In early November these
forces advanced against Mulla Mustapha's men, but they made little
progress and after suffering losses were compelled to retreat. For the next

four weeks there was a lull in the fighting, but in early December Mulla Mustapha took the offensive with a series of successful attacks against police posts, army camps, and government headquarters.[30]

The Iraqi forces did badly in the fighting because they were poorly led by a high command that seriously underestimated the difficulty of a campaign in a remote area with difficult terrain against an enemy that knew the area well and could rely on the local inhabitants for support. Moreover, the Iraqi forces did not have any training in mountain warfare. For the Arabs among them, most of whom were from southern Iraq and had never even seen a mountain before, this was an especially serious problem. For the Kurds among them, who generally were familiar with mountains, this was less of a concern, but they suffered from a strong motivation problem because they were being asked to fight against their compatriots. In the event, a not inconsiderable number of them resolved this dilemma by deserting to the insurgents.[31]

Unable to progress militarily, Nuri al-Said, the Iraqi prime minister, attempted a political solution. On 14 December 1943 he informed Mulla Mustapha that if he stopped his disorderly activities and left the affected area until spring so that the Iraqi government could reestablish its authority, he would be pardoned and allowed to return to his village. As part of the deal, Nuri also promised that Shaykh Ahmad and the other Barzani prisoners would be allowed to return to their homes.[32]

But Mulla Mustapha was suspicious of the government's bona fides. He was also encouraged by his military success, and after his long exile determined to remain in his ancestral territory. Consequently, he rejected Nuri's offer.[33]

Ambassador Cornwallis was sympathetic to Kurdish grievances. Indeed, he and other British officials in Iraq had long attempted to persuade Iraqi leaders to improve conditions in the region and thereby win the loyalty of their Kurdish subjects.[34] However, Cornwallis had no particular love for Mulla Mustapha. He was also eager to end the insurgency because he feared that it might spread to other areas and possibly disrupt British communications and interfere with oil production.[35] Consequently, during the fighting he authorized the grant of some emergency assistance to the Iraqi armed forces. These items consisted primarily of winter clothing, tinned rations, trucks, and Bren carriers (lightly armored tracked vehicles designed to transport troops and a machine gun into battle while under enemy fire).[36] But, as we have observed, this assistance proved ineffectual. Consequently, with Nuri's consent and with the authority of the Foreign Office, on 21 December 1943

Cornwallis warned Mulla Mustapha that his feud with the government was becoming an embarrassment to the war effort, and that if he continued his activities the British government would regard him as hostile and respond accordingly.[37]

Cornwallis's warning had the desired effect, and Mulla Mustapha immediately halted all military operations. He also said that if the Iraqi government pardoned him and released all of the Barzani prisoners he would agree permanently to maintain the peace in his area. But he would not accept Nuri's demand that he temporarily leave the region to permit the Iraqi government to reestablish its control.[38]

Of the leading politicians in Iraq Nuri was one of the most sympathetic to Kurdish aspirations for an improved situation within Iraq.[39] Consequently, in late December 1943 he appointed Majid Mustapha as minister without portfolio with responsibility for Kurdish affairs. Now in his mid-forties, Majid was an energetic and competent Kurd who had been a *mutasarrif* (governor of a province). In 1941 he had served under Rashid Ali and for this reason had not subsequently been given any government appointment. But Nuri now resurrected him because he was a good administrator who was sympathetic to Kurdish aspirations and who knew and was trusted by many of the Kurdish leaders.[40]

Accompanied by a group of Kurdish aides known as liaison officers, in early January 1944 Majid went to the north to meet Mulla Mustapha and other Kurdish leaders. Two weeks later he returned to Baghdad with a series of recommendations including the formal submission of Mulla Mustapha to the regent in Baghdad followed by a pardon; Mulla Mustapha's temporary departure to a village, to be determined by the government, outside of the Barzan tribal area; the return of Shaykh Ahmad and the other exiled Barzanis to their homes; the pardoning of Kurdish deserters from the Iraqi army and police; the reestablishment of the Iraqi civil administration, including police posts, in the affected region; the withdrawal of the Iraqi army from its recently established positions at Mergasur and Bille near Barzan; and the employment of the liaison officers as administrative officials in the Kurdish areas under Majid's direction for the purpose of implementing a more liberal policy. To alleviate some of Kurdistan's poverty, Majid also recommended that the government distribute food, either free or at reduced cost, to the needy; and employ local inhabitants on road and telegraph construction. For the government, of course, the latter projects would have the added benefit of strengthening its control of the area.[41]

Nuri was favorably disposed toward Majid's recommendations, and in February 1944 much progress was made in implementing them. For example, Mulla Mustapha arrived in Baghdad and made formal submission to the regent, and Shaykh Ahmad and the other Barzanis (eighty-six in all) were released and allowed to return to their homes. The government also distributed a considerable quantity of cheap and free grain to hungry villagers in the Kurdish areas and withdrew most of the troops that it had sent to the north the previous autumn. And the government appointed Baha Ud Din Nuri, one of Majid's liaison officers, as *mutasarrif* of the primarily Kurdish inhabited province of Sulaimaniya.[42]

However, the government did not implement all of Majid's recommendations. For example, aside from Baha Ud Din Nuri, the minister of the interior, Umar Nadhmi, refused to give executive power to any of Majid's liaison officers on the grounds that this grant would diminish his own authority because they would then owe their primary loyalty to Majid. Instead, he turned the liaison officers into observers with only the authority to make suggestions. In reality he expected them mainly to use their influence to cajole Kurdish tribesmen into submission to demands that his officials were powerless to make effective. And when they proved unwilling to perform this task, in March and April 1944 he simply withdrew them.[43]

Nadhmi also refused to pardon Mulla Mustapha on the grounds that he had not returned all of the arms that he had captured from various police posts. According to the government, the outstanding weapons amounted to eleven machine guns and more than 140 rifles.[44]

The army too resisted Majid's recommendations. For example, they refused to withdraw troops from Mergasur and Bille on the grounds that these outposts would be useful in the event of renewed hostilities with Mulla Mustapha. And they refused to pardon Kurdish deserters on the grounds that this would be inimical to the maintenance of discipline. But aside from these stated reasons, the army was uncooperative because many officers were angry at the government for having accepted a cease-fire. In their view this action was a humiliating recognition of their defeat and, moreover, entirely unnecessary because they could have crushed Mulla Mustapha in a spring campaign.[45]

Nuri did not press on more vigorously with Majid's recommendations because his Kurdish policy was harshly attacked by leading figures in Parliament. These politicians opposed the government's lenient treatment of Mulla Mustapha on the grounds that this would encourage malefactors elsewhere in the country to create disturbances. They also disliked the idea of giving the Kurds any form of special administration or preferential treatment on the grounds that this would encourage secessionist sentiment in the Kurdish areas and eventually result in the breakup of the country.[46]

Aside from questions of policy and principle, these politicians were motivated by opportunism because they wanted to supplant Nuri and his colleagues in office. For this reason even Kurdish deputies attacked the government's policy. The latter were especially upset because they did not like the idea of a newcomer like Majid occupying one of the two cabinet positions normally reserved for Kurds.[47]

Finally, opposition politicians were encouraged to attack the government by the widespread knowledge that the regent was not pleased with Nuri's cabinet because it contained four men whose behavior during the upheaval of 1941 had been, from his perspective, not irreproachable.[48]

Because Nuri had not fully implemented Majid's recommendations, during the spring of 1944 tension in the north remained high. Mulla Mustapha frequently complained that the government was not faithfully implementing its reform policy; and he was especially angry that Majid's liaison officers were withdrawn, that the army retained its garrisons at Mergasur and Bille, and that his pardon had not yet been granted.[49]

In spite of the considerable amount of opposition that he had encountered, Nuri decided to make a final effort to resolve the Kurdish question on a generous basis. Apparently he hoped that by redressing Kurdish grievances he could not only significantly reduce dissatisfaction in the region but also deprive Mulla Mustapha of much of his support and thereby make him more tractable. Accordingly, in May 1944 he traveled to the north to investigate the situation firsthand. On his journey he visited Kirkuk, Sulaimaniya, Arbil, and Mosul (the four major towns in the region) and talked with numerous army officers, government officials, and local notables. And at each town he accepted a petition from the notables outlining their views on the reforms required. Essentially these notables requested the creation of a new province in northeastern Iraq that would absorb Barzan and other Kurdish inhabited districts of the province of Mosul, the administrators of which had traditionally been unsympathetic to Kurdish grievances; the employment of Kurds as administrators in the Kurdish areas; the creation of a cabinet minister for Kurdistan; the spending of a proportionate share of the country's revenue in the Kurdish areas; and more Kurdish language instruction in the schools.[50]

Nuri returned to Baghdad determined to press ahead with his reform policy in Kurdistan. As an immediate sign of goodwill to Mulla

Mustapha, on 31 May 1944 he prevailed upon the army to withdraw the garrison from Mergasur. However, Nuri did not have the opportunity to do much more because after further virulent attacks in Parliament followed by lack of support from the regent, in early June he felt obliged to resign.[51]

The regent replaced Nuri with Hamdi al-Pachachi. Hamdi was a leading Sunni Arab politician, a former cabinet minister, and a wealthy landowner. In the last few months he had not taken a particularly hard line on the Kurdish question, but three of his ministers—Mustapha al-Umari at Interior, Tahsin Ali at Defense, and Salih Jabr at Finance—had been among the main critics of Nuri's policy. Consequently, on this issue the new government was predisposed toward a considerably harder line than its predecessor. Indeed, from its perspective Mulla Mustapha was a dangerous insurgent who had repeatedly defied Baghdad's authority and who ultimately threatened the territorial integrity of the country. After all, since the cease-fire in January 1944 he had made peremptory demands upon the government, boycotted or treated condescendingly the government authorities in his area, assumed the right to settle disputes between various Kurdish tribes, refused to dissolve his armed bands, refused to return most of the arms which he had captured from the police, and refused to send back any of the army and police deserters whom he was sheltering. Moreover, because of his successful defiance of the government and because he had compelled Iraqi leaders finally to take serious note of Kurdish grievances, he had acquired a large following and was respected and admired throughout Kurdistan.[52]

For these reasons, initially Hamdi's government leaned toward a military solution.[53] However, Major-General J. M. L. Renton, the head of the British military mission in Iraq, warned that the Iraqi forces would need substantial reorganization and training before they would be ready for another campaign in the mountains. Indicating the seriousness of the problem, in July 1944 Renton pointed out that "every unit I have inspected is under strength—untrained—immobile—and quite unfit to take the field. Even when brought up to strength after re-organisation, in my opinion 6 months' hard unit and formation training will be needed before they are fit to take the field against any enemy however weak and ill-armed the latter may be."[54]

Ambassador Cornwallis too urged caution and recommended that the government continue to alleviate legitimate Kurdish grievances. In this manner he hoped that it could reconcile most Kurds to Iraqi rule and thereby separate Mulla Mustapha from the bulk of his supporters.[55]

In view of these considerations, for the moment Hamdi's government decided to refrain from a test of strength. Indeed, in the summer and autumn of 1944 it even made some conciliatory gestures like announcing that it would continue Nuri's reform policy; sending Tawfiq Wahabi, the minister of economics and the only genuine Kurd in the cabinet, to the north to investigate the situation and assure Mulla Mustapha and other Kurdish leaders that the government would remedy legitimate grievances; withdrawing the Iraqi garrison from Bille; and distributing grain and cloth to impoverished inhabitants of the Kurdish regions. And in April 1945 it pardoned Mulla Mustapha.[56]

But in Kurdistan these statements and measures did little to instill confidence because simultaneously the government sent out some important contrary signals. For example, it engaged in conspicuous military exercises in the north and began rebuilding destroyed police posts in the Barzan area; withdrew Baha Ud Din Nuri, the liberal *mutasarrif* of Sulaimaniya whom the previous government had appointed, and in various ways penalized all of Majid's liaison officers; refused to pardon deserters from the Iraqi army and police who were now with Mulla Mustapha; and did not begin any public works projects, improve public services like education, or give badly needed agricultural assistance such as seed, ploughs, and oxen. Even the government's distribution of grain and cloth proceeded very slowly, possibly because of obstruction by local officials.[57]

Angered by the government's behavior, between December 1944 and July 1945 Mulla Mustapha made a continual series of demands. Essentially he insisted upon the fulfillment of the terms of the petitions that the Kurdish notables had handed to Nuri in May 1944. He also had a few new demands designed to enhance his own position, such as a loan of ID 144,000 to himself for agricultural improvements in the Kurdish areas, a halt to the construction of police posts in his area, and the release of some of his followers whom the government was holding prisoner.[58]

The fact that Mulla Mustapha was now making these demands indicates that he was confident of his power and viewed himself as the spokesman for all Iraqi Kurds. Needless to say, Iraqi leaders would not accept this situation. Indeed, his constant importunities simply reinforced their determination to use military means to combat what they viewed as an increasingly serious threat to their prestige and authority.[59]

With tension and suspicion high on both sides, it is not surprising that in August 1945 hostilities broke out between Mulla Mustapha and the government. Ultimately the cause of the conflict was the government's determination to assert full control over the Barzan area and Mulla Mustapha's determination to maintain local autonomy. The proximate cause, however, was Mulla Mustapha's decision in late July to set out on a trip in the direction of Dohuk, fifty miles west of Barzan, to settle a feud between local tribal leaders. The trip itself heightened tension because it was made in defiance of orders from government officials who strongly opposed his moving about the countryside with a large armed band and presuming to act in their stead. Making matters worse and actually provoking the conflict, Shaykh Ahmad, who was much rasher than Mulla Mustapha, took advantage of his brother's absence to attack several government headquarters and police posts in the Barzan area.[60]

In early August 1945 Iraqi leaders, and especially Mustapha al-Umari and Salih Jabr, who dominated the cabinet in the absence abroad of the regent, the prime minister, and the foreign minister, decided to take advantage of these provocative actions to smash the Barzanis. General Renton, however, warned that the army would not be ready until early October because it had just released many experienced troops and absorbed a large batch of untrained recruits. But Iraqi leaders were determined to strike quickly because they feared that Mulla Mustapha would use the interval to gain new adherents and thereby strengthen his position.[61]

In preparation for the assault, by the end of August 1945 the Iraqis had marshaled six army and police brigades in Rowanduz, Aqra, and Amadia, which were situated respectively south, west, and north of Barzan. In all the Iraqi forces numbered 14,000 men, with considerable artillery and air support. Indeed, in the Rowanduz sector alone they had twenty-eight field guns.[62]

By contrast, Mulla Mustapha only had about 1,000 men. True, he was bolstered by around 1,300 men from other Kurdish tribes, but these men were under the command of their own leaders and so he could not depend upon them. And, of course, he did not have any heavy equipment such as artillery or aircraft.[63]

On 26 August 1945 the Iraqi forces at Rowanduz advanced, but after encountering heavy resistance were immediately obliged to withdraw. On 4 September all three Iraqi columns advanced, but they again encountered heavy resistance and within two days halted after making only small gains. Of the three columns the Aqra one was in the worst condition, being actually cut off from its base and surrounded.[64]

The Iraqi forces did badly against their lightly armed and less numerous tribal opponents because they had been thrown into battle precipitately before their units had been brought up to full strength and properly trained. Indeed, some of the Iraqi troops had not even fired a rifle before being sent into combat.[65]

Moreover, their commanders were by no means the best in the army. Several, for example, had not had any recent training and were selected for personal reasons or because they supported the government's desire for an immediate attack rather than waiting until October, which is what Renton had advised. One artillery officer, who had never commanded infantry, was given command of an infantry battalion, with predictable results. And one officer, whom Renton regarded very highly, was deliberately kept away from the entire operation because he was a Kurd and for that reason distrusted by his Arab colleagues.[66]

Another problem was the unsound plan, and especially the advance from Aqra. Although Aqra was a relatively short distance from Barzan, the advance involved crossing two 6,000-foot heavily forested mountains in hostile territory with numerous suitable points for an ambush. Before the hostilities Renton had warned about this danger, but his advice was disregarded.[67]

In spite of their difficulties in the field, the Iraqi forces ultimately triumphed because in middle and late September 1945 Mustapha al-Umari, in his capacity as minister of interior, bribed several important Kurdish tribes, who had been allied with Mulla Mustapha, to come over to the government's side. "Since then," in the words of the British ambassador, "we have been confronted with the ludicrous spectacle of the friendly tribes ejecting Mulla Mustapha from one position after another, with the Army following up." In the final blow, in mid-October the Iraqi forces marched into Barzan, and Mulla Mustapha and his remaining followers fled into Iran where they were given shelter by the occupying Soviet troops and their Iranian Kurdish allies.[68]

Although the campaign in Kurdistan lasted only from late August to mid-October, the fighting was intense. For example, the Iraqi forces suffered approximately 1,000 casualties. Kurdish casualties are unknown, but it is known that damage on their side was extensive because the Iraqi air force dropped forty-five tons of bombs on a total of fifty-five villages. Moreover, the Iraqi army damaged or destroyed many other villages by shell fire and burning as it advanced.[69]

The leading British officials in Iraq supported the Iraqi government's decision to use force against Mulla Mustapha.[70] Although they were sympathetic to Kurdish desires for a better situation within the country and had often pressured Iraqi leaders toward this end, they were not particularly well-disposed toward Mulla Mustapha. They had frequently advised him to abandon politics and devote himself to agriculture, but he had refused to do so. By 1945 they had grown weary of his constant demands and his unceasing efforts to usurp the government's authority. Ambassador Cornwallis, for example, now referred to him as "overbearing and tyrannical;"[71] Cornwallis's successor, Sir Hugh Stonehewer-Bird, described him as "a bandit undeserving of any trust;"[72] G. H. Thompson, the chargé d'affaires, maintained that "his professions of loyalty are insincere;"[73] Stewart Perowne, the oriental counsellor, labeled him an "egregious brigand;"[74] General Renton called him a "cold blooded murderer;"[75] and A. H. Ditchburn, the adviser to the Ministry of Interior, complained of his "gibberish and moaning."[76]

The Foreign Office too supported the Iraqi government's decision to use force against Mulla Mustapha. Indeed, it believed that the Iraqi government was perfectly justified in wanting to maintain order in its outlying tribal areas.[77]

While supporting the government, the British were determined that their people in Iraq should not participate in the actual operations. To begin with, they viewed the matter as an internal affair that the Iraqis should settle among themselves. They also did not want to alienate the Kurdish population of Iraq any more than necessary. In addition, they were not pleased with the prospect of operating on the basis of a military plan that Renton considered unsound.[78]

Although unwilling to participate in military operations, British officials in Iraq provided valuable assistance by advising Kurdish townspeople and tribes that Britain was completely behind the Iraqi government in the conflict, and that they should dissociate themselves from Mulla Mustapha. In this manner they helped avoid a general Kurdish uprising and facilitated Mustapha al-Umari's efforts to win key Kurdish tribes over to the government.[79]

In various ways the British military mission and the British forces in Iraq also provided valuable assistance to the Iraqis. For example, the military mission gave important administrative and tactical advice to Iraqi commanders[80] and did much to maintain and service the Iraqi aircraft involved in the operations.[81] And the British forces in Iraq lent numerous vehicles that greatly facilitated the movement of Iraqi troops to the troubled areas and into combat with the rebels.[82] They also supplied containers that the Iraqi air force required for the air supply of the beleaguered Iraqi army column that had advanced from Aqra.[83]

It is interesting to observe that in spite of the rather nasty nature of this counterinsurgency campaign and the undoubtedly large number of civilian casualties, none of the leading British officials in Iraq demonstrated any moral inhibitions about the valuable assistance that they were providing to the Iraqi armed forces. In adopting this attitude, of course, they reflected the long-standing British policy of support for the regime in Baghdad against the claims and interests of the minority communities. We observed similar behavior in 1933 during the Assyrian disturbances[84] and in 1935-37 during the Shiite tribal uprisings.[85] And in the 1948-51 period we will observe similar behavior during the Iraqi government's campaign against its Jewish community.[86]

However, the assistance that the British provided on this occasion did not win them much goodwill among the Iraqi leadership. On the contrary, in this quarter there was a widespread suspicion that Britain had actually instigated the Kurdish agitation and disturbances in an effort to create an autonomous Kurdish area, or even an independent Kurdish state, to counterbalance the government.[87] The basis of this belief was Britain's frequently expressed wish for the rectification of Kurdish grievances. It was also due to the conspicuous pro-Kurdish sympathies of the British political advisers in the north.[88] In fact, of course, Britain's objective was the integration of the Kurds into the body politic of the nation. But Iraqi leaders were influenced by the example of European support for independence-minded minorities in the Ottoman Empire, and by the Sykes-Picot agreement between Britain and France during the First World War to partition the Fertile Crescent. Consequently, they perceived Britain's interest in the Kurdish question in a more sinister light. In the short run they reacted by redoubling their efforts to stamp out Mulla Mustapha's rebellion. In the long term they reacted by increasing their efforts to end Britain's overweening presence in the country, and especially the stationing of ground troops, so that they would have complete freedom to assert their authority over all of their subjects. But, ironically, in acquiring this freedom Iraqi leaders signed their own death warrant because in 1958, when the army revolted, they did not have anyone to defend them.

While the British did not strengthen their position with the Iraqi leadership, they did not win the goodwill of the Kurds either. On the contrary, in the aftermath of the fighting most Kurds were disabused of the belief that they could ever rely upon Britain for assistance in the alleviation of their grievances. Instead many now turned toward communism and the Soviet Union for succor. After all, in September 1945 the

Iraqi Communists had strongly opposed the government's assault on Mulla Mustapha, and the following January the Soviet Union facilitated the creation of an independent Kurdish state in northwestern Iran. Thus for the regime, and for Britain as a key supporter of the regime, the appeal of this opposing ideology and hostile power to a large section of the population was to prove a continual source of concern.[89]

.5.

The Dispute Over Kuwait
and Umm Qasr

In the late 1930s Kuwait was a quasi-independent shaykhdom of about 70,000 inhabitants covering 5,800 square miles at the head of the Persian Gulf. Most of the population of Kuwait lived in the town by the sea eighty miles south of Basra. At this time Kuwait was firmly under British influence. According to the terms of various agreements between Britain and the ruler (commonly referred to as the shaykh) of Kuwait dating back to 1899, Britain was obligated to protect Kuwait (the entire principality and not just the town) against aggression while, in exchange, the shaykh agreed not to receive the representatives of foreign powers. The shaykh also agreed not to cede or lease any part of his territory, or to give a concession for oil development or pearl fishing, to any foreigner or foreign power without British consent. Thus Britain was responsible, de facto if not de jure, for managing the shaykh's foreign relations and honor bound to uphold his interests generally. Britain's dominant position in Kuwait was further indicated by the fact that the shaykh was not allowed to levy custom dues in excess of 4 percent on goods imported or exported by British subjects. In addition, the British representative in Kuwait had full judicial authority over all British subjects and protected persons in Kuwait. This representative, whose title was political agent rather than ambassador as in Iraq, was a member of the Indian Political Service and was responsible to the political resident in the Persian Gulf at Bushire. Unlike the British ambassador in Iraq, the resident was not responsible to the Foreign Office but rather to the India Office.[1]

In the late 1930s Iraq tried to gain control of Kuwait. Iraqi leaders pursued this objective because, like the leaders of many countries, they sought territorial aggrandizement for the sake of prestige and power. They also believed in Arab unity, especially if it were realized under their auspices. Doubtless too they hankered after the rich oil deposits that, although not yet discovered, were rumored to exist in the shaykhdom. In addition, Iraqi leaders tried to gain control of Kuwait to prevent the smuggling of goods from Kuwait into Iraq. This smuggling cost Iraq a considerable amount of money in lost custom revenues. Indeed, in September 1938 Iraqi officials maintained that the loss was as high as £250,000 per year, plus the cost of preventive measures such as extra police patrols along the frontier. The main reason for this smuggling was that Iraq maintained high tariffs—about 75 percent on such items as tea, coffee, sugar, tobacco, and matches—to raise revenue while Kuwait kept its tariffs low—about 4 percent on most items—because of its agreement with Britain on this subject and to encourage trade. Aside from the loss of revenue from this smuggling, Iraqi leaders were concerned that arms were moving from Kuwait into Iraq and that this illicit traffic was increasing their difficulty in maintaining firm control in the tribal areas of the country along the Euphrates. However, in spite of repeated Iraqi requests, the shaykh of Kuwait refused to do anything to curb smuggling—for example, raise tariffs, institute a quota system for imports, or take active preventive measures—because Kuwait's economy was heavily dependent upon trade, because he believed that it was Iraq's responsibility to control the illicit movement of goods into its own territory, and because he had major outstanding differences with the Iraqi government concerning the ownership and taxation of certain valuable date gardens in Iraq.[2]

As important as these considerations were for Iraq, probably the main reason why it attempted to gain control over Kuwait was to acquire freer access to the open sea. At this time Basra was Iraq's only port. Basra was a well-developed port but it had the disadvantage, from Iraq's point of view, of being situated more than seventy miles up the Shatt al-Arab River from the sea. Although a treaty between Iraq and Iran in 1937 confirmed Iraq's full control of the Shatt al-Arab (except for portions in the vicinity of Khorramshahr and Abadan where the frontier followed the *thalweg* or line of deepest flow), Iraqi leaders were concerned about the ease with which Iran, from its own territory, could impede or block the movement of ships proceeding up the river to Basra. Consequently, by the spring of 1938 they began to consider seriously the possibility of constructing an additional port in order to secure more satisfactory access to the sea. But the length of Iraq's coastline along the Persian Gulf was less than forty miles, and the topography of this area did not readily lend itself to the development of a port. Kuwait, on the other hand, had a much longer coastline along the Persian Gulf and thus more room for the construction of a port.[3]

Iraq based its legal title to Kuwait on the Anglo-Ottoman Convention of 1913. This agreement, which was never ratified, stipulated that Kuwait was an autonomous district of the Ottoman Empire and that the shaykh of Kuwait was an Ottoman official. Since Iraq was the successor state to the Ottoman Empire in this region, Iraqi leaders believed that they had inherited the Ottoman Empire's suzerainty over Kuwait.[4]

The British did not accept Iraq's contention. They pointed out that Ottoman authority in Kuwait had only been nominal, that in the Convention of 1913 the Ottoman government had even recognized the validity of the shaykh of Kuwait's agreements with Britain, and that Turkey had renounced all claims to Kuwait in the Treaty of Lausanne of 1923. They also noted that when Iraq was admitted to the League of Nations in 1932 it had formally accepted the border with Kuwait that Britain had established (although not actually demarcated) in 1923.[5]

Aside from these legal arguments, the British rejected Iraq's claim to Kuwait because they were determined to maintain their own dominant position in the shaykhdom. There were several reasons for this policy: Kuwait occupied an important location on the air route to India, and the British believed that this location might become even more important in the future if an unfriendly government in Baghdad expelled them from their air bases in Iraq; the British envisaged the possibility of moving troops along a motor route from Kuwait to Amman through Saudi Arabian territory if Iraq obstructed transport along the road from Baghdad to Amman; Ibn Saud, the king of Saudi Arabia with whom the British were eager to maintain good relations, preferred that they stay in Kuwait in order to prevent the growth of Iraqi influence in the shaykhdom; by 1938, although Kuwait was not yet exporting oil, prospects for oil development appeared good and the Kuwait Oil Company, which held the concession, was half-owned by the British-owned Anglo-Iranian Oil Company; the British considered the possibility of using Kuwait as a base for defending the large oil fields in southwestern Iran, for which the Anglo-Iranian Oil Company held the concession, in the event of an emergency; and the British feared that their prestige in the Persian Gulf region would fall if they sacrificed Kuwait to Iraq.[6]

In the late 1930s Iraq employed several methods in its efforts to gain control of Kuwait. For example, it waged a vigorous propaganda campaign in the press and on the radio against Shaykh Ahmad, the ruler of Kuwait, accusing him of oppressing his subjects and not spending any of his abundant revenues on education, health, or social welfare. These articles and broadcasts constantly referred to Kuwait as an integral part of Iraq and openly advocated Iraqi annexation of the shaykhdom.[7] The propaganda campaign was accompanied by Iraqi support for dissident elements within Kuwait and by incursions of Iraqi police cars into Kuwait.[8] During this period Iraq also tried to gain British permission to take over a large section of northern Kuwait; station police in Kuwait; maintain a political adviser at the shaykh's court; form a customs union with Kuwait; and build a port on the Bay of Kuwait and a railway linking that port with Iraq, both of which would remain under Iraqi control.[9] All of these efforts failed because Shaykh Ahmad would not yield to Iraqi pressure or accept any Iraqi influences in his country, and because Britain firmly supported him in this matter.[10]

But the British did not want to alienate Iraq unduly. Although they did not have the same legal and moral obligations toward Iraq that they had toward Kuwait, Iraq was a larger and more influential country and one in which they had important military and commercial interests. The British were also sympathetic with Iraq's desire to develop a port outside of the Shatt al-Arab that would therefore be less vulnerable to Iranian harassment. Consequently, in October 1938 they suggested that Iraq should consider the possibility of building a port on the Khor Abdullah. The Khor Abdullah was a channel of water jutting into the mainland west of the Shatt al-Arab. With its northwest arm, the Khor Shetana, it was bordered on one side by Iraq and on the other side by the Kuwaiti islands of Bubiyan and Warba. The British believed, and tried to persuade the Iraqis, that the Khor Abdullah was a better location for a port than the Bay of Kuwait because the water was deeper, both on the approach and near the shore, and therefore dredging costs would be lower. Indeed, the Khor Abdullah would require relatively little dredging because it was already about nineteen feet deep at low tide and twenty-nine feet at high tide, which was adequate for most of the ships that used the Persian Gulf. By contrast, the construction of a modern port on the Bay of Kuwait would necessitate large-scale dredging and the building of a long breakwater to provide shelter against unfavorable winds. In addition to this factor, the British argued that the Khor Abdullah was a better location for a port because it lay appreciably closer to the Iraqi railway system than did the Bay of Kuwait.[11]

The Iraqis delayed their response to the British suggestion regarding the construction of a port on the Khor Abdullah because they wanted to await the results of a survey they were making of the area. Finally, in November 1939 they informed Britain that they had decided to build a port near the Umm Qasr Creek, which flowed into the Khor Abdullah by way of the Khor Zubair. The mouth of the creek was six miles north of Warba Island, near the remains of an old Ottoman fort also known as Umm Qasr. Although the border between Iraq and Kuwait had not been demarcated on the ground, at the time it appeared to the British that while the northern side of the creek and the creek itself were in Iraq, the southern side might be in Kuwait. Although the Iraqis did not specify where in the vicinity of the Umm Qasr Creek they intended to construct the port, Kuwaiti ownership of the islands of Bubiyan and Warba meant that Kuwait controlled half of the channel leading to any port site in the area of Umm Qasr. Consequently, to gain complete control of the access route to the envisaged port they informed Britain that for security and navigational reasons they would like to acquire Bubiyan and Warba. Although these islands constituted a significant proportion of Kuwait's total territory, the Iraqis did not offer a quid pro quo to Kuwait for their cession. In their opinion compensation was unnecessary because the islands were barren and uninhabited and therefore valueless to Kuwait. Indeed, at certain times of the year large sections of the islands were under water at high tide.[12]

Foreign Office officials opposed Iraq's demand for Bubiyan and Warba because they could not envisage a threat to Iraq from a small and weak state like Kuwait that was in close treaty relationship with Britain. However, they sympathized with Iraq's desire for navigational reasons to control the entire channel leading to Umm Qasr. They also believed that Iraqi possession of undivided control of at least one good means of access to the sea would result in stabler conditions in that region in the future. In addition, they thought that ownership of half of the Khor Abdullah was useless to Kuwait. Consequently, in December 1939 the Foreign Office suggested that the British government should urge Kuwait to cede its rights in the Khor Abdullah in exchange for a monetary payment from Iraq.[13]

However, in February 1940 Lieutenant-Colonel C. G. Prior, the political resident in the Persian Gulf, who was responsible for protecting Kuwait's interests, strongly objected to the Foreign Office's proposal. He pointed out that in the future Kuwait might wish to construct its own port on the Khor Abdullah for the purpose of exporting oil and would not want the sea approaches to be completely controlled by Iraq; that Kuwaiti and thereby British control of one bank of the sea approaches to Umm Qasr was desirable because Britain would then possess a useful means of pressure on Iraq; that Ibn Saud would resent any Kuwaiti concession to Iraq on this issue because he strongly opposed an increase in Iraqi territory or privileges at the expense of Kuwait; and that any extension of Iraqi influence at the expense of Kuwait was inherently undesirable because Iraq's policy was ultimately to gain complete control of Kuwait.[14]

Prior's opposition to the Foreign Office's proposal to encourage the shaykh of Kuwait to yield his rights in the Khor Abdullah to Iraq was supported by the government of India, the India Office, and the British ambassador in Iraq.[15] In addition, the Kuwait Oil Company urged the British government to preserve the shaykh's rights in the Khor Abdullah because it wanted to retain the option of exporting Kuwait's oil through that waterway.[16] Finally, in March 1940 the shaykh of Kuwait adamantly refused to concede to Iraq any part of his territory or his territorial waters.[17] As a result of this opposition, in May 1940 the Foreign Office agreed that Britain should not press the shaykh to surrender his rights in the Khor Abdullah.[18]

By this time it was apparent to the British government that the Iraqis preferred to construct their port immediately south of the Umm Qasr Creek at a point on the Khor Zubair that was not clearly in Iraqi territory.[19] The Foreign Office wanted to obviate the problem of the undemarcated border at this sensitive point and also alleviate the disappointment of the Iraqi government with its failure to secure Bubiyan and Warba or Kuwait's rights in the Khor Abdullah. Consequently, in May 1940 the Foreign Office suggested that the British government should recommend that Iraq and Kuwait demarcate their common frontier in a manner that would clearly place in Iraq not only the southern side of the Umm Qasr Creek but also the entire length of the Khor Zubair including the southernmost section between the Umm Qasr Creek and Warba Island.[20]

We must now digress briefly to note that the Iraqi-Kuwaiti border was first defined in the Anglo-Ottoman Convention of 1913. (At this time, of course, the territory that eventually became Iraq was still part of the

Ottoman Empire.) According to the convention, "La ligne de démarca-tion part de la côte à l'embouchure du Khor-Zoubair vers le nord-ouest et passe immédiatement au sud d'Oumm-Kasr, de Safouan et de Djebel-Sanam, de façon à laisser ces endroits et leurs puits au vilayet de Basra."[21]

The Iraqi-Kuwaiti border was next defined in 1923, when Iraq was still a British mandate, by Sir Percy Cox, the British high commissioner in Iraq. At that time Cox declared that the Iraqi-Kuwaiti frontier should run "from the intersection of the Wadi-el-Audja with the Batin [a great depression] and thence northwards along the Batin to a point just south of the latitude of Safwan; thence eastwards passing south of Safwan wells, Jabal Sanam and Um Qasr, leaving them to Iraq and so on to the junction of the Khor Zubeir with the Khor Abdullah." In 1923 Cox also stated that his frontier line was identical to the line established by the Anglo-Ottoman Convention of 1913, although the wording of that agreement was not identical to his wording.[22]

In 1932 both Iraq and Kuwait formally accepted Cox's definition of their common frontier.[23] However, this did not solve the problem of the border because Iraq later maintained that its acceptance only meant that it recognized Kuwait as an autonomous subdivision of Iraq and not as an independent state. Iraq later also maintained that its acceptance was not binding because at the time it was still under the mandate and therefore not a completely free agent.[24]

Cox's definition of the common frontier did not solve the problem of the border also because it was imprecise and open to varying inter-pretations. For example, and most important for our purposes, Cox did not specify how far south of Umm Qasr (presumably he was referring to the fort and not to the creek) the border should run. The line estab-lished by the Anglo-Ottoman Convention of 1913, which Cox main-tained was identical with his line, passed "immédiatement au sud d'Oumm-Kasr." But Cox's formula of 1923 omitted the word imme-diately and merely stated that the frontier should run "south of . . . Um Qasr." Thus emphasis on the Anglo-Ottoman Convention for purposes of interpretation and clarification would favor Kuwait, while accent on Cox's formula alone would favor Iraq. Generally the India Office inclined toward the former course because it was acutely conscious of Britain's legal and moral obligation to uphold the interests of the shaykh of Kuwait, and in this regard to consider fully any evidence that might support those interests. However, the Foreign Office, which was very concerned with not alienating Iraq, maintained that Cox's definition of the Iraqi-Kuwaiti frontier in 1923 was the only binding text because it superseded the Anglo-Ottoman Convention that, in any case, had no legal validity because it had not been ratified.[25]

Another difficulty in establishing the northern border of Kuwait arose from the fact that the exact location of the two terminal points mentioned by Cox, that is, "a point just south of the latitude of Safwan" and "the junction of the Khor Zubeir with the Khor Abdullah" was unclear. The imprecision of the phrase "a point just south of the latitude of Safwan" is, of course, obvious. Similarly, the phrase "the junction of the Khor Zubeir with the Khor Abdullah" was unclear because it could refer to their median lines or to their *thalwegs* or even to a point on the shore near their confluence. However, the junction of the Khor Zubair with the Khor Abdullah was even more difficult to locate than appeared at first glance from Cox's text because a difference of opinion existed over the proper nomenclature to adopt for the various bodies of water in the region. For example, in November 1941 E. B. Wakefield, a member of the Indian Civil Service who studied the question at the request of the political agent in Kuwait, stated that the Khor Zubair terminated at the mouth of the Umm Qasr Creek, and that the channel between the Umm Qasr Creek and Warba Island was actually part of the Khor Abdullah. This definition would place in Kuwait the site of Iraq's envisaged port just south of the Umm Qasr Creek. Although Wakefield's position was carefully argued with detailed references to the negotiations preceding the Anglo-Ottoman Convention, the other British officials who studied the matter maintained that the Khor Zubair extended all of the way to Warba Island. Still, Wakefield's views on the question of nomenclature, and the logical consequence of these views, could not be dismissed lightly, and they further complicated an already tangled dispute.[26]

An added element of confusion arose from the fact that Cox did not indicate whether the northern border of Kuwait should be straight, following the shortest line between the two terminal points (wherever they were), or oblique. If one assumes the generally accepted definition of the Khor Zubair, a straight line would place the frontier about two miles south of the Umm Qasr fort and the creek and thereby favor Iraq. Conversely, and even under the same definition of the Khor Zubair, a line that curved southward after reaching the Umm Qasr fort could easily establish the border only a few yards south of this point and thereby favor Kuwait. In support of the latter position, in 1942 Lieutenant-Colonel W. R. Hay, the officiating political resident in the Persian Gulf, and the India Office pointed out that the Anglo-Ottoman Convention contained a map that, although of poor quality, did indicate that the northern frontier of Kuwait was oblique, with a definite curve toward the south in the vicinity of Umm Qasr, rather than straight. The Foreign Office, however, was disinclined to consider this point because it believed that Cox's definition of 1923 was the only authoritative text for establishing the Iraqi-Kuwaiti border, and that in any case the map attached to the Anglo-Ottoman Convention was drawn on a very small scale and was notoriously inaccurate.[27]

For many years, including the most trying period of the Second World War, various representatives and departments of the British government debated the question of the proper location of the Iraqi-Kuwaiti frontier. If Cox had been more precise while defining the border in 1923, or if he had appended a clearly drawn map to his description, he would have obviated considerable difficulty and much trouble for his government.[28]

We have observed that in May 1940 the Foreign Office proposed that Britain adopt a pro-Iraqi interpretation of Cox's definition of the Iraqi-Kuwaiti border. Specifically, the Foreign Office's interpretation drew a straight line from a point 1,050 yards south of the southernmost palm of Safwan (where a frontier notice board had stood until the Iraqis removed it in March 1939) to the western or right bank of the Khor Zubair about midway between the Umm Qasr Creek and Warba Island. The line then extended south along the low-water line on the right bank of the Khor Zubair until it reached the vicinity of Warba Island, at which point it moved into the channel to intersect the *thalwegs* of the Khor Zubair and the Khor Shetana. This line passed about two miles south of the Umm Qasr fort and clearly placed in Iraq the territory south of the Umm Qasr Creek where the Iraqi government planned to construct a port. It also placed in Iraq the entire length of the Khor Zubair including the southernmost section between the Umm Qasr Creek and Warba Island.[29]

Although they would soon change their positions, initially the political resident, the government of India, and the India Office supported the Foreign Office's proposal. They were eager to secure Iraq's agreement to demarcate the border to eliminate possibly serious complications if Iraq built a port on the Khor Zubair or if either country discovered oil in the vicinity of the frontier. They also hoped that demarcation would end or at least reduce the considerable number of border violations by Iraqi police cars that had occurred in recent years. In addition, they believed that demarcation would connote abandonment of Iraq's claim to the entirety of Kuwait.[30]

With the British now in agreement among themselves, in June 1940 they asked the shaykh of Kuwait to agree to the Foreign Office's interpretation or, as it was actually phrased, "clarification" of the existing definition of the Iraqi-Kuwaiti border. Trusting Britain to uphold his interests, unaware of the existence of the Anglo-Ottoman Convention or of Cox's statement that his frontier line was identical with the line drawn in that agreement, and possibly not fully comprehending the British proposal because it was unaccompanied by a clearly drawn line on a map, the shaykh agreed.[31]

With the shaykh now on board, in October 1940 and February 1941 the British government asked Iraq to agree to demarcate the Iraqi-Kuwaiti frontier on the basis of the Foreign Office's pro-Iraqi interpretation. However, the Iraqis, while not commenting on the accuracy or equitableness of the British interpretation, refused to demarcate the border until they had received territorial concessions from Kuwait that would enable them to secure full control over the Khor Abdullah. The Iraqis were probably also concerned that demarcation would involve recognizing the legitimacy of Kuwait, thereby making it more difficult for them later to claim sovereignty over all of Kuwait. In addition, the Iraqis probably refused to demarcate the frontier because at this time they lacked the financial resources to build a port at Umm Qasr, and therefore from their perspective there was no pressing need to establish the exact location of the border.[32]

And speaking of Iraq's inability to fund the construction of a port at Umm Qasr, in June 1940 the British government had refused an Iraqi request to contribute most of the cost because British military leaders stated that the project was unnecessary for the British war effort and would be an unjustifiable expense. They pointed out that Britain had to keep the Shatt al-Arab open in order to maintain access to the vital oil refinery at Abadan in Iran, and that as long as the Shatt al-Arab was open British forces had available a well-developed port at Basra. They also believed that it would be difficult for an enemy permanently to block the Shatt al-Arab by sinking a ship in the channel because the Iraqi government's Basra Port Directorate (the key positions in which were held by British officials) maintained four large and powerful dredges at Fao, near the mouth of the Shatt al-Arab, that would be able to cut a new passage or displace the blocking ship in a few days. In addition, they postulated that a heavy enemy air attack in this region, which might prevent the movement of ships up the Shatt al-Arab, was most unlikely. Soon, however, the eastward extension of the war made British military leaders reconsider their views on the need for a port at Umm Qasr.[33]

We have observed that during the Anglo-Iraqi hostilities of May 1941 the Germans sent two squadrons of warplanes to an airfield in northern Iraq to aid Rashid Ali. Because of their small number and late arrival, these aircraft did not have much effect on the course of the battle. Nevertheless, they gave Germany the ability to drop mines in the Shatt al-Arab and thereby impede access to Basra. Spurred by this danger, in May 1941 British military leaders in Iraq and Egypt expressed for the first time a desire to build a port at Umm Qasr to supplement the existing facilities at Basra. The following month the British military authorities in India and the Chiefs of Staff in London endorsed this request, although the fighting in Iraq was now over. These military leaders supported the construction of a port at Umm Qasr because, in addition to the fear of mines in the Shatt al-Arab, they wanted to provide more harbor facilities to supply the increased number of troops that the British government was planning to station in Iraq to defend the country against an anticipated renewed German offensive. It is interesting to observe, parenthetically, that British military leaders wanted to develop a port at Umm Qasr before the German attack on the Soviet Union on 22 June, indicating therefore that initially they were not concerned with using the port to facilitate the movement of war matériel to the Soviet Union.[34]

In mid-July 1941 the War Office, with the support of the Admiralty, ordered that work should begin at once on the construction of a British-controlled port at Umm Qasr and on a railway linking the port with the Iraqi railway system at Shaiba near Basra. Neither the government of Iraq nor the shaykh of Kuwait was consulted before the decision was taken, nor for that matter were the Foreign Office, the India Office, or the government of India. In deciding to develop a port at Umm Qasr the War Office and the Admiralty disregarded the fact that the narrow waters of the Khor Shetana and Khor Zubair could be mined almost as easily and effectively as those of the Shatt al-Arab, although this point was emphasized by the commander of the British naval forces in the Indian Ocean. The latter wanted to construct a port in the less confined waters of the Bay of Kuwait, but the Admiralty, while agreeing that the Bay of Kuwait was preferable to Umm Qasr from a minesweeping aspect, maintained that Umm Qasr could be built more quickly because plans for the port already existed. The Admiralty also believed that the Bay of Kuwait was too far from the Iraqi railway system and that the Iraqi government would be irritated if Britain developed a port in this area that was clearly outside of Iraqi territory.[35]

In late July 1941 Britain informed the Iraqi government and the shaykh of Kuwait about its intention to build a port at Umm Qasr that would remain under British control during the war. The Iraqi government welcomed this step, probably because it hoped to secure the port free of charge after the war. However, the shaykh of Kuwait, while not objecting to the construction of a British-controlled port at Umm Qasr, was concerned that Iraq would eventually gain control of it. He believed that an Iraqi port at Umm Qasr would attract trade and population from Kuwait and thereby gravely weaken his state. Consequently, in August 1941 he asked the British government to destroy the port after the war rather than hand it over to Iraq. The political resident and the government of India were sympathetic with this view, but the India Office and the Foreign Office were unwilling to commit themselves and instead gave the shaykh a general and rather vague assurance that his interests in this matter would be fully protected.[36]

The actual construction of the port was undertaken mainly by American contractors under the supervision of the British military authorities in Iraq. The Basra Port Directorate assisted the work, especially in the area of dredging and buoying, because it had conducted an earlier survey of the area and had much of the necessary equipment readily available. For technical reasons indicated by the earlier survey, such as the flow of the tides, the nature of the land approaches, the suitability of the soil to hold piles, and the slope of the seabed, in August 1941 the British military authorities chose a site for the port on the Khor Zubair immediately south of the Umm Qasr Creek. This location was precisely where Iraq had intended to build its port and, according to the line of demarcation that the British government had proposed to Iraq in October 1940, was clearly in Iraq.[37]

However, in October 1941, a few months after the British decision to build a port at Umm Qasr, Prior, the political resident in the Persian Gulf, recommended that the British government withdraw its proposal of October 1940 to demarcate the Iraqi-Kuwaiti frontier. He maintained that the proposal was based on an inaccurate interpretation of the border that was unfair to Kuwait, and that since Iraq had not accepted it the British government and the shaykh of Kuwait were not bound by it. Influenced by Prior's arguments, the India Office reversed its earlier support for the Foreign Office's pro-Iraqi interpretation. It now maintained that the 1940 formula was inconsonant with the Anglo-Ottoman Convention because the latter stipulated that the frontier should pass "immédiatement au sud d'Oumm Kasr." Consequently, the India Office recommended that the British government propose a new and fairer basis for the demarcation of the border.[38]

Responding to the India Office, in the spring of 1942 the Foreign Office continued to uphold the 1940 formula as a reasonable and accurate interpretation of Cox's definition of the Iraqi-Kuwaiti frontier. The Foreign Office also believed that since the British government had already communicated the 1940 formula to Iraq, the latter would not now accept a less favorable interpretation; that it would be most embarrassing for the British government to admit that in 1940 it had inadvertently neglected to read the relevant provisions of the Anglo-Ottoman Convention or that it had now changed its mind about the proper nomenclature to employ for the various bodies of water in the region; and that if Britain were bound to offend either Iraq or Kuwait in this matter it was more sensible to offend Kuwait, the weaker and less important country, especially since Kuwait had no option but to continue to rely on Britain for protection against its large and covetous neighbors. Finally, the Foreign Office emphasized that the 1940 formula had been accepted at the time by the India Office, the government of India, the political resident, and the shaykh of Kuwait.[39]

The disagreement between the Foreign Office and the India Office over the proper location of the Iraqi-Kuwaiti border continued throughout the Second World War. As a result, and also because the area around Umm Qasr port was being successfully administered by the British military authorities without hindrance, during the war the British government did not again press Iraq or Kuwait to demarcate their common frontier. Thus the question of whether the British government still adhered to the 1940 formula was left in abeyance.[40]

Ironically, after all of this dispute and contention Britain did not use the port of Umm Qasr to any appreciable extent during the Second World War. Although in March 1942 the British military authorities in Iraq declared the port open to shipping, at this time only two berths of an envisaged six-berth port were completed, and even these two berths were not put into full operation. In the spring of 1943 construction at Umm Qasr was halted, and work at the port was limited to care and maintenance. The British did not complete the development of the port because the Shatt al-Arab was not blocked during the war, and the large and modern port at Basra was able to handle all necessary shipping for Iraq. Moreover, the decisive Allied victories in North Africa and the Soviet Union in late 1942 and early 1943 essentially eliminated the German threat to Iraq and to navigation on the Shatt al-Arab.[41]

In the summer of 1943 the British began to consider the possibility of completing Umm Qasr after the war and then retaining the port for their own purposes. The Foreign Office favored this course of action because it feared that Anglo-Soviet relations would deteriorate after the war, and that in an emergency Umm Qasr would be a useful base for organizing the defense of the oil fields in southwestern Iran. The defense of these oil fields could not be organized from inside Iran because Britain was pledged to withdraw all of its military forces from that country within six months of the conclusion of hostilities. Nor could the defense of the Iranian oil fields be organized from Iraq because the Treaty of 1930, which gave Britain control over two air bases, did not permit it to station ground troops in Iraq in peacetime.[42]

However, the British military authorities in London, while not opposing the retention of Umm Qasr, were only lukewarm in their support of the scheme. In September 1943 the War Office estimated that it would cost about £1 million to complete the port, and all of the services had competing priorities for their limited resources. The Admiralty also had a developed and generally more suitable naval base in the Persian Gulf about 300 miles away at Bahrain, while the Air Ministry believed that it could supply its bases in Iraq by air from Egypt if the Shatt al-Arab were temporarily closed to shipping. Moreover, in March 1944 Cornwallis maintained that Umm Qasr was unsuitable as a permanent station for British troops because it was desolate and barren, and that the British military authorities in Iraq did not regard it favorably as a future base. As a result of these considerations, the British government abandoned the idea of completing the port of Umm Qasr and retaining it after the war as a British military base.[43]

The British government was now confronted with the option of dismantling the port of Umm Qasr or, alternatively, giving it to Iraq or Kuwait. In November 1944 Lieutenant-General Sir Arthur Smith, the commander of the British forces in Iraq and Iran, reported that the port was not only militarily useless in the present conflict but that it was actually a liability because it required British troops to guard it against pilfering. He also believed that the equipment and material at Umm Qasr, including some 6,000 tons of timber, could be better utilized elsewhere in his command or in other theaters of the war. In addition, Smith pointed out that soon it would be difficult to dismantle the port because after the war all of the British military personnel capable of such a task would leave the area. Consequently, he recommended that the British government begin to dismantle the port as soon as possible.[44]

Cornwallis supported Smith's recommendation and added that Britain should not consult the Iraqi government in advance because the latter would probably request that all of the port facilities remain in place. This request, Cornwallis believed, would inevitably reopen the troublesome and complicated matter of the undemarcated frontier between Iraq and Kuwait that for some years the British government had been attempting to keep quiescent.[45]

In March 1945 a committee of the War Cabinet, specially constituted to consider the matter of the ultimate disposal of the installations at Umm Qasr, also recommended that the port be dismantled. In addition to the reasons cited by General Smith, the committee emphasized that unless the port were dismantled its ownership would prove to be a continual source of trouble and dispute between Iraq and Kuwait. The committee conceded that the port might be useful in some future war in that region but this factor was insufficient to alter its recommendation, especially because of its belief that the lifespan of the existing facilities was rather limited.[46]

The political resident, the government of India, and the Chiefs of Staff all agreed that the port of Umm Qasr should be dismantled. The Foreign Office, which by now had abandoned its earlier proposal to retain the port under British control, did not object to this solution. Consequently, in April 1945, one month before the cessation of hostilities in Europe, the War Office instructed the British military authorities in Iraq to dismantle the port.[47]

Throughout the dispute over Umm Qasr and the Iraqi-Kuwaiti frontier between 1938 and 1945, Britain was confronted with the difficult task of reconciling its obligation to protect the interests of Kuwait with its desire not to alienate Iraq. During this period the political resident in the Persian Gulf, the government of India, and the India Office generally gave priority to upholding the interests of Kuwait, while the British ambassador in Iraq and the Foreign Office were usually more concerned with maintaining good relations with Iraq. However, in the final analysis all of the British representatives and departments that dealt with this question agreed that it was essential to maintain the independence of Kuwait under British protection and therefore necessary to prevent any serious Iraqi encroachment on Kuwait. Thus Britain refused to allow Iraq to construct a port on the Bay of Kuwait under its own control, refused to countenance Iraq's claims to the Kuwaiti islands of Bubiyan and Warba or to Kuwait's rights in the Khor Abdullah, and insisted upon retaining complete control over the operation of the port of Umm Qasr. Britain's dismantling of the port at the end of the war was also designed at least in part to protect the interests of Kuwait. By safeguarding Kuwait from Iraq, these measures helped Britain to maintain its own dominant position in the shaykhdom until well into the postwar period. Ultimately, in 1961, at the request of Kuwait, Britain withdrew its protectorate and Kuwait became a completely independent state.

While Britain was successful in upholding Kuwait's interests, it could only achieve this goal at the expense of its relations with Iraq. Indeed, from Iraq's perspective Britain was depriving Iraq of much needed custom revenues, increasing Iraq's internal security problems, blocking Iraq's path to the open sea, preventing Iraq from increasing its oil resources, and impeding the advancement of Arab unity. Even Britain's efforts in 1940 and 1941 to demarcate the frontier on the basis of the Foreign Office's pro-Iraqi interpretation of Cox's 1923 definition angered the Iraqis because it would have denied them Bubiyan and Warba, and entailed the abandonment of their claim to the entirety of Kuwait.

During the remaining tenure of the old regime the question of the Iraqi-Kuwaiti border, and indeed the very existence of Kuwait as a quasi-independent shaykhdom under British protection, continued to trouble Anglo-Iraqi relations. In the 1950s, as Kuwait grew richer and Iraq became increasingly interested in constructing its own port at Umm Qasr, Iraq intensified its efforts to gain control of all or part of the country. Because of continued British and Kuwaiti opposition, these efforts too were unsuccessful. Still, they indicate that Iraq's expansionist tendencies toward the south, which were so clearly manifested in 1990, were of long duration and not simply a product of the Baathist ascendancy.[48]

Part II

THE END OF THE SECOND WORLD WAR AND THE BEGINNING OF THE DECLINE IN BRITISH INFLUENCE 1945–48

.6.

Britain's Weakened Position

For Britain the human and economic costs of the Second World War were very high. Nearly 400,000 British soldiers and civilians were killed. Nearly 500,000 houses were destroyed or rendered uninhabitable, and more than 3.5 million others were damaged. In all, this amounted to about one-third of the houses in Britain.[1]

Many industrial plants, which were of course one of Germany's main objectives, were also destroyed. In all, the total damage to property, at postwar replacement costs, amounted to £1.45 billion.

Over and above such losses, Britain's industrial capacity was severely run-down because the urgent demand for immediate and maximum production, coupled with shortages of materials and labor, meant that most repair and maintenance had to be deferred. In all, this type of domestic industrial disinvestment, excluding deliberate destruction by the enemy, amounted to nearly £900 million.

During the war Britain had devoted the great majority of its productive facilities to military supplies and essential domestic needs. As a result, its export trade had fallen off substantially, plunging in 1943 to only 29 percent (by volume) of the prewar figure. In spite of the radical decline in exports, during the conflict Britain was still able to maintain a high level of imports because of Lend-Lease from the United States, Mutual Aid from Canada, and sterling credits from numerous other countries, including Iraq. After the war, however, when foreign aid was reduced, when many of its industrial plants had deteriorated and many of its overseas markets had been lost to import substitution or American competition, and when domestic reconstruction needs were very great, Britain was confronted with the formidable task of once again having to pay its own way in the world.

This task was made even more difficult because as a result of the war Britain had accumulated an enormous amount of overseas debt. The extent of this development is illustrated by the fact that on the eve of the conflict Britain's total external liabilities were £476 million, while at the end of the war they stood at £3.355 billion. Most of this debt was the result of large-scale military campaigns in the Middle East and Far East. To wage these campaigns Britain had to spend a great deal of money in these areas on the building of airfields, railways, roads, and harbors, the payment of local labor, and the acquisition of supplies. For the most part this expenditure took the form of huge debts or sterling balances that the countries of the region accumulated in London. Now, at the end of the war, when Britain needed to devote all of its energies to domestic reconstruction and earning precious dollars to pay for vitally needed imports from the United States and other countries that demanded payment in dollars, these sterling balances represented a tremendous drain on Britain's productive capacity.

Traditionally income from overseas investments had greatly helped Britain to pay for imports. However, during the war, when Britain was no longer able to export much, the country had been obliged to liquidate many of its overseas assets in order to acquire enough foreign exchange to pay for essential imports. In all, Britain sold more than £1.1 billion worth of overseas investments. As a result of this wholesale liquidation, in 1945 Britain's income from overseas investments was less than half that received in 1938.

Traditionally income from shipping had also helped Britain to pay for imports. However, during the war Britain lost more than half of the prewar tonnage of its merchant marine. Although Britain built or acquired many ships during the conflict, at the end of the war, and after allowing for the return of ships belonging to other countries, its tonnage was still only 71 percent of the prewar figure. Thus Britain's long-standing ability to earn foreign exchange from shipping services was now reduced.

Nor did Britain have sufficient gold and dollar reserves to deal with these serious problems because it had spent these holdings freely in the early period of the war, mainly for the purchase of vital supplies from the United States. The extent of this development is indicated by the fact that at the outset of the war in September 1939 Britain's gold and dollar reserves amounted to more than £600 million, while in April 1941 they stood at only £3 million. Although Britain increased these holdings during the latter part of the war because of the large-scale stationing of American troops in Britain, at the end of the conflict they still amounted to only £450 million. In view of Britain's tremendous obligations and needs, this sum was relatively small.

If we add up Britain's debts in the form of sterling balances, loss of overseas investments, and the running down of its gold and dollar reserves, we arrive at a figure of nearly £4.2 billion. This sum represents Britain's total wartime capital loss in its overseas financial position.

If we add to this figure the cost of physical destruction in Britain, internal disinvestment as a result of deterioration of industrial facilities due to inadequate maintenance, and loss of shipping (including cargoes), we arrive at a total loss of national wealth of approximately £7.3 billion. Since prewar British national wealth was roughly £30 billion (at postwar prices), this means that during the war Britain lost about 25 percent of its national wealth.

We have observed that during the war Britain had to make large overseas payments to support its military forces abroad. But the conclusion of the conflict did not terminate this drain on the exchequer. On the contrary, for various reasons Britain continued to maintain garrisons, sometimes quite sizable, in numerous places in continental Europe, the Middle East, South Asia, and the Far East. The sums involved in these deployments are indicated by the fact that in 1946 Britain's overseas military expenditure amounted to £216 million, of which £61 million was spent in the Middle East.[2]

In addition to costing money, these overseas deployments created the need for large armed forces at a time when Britain was suffering from an acute labor shortage due to an all-out effort to produce enough goods to facilitate domestic recovery and pay for essential imports. The numbers involved are indicated by the fact that in June 1946, over a year after the surrender of Germany, there were still 1.9 million men in the armed forces.[3] By contrast, before the war, in March 1936 there were only 344,000 men in the armed forces.[4]

Thus in the immediate postwar period Britain's weak economic position was further weakened by an overextended and expensive military position. And in this difficult situation the British had to confront serious challenges to their dominant position in the Middle East. For example, in Greece they had to conduct a counterinsurgency campaign against Communist guerrillas; in Turkey they had to assist the government in resisting Soviet pressure for territorial concessions in the eastern part of the country and military bases at the Straits; in Iran they had to press the Soviets to evacuate their wartime zone of occupation in the northern part of the country; in Palestine they had to combat an uprising by the Jewish community over the issue of immigration; in Egypt they had to resist a strong nationalist movement pressing for the evacuation of all

British military forces from the country; and in Iraq they had to deal with increasingly loud demands for the revision of the Treaty of 1930.[5]

For Britain the difficulty in Iraq was in part due to the fact that with the end of the war in sight, in the summer and autumn of 1944 the government eased press censorship, permitted the formation of labor unions, and released some of the internees. But it did not combine this liberalization with meaningful political reforms such as free elections, or serious economic and social reforms to redistribute wealth and improve the condition of the great mass of the population that lived in poverty. And because Britain exercised such a strong position in Iraq and was so closely linked to the regime, the ability of the Iraqi people to write, speak, and organize more freely made it the target of every discontent. This criticism was increased by the fact that the end of the wartime alliance between Britain and the Soviet Union freed the Iraqi Communist from the self-imposed restraints under which they had previously operated in this regard.[6]

For the British the difficulty in Iraq was also due to the fact that the Treaty of 1930 did not give them the right to station ground troops in Iraq in peacetime. For this reason, and also because of nationalist pressure in Iraq and manpower and financial constraints at home, after the war they continued the withdrawal of their military forces that had begun in early 1943 with the termination of the German threat to the area. In May 1946 the number of troops was down to three battalions most of whom were guarding stores that the British had not yet been able to evacuate or dispose of. However, in July 1946, with the permission of the Iraqi government the British temporarily reinforced their garrison by dispatching a brigade of Indian troops to the Basra area because of disturbances in the Iranian oil fields. But the situation in Iran soon quieted down, and pressure from India for the return of the troop mounted. Consequently, the withdrawal soon resumed, and in October 1947 the last Imperial troops left Iraq. Although Britain still retained control of two air bases, clearly its ability to safeguard its position an influence events in the country was now reduced.[7]

It should be noted that the Indian troops that left Iraq in 1947 were the last ones that Britain was ever able to use to assist in maintaining it dominant position in the Middle East because in August of that yea

India and Pakistan became independent states. For Britain the loss of the Indian army was a considerable blow because during the First World War most of the troops that conquered Iraq from the Ottoman Empire were Indian. In 1920 most of the troops that suppressed a widespread uprising against British rule in Iraq were Indian. During the Second World War most of the troops that conquered Iraq and Iran and then remained to defend them against a German attack were Indian. And as we have just observed, as late as the winter of 1946-47 Britain retained a substantial Indian force at Basra to intervene in the event of disturbances in the Iranian oil fields.[8]

Aside from the withdrawal of its ground troops, Britain's influence in Iraq was reduced because, in deference to nationalist sentiment, in March 1946 the ambassador terminated his political advisory organization in the provinces. Although he replaced the political advisers with a number of vice-consuls, the latter were fewer in number and did not have the authority or status of their predecessors.[9]

Further reducing Britain's influence in Iraq, for nationalist reasons in 1946 and 1947 Iraqi leaders dismissed nearly all of the British advisers whom they had employed during the war and did not replace them. For example, in September 1946 they dismissed the adviser in the Ministry of Education and the assistant adviser in the Ministry of Interior, in October 1946 the adviser in the Ministry of Communications and Works, and in June 1947 the adviser in the Ministry of Finance. During this period they also dismissed the last three senior British police officials in the Ministry of Interior. As a result, in September 1947 Douglas Busk, the British chargé d'affaires in Baghdad, observed that "the time is past when we can hope to induce the Iraqis to consider the appointment of British experts, except in technical subjects."[10]

In view of all these considerations and developments, after the war Clement Attlee, prime minister in the new Labour government, believed that Britain was no longer strong enough to maintain its dominant position in the Middle East. Nor, in his opinion, was it still necessary to protect the route to India because India would soon become independent. In addition, he feared that a strong British military position in the Middle East might frighten the Soviets and thereby actually provoke their aggression. Consequently, Attlee concluded that Britain should essentially withdraw from the area. As he put it in March 1946, the cabinet should now "consider the British Isles as an easterly extension of a strategic area the centre of which is the American continent rather than as a power looking eastwards through the Mediterranean to India and the East."[11]

Attlee's proposal was supported by Hugh Dalton, the chancellor of the exchequer, who for reasons of economy wanted to reduce overseas military expenditure. Indeed, Dalton felt so strongly about this question that in February 1946 he warned the cabinet that "unless we can reduce our overseas military expenditure drastically and rapidly, and avoid further overseas commitments, we have no alternative but to cut our rations and reduce employment through restrictions in the import of machinery and raw materials."[12]

However, Attlee's proposal was not adopted because it encountered strong opposition elsewhere in the government, and in the end he did not press it hard.[13] The dominant view, which was held by Foreign Secretary Ernest Bevin[14] and the permanent officials in the Foreign Office,[15] the Chiefs of Staff,[16] and the Ministry of Fuel and Power,[17] was that the Middle East was too important to abandon.

To begin with, there was the matter of the protection of the oil facilities. While the Middle East was now producing only about 10 percent of the world's supply, it was common knowledge that this figure would soon increase substantially because the region contained vast reserves and production in other areas would not be able to keep pace with rising world demand. Indeed, in 1946 the Middle East was already supplying 60 percent of Britain's requirements, and British officials estimated that by 1955 this figure would increase to 70 percent. Moreover, British companies held the concessions for Iraq, Iran, and Kuwait. True, in Iraq the Anglo-Iranian Oil Company (AIOC) and Shell, the British interests in the Iraq Petroleum Company, only had access to about half of the production. But this amount was a great deal because Iraq was already producing more than 4 million tons per year, and according to British calculations by 1955 this figure would rise to nearly 27 million tons per year. And in Iran the AIOC had access to all of the production, and in Kuwait to half of the production. The quantities involved and the consequent importance of the British concessions are indicated by the fact that in 1946 the combined production of Iraq, Iran, and Kuwait totalled 24.7 million tons, while British requirements for that year were only 16 million tons. But better was yet to come because, according to British estimates, by 1955 the combined production in these three countries would increase to 91.8 million tons, while British requirements would only rise to 32 million tons. And from the sales of the products of this production in 1946 the AIOC and Shell earned £109 million, and British officials estimated that by 1950 this figure would more than double. All of this income was, of course, taxable in the United Kingdom. Moreover, the British government gained from the AIOC's dividend distribution because it was the majority stockholder in the company. The importance of the concessions is further indicated by the fact that in all three countries Britain and other members of the sterling area could purchase oil for sterling and thereby conserve their precious dollar supplies. But the concessions also meant that the British oil companies had extremely valuable and vulnerable physical assets in the region. For example, the AIOC's refinery at Abadan in southwestern Iran alone had a 1946 replacement cost of £120 million, which was roughly the sum required to retool and modernize the entire British coal industry.[18]

For Bevin the need to protect Britain's oil assets in the Middle East was linked to his belief that their loss would lead to a decline in the standard of living at home. As he put it in May 1947, "the British interests in the Middle East contribute substantially not only to the prosperity of the people there, but also to the wage packets of the workers in this country. . . . I cannot be a party to an act or policy which would result in lowering the wages and purchasing power of Great Britain."[19]

Aside from oil, there was the matter of communications because the Middle East controlled the shortest sea and air routes to India. Even after India became independent communications through the Middle East would be important because Britain would still retain possessions and Commonwealth associates in the Far East such as Malaya, Singapore, Hong Kong, Australia, and New Zealand.[20]

At this time the British also viewed the Middle East as a bulwark separating a hostile and possibly aggressive Soviet Union from Africa. Because they intended to develop their African colonies to help facilitate domestic recovery, this consideration was important.[21]

In addition, the British were eager to retain their dominant position in the Middle East because the region contained bases from which they could launch air attacks on valuable oil and other installations in the southern part of the Soviet Union in the event of war. Because Anglo-Soviet relations deteriorated rapidly after 1945, this consideration too was important.[22]

And so in spite of their weakened condition, in the postwar period the British had no intention of abandoning their dominant position in the Middle East. But Bevin believed that in the long run Britain could only secure this position by accommodating local nationalists and eliminating some of the more objectionable features of its former imperium in the region, such as interfering in the internal affairs of the local countries. He also wanted to promote political democracy, economic development, and social reform so that it would not appear, as it so often had in the past, that Britain was relying exclusively upon small numbers of wealthy, corrupt, and repressive individuals to maintain its influence. In other words, Bevin wanted to secure Britain's dominant position in the Middle East by appeasing nationalist sensibilities and broadening Britain's local basis of support. His failure to do so has been discussed at length in a distinguished work by William Roger Louis.[23] Perforce Louis was only able to devote a relatively small amount of attention to Iraq, and it is to filling this gap that the following chapters are devoted.

.7.

The Iraqi Opposition

D uring the Second World War political liberty in Iraq was severely restricted. For example, there was martial law, internment without trial, censorship of the press, rigged elections, and a ban on political parties. Paradoxically, while these restrictions were in place Iraq was allied with a group of nations ostensibly fighting for freedom and against repression, and British propaganda extolling the merits of democracy was infusing the country. Consequently, by the end of the war there was much discontent with the continued domination of the country by the small group of conservative politicians who enforced these restrictions and also resisted vitally needed economic and social reforms. In the summer of 1945 this discontent increased when the victory of the Labour party in the elections in Britain drew a stark contrast with the lack of similar change in Iraq.[1]

British officials in Iraq supported the liberalization of political life and the implementation of economic and social reforms because they believed that such measures were necessary to ameliorate the widespread discontent with the regime and stave off revolutionary upheaval. For example, in February 1944 G. H. Thompson, the counsellor, maintained that "there is undoubtedly growing weariness of the 'old gang,' which one day is likely to find violent expression in some form or another."[2] In March 1945 Ambassador Cornwallis warned that "unless they [the Iraqi ruling class] do make some concessions, a violent clash between the 'haves' and the 'have-nots' is inevitable in time."[3] And in September 1945 Thompson pointed out that "members of this embassy lose no opportunity of impressing on Ministers and all responsible Iraqis with whom they come in contact that their first line of defence against communism is an advanced social programme."[4]

The Foreign Office officials in London who dealt with Iraq generally held a similar view. For example, in March 1945 C. W. Baxter, the head of the Eastern Department, maintained that "the comparatively small clique of politicians which governs the country is not really representative of the people or of the younger generation. It looks as if there is bound to be trouble before long."[5] And in less clinical language, the following month R. M. A. Hankey, also from the Eastern Department, railed against "the fat and socially callous pashas who form the Governments [in the Middle East] which we keep in power."[6]

As we observed in the previous chapter, Foreign Secretary Ernest Bevin, who came to power with the Labour government in July 1945, also favored progressive reforms. He was especially interested in broadening Britain's base of support in the Middle East by reducing its dependence upon small groups of wealthy, reactionary, repressive, unpopular, and corrupt leaders.

In response to the pressure for liberalization from within Iraq and from Britain, in December 1945 the regent gave a speech to Parliament calling for the formation of political parties, the holding of free elections, and the implementation of economic and social reforms to provide at least some redistribution of the country's wealth. Two months later, in February 1946, he appointed Tawfiq al-Suwaydi as prime minister to implement this new policy. Now in his late fifties, Tawfiq was a lawyer by training. Having first held cabinet office in 1928 and having served as prime minister in 1929, he was very much part of the ruling class. However, he was more liberal than most of its members, and presumably for this reason was now the regent's choice.[7]

In accordance with the regent's desire, popular demand, British pressure, and his own views, Tawfiq liberalized political life in Iraq. For example, immediately after coming to power he eliminated martial law, internment, and censorship of the press. These actions quickly led to the establishment of a large number of newspapers. Indeed, by April 1946 there were as many as nineteen appearing regularly in Baghdad. Reflecting as well as creating public opinion, nearly all of these newspapers advocated the great reduction or complete elimination of British influence in Iraq. Specifically, they demanded the revision or abrogation of the Treaty of 1930, the withdrawal of all British military forces from the country, and the dismissal of the numerous British subjects whom the Iraqi government employed at high salaries.[8]

While the British supported the liberalization of political life in Iraq, they did not like the results and especially the constant and bitter attacks on Britain's position in the country. Consequently, they now pressed Iraqi leaders to curb the press. But Tawfiq was unwilling so quickly to reverse a policy that in response to widespread demands he had just implemented. He may also have feared incurring unpopularity by appearing to act at the behest of the British. In any event, he did little to restrict the press.[9]

Continuing his policy of liberalization, in April 1946 Tawfiq sanctioned the formation of five political parties. The strongest was the Istiqlal or Independence party, an extreme nationalist pan-Arab organization composed largely of supporters of former prime minister Rashid Ali. It emphasized support for Arab rights in Palestine and opposition to the British bases in Iraq. The Istiqlal had considerable support among the urban, middle-class, Sunni Arab section of the population, including government officials, army officers, and students. But the party's pan-Arabism had little appeal to the Kurds or other minorities, and its lack of stress on social reform reduced its support from the lower classes.[10]

Of the other parties, the Liberals were a weak center group of little consequence. The remaining three, the National Democratic party, the National Union party, and the People's party, were left-wing. Of them, the largest and most moderate were the National Democrats. They supported distribution of state lands to the peasantry, limitations on future accumulations of large quantities of private land, government planning for economic development, graduated income and inheritance taxes, improvement of working and living conditions for the peasantry and urban proletariat, and expansion of public health and education. They opposed the use of violence and did not advocate the nationalization of private estates. Indeed, the latter proposal would have been difficult for them to support because their leader, Kamil Chadirchi, was a large landowner. Because the National Democrats were concerned with social reform and did not emphasize pan-Arabism, they had more appeal to the Shiites and minorities than did the Istiqlal. Indeed, even British officials generally sympathized with the party's domestic program, but they felt unable to support the party because it advocated the withdrawal of all British military forces from Iraq.[11]

The People's party was the most radical of the three legal left-wing parties. Although in many respects its platform was similar to that of the National Democrats, its leader, Aziz Sharif, was a poor man who questioned the wealthy Chadirchi's sincerity and true commitment to the cause of reform. He also believed that ultimately a certain degree of violence would be necessary to rid the country of its present ruling class.

Moreover, in his newspaper articles he was a closer follower of the virulently anti-British line propagated by Moscow radio than was Chadirchi.[12]

In the spring of 1946 the underground and illegal Communist party applied for legalization under the name of the National Liberation party. However, Tawfiq's liberalization policy did not extend this far, and the government denied the application.[13]

Nonetheless, Tawfiq's measures alarmed the conservative forces in Iraq. Unlike him, most of them were unwilling to jeopardize their political and economic control of the country by making serious concessions to the opposition. Consequently, in late May 1946 they engineered his defeat on a money bill in the Senate and in this manner forced him to resign.[14]

Apparently frightened by the repercussions of the policy that originally he himself had proposed, the regent now requested Arshad al-Umari to form a new government. Now in his late fifties, Arshad came from a prominent family in Mosul. Trained as an engineer, he had served in the Ottoman army during the First World War. He first held cabinet office in 1934, and then for many years served as mayor of Baghdad. On 30 May 1941, after Rashid Ali had fled to Iran, he performed a valuable service for Britain by persuading Iraqi military commanders to seek an armistice. Three days later, on 2 June, when leading police officials and army officers were refusing to suppress serious anti-Jewish rioting in Baghdad, he again acted decisively in favor of the established order by prevailing upon the regent to issue a written directive commanding them to fire upon the rioters. Of the leading politicians in Iraq he was one of the most authoritarian, and because of the prevailing circumstances this was an important reason for his appointment.[15]

On 28 June 1946 there was an antigovernment and anti-British demonstration in Baghdad organized by the illegal National Liberation party and its legal front group the Anti-Zionist League. The demonstrators numbered about 800, approximately 100 of whom were soldiers. Prominent among their demands were the withdrawal of all British military forces from Iraq, the legalization of the National Liberation party, and the creation of an Arab state in Palestine. To prevent the demonstrators from reaching their destination of the British embassy, the police opened fire killing one and wounding six. The police then arrested ninety-seven of the demonstrators, twenty-nine of whom were soldiers. At the same time a group of soldiers gathered at the railway station at the outskirts of Baghdad with the intention of moving into the city to join the demonstration. However, the police prevented them from moving and eventually the military police arrived and took about 100 of them into custody.[16]

For Arshad the Baghdad demonstration, and especially the comparatively large number of soldiers who were involved or who attempted to
become involved, was an ominous sign. Adding to his concern, a few
days later about 5,000 workers at the Iraq Petroleum Company's facilities at Kirkuk went on strike for increased wages and improved working conditions. Here too there was violence when on 12 July 1946 the
police opened fire on a meeting of strikers killing six and wounding
twenty-eight.[17]

Alarmed by the Baghdad demonstration and the IPC strike, and angered
by strong criticism from the opposition parties and newspapers, Arshad
decided to crack down. But before embarking upon a test of strength with
the opposition, in July 1946 he explained his plans to the British and
sought an assurance of support. To help persuade them, he argued, correctly, that the opposition was not only opposed to his government but to
Britain's dominant position in Iraq. He also maintained, this time with less
truth, that all three of the legal left-wing opposition parties were really
Communist and in close contact with the Soviet legation.[18]

The British rejected Arshad's request. True, they supported strict
measures against specific individuals who were fomenting disturbances
and firm dealing with particular breaches of the law. For example, during the IPC strike they recommended that the government arrest the agitators whom they believed were largely responsible for the trouble.
However, they opposed general restrictions on liberty because, as they
saw it, repressive measures of this nature would only increase anti-
regime and anti-British sentiment. They also feared that such measures
would drive the left-wing parties underground where they would be
more difficult to monitor and where their influence would grow in
secret. In addition, they were concerned that the Soviet Union would
respond by intensifying its propaganda against both Iraq and Britain, and
by attempting to stimulate unrest among discontented groups like the
oil-field workers and the Kurds. Rather than a policy of general repression, the British recommended that the government implement social
and economic reforms to improve the standard of living of the working
class. By thereby satisfying legitimate grievances, especially in the areas
of pay and housing, they hoped to separate the relatively small number
of extremists from the great bulk of their potential supporters.[19]

Like most members of the ruling class, Arshad had little interest in
remedial measures of this sort. He may also have suspected the British
of hypocrisy because they advocated tough steps when trouble
occurred at a British-controlled company like the IPC but not in Iraqi

affairs generally. In any event, he did not believe that remedial measures would be effective in time to meet the immediate danger.[20] And
in August 1946 this danger appeared to increase when the opposition
severely criticized him for allowing Britain to bring a brigade of Indian
troops into the country to act as a possible force of intervention in a
bitter labor dispute in the Iranian oil fields.[21]

Consequently, in the summer of 1946 Arshad adopted a policy of
strict repression. The comprehensiveness of the policy is illustrated by
the fact that by August he had suppressed ten newspapers, including
those of four of the five legal opposition parties. He also took legal
action against many of his opponents, including Kamil Chadirchi.
Chadirchi, it will be recalled, was a man of considerable wealth and
stature, a former minister and former president of the Press Association,
and currently head of the only mildly reformist National Democratic
party. Nonetheless, on 11 August he was charged with violating the
penal code by publishing false reports in his party's newspaper about the
government's handling of the strike by the IPC workers and "thus
estranging the people from the Government." His trial resulted in a
sentence of imprisonment of six months at hard labor followed by a year
of police surveillance. He was permitted to appeal but was denied bail,
and his party's newspaper was suspended indefinitely.[22]

As another example of Arshad's determination to stamp out even moderate opposition, in September 1946 he suspended the anticommunist
newspaper *Al-Nahdha* because of a mildly critical article of the government that it had published. This newspaper, it should be noted, was
partly founded by, and had published articles by, Fadhil al-Jamali, his
own foreign minister.[23]

Arshad had considerable success in suppressing opposition newspapers. Indeed, by October 1946 all of the remaining newspapers were
well-disposed, or at least not hostile, to his government. However, he was
less successful in imprisoning his opponents because often judges, many
of whom opposed his repressive policies, would not convict them. For
example, Chadirchi's conviction was overturned upon appeal to a higher
court. Iraq, it must be remembered, for all its faults and injustices—domination by a small wealthy group, rigged elections, harassment of the
opposition, terrible corruption, extreme maldistribution of wealth, and
lack of social measures to improve the lot of the poor—was, interestingly,
and largely because of its British heritage, still a *Rechtsstaat*.[24]

In late September 1946 Arshad attempted to circumvent the judicial
obstacle by obtaining a grant of dictatorial powers from the regent. He

then planned to banish his opponents to remote parts of the country or intern them in concentration camps like those that had existed in Iraq during the Second World War.[25]

The British were pleased that Arshad was bringing some discipline and order to public life after what they considered to be the excessive tolerance of Tawfiq's government.[26] Nonetheless, they opposed his crackdown because they thought that it went too far and included the suppression of legitimate dissent. They were also concerned that it was creating anti-British sentiment because it was unpopular in the country, and many Iraqis automatically assumed that Britain was behind every government action. They were worried too by signs that it was uniting the opposition parties that previously had had considerable difficulty cooperating. For example, on 30 August the three legal left-wing parties met in a large assembly to condemn the government. In addition, they were alarmed by indications that it was arousing sympathy for the victims of prosecution and thereby gaining adherents for the opposition. For example, in September the printers and railway workers went on strike in protest against the suppression of the newspapers and the prosecution of the editors.[27]

Aside from the crackdown on dissent, the British were concerned because Arshad was refusing to conduct free elections in accordance with the regent's pledge of December 1945. They believed that free elections in Iraq were necessary for a healthy political life, and they feared that a refusal to hold them would increase discontent within the country and cause an unfavorable impression abroad. While recognizing that some left-wing candidates would probably win seats, they thought that this result would actually be desirable to spur the government into reforms. They also considered it preferable for opposition leaders to make their speeches publicly in Parliament rather than secretly in more conspiratorial settings. Moreover, they believed that service as deputies would be a valuable education for these people and a moderating influence on their temperaments and policies.[28]

In addition to the crackdown on dissent and refusal to conduct free elections, the British were upset because Arshad was not making any effort to implement social and economic reforms that would improve the standard of living and thereby make the poor less vulnerable to appeals by radical agitators. On the contrary, Arshad seemed to feel that "if you encourage labourers in any way at all they will turn and rend you," and that "it was not worth worrying about fifty thousand or so industrial workers, who should be kept severely in their place."[29]

But the British were unable to alter Arshad's policies very much because the prime minister was almost impervious to their advice and suggestion. For example, in August 1946 Douglas Busk, the chargé d'affaires, complained that

> he switches the subject of conversation before one can get down to it, and is inclined to weird outbursts. It is impossible to get a word in edgewise, and he has a habit of declaring an interview at an end without the business in hand having been properly settled. On one occasion, when the commercial secretary and I were having a meeting with him and several of his colleagues, we were compelled to resist our ejection and carried on the discussion, shaking hands vigorously all the time, down the corridor until we were able to achieve the result we wanted at the front door. I am sure that the ambassador will agree with me that it is rare for one to leave an interview with the Prime Minister without a feeling of frustration.[30]

And the following month, after a dinner party with the prime minister, Stewart Perowne, the oriental counsellor, observed that

> Arshad was completely uncompromising. He would hardly even discuss anything political, and said that he understood in Britain it was a custom that you did not talk politics in the evening. . . . When I suggested that perhaps some of them [the left-wing politicians] might be ready to play ball with us he waved the idea aside, said they were all dogs and that I did not understand the people.
> The mention of elections sent his blood pressure rocketing. "Impossible until these people are beaten," he said.[31]

Nor could the British influence Arshad through other cabinet members or permanent officials because he did not listen to them either. In August 1946 Busk indicated the extent of the problem when he reported that

> the Prime Minister is ruthless, and, I understand, even offensive to his colleagues and subordinates. His colleagues are terrified of him and have on occasion actually asked us to speak for them in matters concerning their departments. It is doubtful if any of them, including the Minister for Foreign Affairs, dare to pass on our remarks to the Prime Minister, though they say, apparently with the utmost sincerity, that they agree with them.[32]

While the British frequently pressed Arshad to moderate his crack-down and conduct free elections, this was not widely known in the country and so they did not receive much credit for it. On the contrary, in Iraq it was generally assumed that the British were responsible for Arshad's repression because they wanted to limit opposition to their Palestinian policy and prevent the spread of Soviet influence in the Middle East.[33]

Unable to sway Arshad and fearful for their standing in Iraq, in October 1946 the British persuaded the regent to refuse Arshad's request for dictatorial powers. And the following month they prevailed upon him to remove Arshad from office.[34]

The regent replaced Arshad with Nuri al-Said. A more subtle politician than Arshad, Nuri immediately announced that his purpose was to serve as the head of a caretaker administration which would conduct free elections and then resign. To divide and thereby weaken his opponents, he accepted representatives of the National Democratic and Liberal parties into the government. In a further effort in this direction, he allowed all of the suppressed newspapers to resume publication, and he dropped all of the cases which Arshad had brought against newspaper editors.[35]

Thus at the end of 1946 the British achieved several important goals: the ouster of Arshad, his replacement with a more effective leader, the co-option of two of the opposition parties, a reduction in the amount of repression, and the scheduling of elections. They did not, however, get the free elections that they wanted. Old habits died hard in Iraq and, despite the government's pledges and the existence of a more liberal electoral law, as usual the prime minister and minister of interior managed to secure a favorable result. And in this case Nuri held both offices so, not surprisingly, the new Parliament that assembled in March 1947 was favorably disposed toward him. Indeed, because of government interference in the elections the representatives of the National Democratic and Liberal parties had resigned from the cabinet, and four of the five legal parties had refused to participate in the voting. The regent now requested that Nuri remain in office but, physically exhausted and in poor health, he refused. With the encouragement of the British embassy, the regent then turned to Salih Jabr, who eagerly accepted.[36]

Now in his mid-fifties, Jabr was probably the foremost Shiite politician in Iraq. He came from a poor artisan family, which was unusual for a leading figure. A lawyer by training, he had been a judge and a *mutasarrif* and had held numerous cabinet positions dating back to 1933.[37]

The British were well-disposed toward Jabr because in the upheaval of May 1941 he had sided conspicuously with the regent. Moreover, as minister of interior in Nuri's government, between October 1941 and October 1942 he had played a major role in interning suspected opponents of the regime. The British favored Jabr also because, unlike most of the leading politicians in Iraq, he appeared to be interested in implementing vitally needed economic and social reforms. For example, as minister of finance in Hamdi al-Pachachi's government, in August and September 1944 he had played an important part in securing the legalization of numerous trade unions.[38]

Jabr remained in office until January 1948. During this period the opposition parties strongly criticized him for failing to introduce meaningful reforms, failing to halt the rise in the cost of living, failing to prevent a serious bread shortage, failing to prevent the loss of Arab rights in Palestine, and being determined to conclude a new treaty of alliance with Britain. Like Arshad, Jabr felt threatened and responded with a crackdown. For example, in June 1947 he obtained convictions against the leaders of the Communist party whom Nuri had apprehended the previous January. By July he had suspended all but one of the newspapers of the legal political parties. And in September he prosecuted the leaders of the National Democratic party and the National Union party (the leader of the People's party fled the country to avoid prosecution) and proscribed the National Union party and the People's party.[39]

As we shall observe in chapter 11, Jabr's repression did not prevent a large-scale uprising in January 1948. Indeed, by then the accumulation of grievances was so great that it was not until May 1948, when the beginning of the Arab-Israeli war gave the government the opportunity to declare martial law, that the authorities were able to stop the constant series of strikes and demonstrations.[40]

The government's use of martial law to end the strikes and in the process weaken the labor movement is indicated by its action in May 1948 when it arrested the presidents of the three trade unions in Basra, and many other labor leaders in that area, and sentenced them to terms of imprisonment of up to five years.[41]

For the government martial law had the additional advantage of enabling it to suppress more easily the opposing political parties. For example, in May 1948 the authorities imprisoned the president and several other prominent members of the Basra branch of the National Democratic party. The following month they imprisoned the head of the Amara branch of the party. In October 1948 party members in the towns of Karbala, Hilla, Samawa, and Nasiriya suffered a similar fate. In addition, other National Democratic party members had their business with the government delayed until they had severed their ties with the party, and the editorials in the party's newspaper were regularly suppressed. As a result of this type of persecution, by December 1948 the membership of the National Democratic party had dropped to as low as 100. And in that month the National Democrats and the Liberals suspended their activities because they did not believe that they could function effectively any longer in this kind of environment.[42]

At the end of the Second World War the British supported the democratization of political life in Iraq and the implementation of economic and social reforms because they believed that these measures were necessary to win widespread support for the regime and thereby strengthen Britain's position in the country. However, most politically conscious Iraqis wanted to break the power of the ruling class and end Britain's overweening presence in Iraq. So, not surprisingly, democratization produced a proliferation of antigovernment and anti-British newspapers and parties. This development alarmed Iraqi leaders. For the most part they had never believed in democratization and other reforms, and had only accepted movement in this direction under pressure from the British, the regent, and popular forces within Iraq. Now they were convinced that these measures jeopardized their political and economic hold on the country, and consequently beginning with Arshad's government in June 1946 they made a serious effort to halt the reforms and suppress the opposition.

Initially British officials resisted this effort because they believed that it was strengthening the opposition and increasing anti-British sentiment. Indeed, they had much to do with the fall of Arshad's government in November 1946. However, British officials realized that they could not continually undermine the Iraqi ruling class without weakening it to the point where the opposition, all of which was anti-British, might attain power. They were especially reluctant to undermine Salih Jabr, who became prime minister in March 1947, because he was a good friend of Britain's and seemed more aware of the importance of reforms than most Iraqi leaders. They also needed his support to secure a satisfactory revision of the Treaty of 1930, and to refrain from military intervention in Palestine while Britain was still responsible for the country. Consequently, despite Jabr's suppression of the opposition and failure to introduce meaningful reforms, in 1947 British officials ended most of their pressure for liberalization.[43] The serious antigovernment and anti-British rioting in January 1948 that forced Jabr's resignation, and the wave of demonstrations and strikes that followed for the next few months, only reinforced their conviction that now the main need was for firm government to suppress disorder. So too did the worsening international situation, and especially the Communist coup in Czechoslovakia in February 1948 and the Berlin blockade the following June.[44]

With little democracy or reform, and with increasing repression, the regime soldiered on for another decade lurching from crisis to crisis. Britain's continued intimacy with the ruling class made it virtually inevitable that it would incur much of that class's unpopularity; and that, as far as Iraqi history was concerned, it would follow that class into oblivion.

.8.

The Reconstruction of Iraq's Armed Forces

After the fighting against Britain in May 1941 the Iraqi armed forces contracted significantly. For example, the number of personnel declined from 43,400 in the summer of 1940 to 28,000 in the summer of 1944. To a considerable extent this decline was caused by the government's failure to enforce the conscription law strictly. The results of this policy are illustrated by the fact that in the spring of 1944 the British military authorities in Iraq estimated that if the conscription law were strictly enforced the average annual intake of recruits would be 25,000, while in the previous three years the average annual intake had been only 4,000. Of these 4,000, 75 percent paid ID 50 and thus were legally entitled to leave the army after only three months of basic training.[1]

During this period the government did not enforce the conscription law strictly because there was much opposition to it, particularly in the Shiite areas in the southern part of the country.[2] Shiites were especially resentful of conscription because, although their sect constituted a little more than half of the total population, the Sunnis, and in particular the Sunni Arabs, controlled the army. The extent of this control is indicated by the fact that in a sample of sixty-one officers serving in 1936 one scholar could discover only one Shiite.[3] In 1941 a leading Shiite politician maintained that out of roughly 2,000 officers in the army there were only about thirty Shiites.[4] According to another account, in 1946 out of eighty staff officers there were only three Shiites.[5] And in 1953 the British ambassador observed that there were no Shiite officers with the rank of brigadier-general or higher.[6]

In the Shiite areas tribal shaykhs were especially hostile to conscription because it took away their followers and thereby weakened their private armies. It also took away their workers and thereby reduced their agricultural production. And for the shaykhs the loss of labor was usually permanent because after their release from the army agricultural workers, whose horizons had now been broadened, rarely returned to the drudgery and low pay of their former occupation.[7]

After the restoration of the old regime the Shiites were able to gain concessions on the conscription issue because they now had more and stronger representation in the cabinet. The extent of the problem in the past is indicated by the fact that, excluding the premiership, which was always held by a Sunni, between 1921 and 1932 Shiites had held only 17.7 percent of the ministerial appointments, and between 1932 and 1936 this figure had declined to 15.8 percent.[8] Now, however, Britain wanted to improve the condition of the Shiites because for the most part they had not sided strongly with Rashid Ali in the fighting of May 1941. By improving their condition Britain also hoped to bind them closer to the regime. Consequently, in his cabinet of October 1941, during the formation of which he closely consulted the British ambassador, Nuri al-Said gave Shiites four out of a total of ten portfolios. Perhaps more important, he appointed Salih Jabr, one of the Shiites, as minister of interior. This was the first time that a Shiite had held this key position, and Jabr promptly instructed the *mutasarrifs* in the Shiite areas to ease up on conscription.[9]

Aside from popular and especially Shiite opposition, the government did not strictly enforce the conscription law because the British exerted pressure to reduce the size of the army. The British were, of course, motivated by security considerations because they did not trust the army. They also believed that Iraq could spend its limited resources more profitably in the civilian sphere.[10]

Many leading Iraqi politicians, including Jabr, wanted to reduce the size of the army for the same reasons as the British did. Some of these politicians may also have been motivated by the desire to punish the army for its constant interference in the political process between 1936 and 1941.[11]

While lax enforcement of the conscription law accounted for much of the army's contraction, there were other factors as well. For example, of those men who were conscripted and were unable to purchase their way out, many deserted because conditions in the army were bad. In particular, food was inadequate, accommodations insufficient, leave nonexistent, health care minimal, clothing and boots in poor repair, and mosquito nets unavailable. Moreover, to compensate for manpower shortages soldiers were generally held in service considerably beyond the stipulated period of their engagement. As a result, by 1944 the army had over 20,000 deserters on its books.[12]

Aside from the bad conditions in the army, many Iraqis evaded conscription or bought their way out or deserted because they could find alternative, higher paying, more congenial employment. Many of these jobs were with the British military establishment, which at its peak in 1943 employed nearly 70,000 Iraqis as laborers and servants. At this time the British also employed about 6,000 Iraqis in the levies, a locally recruited military force under British officers and control. In the levies, it should be noted, an entry level soldier earned ID 6 per month compared with ID 4 per month in the Iraqi army, and average daily food portions were 1,000 calories higher.[13]

While overall the Iraqi army contracted radically, the number of senior officers and administrative units remained relatively constant. As a result, by 1944 there were approximately twice the number of units complete with administrative staff than there were enlisted men available to fill them. There were even some infantry units with practically a full complement of officers and noncommissioned officers and a mere handful of privates. Because all of the units were so much understrength they could not train effectively.[14]

In addition to a severe reduction in numbers and a malapportionment of the remaining personnel, the Iraqi army was weakened because Jamil al-Midfai, who was prime minister between June and October 1941, and Nuri al-Said, who succeeded him and served until June 1944, dismissed many officers whose loyalty to the regime they suspected or whom they personally disliked. For example, between June and December 1941 they discharged about 160 officers.[15] In the regent's view, these included most of the best officers in the army.[16] Nuri then replaced these men with elderly trustworthy officers whom he brought back from retirement. However, in the opinion of two successive heads of the British military mission, most of the replacements were not competent or qualified.[17] The Amir Abdullah of Transjordan had a similar view, and at one point commented that many of them were so fat that "they had to support their stomachs with their hands when walking."[18]

Aside from these personnel difficulties, in May 1941 the Iraqi army lost much of its equipment during the fighting against Britain. Then in March 1942 it lost a considerable additional amount of equipment when the bund protecting the Rashid camp near Baghdad, which was the army's largest base, broke in several places and flood water enveloped the entire area. Because of these reverses, and because of normal wear and tear, poor maintenance, and an inability in wartime to obtain spare parts or replacements, the Iraqi army was desperately short of vehicles of all sorts. The dimensions of the problem are indicated by the fact that out of a total of approximately 830 vehicles (excluding motorcycles) in the Iraqi army, by the beginning of 1945 only about 250 were in running condition and even most of these were virtually worn out.[19]

As a result of the fighting against Britain in May 1941, subsequent attrition, and the flood at the Rashid base in March 1942, the number of planes in the Iraqi air force declined from 116 in early 1941 to fortynine in early 1943. None of these planes were truly modern, and owing to a lack of spare parts and indifferent maintenance only twenty-nine were serviceable.[20]

During his premiership between 1941 and 1944 Nuri made several efforts to obtain up-to-date weapons. For example, in November 1941 he informed the British authorities in Iraq that he wanted to equip one brigade of the army with modern tanks and one squadron of the air force with modern bombers and one with modern fighters.[21] In May 1942 he again asked Britain for tanks, and this time for armored cars too.[22] In January 1943 Nuri declared war against the Axis powers, in part no doubt because he thought that it would help him pry more military hardware out of Britain.[23] In another effort to get more arms, the following month he offered to place two brigades of the Iraqi army at the disposal of British military commanders for deployment outside of Iraq.[24] And in August 1943 he again requested modern aircraft.[25]

As we observed in chapter 1, Nuri's efforts were not very successful because in the 1941-43 period the British were determined not to provide many weapons for Iraq. To recapitulate, they preferred to allocate their limited quantities of surplus war matériel to countries like the Soviet Union and India that were making substantial contributions to the Allied war effort; they believed that the Iraqi army could be most profitably employed maintaining internal order and guarding Britain's lines of communication within Iraq for which purposes particularly wellequipped forces were not necessary; they did not trust the Iraqi army and feared that under certain circumstances it might become a threat to their position in the country; and they were apprehensive that one day a wellequipped Iraqi army might intervene in Syria or Palestine to secure the independence of those countries from French and British rule.

However, the British were concerned about winning the loyalty of the Iraqi army, tying it closely to Britain, and facilitating its efforts to accomplish the limited tasks that they had assigned to it. Consequently, during this period they did provide some military assistance. For example, in January and February 1942 they returned most of the military equipment that they had captured in the fighting against Rashid Ali's forces.[26] And in July 1942 they gave Iraq forty armored cars and the following November nine cruiser tanks, in both cases without asking for payment. While the armored cars were not up-to-date, they were in good running order and useful for internal security purposes. The cruiser tanks, although less useful for operations because of their obsolescent design, mechanical unreliability, and lack of spare parts, still had some value for training purposes in preparation for the time when Iraq would be able to acquire more modern tanks.[27]

In addition, the British allowed Iraq to use a financial credit, which they had made available in 1939 for military purchases in the United Kingdom, to buy military supplies in India. For Iraq this decision was important because owing to their own needs the British had not permitted Iraq to use much of the credit for purchases in the United Kingdom. Moreover, many of the relatively minor items that the Iraqi army needed, such as clothing, horseshoes, and horse nails, were readily available in India.[28]

Besides providing some arms and other items, the British allowed a limited number of Iraqi soldiers to study at their military schools. For example, in February 1942 they accepted four Iraqi army officers for training at a mountain warfare school in India.[29] In July 1943 they accepted ten Iraqi soldiers for a craftsman's course at the British army's engineering workshop in Egypt.[30] And in October 1943 they accepted six Iraqi air force officers for pilot training at a flying school in Britain.[31]

As another form of assistance, the British allowed some Iraqi soldiers to serve temporarily with their military units in Iraq and thereby acquire valuable training and experience. For example, in February 1942 several dozen Iraqi army officers and noncommissioned officers were serving a one-month's attachment with a British armored formation in northern Iraq in preparation for the creation of an armored unit in the Iraqi army.[32] And in May 1942 sixty Iraqi army officers were attached to the British forces in the Mosul district.[33]

Finally, as we observed in chapter 4, in late 1943 the British provided the Iraqi armed forces with important assistance in their military operations in Kurdistan against Mulla Mustapha and his followers.

In early 1944 the British decided to make a serious effort to increase the effectiveness of the Iraqi armed forces. The main reason for this change of policy was the Iraqi army's poor performance against Mulla Mustafa in late 1943. During the campaign it suffered badly from a lack of equipment, insufficient training in mountain warfare, and a shortage of personnel in infantry units.[34] Because of the disordered conditions resulting from the rebellion, the British authorities in Iraq felt obliged to move eight armored cars and several hundred troops to a town in the disturbed area to protect one of their intelligence officers and some families of Assyrians who were serving in the levies.[35] They also became concerned that if the Iraqi government were unable to triumph, the rebellion might spread to other Kurdish districts in northern Iraq or to the Shiite tribal areas on the middle and lower Euphrates. Such a break-down in the Iraqi government's authority, they feared, might endanger the valuable largely British-owned oil fields in northern Iraq and the important British lines of communication across Iraq, and therefore possibly necessitate an increased British military commitment in Iraq.[36] In view of these considerations, British officials in Iraq, and in the Foreign Office and War Office in London, concluded that it would be prudent to strengthen the Iraqi armed forces so that in the future they would be better able to deal with disturbances of this nature.[37]

While in early 1944 the British decided to make a concerted effort to strengthen the Iraqi armed forces, they believed that these troops should be organized, trained, and equipped primarily for the maintenance of internal security. They opposed the development of a really powerful military establishment because they feared that strong forces might one day menace the civil authority in Iraq as they had in the 1936-41 period, or even threaten Britain's position in the country as they had in 1941. They also thought that the expense of acquiring and maintaining large quantities of sophisticated weapons would have adverse economic reper-cussions for Iraq. Finally, they did not believe that strong forces were nec-essary because for protection against external aggression they wanted Iraq to rely on its treaty with Britain.[38]

In order to improve the effectiveness of the Iraqi army while still tai-loring it primarily for internal security purposes, in July 1944 Major-General J. M. L. Renton, the head of the British military mission in Iraq, drew up a reorganization scheme. Specifically, he recommended recon-figuring the existing four division army into a mountain division for oper-ations in the north, a plains division for operations in the south, and a cadre division for training purposes and the control of a small mechanized

force. Renton also recommended reducing the size of the higher ranks of
the army because he believed that most of these men were lazy and
incompetent and by remaining in office were holding up the promotion
of younger more efficient officers. In addition, he wanted to increase the
number of enlisted men in the various units like battalions and platoons,
all of which were seriously understrength and consequently unable to train
properly. And among the enlisted men he wanted to increase the percentage of volunteers (currently about 40 percent) in order to reduce the
army's dependence upon conscripts who, he believed, were usually poorly
motivated and contributed very little because most of them bought their
way out after three-months' service. To help achieve these aims, Renton
recommended significantly improving conditions of service for enlisted
personnel in the areas of pay, rations, clothing, accommodations, leave, and
facilities for sport.[39]

In August 1944 the Iraqi government accepted Renton's plan for the
reorganization of the army. As a result, in the next few months 120
colonels and generals were retired from active service; training was
intensified, especially in mountain warfare; rations were increased to the
level of those given to the levies; better clothing was issued; facilities for
games were made available; and annual leave with a free return passage
home was instituted.[40]

The Iraqi government's rapid acceptance of Renton's proposal was
probably due in part to the fact that the previous June Nuri had resigned
as prime minister and minister of defense. Nuri had placed many of the
elderly senior officers in office and was reluctant to remove them because
they were his personal favorites and loyal to the regime.[41]

Iraqi leaders accepted the British plan for army reorganization also
because by the summer of 1944 they were becoming increasingly convinced that in order to preserve their complete and undisputed control
over the entire country they would have to defeat Mulla Mustafa and
they would be well-advised to spend the next few months preparing as
best as possible for this campaign. Arshad al-Umari, the minister of
foreign affairs, and Salih Jabr, the minister of finance, were particularly
strong proponents of this point of view. They especially liked Renton's
idea of forming a mountain division because this force would be particularly useful for combat against the Kurds in northern Iraq.[42]

The regent, too, supported the reorganization of the army. He was
especially interested in securing advancement for the younger officers
because he feared their discontent and wanted to win their loyalty to the
regime.[43]

In addition to these considerations, the Iraqis accepted Renton's proposal for army reorganization because they believed that the British would then feel obligated to provide the arms necessary to make the reorganization a success. And indeed in 1944 and afterward British officials in Iraq, and in the Foreign Office and War Office in London, did want to strengthen the Iraqi government's ability to maintain internal security. But they had certain important problems that limited their ability to provide weapons to Iraq.[44]

To begin with, without American permission Britain could not give Iraq any of the military equipment it had received from the United States under the Lend-Lease program or any British-manufactured item if it had received similar items from the United States under the Lend-Lease program.[45] To gain American permission for the shipment of British arms to Iraq, in May 1945 British military leaders pointed out to their American colleagues that the Iraqi government's ability to maintain domestic order was important because Iraq had considerable quantities of oil and was a staging point for the movement of British troops to the Far East; that most of the equipment they were planning to give to Iraq would come from their surpluses in the Middle East and therefore would not have a detrimental effect on military operations in the Far East; and that Britain would not have to draw on greater quantities of American arms as a result of these shipments to Iraq. However, in spite of British appeals, until a few days before the conclusion of hostilities against Japan in August 1945 the United States used its authority to block the delivery of a considerable amount of military equipment to Iraq on the grounds that Iraq was not actively participating in the war.[46]

In addition to the problem of Lend-Lease, after the end of the Second World War in August 1945 the British government discontinued production of many types of military equipment in order to devote scarce labor and raw materials to the production of civilian goods for the long-deprived domestic market and the dollar-earning export market. Thus until the beginning of the significant measure of rearmament that occurred with the onset of the Korean conflict in 1950, to a considerable extent the British army had to live on the stockpiles that it had accumulated during the war. Because so many items were not now being produced, and because so many other countries also wanted to purchase British weapons, the War Office was often reluctant to permit the export of military equipment to Iraq.[47]

For example, as part of Renton's reorganization scheme, in September 1944 the Iraqi government attempted to purchase twenty new light tanks. However, the War Office refused to permit the sale of any new tanks to Iraq on the grounds that it could not spare any while the war lasted. But even after the end of the conflict in August 1945, the War Office refused to permit the sale of any new tanks to Iraq on the grounds that it still did not have any to spare, and that its entire anticipated production for the next two or three years would have to be reserved exclusively for British and Commonwealth forces. The War Office was now particularly worried about the tank situation because during the war it had become quite dependent upon American tanks that, with the end of hostilities and the simultaneous termination of Lend-Lease, would no longer be forthcoming. Nonetheless, to appease the Iraqis, in October 1944 and again in August 1945 the War Office agreed to sell used Valentine tanks. The Valentine was a medium tank that became operational with the British army in 1940. The British manufactured 6,855 (Canada manufactured an additional 1,420) and did not discontinue production until early 1944. About 2,700 Valentines were sent to the Soviet Union, and the Soviets preferred them to the other three types of British tanks that they received. Although now obsolescent and no longer in frontline service with the British army, it was reliable and easy to maintain. Still, the Iraqis refused the Valentine because, aside from its weight, they did not want used machines of an out-of-date type.[48]

Because of its own shortages and requests from other countries whose needs it considered more pressing or whose leaders it considered more important to propitiate, for nearly two years after the end of hostilities the War Office continued to refuse to offer Iraq any other tank. This refusal greatly upset the Iraqis, who could not understand why a major power like Britain had so much trouble releasing so few new light tanks to an allied country.[49]

However, in May 1947, in an effort to facilitate the conclusion of a new treaty of alliance, the War Office offered Iraq either twenty used Churchill tanks in good condition or twenty new Challenger tanks. Having become operational in 1941, the Churchill was a reliable vehicle that performed well in extensive combat and was produced in large numbers. Having become operational toward the end of the war in 1944, the Challenger was produced in smaller quantities, though it too was used in combat. But the Iraqis did not order either of these types because both were expensive, difficult to maintain, and heavier than they required.[50]

As a result of the War Office's refusal to release any tanks that Iraq considered suitable and Iraq's unwillingness to allocate funds for machines that it considered less than optimum, in May 1948, when Iraq intervened in Palestine to prevent the establishment of a Jewish state, its army did not have any tanks.[51] In view of the fact that in its early stages the war in Palestine was a very close contest and that initially the Israelis did not have any tanks, this point is of some importance.[52]

Britain's ability to deliver other military vehicles was also limited, and here too there were substantial delays and Iraq often had to accept second-hand merchandise when it preferred new equipment. For example, in September 1944, immediately after the commencement of the reorganization scheme, Iraq ordered a sizable number of new armored cars, scout cars, trucks, trailers, ambulances, and motorcycles. But these vehicles did not arrive until the spring of 1946, some eighteen months after the order had been placed, and even then many of them were in used condition. The Iraqis were especially irritated about the slow delivery of these vehicles because in the summer and autumn of 1945, when they again campaigned in Kurdistan against Mulla Mustapha and his followers, they suffered from an acute shortage of vehicular transport.[53]

After the war the British government still had difficulty providing military vehicles for Iraq because most types were no longer being produced in Britain, and the British army did not believe that it had enough stockpiled even for its own needs.[54] Nonetheless, under pressure from the Foreign Office and British representatives in Iraq,[55] and in a further effort to facilitate the conclusion of a new treaty of alliance, in May 1947 the War Office offered to sell nearly 1,000 used vehicles, most of which belonged to the British forces that were then evacuating Iraq.[56] However, Iraqi military leaders disliked acquiring secondhand equipment, even if the British army considered it good enough for its own use. Consequently, they only bought about 200 of the vehicles that Britain offered.[57]

Two months after this offer, in July 1947 the Ministry of Supply, at the behest of the Foreign Office, put Iraqi officials in touch with a private firm in Britain that offered to sell reconditioned vehicles at the rate of 150 per month with deliveries beginning within two months of the receipt of the order. In addition, another British firm informed Iraqi officials that within ten or twelve months it could manufacture for them new vehicles identical to those currently being used by the British army. Iraqi military leaders were interested in these offers and wanted to buy various types of vehicles including armored cars and 500 reconditioned trucks. However, Prime Minister Salih Jabr, while approving the other purchases including the armored cars, refused to accept the trucks because he wanted to buy trucks from a company in the United States. At first glance this preference was surprising because the British trucks had the important advantage of four-wheel drive while the American trucks were two-wheel drive vehicles. Moreover, an American order would entail a severe drain on Iraq's scarce dollar holdings. Nonetheless, Jabr was determined to proceed with the American purchase because, it was widely believed, he had arranged with the manufacturer to share in the profits of the deal. In any event, in February 1948, after Jabr had fallen from power, the new government cancelled this order. But by now it was too late to get any more British trucks because, with the developing crisis in Palestine, the British government had prohibited the export of military equipment to Iraq except under the terms of existing contracts.[58]

During the war in Palestine in 1948 the shortage of vehicular transport was one of the reasons why Iraq did not bring greater strength to bear at the outset, when the Israelis were weakest. Thus Iraq's two missed opportunities in 1947 to acquire more vehicles were of some consequence.[59]

As far as artillery was concerned, in 1944 Britain gave Iraq twelve 25-pounder guns. This gun entered service with the British army in 1939 and was produced in large numbers and widely used in combat. In the spring of 1946 Britain delivered thirty more 25-pounders for a total of forty-two. However, the Iraqis were annoyed because of the long delay in receiving the second shipment, and because two of the gun barrels in this shipment were red with rust and unserviceable and had to be replaced immediately. They were also upset because they now had to wait two more years before they received the third and final shipment of thirty additional 25-pounders. Thus while Britain eventually fulfilled Iraq's needs in this important category, the lengthy delays did much to mitigate any sense of gratitude on the part of the Iraqis.[60]

While the Iraqis complained about the artillery situation, during the campaign in Palestine in 1948 their 25-pounders proved far superior to Israel's main artillery piece. The latter, for example, was much older, of a type that had originally entered production in France in 1906. Moreover, Iraq's 25-pounders had twice the range, and their shell had nearly five times the weight.[61]

Quantitatively, too, the Iraqis had superiority in artillery. True, they only sent twelve of their 25-pounders to Palestine because a shortage of ammunition prevented them from adequately supplying more than this number in the field. However, they also sent twelve other artillery pieces that, while older than the 25-pounders, were more modern than the Israeli field guns. Supporting the Iraqis in the northern section of Palestine, the Syrians and the Lebanese each had twelve artillery pieces and the Arab Liberation Army (volunteers from various Arab countries including Palestine) had six.

By contrast, it was not until 22 May 1948, a week after the outset of the war, that the Israelis were able to deploy even two field guns against the Iraqis. And even in July 1948, during the fighting following the expiry of the first truce, in the entire northern part of the country the Israelis still only had a total of four field guns (including one in repair) and three anti-aircraft guns that they used for other purposes.[62]

As far as aircraft were concerned, in July and November 1944, immediately after the commencement of the reorganization scheme, the British sold Iraq a total of thirty Ansons. Having entered service with the Royal Air Force in 1936, the Anson was not a particularly new aircraft. However, it was a durable multipurpose machine that functioned effectively as a trainer, reconnaissance, and transport aircraft. It could also be used for ground attack because it had a machine gun in the nose and carried bombs. It even had an air-to-air capability because, aside from the machine gun in the nose, it had a second machine gun in a turret in the roof. The British were quite pleased with the Anson, and in spite of the age of the design continued production until 1952. In all, they manufactured 8,138 (Canada manufactured an additional 2,882), and did not finally retire the aircraft from service until 1968.[63]

The Anson fit in well with British plans because they wanted the Iraqi air force to be a small efficient body of about fifty-three planes configured primarily for the task of assisting the army to maintain internal security. They did not want Iraq to acquire large numbers of modern sophisticated fighter and bomber aircraft because they believed that these machines would be too expensive to purchase and too difficult to maintain. They also feared that a powerful Iraqi air force, like a strong Iraqi army, might become a serious threat to the civil authority in Iraq or to the British position in the country. Even if this threat did not materialize, they were concerned that a large air force would quickly outgrow its existing bases, and to acquire more facilities would soon press for the return of Habbaniya and Shaiba to Iraqi control.[64]

The British delivered the Ansons to Iraq in the spring of 1945.[65] In the next few years the planes performed well in Iraqi service, including during military operations in Kurdistan.[66] In 1948 the Iraqis also used the Ansons in their campaign in Palestine[67] where, incidentally, initially the Israelis did not have any warplanes, or at least none that were designed for that purpose.[68]

In spite of the planes' good performance, Iraqi leaders were not happy with the Ansons. To begin with, although Iraq paid for new aircraft, the British gave planes that, while not used, had been stored in the open in

England and therefore looked used. The fact that in order to expedite delivery the British flew the planes to Iraq contributed to their weather-beaten and untidy appearance. Moreover, although the planes themselves were new, twenty-one of them had used tires. Finally, and probably most important from Iraq's point of view, within a few months of their arrival the wooden wings began to shrink and crack as a result of the strength of the hot sun in the desert climate.[69]

In order to repair the wings, the British Air Ministry gave Iraq an effective compound called Madapolin. But the British were also concerned with salvaging their reputation for ethical dealing and preserving their monopoly on the Iraqi market for future aircraft exports. Consequently, in November 1945 they gave Iraq, without charge, newly designed wooded wings that, being stronger, were less likely to deteriorate. RAF technicians at Habbaniya then installed the new wings on the Ansons.[70]

But the Iraqis were still not satisfied. At first they wanted to exchange their wooded-wing Ansons for a metal-wing version of the same aircraft. To accommodate the Iraqis, in January 1946 the British agreed to such a transaction.[71] However, the following July, before any of the metal-wing Ansons were delivered, the Iraqis changed their minds and cancelled the order. Instead, they now wanted to return all thirty Ansons, including eight that were inoperable as a result of damage received during operations while in Iraqi service, in exchange for a full refund of the purchase price of the planes. In another effort to accommodate the Iraqis, the British agreed to this proposal and further agreed that the Iraqis would not have to return the Ansons until they had received replacement aircraft.[72]

To replace the Ansons, in October 1946 the Iraqis placed an order for thirty-four Sea Furies.[73] The Sea Fury was a modern fighter-bomber that was still in development and did not enter service with the Royal Navy until August 1947. It performed well in extensive combat operations during the Korean War and remained in service with the Royal Navy until 1957. Aside from Iraq, it was purchased by Canada, Australia, and Pakistan. Total British production, including those for export, numbered 860.[74]

The British believed that the Sea Fury was too advanced for Iraq but nonetheless gave that country a high priority for deliveries. In accordance with this policy, they sent the first Sea Furies to Iraq in February 1948, only six months after the plane entered British service and considerably before the Royal Navy had received all that it needed.[75]

In addition to the Sea Furies, at the end of 1946 the British sold Iraq thirty-one unarmed training, transport, observation, and liaison aircraft.

Although less glamorous than sleek and imposing fighter-bombers, these types were essential for counterinsurgency and communications work within Iraq.[76]

In spite of Britain's efforts to heal the damage caused by the poor initial appearance and subsequent rapid deterioration of the wooden-wing Ansons, the affair harmed Anglo-Iraqi relations. In Iraq it was widely believed that the British had deceitfully attempted to unload obsolete used planes for high prices on their unsuspecting ally. Thus even in the matter of aircraft, where after 1944 the British could reasonably argue that they did a creditable job of satisfying Iraq's requirements, they were subject to widespread accusations of bad faith and sharp practice.[77]

In addition to providing weapons, to help make the reorganization scheme a success and enable Iraq to maintain internal security the British stepped up their training programs for the Iraqi armed forces. The extent of the operation is indicated by the fact that in September 1944 they were training or had just completed training thirty-seven Iraqi soldiers in vehicle maintenance, thirty-six as craftsmen, twenty-eight in antiaircraft warfare, four in military engineering, and several army doctors in advanced medical techniques.[78]

Besides arms and training, we observed in chapter 4 that between August and October 1945 Britain provided valuable assistance to the Iraqi armed forces when they engaged in a second military operation in Kurdistan against Mulla Mustapha and his followers.

In spite of Britain's efforts after 1944 to strengthen the Iraqi armed forces, many influential Iraqis retained a strong sense of grievance against Britain. They believed that Britain had given too few arms too slowly and too often in used condition. They neither understood nor sympathized with Britain's difficulties concerning the American veto on the shipment of Lend-Lease items or British-manufactured equipment of the same type, the severe economic problems that dictated a discontinuation or great reduction of production of military equipment, and the incessant demands of numerous other allied and friendly nations for arms. Attributing a more sinister motivation to British behavior, they believed, and not always incorrectly, that Britain did not sincerely want to strengthen the Iraqi armed forces because it feared a repetition of the events of 1941, or because it feared that Iraq would intervene in Syria against the French or in Palestine against the Jews. To them it appeared that Britain was attempting to keep the Iraqi armed forces as a type of police, equipped and trained only for internal security, and therefore incapable of threatening Britain's position either within Iraq or elsewhere in the Middle East. Even when Britain did deliver weapons, the Iraqis complained about the continual delays, the frequent receipt of second-hand merchandise, the difficulty in obtaining spare parts, and the fact that they had to pay what they considered to be excessively high prices. They were also angry that their freedom of choice was restricted by the Treaty of 1930 that compelled them to purchase virtually all of their military equipment from Britain.[79]

In fact, after 1944, in the important area of aircraft Iraq did not do at all badly. Indeed, with the Ansons, Sea Furies, and other planes Iraq probably received about as much equipment, and as rapidly, as it could afford and maintain. With artillery delivery was slower, but by the outbreak of the Arab-Israeli war in May 1948 Iraq had received seventy-two modern pieces, which was the number it had been seeking. With tanks it is true that the British would not provide the type that Iraq wanted, but in 1944-45 and 1947 they did offer substitutes that Iraq rejected. With other vehicles it is true that initially the British were not very forthcoming, but in 1947, when the gates were finally opened, Iraq ordered considerably fewer than the British offered.

Regardless of the extent of, and the question of responsibility for, the deficiencies in Iraq's armaments, the fact remains that during this period the matter of arms supply was a source of continual contention and bitterness in Anglo-Iraqi relations. As we shall observe in chapter 13, in February 1948 the problem became worse because the British government suddenly prohibited the export of war matériel to Iraq except under the terms of existing contracts, and the following May refused even to deliver weapons previously ordered.

In addition to their complaints over the matter of arms supplies, many influential Iraqis strongly resented the power of General Renton, the head of the British military mission between 1944 and 1948.[80] The British military mission was in Iraq by virtue of a provision that Britain had insisted upon including in the Treaty of 1930. Legally, Renton's power was limited to giving advice and inspecting Iraqi army units.

Technically, he was a servant of the Iraqi government whose uniform he wore and whose salary he collected. In reality, however, he was a military representative and agent of Britain, the dominant foreign power in Iraq. This fact, combined with his forceful personality and good relations with the regent, enabled him to extend his authority considerably. For example, on his recommendation, in the second half of 1944 the army was reduced in size by two divisions; numerous high-ranking officers whom he claimed were incompetent or inefficient were dismissed; his favorite, Ismail Namiq, was appointed minister of defense; living conditions and privileges for the enlisted personnel were significantly improved; and military exercises in cold weather in the mountains, which he personally planned and directed, were held.[81]

Not surprisingly, those officers who on Renton's recommendation were retired from active duty were among his most vocal critics.[82] They were fully supported by the Istiqlal, the strongest of the political parties. For example, in August 1946 the party newspaper accused Renton of exceeding his authority and in the process gravely damaging the Iraqi army. Specifically, it said that he had fired numerous competent officers and terrified the remainder into submission to him with threats of dismissal. It also maintained that he had encouraged insubordination and indiscipline in the ranks (a reference to Renton's efforts to improve living conditions and privileges for the enlisted personnel that apparently motivated some of them to be more vocal in expressing their grievances to their officers); sent the army on maneuvers in inclement weather without adequate provisions (previously most high-ranking officers had rarely suffered the discomfort and inconvenience of leaving their offices, cabarets, and families in Baghdad); refused to train the army for modern warfare (somewhat incongruous in view of the preceding accusation); and generally interfered in army matters where he had no jurisdiction. It concluded the article by calling upon the Iraqi government to dismiss Renton immediately.[83]

In its campaign against Renton and the military mission the Istiqlal was unremitting. For example, in January 1947 the party newspaper maintained that "no calamity has befallen on the Iraqi Army ever since its creation similar to that encountered during the last five years as a result of the activities of the Members of the B. M. M. whose head is General Renton."[84] And at its annual conference the following June the party called for the immediate abolition of the entire mission.[85]

Needless to say, Renton's view of the achievements of the military mission during his tenure was different. Indeed, in March 1948 he maintained that in 1944 the Army was a half-starved, depressed, untrained and unorganized collection of units, disliked and despised by the entire nation for the successive coups d'etat culminating in the disasters of May 1941 and with over 20,000 deserters on their books. They are now a compact well-disciplined and well-trained force with a high morale, good food and clothing and excellent welfare arrangements, clear of politics and respected by the country.[86]

The Istiqlal party, incidentally, was not alone in its hostility to the military mission. By the beginning of 1948 even the pro-British members of the ruling class considered it an affront to national sovereignty and wanted it withdrawn.[87] And in March 1948, when the British announced the withdrawal of the mission to avoid what they feared would be eventual expulsion,[88] only one newspaper in Baghdad mentioned its considerable services to the Iraqi army, such as training Iraqi military personnel and helping to maintain Iraqi military equipment. In extremely intemperate remarks reflecting great animosity, four other newspapers accused the mission of ruining the Iraqi army, two of them singling out Renton for personal attack.[89]

The Renton affair illustrates the difficulty that a great power is likely to encounter when it attempts to play a large role in the affairs, and especially the military affairs, of a minor power. In this case Britain's efforts to use the military mission to maintain influence in the Iraqi army, while successful in the short run, generated hostility and in the long term contributed to the diminution and eventual elimination of that influence.

.9.

The Financial Agreements

During the Second World War the sterling area comprised the whole of the British Empire (except Canada and Newfoundland), Egypt, and Iraq.[1] The system had various features, such as the basing of the members' currency on sterling and the maintenance of close banking relations with London. But the key to the system was the members' obligation to turn in all of their receipts of nonsterling area currencies to a central pool in London that was held by the British government on behalf of the entire sterling area. The members' essential requirements of these currencies were then met from this pool.

Of the nonsterling area currencies United States' dollars, Canadian dollars, Swiss francs, Swedish kronor, and Portuguese escudos were considered scarce or hard currencies because they represented countries whose productive capacity had been undamaged by the war. And of these scarce currencies United States' dollars were by far the most important because the United States' productive capacity was so much greater than that of any other country.

In order that members of the sterling area would be able to draw upon the central pool for their essential needs of scarce currencies, it was necessary for them to avoid making unessential purchases from the scarce currency countries. And to insure that this was done, all members were obliged to establish strict import controls.

Of the sterling area countries Iraq was unique in that it was permitted, or rather obliged, to maintain its own United States' dollar pool based entirely upon its own earnings. In other words, unlike the other members it was not required to turn in its receipts of dollars to the central pool, and it could not draw upon this pool for its dollar requirements. Thus as far as dollar imports were concerned, Iraq was compelled to live within its means. The British insisted upon this arrangement because in

November 1941, when Iraq was readmitted to the sterling area after the upheaval of the previous May, they feared that it would not vigorously restrict its dollar purchases. Because of the existence of this arrangement, Iraq could not be considered a full member of the sterling area.[2]

In March 1944 Iraq had a reserve of $9 million. It had accumulated this money from exports of dates, wool, and hides to the United States, from a fee on the passage of Turkish tobacco through Iraq on the way to the United States, and from the expenditures of American military personnel in Iraq. However, this reserve was declining rapidly because with the Mediterranean now open to shipping Iraq was no longer earning dollars from the Turkish transit trade, and by the latter stages of the war very few American military personnel were stationed in Iraq. Moreover, Iraq's dollar imports were appreciable because British industry, which before the war had supplied much of Iraq's needs, was now devoted almost exclusively to military production and therefore exporting very few consumer goods. Consequently, by the end of 1944 Iraq's reserve had declined to $6 million, and British officials calculated that during 1945, and taking into account Iraq's anticipated earnings of $4 million, the reserve would disappear entirely and leave Iraq with a deficit of $3 million.[3]

In December 1944 the British offered to make good this deficit, but only as part of an arrangement whereby Iraq would accept full membership in the sterling area. In other words, Iraq's separate dollar pool would be eliminated and instead Iraq would contribute its dollar reserve and all of its dollar earnings to the central pool in London. Iraq would then draw all of its dollar needs from the central pool, but this would be done in close consultation with the British government to insure that Iraq restricted its dollar imports to goods that were essential and could not be procured from Britain or other sterling area countries. To be precise, for 1945 the British offered to provide Iraq with $13 million, of which $6 million would come from Iraq's former dollar pool, $4 million from Iraq's anticipated dollar earnings, and $3 million from the central pool. (The latter $3 million would, of course, be provided against payment in sterling.) According to British calculations, in 1945 this arrangement would enable Iraq to increase its imports from the United States by 30-40 percent over 1944.[4]

The British were willing to offer Iraq more dollars than the total of its dollar pool and its anticipated dollar earnings because, with the war ending and all of their ground troops likely to be withdrawn from the country soon, they wanted to tie Iraq firmly to the sterling area and thereby to the British sphere of influence. They were also concerned that if Iraq left the sterling area it would begin to charge dollars for its oil at a time when Britain was desperately eager to continue paying in sterling in order to conserve its precious dollar supplies.[5]

The negotiations over the British proposal began in December 1944 and continued until their successful conclusion the following May. They were difficult because the Iraqi minister of finance, Salih Jabr, was a hard bargainer and determined to obtain as many dollars as possible for Iraq. For example, at one point he suggested that Iraq should be able to draw on the central pool for its essential dollar needs but should only have to surrender to the pool its current dollar earnings and not the $6 million that it held in reserve. At another point he wanted a commitment that Britain would make good Iraq's likely dollar deficiency; but in the event, admittedly improbable, that Iraq's dollar earnings were greater than its dollar expenditures Iraq would be able to retain the surplus rather than surrender it to the central pool. And at still another point he wanted the right to retain any dollars that Iraq secured from noncommercial transactions.[6]

For Jabr the latter point was especially important because he hoped to obtain substantial quantities of additional dollars in the form of a loan from the United States government. Although in February 1945 Washington informed him that it would not give Iraq a loan, he apparently still hoped that some American businesses or banks would extend dollar credits to Iraq.[7]

The negotiations were difficult too because Jabr resisted some subsidiary British demands like the prohibition of imports from Turkey and Iran which originated in scarce currency countries. In the event that these products did enter Iraq, the British wanted Iraq to confiscate them or at least deduct their value from Iraq's annual quota of scarce currencies. The British justified their position with the argument that in the proposed arrangement they would be providing for Iraq's essential needs from scarce currency countries, and that consequently all imports above this figure that originated in scarce currency countries were unessential. In other words, as the British saw it, if Iraq did not prohibit imports from Turkey and Iran that originated in scarce currency countries Iraq would be using valuable funds from the sterling area's central pool to import more from scarce currency countries than it required, and in the process would be depriving Britain and other sterling area countries of essential imports from these countries. But Jabr disliked the idea of not being able to import freely from Turkey and Iran because such imports were convenient and Iraq, like so many other countries at the end of the war, was very short of many types of consumer goods.[8]

For the same reason, Jabr resisted Britain's demand that Iraq restrict imports from Turkey and Iran even of goods that originated in those countries. Here the British were concerned about preventing Turkey and Iran, which were not members of the sterling area, from accumulating significant additional quantities of sterling because, according to the terms of various agreements, Britain was obliged to convert some of this sterling into gold.[9]

Jabr's reluctance to commit Iraq fully to the sterling area was supported by much of educated public opinion. For example, in January 1945 the newspaper *Al-Nida*, which was under the influence of Jamil al-Midfai, one of the leading politicians who was currently out of office, maintained that

> any country which ties its currency to that of another will not enjoy economic independence. . . . We would attain this independence if we were to move the headquarters of our currency control to the homeland and make our own currency the sole medium for our foreign transactions, after taking over our credit balances from the Bank of England which balances we could use as a currency in our international trade. In doing this we would be in a position to organize our export trade and to obtain in exchange for our exported products suitable currency which we could use with complete freedom in importing goods to help in the improvement of our domestic produce and raise our standard of living.[10]

And in March 1945 the newspaper *Sawt al-Ahali*, which was the organ of Kamil Chadirchi and other moderate leftists who were soon to form the National Democratic party, declared that

> it is in Iraq's interest that obstacles in the way of world exchange be removed and the competition of great industrial countries in exports carried on in a natural manner unhampered by artificial barriers, so that Iraq and other importing countries shall have full freedom in purchasing goods from countries whose prices are more favourable. . . . It is not in Iraq's interest to take sides in its import policy.[11]

Ultimately, however, Iraq had to accept Britain's offer and yield on all of the disputed points because the British cared a great deal about this question and were willing to apply considerable pressure to get their way. For example, they made it clear that if the Iraqis rejected the offer Britain would not deal favorably with them in the matter of the disposal of their sterling balances in London. Specifically, the British indicated that they would not agree to exchange these balances for dollars or gold, or make them available for use outside of the sterling area.[12]

At the end of the Second World War Iraq's sterling balances totalled about £65 million. Iraq had accumulated so much because during the war the British had purchased substantial quantities of Iraqi foodstuffs like barley and dates; spent considerable amounts in Iraq for various purposes like transportation, construction, and recreation; and paid wages to thousands of Iraqis as laborers, servants, and guards. The fact that Iraq had not purchased much from Britain because British industry was almost entirely devoted to military production and a serious shortage of shipping impeded exports from Britain to Iraq contributed to the accumulation. While the British never disputed that Iraq owned this money, as we have observed, their control over the release and convertibility of it gave them an important lever over Iraq.[13]

Thus the financial agreement of May 1945 was based on Britain's offer of the previous December. Specifically, the agreement stipulated that Britain would provide Iraq with the scarce currency equivalent of £3.5 million during 1945. This sum was worth about $14 million, which was slightly more than the British had originally proposed. In return, Iraq agreed to conform to the principles of the sterling area, which meant that all of the dollars and other nonsterling area currencies that it acquired would be turned over to the central pool. Iraq's allocation would then be met from that pool.[14]

For the British this agreement was favorable because it firmly integrated Iraq into the sterling area, thereby strengthening British influence in the country and ensuring that they could continue to purchase Iraqi oil with sterling. Moreover, they did not risk a serious hemorrhage of their precious scarce currency reserves because, unlike most of the other members of the sterling area who could draw at will upon the central pool, Iraq had a quota or target figure that it was not permitted to exceed.[15]

For Iraq this agreement entailed the surrender of a considerable amount of sovereignty. Still, Iraq gained because in the immediate postwar period it was not a net dollar earner. Indeed, between 1946 and 1949 Iraq drew a net total (that is, after allowing for its contributions) of $77 million from the central pool.[16] Thus by associating with the sterling area, Iraq acquired more dollars than it otherwise would have had.

Britain was able to provide these dollars because other members of the sterling area, such as Malaya and the Gold Coast, habitually had a trade surplus with the United States.[17] It was these countries, whose membership in the sterling area was involuntary because they were not self-governing, and not Iraq, who paid the price for the existence of the central pool.[18]

The financial agreement of May 1945 was later extended to cover the entire period between 1 January 1945 and 15 July 1947. During this time Britain provided Iraq with the scarce currency equivalent of about £9 million, which was worth approximately $36 million.[19]

We have observed that due to unavailability of supply and shipping problems, during the war Iraq's imports of consumer goods fell sharply. The extent of the decline is indicated by the fact that during the 1942-45 period imports of textiles were only 56 percent in quantity of their prewar level, while imports of sugar, tea, and coffee were only 58 percent. In reality, however, the situation was even worse than these figures suggest because of the increase in population. Needless to say, these shortages resulted in significantly higher prices.[20]

In the area of capital goods Iraq's situation was also bad. For example, during the 1942-45 period imports of iron, steel, cement, timber, machinery, electrical equipment, and vehicles were only 15 to 20 percent in quantity of their prewar level. As a result, economic development schemes were halted, existing equipment was not repaired or maintained properly, and new houses were not constructed.[21]

In 1946 the situation improved but there were still serious problems. For example, in the area of consumer goods imports of sugar, tea, and coffee rose to 85 percent in quantity of their prewar level, but imports of textiles remained at only 55 percent. In the area of capital goods imports of iron and steel rose to 7 percent in quantity above their prewar level, and imports of cement rose to 13 percent above. But imports of timber, machinery, electrical equipment, and vehicles remained far below their prewar level.[22]

Because Iraq's needs were so pressing, Iraqi leaders wanted more dollars to pay for more imports from the United States. Aside from furthering agricultural and industrial development, the greater availability of consumer goods would keep down the cost of these products to the public. They would also increase the government's custom revenues. In addition, if Iraqi merchants could import more from the United States they could increase their sales and, presumably, profits. Because many leading Iraqi politicians were either personally involved in these mercantile activities or had friends and relatives who were, this consideration was important.[23]

If Britain had been able to supply most of Iraq's needs, Iraqi leaders might have been less insistent in their demands for more dollars. But in the first few years after the war Britain had great difficulty supplying Iraq because many laborers were still in the armed forces and many factories had not yet completed the conversion to civilian production. Moreover, British industry did not manufacture certain types of goods, such as inferior quality inexpensive textiles, which were popular in Iraq. And even when Britain was able to supply suitable products to Iraq, British officials, and especially those in the Treasury, were not always eager to do so because they wanted to devote most production to the dollar-earning export market and to the long deprived domestic market. In other words, while the British were restricting the amount of dollars that they provided Iraq for imports from the United States, they were also attempting to restrict the amount of goods that Iraq could purchase in Britain.[24]

To avoid having to export too much to Iraq, in early 1947 the British attempted to reduce the size of Iraq's sterling balances by persuading Iraq to write off about one-third of them. They also tried to freeze most of the remaining money. To achieve these objectives, they proposed to conclude a new financial agreement that would apply to the period after 15 July 1947.[25]

Aside from Britain's desire to restrict its exports to Iraq, a new Anglo-Iraqi financial agreement was necessary at this time because the Anglo-American financial agreement of December 1945 stipulated that by 15 July 1947 all sterling that sterling area members acquired from current transactions would be freely convertible into dollars and other currencies. Thus the existing system whereby Britain periodically provided Iraq with a specified amount of dollars against payment in sterling would have to be altered.[26]

The negotiations for the new financial agreement began in March 1947 and continued until their successful conclusion the following August. Because of their nature, on the British side they were conducted primarily by Treasury officials and on the Iraqi side primarily by officials from the Ministry of Finance.[27]

The negotiations were difficult because the two sides had widely different perspectives. For example, the British justified their desire for a partial write-off of Iraq's sterling balances by arguing that these balances were war debts that they had incurred in the process of defending Iraq and the rest of the Middle East against aggression. They also pointed out that unlike most commercial debts, Iraq's sterling balances did not leave behind any revenue-producing assets that would assist in their amortization.[28]

As far as their desire to freeze most of Iraq's remaining sterling balances, the British maintained that in their weakened position, when they were struggling to recover from the ravages of the war, they simply could not afford to export much to Iraq because these exports did not earn dollars or contribute to domestic reconstruction. They also pointed out that numerous other countries had large sterling balances; and that, according to the terms of the Anglo-American financial agreement, after 15 July 1947 all sterling balances that Britain released and thereby made available for current payments would be convertible into dollars. Thus if the bulk of these worldwide balances were not frozen, there would be a tremendous amount of freely convertible sterling available, and much of this money would undoubtedly be converted into dollars. Then, of course, the value of sterling would decline precipitously and, the British said, as a major holder of sterling Iraq would suffer. In other words, the British argued that the freezing of most of Iraq's sterling balances would contribute to limiting the amount of freely convertible sterling in the world and thereby serve Iraq's interests. They also emphasized that they could not give Iraq unusually favorable treatment in the matter of sterling releases because other countries holding large quantities of sterling would then demand similar treatment for themselves.[29]

While the British believed that their precarious economic situation justified the freezing of all of Iraq's sterling balances that were not written off, they realized that this action would inflict grave harm on the Iraqi economy and on Anglo-Iraqi relations. Consequently, they offered to release £15 million (out of a total of about £65 million) over a five-year period, with Iraq being allowed to take the money in sterling, dollars, or any other currency. In what they interpreted as a further concession, they also agreed to release .5 percent interest on the sterling balances that Iraq had accumulated during the war, with the remainder of the interest being frozen.[30]

Unlike the British, Iraqi leaders did not believe that their sterling balances were war debts, and they strongly resisted the idea of writing off any of them. Moreover, on this issue Iraqi leaders were constrained by public opinion because feeling in the country ran high. For example, in February 1947 *Sawt al-Ahali*, the newspaper of the National Democratic party, warned that "it would be political suicide for any cabinet to consent to a scaling down of any part regardless of how infinitesimal it might be of the sterling balances due to our country."[31]

Aside from refusing to write off any of their sterling balances, Iraqi leaders sought £32.5 million in releases over a five-year period, rather than the £15 million that the British offered. They also wanted all of the interest on their British government securities and other assets in the United Kingdom to be freely available because they did not believe that the British government had the right unilaterally to modify these contractual obligations.[32]

In the discussions, the Iraqis pointed out that when they were accumulating their sterling balances they had never been told that these sums were war debts subject to involuntary reduction or any other limitation on their use. They also maintained that due to the recent conflict Iraq was desperately short of consumer and capital goods; that current earnings were insufficient to make up for the extreme wartime deprivation; and that consequently a large draw upon the sterling balances was essential to raise the standard of living and develop the country. In this context they stressed that most of their people were impoverished because during the war the cost of living had increased by a factor of six while wages had only increased by a factor of three, and that only by increasing the amount of goods available could the cost of living be reduced. Reinforcing their contention that they needed considerably more than the £3 million in releases per year that Britain had offered, the Iraqis pointed out that in the first three months of 1947 alone they had withdrawn £2.6 million from their sterling balances. Finally, they argued that Britain would gain from generous treatment because only if Iraq were prosperous and contented could the government prevent revolutionary agitation and upheaval.[33]

The British were unsympathetic to Iraq's request for larger sterling releases because since the war Iraq had imported sizable quantities of luxury items. For example, between 1945 and 1947 Iraqi imports of silk cloth had risen from 521,000 square meters to 4,110,000 square meters. The British also considered some of Iraq's scheduled development projects unessential. For example, the Iraqis wanted to construct an oil refinery to free themselves from dependence upon the refineries at Alwand and Abadan, both of which were British-owned and the latter of which was situated in Iran. In addition, the British believed that the

Iraqis would not need to draw upon their sterling balances to the extent that they maintained because over the next five years they would receive £12 million more in oil revenues than they had calculated. Finally, the British were concerned that if they allowed Iraq access to £32.5 million, which was half of Iraq's sterling balances, then other countries would demand access to a similarly large percentage of their sterling balances.[34]

Nonetheless, the British were willing to make further concessions because they needed Iraqi goodwill to ensure the success of the contemporaneous negotiations to revise the Treaty of 1930. The Foreign Office in particular was conscious of the connection between the two sets of negotiations, and it applied pressure on the Treasury to be more accommodating in the financial talks.[35]

Accordingly, on 13 August 1947 the two sides concluded an agreement with a five-year duration on the basis of Britain's original offer of £15 million in releases, but with a number of important sweeteners for Iraq. For example, the British also released £5 million to facilitate Iraq's transition to the new arrangements, and £2 million as a working balance on which Iraq could draw to meet any temporary shortage. In addition, the British allowed Iraq to use its unreleased sterling balances to repay £4.2 million in loans to the Iraq Petroleum Company; to pay off the £108,000 outstanding of its debt to the British government for the port of Basra; to pay for nonmilitary orders in Britain on which deposits had been made before 15 July 1947; to pay for any military equipment ordered in Britain before 15 July 1947; and to purchase at any time British military stores, equipment, or assets that were currently in Iraq.[36]

(It should be noted that Iraqi sterling in Britain that was released and thereby freely available to Iraq was placed in what were referred to as number 1 accounts, while Iraqi sterling in Britain that was not released and thus not freely available to Iraq was placed in what were referred to as number 2 accounts.)

Aside from making much greater releases than they had originally envisaged, the British accepted Iraq's position that the agreement should say nothing about writing off any of the sterling balances. However, in a secret letter attached to the agreement the British reserved the right to raise this point again in the future.[37]

The only point on which the British really triumphed was the stipulation in the agreement that they would only release .5 percent interest on Iraq's wartime accumulation of sterling balances. In a secret letter attached to the agreement the British also insisted that they did not have any liability for interest over .5 percent that was credited to Iraq's number 2 accounts.[38]

Thus except for the question of interest on its sterling balances, from Iraq's perspective this agreement was quite good because, including its current earnings, the country would now have a considerable amount of freely convertible sterling at its disposal. Indeed, *The Times* commented that the agreement "appears on the face of it to be almost quixotic generosity in view of the foreign exchange position in which this country now finds itself."[39] *The Financial Times* maintained that "cash releases from accumulated sterling balances on this scale applied over the whole field of the sterling debts would impose an intolerable burden upon this country even assuming further dollar aid."[40] And *The Economist* observed that "the terms conceded to Iraq are certainly favourable by comparison with those afforded by some of the other sterling agreements."[41]

In accordance with the terms of the Anglo-American financial agreement of December 1945, since the autumn of 1946 the British government had concluded financial agreements with numerous countries that, like the one with Iraq, provided for the release of a certain amount of sterling balances, the free convertibility of the released balances, and the free convertibility of all sterling acquired in current transactions. However, in order to purchase more in the United States, where far more goods were available than in Britain, these countries rapidly exchanged large quantities of their sterling for dollars. The extent of the drain on the sterling area's dollar supplies is indicated by the fact that in the second half of 1946 the loss amounted to $580 million, while in the first half of 1947 it increased to $1.84 billion. Measured differently but painting the same general picture, in the second quarter of 1947 the loss averaged $77 million a week, in the six weeks prior to 8 August it rose to an average of $115 million a week, and in the next week it climbed to $175 million.[42]

To halt this terrible hemorrhage, on 20 August 1947, only a week after the conclusion of the Anglo-Iraqi financial agreement, the British government suspended indefinitely the free convertibility of sterling. Consequently, to the disappointment of Iraq, the convertibility provisions of the agreement were only operative for a few days.[43]

Britain and Iraq now opened negotiations for an agreement based on the previous arrangement whereby Britain had provided Iraq with a specified amount of dollars for a specified period of time. The negotiations were held in Baghdad between September and November 1947, and once again they were conducted primarily by British Treasury and Iraqi Ministry of Finance officials. The importance of the negotiations for Iraq is indicated by the fact that at times Salih Jabr, the former minister of finance who was currently prime minister, participated.[44]

The main problem in the negotiations was the amount of dollars and other scarce currencies that Britain would provide to Iraq. During the period between 1 January 1945 and 15 July 1947 Britain had provided Iraq with £3.5 million in dollars and other scarce currencies on an annual basis. However, in the last extension of the agreement, which covered the period between 1 April 1947 and 15 July 1947, Britain had provided Iraq with these currencies at an annual rate of £4.5 million to compensate for a significant rise in prices in the United States.[45]

In early October 1947 W. A. B. Iliff, the Treasury official who was Britain's chief negotiator, offered to continue to provide Iraq with £4.5 million in dollars and other scarce currencies on an annual basis. In view of the sterling area's grave shortage of dollars (in 1947 the drain was $4.1 billion), Treasury officials in London viewed this offer as a major concession. Indeed, initially they had recommended that the British government should insist that Iraq accept £3.5 million on an annual basis.[46]

While the British considered £4.5 million in dollars and other scarce currencies on an annual basis to be a generous offer, the Iraqis rejected it as too low because of the continuing rise in American prices; and because Belgium, from which they had been making substantial purchases, was now a scarce currency country. Moreover, at this time Iraq was obliged to purchase a large quantity of cotton piece goods from Japan, which was now also a scarce currency country, because recently India had significantly cut its exports of cotton piece goods to the Middle East, and Britain did not manufacture the inexpensive types that Iraq needed. For these reasons, the Iraqis requested £7.5 million.[47]

Naturally the British considered this figure way out of line. However, on 17 November 1947 the two sides compromised on £5.75 million in dollars and other scarce currencies on an annual basis, with the agreement itself covering the period from 15 July 1947 to 30 June 1948.[48]

The British were willing to give considerably more than they had originally proposed because if the negotiations failed Iraq threatened to demand that the Iraq Petroleum Company pay nearly one-quarter of its royalties and local expenditures in dollars. This figure currently amounted to $8 million per year, and it was likely to rise considerably in the near future as Iraq's oil production increased. Moreover, from Iraq's perspective a demand for this money would have a logical basis because

American companies owned nearly one-quarter of the IPC, and they paid their share of the IPC's royalties and local expenditures in dollars. But all of these dollars went to the IPC and, in turn, to the sterling area's central pool. The IPC then paid Iraq entirely in sterling.[49]

The British were so accommodating also because the Foreign Office again emphasized the importance of satisfying the Iraqis on financial matters in order to gain their agreement to a revision of the Treaty of 1930. Foreign Office officials were especially eager to place Britain's relations with Iraq on a sound footing because recently relations with Egypt had deteriorated badly, and they now envisaged making Iraq the keystone of their position in the Middle East.[50]

In addition, Foreign Office officials were inclined to be generous to Iraq on financial matters because they wanted to promote economic development and thereby, hopefully, political stability and pro-British sentiment. Indeed, as we observed in chapter 6, the promotion of economic development for these purposes was an important feature of Foreign Secretary Ernest Bevin's policy throughout the Middle East.[51]

As with the financial agreement of May 1945, Britain gained because it retained Iraq in the sterling area and thereby strengthened British influence in the country. It also ensured that it would be able to continue to purchase Iraqi oil with sterling, and retain for the sterling area all of the dollars that the American companies in the IPC paid to Iraq in royalties and local expenditures. In addition, Britain did not risk too serious a loss of dollars because once again Iraq was given a quota that it was not permitted to exceed.

For Iraq the financial agreement of November 1947, like the one in May 1945, entailed a loss of sovereignty because it had to surrender all of its dollar earnings to the sterling area's central pool. Nonetheless, as in May 1945, Iraq gained because Britain provided more dollars than Iraq would otherwise have had. Indeed, according to British calculations, for the period of the agreement, and including the $8 million that Iraq earned from the American companies share of the IPC's royalties and local expenditures, Iraq would receive $6 million more on an annual basis than its actual earnings.[52]

Still, in order to develop the country and raise the standard of living, all through the immediate postwar period Iraqi leaders agitated for more dollars and more sterling releases. The fact that Britain, in the reduced economic state in which it emerged from the war, was unable to give more created dissatisfaction in Iraq and was a major irritant in Anglo-Iraqi relations.[53]

.10.

The Treaty of Portsmouth, Phase 1: The Negotiation

The Treaty of 1930, which governed Anglo-Iraqi relations, was scheduled to remain in effect until 1957. It was only in 1952, twenty years after the treaty entered into force, that either party was entitled to insist upon the commencement of negotiations for the purpose of revising the agreement.

Nonetheless, after the end of the Second World War in 1945, Iraqi leaders pressed Britain to revise the treaty. Their main objective was to create the appearance that the agreement governing Iraq's relations with Britain was one concluded between equals and not, as currently seemed to be the case, one imposed by a senior upon a junior partner. In other words, while they wanted to remove some of the treaty's restrictions on Iraq's sovereignty, they still desired to maintain close ties with Britain for the purpose of assisting external defense, internal security, and economic development. Indeed, their request for treaty revision probably resulted more from a perceived need to deflect attacks by their political opponents in Iraq and other Arab countries, who frequently accused them of being tools of the British and insufficiently nationalistic, than from a profound dissatisfaction with their existing relationship with Britain. The fact that at this time Egypt was pressing Britain for treaty revision made them all the more vulnerable to this type of criticism unless they did likewise.[1]

British Foreign Office officials and military leaders were not happy about the prospect of revising the treaty because the existing agreement satisfied nearly all of their requirements and ensured the continuation of Britain's dominant position in Iraq. In particular, they were pleased with their complete control over the air bases at Habbaniya and Shaiba because this enabled them at any time rapidly to move large air and ground forces into Iraq. In the event of war with the Soviet Union they could then use these forces to protect, and in extremis to destroy, the very valuable oil fields and related facilities in northeastern Iraq and southwestern Iran. In the event of such a war they could also use these forces to conduct offensive air operations against important targets in the southern part of the Soviet Union.[2]

Aside from being useful in a conflict with the Soviet Union, control of Habbaniya and Shaiba could help Britain to defend the oil fields in Iraq and Iran against an internal menace. For example, in chapter 6 we observed that as a result of Communist-led strikes in the oil fields in Iran, in July 1946 the British government dispatched a brigade of Indian troops to Shaiba to serve as a possible force of intervention. And as a result of Iran's nationalization of the British-owned Anglo-Iranian Oil Company's concession, in the summer of 1951 the British government again contemplated using the base at Shaiba to intervene in Iran.[3]

Britain could also use Habbaniya and Shaiba to defend the pro-British regime in Iraq against its internal opponents. Indeed, in the Introduction we observed that in May 1941 the bases proved invaluable when British military forces overthrew Rashid Ali's anti-British government and reinstated the regent and Britain's other friends in power.[4]

In addition to enabling Britain to conduct various types of military operations, control of Habbaniya and Shaiba allowed the Royal Air Force to maintain the integrity of the air route to Bahrain, Britain's key position in the Persian Gulf, and onward to Britain's dominions and possessions in South Asia and the Far East. Although long-range military aircraft could fly from Britain's air bases in Palestine and western Jordan directly to Bahrain without refueling, medium-range aircraft could only do so with a reduced payload, and short-range aircraft could not do so at all.[5]

Nonetheless, after the Second World War the British agreed to revise the treaty because they realized that, regardless of the legal position, the rising tide of nationalist sentiment in Iraq would not enable them to maintain the agreement intact until it expired in 1957. They also feared that if they refused to yield to the importunities of moderate Iraqi politicians for relatively minor alterations that essentially left Britain's dominant position intact, soon extremist politicians would come to power who would demand the immediate abolition of the treaty and the wholesale withdrawal of British military forces and political influence. The fact that the Palestinian issue was likely to come to a head soon, quite possibly with distasteful results for most Arabs and consequent bad feeling against Britain, made them especially eager to conclude an agreement with Iraq now. Moreover, because they had agreed to revise the Anglo-Egyptian treaty, they felt that they could not now refuse to revise the Anglo-Iraqi treaty without inviting invidious comparisons that would damage the position of Britain's friends in Iraq. And since the Anglo-Egyptian negotiations had gone badly, they believed that a treaty with Iraq would set a useful precedent for similar arrangements with other Arab countries, including possibly Egypt, and thereby contribute greatly to Britain's ability to defend the Middle East in the event of war. Finally, as we observed in chapter 6, treaty revision was consonant with the outlook of Foreign Secretary Ernest Bevin who, in the spirit of the more liberal age after the Second World War and in accordance with the philosophy of the Labour party to which he belonged, wanted to upgrade countries like Egypt and Iraq, which in the eyes of many were still little more than British dependencies or protectorates, into equal partners with Britain in the defense of the Middle East.[6]

For Iraqi leaders the clauses requiring them to give precedence to the British ambassador in Baghdad over the representatives of all other nations and preventing them from elevating the status of their legation in London to that of an embassy were some of the annoying features of the treaty. Although these diplomatic provisions did not have much practical effect, they symbolized Britain's dominant position in Iraq and Iraq's subordinate status. The fact that Egypt had an embassy in London, and thereby a superior status to Iraq, made this restriction particularly irritating.[7]

In May 1946, before the onset of negotiations to revise the treaty and without requesting a quid pro quo, the Foreign Office informed Iraqi leaders that it would give them satisfaction on these two points. Accordingly, the following August Britain and Iraq exchanged notes modifying the provisions of the relevant notes exchanged at the time of the signature of the Treaty of 1930.[8]

This matter was easily resolved because by 1946 the Foreign Office believed that these diplomatic clauses annoyed the Iraqis without contributing significantly to the maintenance of British influence in Iraq. It was also under pressure from the United States which, commensurate with its increasing role in world affairs, since 1944 had wanted to raise the status of its legation in Baghdad to that of an embassy. Because it would then be difficult for the Iraqis to continue to grant precedence to the British ambassador, the Foreign Office decided gracefully to yield this relatively unimportant position that, in the face of increasing Iraqi and American pressure, it did not believe that it could readily maintain much longer in any case.[9]

Initial discussions for a new treaty began in Baghdad in May 1947 and continued, either in Iraq or in England, until their successful conclusion in January 1948. During this period the Iraqi government was led by Prime Minister Salih Jabr, Defense Minister Shakir al-Wadi, and Foreign Minister Fadhil al-Jamali, all of whom wanted to preserve close ties with Britain. Jabr, it will be recalled, had served Britain well in 1941-42 when, as minister of interior, he had arrested many supporters of former prime minister Rashid Ali and incarcerated them in concentration camps. Shakir, a former colonel in the army, had many British friends as a result of studying at the Camberley Staff College in 1936 and serving as chargé d'affaires at the Iraqi legation in London during the Second World War. He had also done much to keep the army friendly to Britain since becoming minister of defense in November 1946, in spite of numerous complaints from officers about Britain's failure to supply enough arms. And Jamali, a former official in the Ministry of Education, had a Ph.D. from Columbia University and a Canadian wife and was similarly a staunch upholder of the existing order.[10]

The main stumbling block in the talks in May 1947, and in all of the subsequent negotiations over the treaty, was the British air bases at Habbaniya and Shaiba. These facilities were the most conspicuous example of Britain's overweening presence in Iraq, and for many Iraqis an egregious affront to their country's sovereignty. For Iraqi leaders the bases were especially problematic and difficult to justify because in 1946 Britain withdrew all of its military forces from Syria and Lebanon, and promised to remove all of them from Egypt. While in their discussions with Britain Iraqi leaders did not dispute the importance of the bases to their country's security, they were apprehensive that they would be vulnerable to strong criticism and considerable loss of prestige if British military forces remained in Iraq after they had been withdrawn from most of the other Arab states. If only agreement could be obtained for the presence of British bases in these other countries, they said that then they would easily be able to permit Britain to retain its bases in Iraq. But aside from Jordan, where for various reasons Britain still retained considerable influence, none of the other independent Arab states were willing to accept British bases. Consequently, for Britain this recourse was not viable.[11]

As an alternative to establishing British bases in all of the other Arab states, Iraqi leaders proposed that Britain simply replace its base at Habbaniya with a similar one in Jordan and its base at Shaiba with a similar one in Kuwait. Since the rulers of both countries were friendly to Britain, the Iraqis thought that this proposal was politically feasible. They also believed that in this manner they could free their country from foreign military forces while still ensuring that Britain remained close enough to assist them in the event of an emergency.[12]

However, British military leaders would not accept this proposal. To begin with, they calculated that the cost of developing adequate bases in Jordan and Kuwait—including the required airfields, workshops, hangers, fuel tanks, munition dumps, accommodation facilities, special provisions for the supply of water, and improved lines of communications—would be very expensive, probably more than £12 million, and would conflict with numerous other urgent construction projects. They also pointed out that a base in Jordan, even one located in the extreme eastern part of the country near the Iraqi frontier, would impair the integrity of the air route to Bahrain and onward to the Far East because it would be too far from Kuwait for short-range aircraft to fly without refueling. In addition, they argued that a base in Jordan, which even at the Iraqi border would be some 320 miles from Baghdad, would not be as well-situated as Habbaniya for the purpose of acting as an assembly point for British troops being moved into central Iraq or for organizing the air defense of the oil fields near Kirkuk. Similarly, they believed that a base in Kuwait would not be as well-situated as Shaiba for the purpose of acting as an assembly point for British troops being moved into southern Iraq or for organizing the air defense of the port of Basra, the oil refinery and export facilities at Abadan, and the oil fields in southwestern Iran.[13]

As another option, Iraqi leaders suggested that Britain forego the permanent stationing of British aircraft at Habbaniya and Shaiba in peacetime while retaining the right to use the facilities freely in wartime or when hostilities appeared imminent. The Iraqis believed that this proposal would enable them to free their country from foreign military forces while still ensuring that Britain would have the ability to assist them in the event of trouble.[14]

However, the British did not believe that this proposal would enable them properly to fulfill the obligation that they would be assuming in a new treaty, as in the old one, to defend Iraq. In particular, they doubted that their aircraft would be able to rush to Iraq in a crisis and perform well if the pilots and other key personnel had not had previous experience in operating there. They also doubted that they could successfully improvise a modern air base at short notice in an emergency at a great distance from their source of supply. In addition, they were concerned that in a period of tension when war appeared imminent the Iraqi government, fearing to exacerbate the tension and possibly provoke hostilities, would ignore or dispute its treaty obligation and not actually invite British forces into the country. To understand British thinking on this subject, it must be recalled that in April 1940 Germany's lightening descent upon Norway immediately deprived the RAF of suitable air bases from which to resist the advance; and in May 1940 Belgian leaders refused to invite Anglo-French forces into their country until Germany had actually attacked, thereby making a successful Allied defense far more difficult.[15]

The Anglo-Iraqi talks in May 1947 ended without any agreement on the question of the British air bases. As a result, Douglas Busk, the counsellor at the British embassy in Baghdad who ran the embassy for most of 1947 due to the illness of the ambassador, became concerned that Iraq might confront Britain with a formal demand for complete evacuation. To avoid this possibility, in late May 1947 he suggested to the Foreign Office that Britain invite the Iraqi air force to station its aircraft at Habbaniya and Shaiba alongside British aircraft. Busk believed that this concession would go far to meet Iraq's desire for greater control over the facilities without seriously inconveniencing the RAF. He also believed that shared bases would have the additional advantage that the Iraqi air force would then be maintained in a higher state of efficiency because its ground staff would be working close to British technicians.[16]

British military leaders did not like the idea of having Iraqi military personnel stationed within the confines of the British bases because of the security risk. They also believed that shared bases would inevitably make Britain's use of the facilities more dependent upon Iraqi goodwill than at present. However, British military leaders realized that they would not be able to maintain the status quo in Iraq much longer, and they were fearful of complete eviction. They also saw advantage in the prospect of developing closer ties with, and possibly some control over, the Iraqi air force. Consequently, in July 1947 they endorsed Busk's proposal to share Habbaniya and Shaiba with Iraq provided that they retained final responsibility for the issue of all orders affecting British personnel and the movement of British forces.[17]

Influenced by the position of the military, the Foreign Office also supported Busk's recommendation. Accordingly, in August 1947 it informed Iraqi leaders that Britain was now willing to share the bases with Iraq.[18]

However, for Jabr shared bases were insufficient. Indeed, between October and December 1947 he repeatedly informed the British government that, aside from a few technicians to help operate the bases, British forces must not have the right to be stationed in Iraq in peacetime. Although in time of war or the imminent threat of war he was willing to agree that Iraq "will invite" British forces to use the bases, during peace he was only willing to agree that Iraq "may invite" British forces to use the bases. This solution was one of several that Jabr had mentioned as possible during the initial discussions in May, and it was the one to which he now strongly adhered. Jabr maintained this position because he wanted to be able to claim publicly that now at long last Iraq was freed from all trace of foreign occupation and completely master of its own destiny, and that any British forces that remained in the country were there only on sufferance rather than on right. He was also concerned that if he concluded a treaty without this provision—in other words, a treaty that was too favorable to Britain—it would not be ratified by the Iraqi Parliament, and even if ratified would not long survive the strong public protest that it would arouse. The fact that Jabr was Iraq's first Shiite prime minister, and for this reason probably expected a fair amount of criticism on purely sectarian grounds, may have further influenced his desire to obtain an agreement that, from Iraq's perspective, on the vital question of the air bases was clearly superior to the existing treaty.[19]

To reassure the British, in late November and early December 1947 Jabr maintained that their essential interests would be safeguarded because they had the friendship of the royal family and most Iraqi political leaders, and because these groups recognized Iraq's great need for British assistance in the area of defense. He also said that immediately after an agreement was concluded he planned to request that the RAF continue to station its operational units and maintenance personnel at the bases.[20]

But the British were not reassured. To begin with, they did not believe that they could depend upon future Iraqi governments being as friendly as Jabr's and adopting the same policy. After all, in 1941 the regent had to flee Baghdad to escape capture and probably execution by anti-British military conspirators, and Rashid Ali had aligned Iraq with Nazi Germany. They also emphasized that they were being asked to undertake a commitment to defend Iraq, and that in return they would have to insist upon wording that was more definite, and that consequently provided more assurance, than Jabr's imprecise formulation. In addition, they wanted tighter wording because they viewed the prospective Iraqi treaty as a model that would eventually be extended to other Middle Eastern countries, and they did not want to set an undesirable precedent.[21]

In late December 1947 Jabr asked Nuri al-Said, the pro-British elder statesman and longtime former prime minister, who currently did not hold a cabinet position, to become involved in the negotiations. Nuri thereupon proposed a compromise that would retain Jabr's insistence that during peace Iraq "may invite" British aircraft to use the bases, but to compensate the British would define peace as beginning on the date when the last peace treaty that Britain concluded with the former enemy countries from the Second World War entered into effect. Since with the onset of the cold war a peace treaty with a united Germany did not appear imminent, and since until then the RAF would have unrestricted use of the bases, Nuri believed that this formulation would satisfy Britain's needs. Moreover, from his perspective it would still place a reasonable and politically defensible limitation on Britain's right to station military aircraft in Iraq.[22]

The final negotiations for the treaty were held in London in January 1948. In addition to Prime Minister Salih Jabr, Defense Minister Shakir al-Wadi, Foreign Minister Fadhil al-Jamali, and Nuri al-Said, the Iraqi delegation included Tawfiq al-Suwaydi, another elder statesman and former prime minister whom Jabr brought along to widen his base of political support at home. Most of the discussion at these talks centered around Nuri's proposal, which was now the official Iraqi position, to define peace as beginning when the last peace treaty between Britain and the former enemy countries entered into effect. To help persuade the British, the Iraqis now suggested that even after peace officially arrived they might continue to permit British aircraft to remain in Iraq. They also mentioned the possibility of extended visits by British aircraft to Iraq in peacetime for training purposes.[23]

But Foreign Secretary Ernest Bevin, who participated in the talks, disliked the sort of ambiguity that the Iraqis, because of their need to satisfy opposing constituencies, were so fond of. He was also concerned that peace treaties with all of the former enemy countries would not usher in a state of international amity warranting Britain's withdrawal from the bases in Iraq. After all, Britain had already concluded peace treaties with five former enemy countries in Europe (Italy, Bulgaria, Romania, Hungary, and Finland) without any noticeable amelioration of international tension. Consequently, Bevin insisted upon firm arrangements that would definitely permit British aircraft to use the bases in Iraq, not merely until peace treaties were concluded with all of the former enemy countries, but also until the setting up of arrangements for international collective security in accordance with article 43 of the United Nations Charter.[24]

The members of the Iraqi delegation would not accept Bevin's proposal because, with international relations so tense, they did not believe that article 43 of the United Nations Charter would be implemented at any time within the foreseeable future. In other words, they feared that if this proposal were adopted the withdrawal of British forces from Iraq would be indefinitely delayed, and therefore to many Iraqis the new treaty would not be meaningfully superior to the existing one.[25]

In an effort to reach an agreement, the British now abandoned their insistence on linking a definition of peace—which was the time when they would no longer have the right to station their aircraft in Iraq—with the establishment of a system of international collective security under the terms of article 43 of the United Nations Charter. However, they were still not satisfied with the Iraqi proposal to define peace as the time when Britain concluded the last peace treaty with the former enemy countries because they feared that this date might be too imminent and might not bring about sufficiently secure international conditions. Consequently, they proposed to define peace as the conclusion of peace treaties with all of the former enemy countries plus the complete withdrawal of all Allied troops from these countries.[26]

To the members of the Iraqi delegation this definition of peace was little better than Bevin's earlier one, which mandated the establishment by the United Nations of an effective system of international security, because both seemed equally unlikely to materialize within the foreseeable future. To improve these prospects, at least slightly, they suggested that the definition be limited to the conclusion of the peace treaties plus the withdrawal of all British troops, rather than all Allied troops, from the former enemy countries. However, Foreign Office officials would not accept this modification because they were concerned about the possibility that American occupation troops might replace their British counterparts in Germany and Austria as they had already done in Japan.[27]

Apparently worn down by Bevin's obduracy, and eager to achieve the agreement that was now so close and upon the conclusion of which he had staked his prestige, Jabr finally yielded and accepted the British wording. In this manner the two sides surmounted the last obstacle, and on 15 January 1948, in Portsmouth, they signed the treaty.[28]

The treaty was due to remain in effect for twenty years with either party permitted to request revision after fifteen years. If the treaty had not been revised at the expiry of the twenty-year period it was scheduled to remain in force indefinitely, although either party then had the right to give one-year's notice of a desire to terminate it.

As we have observed, on the question of the air bases, which for both sides was the most vital issue, the British did well. At the price of allowing the Iraqis to share the bases, they received the unrestricted right to use the facilities in war or peace, for purposes of transit or permanent basing and with no limit on the number or type of aircraft, for what gave every indication of being a very prolonged period. Moreover, while the British had to share the bases, they were not placed under overall Iraqi command. On the contrary, the treaty specified that their operation and security arrangements would be managed jointly by the British and Iraqi commanding officers with each retaining responsibility for the movement of his own country's aircraft. Therefore, the British would be able to keep all of their units firmly under their own command.[29]

The Treaty of 1930 stipulated that "His Majesty the King of Iraq agrees to afford, when requested to do so by His Britannic Majesty, all possible facilities for the movement of the forces of His Britannic Majesty of all arms in transit across Iraq." British officials wanted to retain this provision, not only because they envisaged using it to move British troops across Iraq, but also because under certain circumstances they envisaged using it as a guise to place British troops in Iraq, even though the Treaty of Portsmouth did not specifically give them the right to do so. But Iraqi leaders disliked the peremptory phrasing of this article because it took the decision entirely out of their hands. Instead, they wanted the right to decide whether any particular British troop movement across Iraq was necessary.[30]

In the end the two sides agreed to an ambiguous formula that stipulated that "His Majesty the King of Iraq agrees to afford, in case of need and on request, all necessary facilities for the movement of units of His Britannic

Majesty's forces in transit across Iraq." What was left unsaid, of course, was which party had the right to determine the "need" for the troop movements. Thus the Iraqis could maintain that they had the right to determine the "need," and that consequently they now had a veto over British troop movements across Iraq. In a crisis, however, the British could assert that the "need" to move their troops across Iraq was apparent, and that therefore they had the right to proceed on their own accord.

Aside from the air bases and the movement of troops across Iraq, in various other security-related areas the British retained important privileges from the Treaty of 1930. For example, they kept the right to send their warships into the Shatt al-Arab, which was an Iraqi waterway, without obtaining prior permission. For the British this provision was desirable because it enabled them in an emergency to dispatch forces quickly to protect the large British-owned oil refinery at Abadan in southwestern Iran.

The British also retained a provision from the earlier treaty requiring Iraq to ensure that its military equipment not differ in type from that used by the British armed forces. In reality, of course, this meant that Iraq had to purchase virtually all of its arms from Britain. For the British this provision was desirable because they believed that the two armed forces would be able to operate more efficiently together in wartime if they used similar equipment, because they calculated that it would make Iraq dependent upon Britain for spare parts and therefore eager to retain Britain's friendship, because they wanted to prevent other countries from using the supply of arms to acquire political influence in Iraq, and because they wanted to preserve the Iraqi market for British arms manufacturers for purely commercial reasons.[31]

In the past the Iraqis had been upset by the slow delivery of arms that they purchased from Britain. In an effort to ensure that in the future they received weapons more promptly, they tried to insert a provision in the treaty stipulating that Britain would give Iraqi orders for military equipment the same priority as orders from its own armed forces. However, British military leaders would not agree invariably to give Iraq such a privileged position. Consequently, Iraq had to be content with a loophole-filled statement to the effect that Britain would provide arms to Iraq "on a priority which, having regard to the relative needs of each force, shall treat both forces equally."[32]

Other security-related provisions of the Treaty of 1930 that Britain was able to retain were those stipulating that all of Iraq's foreign military instructors would be British and that all Iraqi soldiers sent abroad for military training would be sent to British schools. Combined with Iraq's obligation to purchase virtually all of its military equipment in Britain, these provisions helped to ensure considerable British influence in the Iraqi armed forces.

In a final effort to achieve this objective and tie Iraq as closely as possible to Britain in the area of defense, the British inserted a clause in the treaty, which was not contained in the earlier agreement, calling for the establishment of a Joint Defense Board. This body, which was to be composed of military representatives of the two countries in equal numbers, was supposed to coordinate military matters between the two countries such as making plans for the defense of Iraq, arranging joint-training exercises, and determining the type of military equipment best suited for Iraq.

Thus the Treaty of Portsmouth did much to ensure the continuation of Britain's dominant position in Iraq and the Middle East generally. Indeed, compared with the agreement that Bevin had concluded with Egyptian Prime Minister Ismail Sidky in October 1946, which called for the withdrawal of all British military forces from Egypt, the terms of the Treaty of Portsmouth were especially advantageous for Britain.[33]

Britain was able to conclude such a favorable treaty because Jabr badly wanted an agreement to boost his prestige within Iraq. He was particularly eager for a success because he had suffered a major blow in August 1947 when the British suspended indefinitely the free convertibility of sterling, thereby obviating the main provisions of a financial agreement that with considerable fanfare he had concluded with them only one week previous. The following November he had suffered another setback when the United Nations General Assembly recommended the creation of a Jewish state in Palestine. On the domestic front too he was incurring considerable criticism because of a serious bread shortage.[34]

Britain's success was also attributable to the fact that, unlike most Egyptian leaders, Iraqi leaders generally perceived a serious external threat because of their relatively close proximity to the Soviet Union. After the Second World War this concern was increased by various Soviet actions, such as making territorial demands on Turkey, delaying the withdrawal of their troops from Iran beyond the permitted time, and setting up pro-Soviet regimes in the Azerbaijani and Kurdish districts of northwestern Iran near Iraq's border. In addition to the external threat, Iraqi leaders generally perceived an internal threat from dissident elements within their society such as the Kurds, the Communists and their followers among the urban poor, and their own armed forces. Consequently, they were not entirely unwilling to see British forces stationed in Iraq to counterbalance, and conceivably to combat, these elements. During the Rashid Ali incident in 1941 they had learned how valuable the British bases could be for this purpose.[35]

Aside from these factors, the British were able to conclude such a favorable agreement because they made some concessions. For example, they agreed to eliminate the provision of the Treaty of 1930 that stipulated that "there shall be full and frank consultation between them [Britain and Iraq] in all matters of foreign policy which may affect their common interests." The Iraqis had pressed for the elimination of this provision because they viewed it as a restriction of their sovereignty. Although this provision helped to tie Iraq closer to Britain, Foreign Office officials agreed to abandon it as part of a general policy of accommodating Iraq on nonvital matters in order better to preserve what they considered to be essential British interests.[36]

The British also agreed to the disbandment of the levies and their replacement by Iraqi troops. As we observed in chapter 1, the levies were a military force under British control that the British recruited in Iraq for the purpose of guarding their air bases. There were now about 2,100 men in the levies, down from a peak strength during the war of more than 6,000. Iraqi governments had long disputed the legal status of the levies, and in any case considered them a major affront to Iraqi sovereignty. The fact that the British recruited the levies to a considerable extent from the Assyrian community (a small, imperfectly assimilated, pro-British Christian group with a rebellious history) made them especially unpopular with most Iraqis.[37]

The British were reluctant to agree to the disbandment of the levies because, with their large Assyrian component, these troops were a politically reliable, well-disciplined, financially inexpensive body with a long record of loyal service to the British Crown. Moreover, the British were not pleased with the idea of entrusting the security of their bases to the Iraqi army because it had turned against them in 1941. However, they knew that they would have to yield on this issue because the Iraqis felt so strongly about it. They also wanted to further the integration of the Assyrian community into Iraqi society and realized that this task would be much easier without the levies. In addition, they believed that in an emergency they could introduce British troops to protect the bases by deceitfully claiming that these troops were really in transit across Iraq.[38]

While realizing that as an institution the levies were doomed, the British were concerned about the welfare of the individual soldiers who had served in the organization. In particular, they wanted to obtain a pledge that the Iraqi government would not conscript them into the Iraqi army. However, the Iraqi negotiators refused to give such a pledge because they maintained that this action would involve placing the Assyrians above the law. The most that they would agree to was a vague statement that "it is the intention of the Iraqi Government to give to these men the fairest possible treatment in recognition of their previous service in the Royal Air Force Levies." And with this the British, and the levies, had to be content.[39]

In addition to the disbandment of the levies, the British agreed to eliminate the provision of the Treaty of 1930 requiring Iraq to employ at its own expense the services of a British military mission. The British agreed to this because they feared that otherwise Iraq would soon demand the withdrawal of the mission, like Egypt had recently done, and that for reasons of prestige it would be preferable to yield gracefully rather than under compulsion. They also believed that other portions of the treaty, and especially the clause obligating Iraq to hire exclusively British subjects for its foreign military instructors, would still enable them to retain influence in the Iraqi armed forces.[40]

As another concession, the Foreign Office agreed to eliminate the section of the Treaty of 1930 requiring Iraq to employ British subjects whenever it needed foreign experts in any nonmilitary sphere of its government or administration. True, this obligation had never been absolute because Iraq was allowed to hire nationals from other countries whenever Britain was unable to provide the necessary personnel. Moreover, Iraq had occasionally ignored this obligation by employing non-British experts, especially from other Arab countries, without consulting Britain. Nonetheless, the existence of this provision still grated on Iraqi sensibilities because it emphasized Iraq's subservient status.[41]

Foreign Office officials were not pleased about abandoning this section of the earlier treaty because the presence of British subjects in many branches of the Iraqi government was an important source of British influence. This presence was also a boost to the British economy because often these men were able to steer orders for machinery and equipment to British companies. Indeed, partly for this reason in the period 1946-51 Britain supplied 42.9 percent of Iraq's imports. In addition, Foreign Office officials feared that if they abandoned this provision Iraq would not continue to employ British subjects on dredging operations in the Shatt al-Arab, which for Britain was a matter of considerable importance because large numbers of British tankers regularly used this waterway to reach the Anglo-Iranian Oil Company's refinery and export terminal at Abadan in southwestern Iran.[42]

However, as in the matter of consultation about foreign policy, the levies, and the military mission, Foreign Office officials believed that it would be advisable to give way on the issue of advisers in order better to take a firm stand on the truly vital question of the air bases. They also calculated that if they did not yield they would simply anger the Iraqis without achieving much because the Iraqis would then proceed to hire whomever they pleased with Britain reduced to the undignified position of constantly making ineffectual protests. In addition, Foreign Office officials thought that it would be invidious to insist upon retaining such a provision in a treaty with Iraq because in 1946 Britain had concluded a treaty with Jordan that did not contain such a provision. Finally, they believed that left on their own the Iraqis would probably continue to employ primarily British subjects because they were accustomed to them, and because the employment of nationals from other countries would usually involve a drain on Iraq's scarce supplies of non-sterling currencies.[43]

A further British concession that made the treaty more palatable to the Iraqis was the handing over free of charge of many of the installations that Britain had constructed in the Basra area for its military forces during the Second World War. This gift included two hospitals, a water filtration plant, an electric power station, and several telecommunications systems. Actually this gift was not as magnanimous as it appeared because the British did not believe that they could sell the installations for any appreciable amount of money either to the Iraqi government or to anyone else. In any event, in return for this gift Iraq was only obligated to maintain the facilities in good working order so that, in case of need, British forces would be able to use them again.[44]

Another British concession was the agreement to pay £20,000 per year for the next four years (with the possibility of continuation after this period) toward the cost of instruction of Iraqi officers at various military schools in Britain. Iraq was required to pay a similar sum and therefore the cost of these courses, which previously Iraq had borne entirely alone, would now be evenly divided. For Iraqi leaders this arrangement seemed only fair because they believed that these officers were performing a joint service for Britain and Iraq. The British yielded on this question, partly in order to accommodate the Iraqis, but also because they wanted to bring as many Iraqi officers to Britain for training as possible in the belief that these men would be pro-British upon their return home.[45]

Finally, the Foreign Office agreed to terminate the Anglo-Iraqi Railway Agreement of 1936. This arrangement obligated Iraq to purchase all of its railway material in Britain and to employ six British officials in important positions on the railways. For Iraqi leaders the termination of the agreement was significant because its provisions, although not terribly consequential, still restricted their freedom and demonstrated their subordinate position vis-à-vis Britain.[46]

As we have observed, for the British the Treaty of Portsmouth was a favorable document because, despite their concessions, it preserved their vital security interests. The Iraqi negotiators believed that the agreement was in the best interests of their country too, and certainly an improvement on the Treaty of 1930. After all, they had secured shared air bases, gained some control over Britain's previously unrestricted right to move troops across Iraq, ended the obligation to consult with Britain on matters of foreign policy, and obtained the elimination of the levies, the military mission, and the requirement to hire only British subjects as advisers and employees (except for the armed forces). They had also received a number of valuable British-owned installations for free, procured financial assistance for the training of their officers in British military schools, and secured the termination of the railway agreement. However, for various reasons a large part of the politically active section of the Iraqi population did not agree that the treaty was in Iraq's best interests, and it is their reaction that we must now discuss.

.11.

The Treaty of Portsmouth, Phase 2: The Collapse

In Iraq the Treaty of Portsmouth encountered a storm of protest. For example, the Istiqlal party maintained that "this Treaty is more oppressive than its predecessor. It is a national catastrophe. . . . It will involve Iraq in avoidable dangers and unsupportable expenditure." The National Democratic party described the treaty as "an openly hostile act against Iraq's existence, sovereignty and political future and an obstacle to national development and the achievement of national aspirations." And the Liberal party maintained that the new treaty is "more onerous and more tyrannic" than the earlier one, and that it constitutes a "series of shackles which disregard Iraq's sovereignty and independence and turn the country into British imperialism's camp."[1]

Probably the most important single complaint against the new treaty was that it gave Britain the right to maintain its existing positions at Habbaniya and Shaiba more or less indefinitely. Indeed, many Iraqis believed that the treaty actually expanded Britain's privileges in Iraq by giving it facilities at other airfields as well. The latter criticism was based on provisions stipulating that "His Majesty the King of Iraq will make available facilities at air bases in Iraq necessary for the purposes of this joint training," and that "His Britannic Majesty shall not be called upon to pay any charges in respect of the use of any other landing grounds in Iraq [that is, other than Habbaniya and Shaiba] by his air forces."[2]

The Iraqi critics were, of course, correct about Britain having the right to maintain its existing positions at Habbaniya and Shaiba for a very extended period. Indeed, this criticism was precisely the sort that Jabr had feared when he continually implored the British to agree to some type of alternative arrangement.

The Iraqi critics were correct too about Britain now acquiring the additional right to train at other Iraqi air bases. However, Foreign Office officials maintained that without this provision the whole idea of partnership and cooperation, which was inherent in the concept of a treaty of alliance, would be meaningless. They also pointed out that the treaty stipulated that Britain would make available its air bases in Britain and the Middle East for training by the Iraqi air force, thereby providing, at least in theory, reciprocity in this matter.[3]

Aside from the air bases, much criticism centered around article 3, which stated that if either country became involved in war the other country would "immediately come to his aid as a measure of collective defence." Conspicuously absent from this provision, or any other provision of the treaty, was any limit on the type of aid that Iraq was required to provide to Britain; whereas the Treaty of 1930 stated that "the aid of His Majesty the King of Iraq in the event of war or the imminent menace of war will consist in furnishing to His Britannic Majesty on Iraq territory all facilities and assistance in his power, including the use of railways, rivers, ports, aerodomes and means of communication." From this omission opponents of the treaty alleged that Iraq would now be obliged to send its army to engage in distant conflicts to defend purely British rather than Iraqi interests. Even mentioned was the possibility that one day Britain, at war with Argentina, might call upon Iraq to send troops all of the way to the Falkland Islands.[4]

In fact, the British had no intention of requesting Iraq to send its forces outside of the country. Indeed, as we observed in chapter 1, during the Second World War they had rejected several such Iraqi proposals because, aside from various political considerations, they believed that the British arms and equipment necessary for such a deployment could be better expended on other Allied forces. Similarly, in the event of a future conflict they only envisaged Iraq providing facilities within the country, just as it had done in the past. However, Foreign Office officials did not incorporate this understanding in the Treaty of Portsmouth because they wanted to give the impression that the agreement was concluded on the basis of equality. In other words, they reasoned that since the treaty specified that in the event of war Britain was obligated without limit to aid Iraq, then Iraq should incur a similar obligation. Still, Foreign Office officials believed that Iraq's concerns were fully covered because article 5 of the annexure, which established the Joint Defense Board to coordinate military relations between Britain and Iraq, stated that one of the board's functions would be "the formulation of agreed plans in the strategic interests *common to both countries*" [my emphasis]. Consequently, they said that it would be open to the Iraqi representatives on the board to argue that any particular plan, for example, one concerning the defense of the Falkland Islands, was not within purview of Iraq's strategic interests. They also pointed out that the board was to be composed of an equal number of representatives of both countries and therefore presumably could not make any plans or insist upon any deployments without mutual consent.[5]

In spite of the fact that the Joint Defense Board was to be composed of an equal number of representatives of both countries, opponents of the treaty alleged that the Iraqi representatives would not be truly equal to their British counterparts because they had less training and experience, and because the two countries were so greatly disparate in strength. This argument may have had merit, although it betrayed a lack of confidence in the ability or willingness of Iraqi officers to assert their point of view that previous discussions between the military representatives of the two countries did not indicate.[6]

Another criticism of the Joint Defense Board was that it would be able to make final decisions binding on both governments, thereby sidetracking normal constitutional procedures. This argument was plausible because the treaty did not explicitly state that the board's decisions would be subject to approval by both governments. However, Foreign Office officials considered it obvious that the military representatives on the board would require ministerial approval before formally committing their governments to any major undertaking.[7]

Still another complaint was that the treaty would involve additional expense because, with the abolition of the levies, Iraq would now have to pay for the guards at Habbaniya and Shaiba. Iraq would also have to pay for the construction and maintenance of installations and buildings at the bases that were exclusively occupied by, or erected for, the use of its forces.[8]

As far as the guards at Habbaniya and Shaiba were concerned, this criticism was correct, but only if Iraq chose to provide them by increasing the size of its army rather than by simply redeploying existing units. In any event, opponents of the treaty were poorly placed to make this argument because they had long opposed the current arrangement whereby Britain paid for, but therefore also commanded, the guards.

As far as the construction and maintenance of installations and buildings at Habbaniya and Shaiba was concerned, this criticism was also correct, but only if Iraq chose to station its aircraft and personnel at the bases. After all, it would be within its rights to choose not to do so. Moreover, the treaty stipulated that "His Britannic Majesty will provide at these bases [Habbaniya and Shaiba] the necessary technical staff, installations and equipment, and subject to paragraph (e) of Article 2 below [which said that Iraq would pay for the construction and maintenance of installations and buildings at Habbaniya and Shaiba which were required exclusively for the use of its forces] will meet the cost of such maintenance." Thus Iraq would have the use of two modern air bases for which Britain had paid the cost of construction and for which Britain would continue to pay nearly all of the cost of upkeep.

Opponents of the treaty also maintained that Iraq would now be bound to Britain in an intimate relationship in perpetuity, because article 7 stipulated that any revision of the agreement after its expiration "shall provide for the continued co-operation of the high contracting parties in the defence of their common interests."[9]

But this charge was incorrect because this sentence read in its entirety stated, "At any time after fifteen years from the date of coming into force of this treaty, the high contracting parties *may* [my emphasis], at the request of either of them, negotiate for its revision, which shall provide for the continued co-operation of the high contracting parties in the defence of their common interests." Thus Iraq was in no way obligated to negotiate a new treaty after the expiry of this one. And even if Iraq did so, the phrase "shall provide for the continued co-operation of the high contracting parties in the defence of their common interests" was vague and open to various interpretations. For example, it could be plausibly argued that a mere exchange of intelligence information would be sufficient to fulfill the requirement.

The Istiqlal, National Democratic, and Liberal parties had opposed the British connection since their inceptions in 1946. They also had strong grievances against Jabr because he had prosecuted their leaders, suppressed their newspapers, and collaborated with Nuri in rigging the election of March 1947 to freeze them out of power. Consequently, their opposition to the treaty was expected. Indeed, even before the treaty was signed they had committed themselves to opposing it on the grounds that the government that concluded it was illegitimate because it had not been democratically elected.[10]

What was notable, however, was the opposition of virtually all of the leading, establishment, essentially pro-British politicians who usually dominated Iraqi governments. Unlike the political parties, these men were not especially concerned about the deficiencies, alleged or actual, of the treaty. Rather, they wanted to use this issue as a means of bringing down Jabr's government and elevating themselves to power.[11] Jabr, it should be noted, had excluded all of the members of this group from office.[12] Moreover, he had not consulted them to any appreciable extent during the course of his negotiations with Britain.[13] Possibly Jabr did not want to share too widely what he hoped would be the glory of his achievement. He may also have believed that consultation would lead to unfavorable publicity about the treaty before it was even concluded. In any event, by not being more solicitous toward this important group he lost a good opportunity to divide his opponents and gain valuable political support for his policy.

Probably these leading politicians, nearly all of whom were Sunni, also opposed Jabr because he was a Shiite—indeed he was the first Shiite prime minister. An example of this type of sectarian prejudice occurred in March 1947, just after Jabr assumed office, when a prominent Sunni member of the Chamber of Deputies remarked to one of the staff of the American embassy that "Perowne [the oriental counsellor at the British embassy] is going too far in shoving a Shia Prime Minister down our throats, but I fear there is nothing we can do about it at the moment."[14] However, Sunni opposition to Jabr was not only based on sectarian prejudice. There was also the more practical concern that in the disposition of offices he would use his powerful position to favor members of his own group.[15]

The leading politicians, nearly all of whom were wealthy landowners or had close family or business ties with this element, also opposed Jabr because in late 1947 and early 1948 he was dealing with a serious bread shortage by enforcing a law requiring farmers to surrender half of their wheat supplies to the government. Because the government-set price for its share of the farmers' wheat was considerably below both the free market price in Iraq and the price that this wheat could command in Syria and Jordan, this policy alienated the agricultural interests. They were aggrieved too because at this time Jabr moved strongly against farmers who were hoarding wheat in an effort to force up prices. For example, in November 1947 in the province of Arbil, in the northern part of the country, his officials imprisoned 200 people for hoarding. And, pertinently, it was the northern part of the country, which was Sunni inhabited, that was the main wheat-growing area. Thus it was Sunni landowners rather than Shiite ones who bore the brunt of Jabr's agricultural policies. And so the sectarian and economic strains in the opposition of the leading politicians to Jabr were again intertwined.[16]

Finally, some prominent politicians opposed Jabr because he did not come from a well-established family. On the contrary, his father had been a carpenter, and his brother still practiced this trade.[17]

It was not only among the leading politicians that Jabr had failed to ingratiate himself. Indeed, most of his own cabinet members were not well-disposed toward him because he had continually insisted upon keeping nearly all of the reins of power in his own hands, and he had not even informed them of the progress of his negotiations with Britain. Because of Jabr's refusal to share his confidence, when he was confronted with a large-scale urban uprising after the signing of the treaty most of his cabinet colleagues refused to defend him or the treaty. In this manner at the moment of crisis they helped to make his position untenable.[18]

Jabr's secretiveness also damaged his standing with the general public because there was a widespread impression in Iraq that the treaty had been concluded with great speed. Indeed, to many it appeared that the Iraqi delegation had been peremptorily summoned to England and imperiously presented with an already prepared British draft with which they had promptly and dutifully concurred. The fact that the Iraqi delegation had departed Baghdad on 6 January, met with the British for the first time on 7 January, and initialed the treaty on 10 January (the treaty was formally signed on 15 January) lent sustenance to this accusation. In reality, of course, the negotiations for the treaty had begun in May 1947, eight months earlier, and by the time that the Iraqi delegation arrived in London agreement had been reached on nearly all points. However, because of Jabr's penchant for secrecy the Iraqi public was unaware of this fact.[19]

Jabr's mistakes did not only extend to the period before the conclusion of the treaty. On the contrary, after signing the treaty he made two errors that played directly into the hands of his opponents. First, and most important, he did not return to Iraq until 26 January, eleven days after the treaty was signed and ten days after the text was released in Baghdad. Jabr delayed because he greatly underestimated the precariousness of his political position in Iraq. He was also under pressure from his wife to remain in London because she needed to stay for medical treatment. In any event, the delay had fateful consequences because it meant that during this vital period Jabr and his leading colleagues were not present in Iraq to defend the treaty and correct honest misconceptions and deliberate distortions.[20]

Jabr's second mistake was to permit the publication of the English text of the treaty before the Arabic version was ready. Because few Iraqis could read English, in their campaign against the treaty Jabr's opponents were now better able to misrepresent various provisions.[21]

In spite of these errors, Jabr's opponents among the legal political parties and the prominent politicians would probably have been unable to instigate the major urban uprising that eventually brought down the government without the assistance of the illegal but still vigorous Communist party. That they received this support was due to the fact that the Communists strongly opposed Jabr because he had repressed their party, imprisoned their leaders, failed to implement progressive social and economic policies, and maintained close ties to Britain.[22]

Even the combined forces of these three groups would probably have been insufficient to foment a major urban uprising unless there had already existed widespread popular opposition to the regime in general, and to this government in particular, for reasons quite apart from the details of the Treaty of Portsmouth. That such opposition did exist was attributable to the fact that to many Iraqis it appeared that their leaders, including Jabr, were kept in power by Britain to serve primarily British interests and consequently were not true nationalists or legitimate representatives of their country. After all, Britain had initially placed the regime in power in 1921 and by force of arms reestablished its authority in 1941. Moreover, British forces still occupied two air bases, British companies still held the oil concessions, and British subjects still occupied numerous government jobs.[23]

Aside from its close ties to Britain, many Iraqis opposed the regime because its leaders were primarily wealthy landowners and businessmen who used a variety of means, such as the tax system, to favor the interests of their own social class at the expense of the vast majority of the population that lived in poverty. Moreover, it was widely, and correctly, believed that Iraqi leaders frequently added considerably to their incomes through a pervasive system of corruption.[24]

The absence of political democracy also generated hostility to the regime. Although the facade of democracy existed, it was common knowledge that governments carefully managed elections to ensure the return of a majority of friendly deputies. Thus meaningful change through legal means was impossible. Jabr's unusually autocratic behavior toward the left-wing opposition merely emphasized this point.[25]

At this time popular opposition to the regime was especially great because Iraq was suffering particularly bad economic conditions. As we observed in chapter 3, during the Second World War the presence of a substantial number of British troops in Iraq with their incessant demands for commodities of all sorts, coupled with Iraq's inability to obtain many types of imports, had led to a serious rise in prices. This inflation brought hardship to large sections of the population whose wages and salaries did not increase enough to keep pace with the rise in prices. During the immediate postwar period this widespread distress was not significantly ameliorated because of the continued shortage of commodities. Moreover, after the war the withdrawal of British troops from Iraq brought additional hardship because many people who had worked for the British were now unemployed.[26]

Added to these difficulties, in 1947 Iraq had a poor wheat harvest because of the unfortunate conjunction of a plague of locusts and a severe drought. The dimensions of the problem are indicated by the fact that in 1946 the wheat harvest had been 370,000 tons, while in 1947 it fell to 235,000 tons. Measured differently but still showing the great decline in production, in the 1935-39 period the average annual wheat harvest had been 18.1 million bushels, while in 1947 it fell to 12.5 million bushels.[27]

Alone the poor wheat harvest would probably have been sufficient to cause a shortage of bread. But the problem was exacerbated by the fact that, in violation of government regulations, some large landowners hoarded wheat to force up prices or smuggled wheat to Syria and Jordan to take advantage of the higher prices prevailing there. Thus to many Iraqis it appeared that government malfeasance and incompetence, possibly combined with the cupidity of Jabr and certain other ministers, was a contributing factor in the food crisis.[28]

Earlier we observed that much of the landowning class criticized Jabr for acting too strongly in collecting wheat. Now we see that much of the urban population criticized him for acting too weakly.

The government aggravated the bread shortage by permitting the free export of barley until late October 1947, by which time the situation was already acute. In allowing these exports the government was motivated by the understandable desire to earn foreign exchange for the country, and perhaps by the less praiseworthy desire to earn large profits for certain influential landowners. In any event, since barley could be used as an adulterant in the manufacture of bread, these exports exacerbated the food crisis and strengthened the popular impression that, motivated by pecuniary interests, ministers were contributing to the problem.[29]

Like any shortage, the bread shortage led to a rise in prices and a consequent further impoverishment of the masses. The dimensions of the problem are indicated by the fact that the wholesale price index rose from 463 in March 1947 (100 was the prewar figure) to 629 in March 1948.[30]

Most politically conscious Iraqis cared deeply about the Palestinian question. Consequently, the United Nations recommendation on 29 November 1947 to establish a Jewish state in Palestine created great anger in Iraq. Although Britain abstained in this vote, its policy of fostering a Jewish national home in Palestine and, allegedly, permitting the Jews to arm was widely held to be ultimately responsible for the unfortunate fate of the Arab cause in that country. Because the Iraqi government was so closely linked to Britain, it inevitably received much of the blame for these developments.[31]

Thus the Treaty of Portsmouth descended upon the Iraqi public, large sections of which were already hostile to Jabr and the British connection. Unsupported by its absent signatories and bitterly attacked by its on site opponents, it was as though a match had been thrown into a tinderbox.

Preceding the uprising by a few weeks, in early December 1947 large-scale student-led demonstrations broke out in Baghdad in opposition to the United Nations recommendation to establish a Jewish state in Palestine. Ironically, the government had encouraged these demonstrations, or at least not discouraged them, in the hope of strengthening its anti-Zionist credentials. But the demonstrations habituated the students to protesting and gave them, and vicariously other discontented elements in the population, some hint of the power of a crowd.[32]

The next phase began on 3 January 1948 when Foreign Minister Jamali issued a statement in London maintaining that "party politics rather than justice were behind much of the criticism levelled in Iraq at the 1930 Treaty. . . . If attacks upon it have continued unabated, a large number of Iraqis have, in the meantime, become sensitive to its merits." In protest against this statement, on 5 January the Istiqlal party organized a large student demonstration in Baghdad that was forcibly broken up by the police with several demonstrators injured and thirty-nine arrested. This development in turn led to a widespread student strike that lasted until 8 January when the government capitulated by releasing the arrested students. Although there was now a period of quiet, the episode increased the students' confidence in their ability effectively to challenge the government.[33]

The uprising proper began in Baghdad on 16 January 1948, immediately after the text of the treaty was published in Iraq. Initially it took the form of student strikes and demonstrations, but quickly working-class elements of the population joined in. The strikers and demonstrators demanded the rejection of the treaty, the resignation of Jabr, the calling of new parliamentary elections, the implementation of democratic freedoms, and firm action in defense of Arab interests in Palestine. As the uprising progressed and more poor people participated, the demand for bread became increasingly heard. In an effort to suppress the disturbances, on 19 January Acting Prime Minister Jamal Baban banned all further strikes and demonstrations. But this act proved ineffectual and the demonstrations continued. Indeed, on 20 and 21 January they became more widespread and for the first time turned violent, with demonstrators stoning police and the police responding with firearms, killing five.[34]

With the situation worsening, on the afternoon of 21 January 1948 the regent called a meeting at the royal palace of leading politicians, representatives of the political parties, and the members of the cabinet present in Baghdad. The regent said that he only wanted to ask for advice and assistance in dealing with the disturbances and did not want to discuss the treaty because that was now a matter for Parliament to decide. Nonetheless, most of the participants immediately proceeded to attack the treaty and maintained that only a statement by the regent repudiating it would curb the uprising. The regent, of course, was a strong supporter of the treaty and the British connection generally. But he was under great pressure from most of the leading politicians. He was also afraid that there would be a massacre of the Jews in Baghdad because it was widely rumored that they had fired on demonstrators from the roofs of their homes. In addition, and perhaps most important, he feared for the existence of the regime and his own personal safety. Largely unsupported by the ministers present and feeling abandoned by Jabr and the other members of the Iraqi delegation, all of whom were still in Britain, after four hours the regent finally yielded. Accordingly, on his instructions that evening, 21 January, the royal palace broadcast a message stating that all of the participants in the meeting had agreed that the treaty "does not realise the aspirations of the country and was not a good instrument to consolidate the pillars of friendship between the two countries." Therefore, the statement continued, the regent "promises the Iraqi people that no treaty whatever not ensuring the rights of the country and its national aspirations will be ratified."[35]

The regent did not consult the British embassy before issuing this important statement. If he had done so, British officials would undoubtedly have advised him not to repudiate the treaty because they were deeply committed to it. But at this vital moment they did not have the opportunity to play any role.[36]

Within Iraq the regent's statement was generally well-received. Even politicians and newspapers not usually well-disposed to him supported his action. Many even believed that his statement had saved the country from anarchy and upheaval.[37]

Although the demonstrations in Baghdad continued, there was now less police interference and consequently less violence. The Communist party now began to play an increasing role, in large part because the regent's statement had temporarily mollified the more moderate elements in the opposition.[38]

In London the members of the Iraqi delegation were extremely upset by the regent's action. In a conversation with Foreign Secretary Ernest Bevin on 24 January, Jabr said that he could not understand how the regent had (1) summoned a meeting at the palace that included opponents of the government and the regime; (2) allowed the participants to discuss the treaty in the absence of the prime minster and the rest of the delegation that had negotiated it; and (3) permitted a statement to be issued from the palace connecting his name with criticism of the treaty. In short, Jabr believed that the regent's action had been both unnecessary and unwise; and on 26 January, five days after the controversial meeting at the palace, he arrived in Iraq accompanied by the other members of the delegation and determined to remain in office and secure parliamentary and royal consent of the treaty.[39]

Foreign Office officials fully supported Jabr in this course of action. They were very disappointed with the regent's declaration, which they considered to be an act of panic and weakness. They now advised the regent to give full support to Jabr, and they even suggested that he issue a statement to the effect that after discussion with the delegation on their return he had been fully satisfied with their explanation of the treaty and had authorized the prime minister to present the agreement to Parliament for approval.[40]

The regent never issued such a statement, possibly because he believed that a public retraction of his statement of 21 January would make him look foolish. But in accordance with Britain's wishes, he did offer Jabr full support. Accordingly, on the evening of 26 January, just after his arrival in Iraq, Jabr broadcast to the nation. Contrary to widespread expectations that he would resign, he announced that he was going to remain in office, restore order, and present the treaty to Parliament for approval. This speech immediately provoked serious riots in Baghdad that lasted into the next day. Police fired on demonstrators, killing more than 100.[41]

Jabr's position now became increasingly difficult. In protest against the government's action, on 27 January four of his own ministers, including

Jamal Baban, resigned. So too did about thirty other members of Parliament, including the president of the Chamber of Deputies. Leading politicians told the regent that only Jabr's resignation could bring an end to the riots. At least one of them also warned the regent that the army would not remain loyal if it were called out in support of the police.[42]

In spite of the rising tide of opposition, Jabr wanted to remain in office and forcibly suppress the disturbances. His temper is indicated by a remark to the regent that if it were necessary to shoot 1,000 people to restore order he would do it so that 5 million Iraqis could remain safe. In his determination to crush the uprising, Jabr was fully supported by Nuri. But by now the regent had no stomach for further struggle. As on 21 January when he repudiated the treaty, he feared revolution and was frightened for his personal safety. He was also influenced by his mother and sisters, who implored him to conciliate rather than fight. Consequently, on the evening of 27 January he requested, and received, Jabr's resignation.[43]

As on 21 January, the regent did not consult the British embassy before acting. If he had done so Douglas Busk, the counsellor who was running the embassy because of the illness of the ambassador, would probably have advised him to change prime ministers because by 27 January he had reluctantly come to the conclusion that Jabr did not have enough support to continue to govern. But once again events in Iraq moved so rapidly that at a vital moment the British did not have the opportunity to play any role.[44]

As on 21 January, within Iraq the regent's action was generally well-received. Once again, it was widely believed that he had served the national interest and saved the country from violent turmoil and perhaps even revolution.[45]

(There was, however, an important exception to this widespread approbation. According to the American consul in Basra, much Shiite sentiment in the south, both of the wealthy in Basra and the tribes in the rural areas, was critical of the regent for having abandoned Jabr and suspected a Sunni plot designed to topple Iraq's first Shiite prime minister.[46] The British consul in Amara, a Shiite-inhabited town on the Tigris about 100 miles north of Basra, also reported a general belief that the uprising was engineered by Sunnis against Shiite influence in the government. Indeed, according to his report, in Muntafiq, a Shiite-inhabited province on the Euphrates just north of Basra, feeling on this matter was so strong that the tribal shaykhs offered the regent armed assistance against the rioters.)[47]

For the next few months parades in Baghdad continued celebrating the deaths of those shot by the police and protesting against the persisting shortage of bread and the high price and poor quality of what was available. In the spring there were also several serious labor strikes. However, with Jabr's resignation the riots ended, and the immediate threat to the regime was over.[48]

To replace Jabr the regent appointed Muhammad al-Sadr. Sadr was a respected elderly politician of a distinguished Shiite family who had sat in the Iraqi Parliament since 1925 and served as president of the Senate. He had played a major role in the anti-British insurrection of 1920 but since then had become better disposed toward the British connection. In part he was chosen because, like Jabr, he was a Shiite, and so it would not appear that Jabr had been removed from office for sectarian reasons.[49]

Although Sadr came to power as a result of a popular uprising, he filled his cabinet largely with well-established political figures. For example, the foreign minister (Hamdi al-Pachachi), the defense minister (Arshad al-Umari), and the minister of interior (Jamil al-Midfai) were all former prime ministers. Thus Sadr's government was neither a reformist administration nor hostile to the British connection. Indeed, in composition and policy it did not differ significantly from its many predecessors. Its main unifying link appeared to be opposition to Jabr and his powerful patron, Nuri al-Said.[50]

In spite of the fall of Jabr, Foreign Office officials did not give up on the treaty. They hoped that after a decent interval for tempers to cool the new government would submit it to Parliament for approval. To facilitate its passage, they were even willing to agree to an additional exchange of notes stating that in the event of war the assistance that Iraq would provide to Britain would be the same as in the Treaty of 1930, and that in no circumstances would Iraq be required to send its forces outside of the country.[51]

As we have observed, the leading members of the Iraqi government were not opposed to the British connection generally or quite possibly even to the Treaty of Portsmouth specifically. However, as a means of forcing Jabr's resignation they had adopted antitreaty positions that they could not easily abandon immediately upon assuming office. Moreover, popular opinion in Iraq was still strongly opposed to the agreement, and ministers were unwilling to argue publicly against this sentiment or to combat forcibly its violent manifestations. Consequently, they never discussed their objections to the treaty in detail with officials from the British embassy or proposed any changes. Instead, on 4 February 1948, after only one week in office, they simply informed the British government that, although they still wanted to preserve close ties and were willing to negotiate a new treaty, they rejected the Treaty of Portsmouth because it was "not a fit instrument for strengthening the ties of friendship between Iraq and the United Kingdom."[52]

And so the Treaty of Portsmouth died. Eventually the Iraqi politicians who had concluded it returned to office, but even they refused to submit it to Parliament for approval for fear of the popular reaction.[53]

Essentially the Treaty of Portsmouth collapsed because of a fundamental and irreconcilable difference in outlook between Bevin, Foreign Office officials, and British military leaders on the one hand, and most of the politically aware section of the Iraqi population on the other hand. Influenced by the Soviet Union's takeover of eastern Europe immediately after the Second World War, the British were genuinely concerned about the possibility of Soviet aggression in the Middle East. Influenced also by the unfortunate fate of neutral nations such as Denmark, Norway, Holland, Belgium, and Greece during the Second World War, they believed that in the event of a future conflict Iraq and other small nations in the line of fire would not be able to save themselves by adopting an unprovocative or neutral policy.[54]

Outside of the ruling class, most politically conscious Iraqis did not agree with this analysis. They did not believe that the Soviet Union had any intention of attacking their country, at least as long as Iraq did not pose a threat to it. Rather than protecting Iraq against attack, by posing a threat to the Soviet Union they believed that the British bases simply invited such an attack. Thus, they concluded, the best way to avoid being dragged into a future war between the great powers was to terminate the British alliance, oust the British military forces, and maintain a policy of strict neutrality.[55]

Most politically aware Iraqis opposed the presence of British military forces in Iraq also because they believed that in an emergency these forces would interfere in Iraq's internal affairs to uphold the authority of the ruling class. In reaching this conclusion they were strongly influenced by the events of 1941 when British military forces had utilized the bases at Habbaniya and Shaiba to crush the nationalist government of Rashid Ali and reinstate the regent and the pro-British regime.[56]

Because the Treaty of Portsmouth still tied Iraq closely to Britain and still permitted a British military presence, it was not surprising that in Iraq it immediately generated widespread opposition. Indeed, there was a common, and not entirely incorrect, view that with minor modifications it was essentially a continuation of the widely hated Treaty of 1930.

Thus to some extent the British brought the defeat of the Treaty of Portsmouth upon themselves. Although they made some concessions to Iraqi nationalism, they still insisted upon terms, especially the more or less permanent retention of their air bases, which were too onerous for most Iraqis to accept. In this manner they created resentment and, ironically, helped to foment the movement that eventually destroyed the treaty.

We have observed that in large part the British insisted upon maintaining their military presence because they were concerned about a threat from the Soviet Union. However, by focusing so much upon this danger, and acquiring the means to combat it, they lost sight of the fact that their military presence helped to make the Iraqi ruling class illegitimate in the eyes of its own people. Thus they inadvertently contributed to the internal, and ultimately greater, threat to the regime that they were trying to protect.

After the defeat of the Treaty of Portsmouth the British fell back upon the Treaty of 1930, which was not due to expire until 1957. In 1955, just before its expiration, they secured most of their strategic objectives by integrating Iraq into a multinational pro-Western alliance known as the Baghdad Pact. Thus at first glance the defeat of the Treaty of Portsmouth did not appear to be consequential.

However, the incident was significant because it revealed the extent and depth of anti-British sentiment in Iraq.[57] It also revealed how narrow was the base of support for the British connection. Indeed, aside from some small minority communities such as the Assyrians, this base appeared to consist essentially of the royal family, a few prominent politicians, and a small group of other wealthy individuals. Even worse for the British, most of these people were unwilling publicly to defend their position for fear of appearing unpatriotic and alienating public opinion. Thus, although the British weathered this storm, the events of January 1948 strongly suggested that in the long run their position in Iraq was unsustainable.

Part III

The Arab-Israeli War and Its Consequences for the Anglo-Iraqi Relationship 1948–50

.12.

Iraq's Intervention in Palestine

On 29 November 1947 the United Nations General Assembly recommended that Britain's mandate for Palestine be terminated as soon as possible, and that Palestine be divided into a Jewish state and an Arab state. The Jewish state was supposed to comprise most of the coastal plain including the port of Haifa, the eastern Galilee, and most of the Negev. Except for Jerusalem, which was to be internationalized, the remainder of Palestine was supposed to constitute the Arab state.[1]

The United Nations recommendation immediately provoked a civil war in Palestine between the Jewish community, which was determined to create a state, and the Arab community, which was determined to prevent it. This phase continued until the termination of the British mandate on 15 May 1948, with the Jews gradually gaining the upper hand in the fighting.[2]

Like the Palestinian Arabs, Iraqi leaders were determined to resist the United Nations recommendation because it entailed the creation of a Jewish state. From their perspective, legal and moral considerations dictated that all of Palestine should be under Arab control, although possibly with some form of autonomous arrangement for the Jewish minority. They also feared that a Jewish state would inevitably be expansionist because it would have to accommodate large numbers of immigrants, and that in time it would present a military threat to Iraq. In addition, they did not want Haifa, the terminus of one of Iraq's two oil pipelines to the Mediterranean, to be under Jewish control because this situation would enable the Jews at will to apply serious pressure on Iraq.[3]

From March 1947 to January 1948 Iraq was led by Salih Jabr. On the Palestinian issue Jabr was very militant. For example, in the autumn of 1947 he threatened to cancel all of Iraq's oil concessions in order to force Britain and the United States to oppose partition. In the words of a British official with whom he spoke, "he realised that it meant temporary ruin for Iraq and abandonment of their many projects for development but the sacrifice would be made." Probably Jabr never seriously contemplated such a drastic step because he always made it contingent on the other Arab states acting similarly, and he knew that they, and especially Saudi Arabia, would not do so. Certainly he never implemented the threat. Nonetheless, the statement shows the extreme position that he adopted on this question.[4]

In Iraq public opinion was strongly anti-Zionist. Indeed, it was one of the few issues that united most of the population. Thus Jabr's militance on this question may have been influenced by his desire to court popularity, or at least avoid criticism, at home. The fact that he was a Shiite meant that he was especially vulnerable to attack if he appeared in any way unsympathetic to, or inactive in the cause of, the Sunni Arab population of Palestine.[5]

(It should be noted that in Iraq the Kurds were generally much less anti-Zionist than the Arabs because they had no interest in extending the boundaries of Arab rule and because they could easily empathize with another non-Arab minority in the Middle East struggling for independence. This difference was illustrated in February 1948 when, just as the government was preparing to go to war to prevent the creation of a Jewish state, there was a demonstration in the Kurdish-inhabited town of Sulaimaniya with the slogan "Up with the partition of Palestine." And the following November, when there was a large Iraqi military force in Palestine attempting to prevent the Israelis from seizing the entire country, there was a demonstration in Sulaimaniya with the slogan "Withdraw from Palestine." But in political matters in Iraq the Kurds usually did not count for much.)[6]

Jabr's use of the Palestinian issue to court popularity may also have been influenced by the fact that his public standing in Iraq was low because on 20 August 1947 Britain had suspended the free convertibility of sterling. In this manner Britain had nullified much of Iraq's gain from the Anglo-Iraqi financial agreement that Jabr had concluded with considerable fanfare only one week previous. Thus Jabr was now particularly anxious to ingratiate himself with the public, and adopting a militant position on the Palestinian question was the ideal way to do it.[7]

It is important to recall that the Palestinian issue came to a head in late 1947 just when Jabr was completing negotiations with Britain for the Treaty of Portsmouth. Because he was vulnerable to nationalist criticism for his decision to maintain close military ties with Britain, possibly he was especially eager to show his nationalist credentials on Palestine.[8]

The Palestinian issue also developed against the background of a serious bread shortage in Iraq. Although Jabr undoubtedly felt deeply about Palestine, possibly he believed that to some extent he could use the matter to divert public attention from growing domestic hardship.[9]

Jabr's stance on Palestine may have been influenced too by the fact the issue unfolded in the context of Iraq's continuing struggle with Egypt for predominance in the Arab world, especially in Syria. Thus if Jabr were conciliatory over Palestine, Iraq would lose prestige among the Arabs and be set back in this contest. By the same token if Jabr were militant over Palestine, Iraq would gain prestige among the Arabs and possibly secure advantage over Egypt in the inter-Arab rivalry.[10]

In November 1947, just before the United Nations recommendation to partition Palestine, Jabr attempted to send troops to Jordan. His intention was to hold these forces in Jordan until the termination of the mandate in May 1948 and then, in conjunction with the Jordanian army (usually referred to as the Arab Legion), occupy all of Palestine, including the areas that the United Nations envisaged as comprising a Jewish state. Aside from preventing the establishment of a Jewish state, for Jabr this step would have the advantage of preventing Haj Amin al-Husayni, the former mufti of Jerusalem and a strong supporter of exiled former prime minister Rashid Ali, from attaining power in Palestine. It would also appease public opinion in Iraq that clamored for strong action. Although the British strongly dissuaded Jabr for fear of exacerbating tension in Palestine while they were still in charge of the country, the prime minister stuck to his position.[11]

However, Jabr was thwarted because King Abdullah of Jordan refused to admit Iraqi troops for fear of compromising his sovereignty. Abdullah may also have believed that the troops were unnecessary because he hoped to conclude an arrangement with the Jews to acquire the Arab sections of Palestine without fighting. In refusing to admit Iraqi troops Abdullah was fully supported by the British government.[12]

Stymied, Jabr now chose a different approach. In January 1948 he sent about 900 volunteers, most of whom were former soldiers or policemen, to Syria. There they were given arms and, together with volunteers from other Arab countries, formed into what was called the Arab

Liberation Army. This force then infiltrated into the Arab-inhabited sections of Palestine.[13]

British officials were upset by this illegal movement of armed personnel into a territory under their control. They were especially afraid that these men might become involved in clashes with British troops. Consequently, they protested to the Iraqi government and requested the withdrawal of the men. However, they did not receive any satisfaction in this matter because Iraqi leaders believed that this was the least that they could do to support the Arab community in Palestine.[14]

In chapter 11 we observed that at the end of January 1948 Jabr was forced to resign because of widespread opposition to his conclusion of the Treaty of Portsmouth. He was succeeded as prime minister by Muhammad al-Sadr, who was also a Shiite.

Like Jabr, Sadr was as determined to assist the Palestinians as any of the leading Sunni politicians in Iraq. For example, in February 1948 he continued Jabr's efforts to insert Iraqi troops into Jordan for the purpose of advancing into Palestine, in conjunction with the Arab Legion, upon the termination of the mandate. To help overcome Jordanian resistance that had thwarted Jabr, Sadr's foreign minister, Hamdi al-Pachachi, informed the British that a disciplined force like the Iraqi army would be required to assist in maintaining law and order in Palestine after Britain withdrew. He also pointed out that Iraqi troops would be able to help in preventing Haj Amin al-Husayni, who was Britain's enemy as well as Iraq's, from taking over.[15]

With their departure from Palestine now imminent, and with increasing conflict and chaos in that country, the British saw more merit in Hamdi's proposal than in Jabr's similar one the previous November. However, they did not accept it because they believed that the appearance of a large Arab force in Jordan would not be conducive to the maintenance of law and order in Palestine. They also feared that after the termination of the mandate the Iraqi forces would advance into the Jewish sections of Palestine, thereby subverting the intention of the United Nations and provoking a conflagration with the Jews. In addition, they were concerned that Hamdi's proposal would anger Ibn Saud, the king of Saudi Arabia, because he was strongly opposed to any strengthening or territorial aggrandizement of his Hashemite rivals in Iraq and Jordan. Because Britain had extensive oil and other interests along the Persian Gulf that Ibn Saud could subvert, for Britain the king's friendship was important.[16]

In spite of the assistance provided by volunteers from Iraq and other Arab countries, by April 1948 the Jews gained the upper hand in the fighting in Palestine. Their success is indicated by the fact that from the beginning of that month to the termination of the mandate on 15 May they seized about 100 Arab villages, the important towns of Tiberias, Safed, Haifa, and Jaffa, and substantial sections of Jerusalem. During this period their dissident forces also massacred several hundred inhabitants of the Arab village of Deir Yassin. Because of these Jewish victories on the battlefield and the terror inspired by the atrocity at Deir Yassin, plus some deliberate expulsions, large numbers of Arabs fled Palestine and poured into neighboring countries.[17]

As a result of these developments, the internal pressure on Iraqi and other Arab leaders to intervene in Palestine became overwhelming. When King Abdullah decided to march, the determination of the Syrians and Egyptians to proceed became even stronger because they wanted to prevent him from seizing Palestinian territory for himself.[18]

In spite of public opinion in the Arab world, King Abdullah was probably still willing to accept a Jewish state in a section of Palestine and did not intend to advance beyond the frontiers that the United Nations had allocated to the Arabs in November 1947.[19] However, Iraqi leaders did not share this view. On the contrary, their public and private statements, coupled with their military plans before the war and their troop movements after the fighting began, indicate that their objective was to prevent the establishment of a Jewish state, regardless of its size, in any part of Palestine.[20]

With Abdullah now granting permission, on 29 April 1948 Iraqi leaders began moving troops to Jordan. Initially the number was relatively small, and by the outbreak of hostilities on 15 May totalled only about 4,500. Putting this figure in perspective, there were 45,000 men in the Iraqi armed forces, another 6,000 in the semimilitary mobile police, and a large number of former soldiers who presumably could have been mobilized. The Iraqis sent such a small force because they underestimated the difficulty of crushing Jewish resistance in Palestine; because they had trouble transporting and supplying troops and equipment so far from their home base; and because they were worried about the possibility of a Kurdish revolt or an urban uprising and wanted to have sufficient strength in reserve to deal with such contingencies. However, in spite of these problems and concerns, gradually they increased the size of their force at the front until by early 1949 it numbered about 20,000. But for the Arab cause in Palestine, the failure of Iraq and the other Arab states, except for Jordan, to bring their full military potential to bear at the outset, before the Israelis had the opportunity to organize and strengthen themselves, proved fatal.[21]

With the termination of the British mandate, on 15 May 1948 the
Iraqi troops in Jordan, in conjunction with Lebanese, Syrian, Jordanian,
and Egyptian forces, entered Palestine. The Iraqis crossed the border
about eight miles south of the Sea of Galilee in an area that the United
Nations had allocated to the Jews. They chose this point because it was
near the place where the oil pipeline from Kirkuk entered Palestine, and
they wanted to control its entire length to Haifa.[22] Numerically they, in
combination with the other Arab armies in the north and the irregular
Arab forces in the area, were probably at least equal to the troops that the
Israelis could divert from other hard-pressed fronts to deploy against
them.[23] Moreover, the Iraqis were fresh while the Israelis had been heavily engaged for nearly six months.[24] They also had air support from twelve
Ansons based at Mafrak in Jordan,[25] while at this stage the Israelis did not
have any warplanes, or at least none that were designed for that purpose.[26]
And with twenty-four field guns, half of which were modern British-
manufactured 25-pounders, in artillery they had great advantage.[27] Indeed,
it was not until 22 May that Israel was able to deploy any field guns
against them, and even then only two short-range ones without sights of
a model that had originally entered production in France in 1906.[28]

However, after a week of fighting the Iraqis failed to capture any
Israeli settlements or make any significant advance into Palestine.
Stymied, they now abandoned this area and repaired to the exclusively
Arab inhabited region around Nablus, about thirty miles north of
Jerusalem. Here they were well-situated for operations westward against
the narrow strip of Israeli-held territory along the coastal plain, or northward against the equally narrow strip of Israeli-held territory linking the
Jewish settlements near the Sea of Galilee with the rest of the country.
But the Iraqi commanders apparently did not appreciate the vital importance of rapidly inflicting a mortal blow on the Israelis before they could
organize and strengthen themselves. Consequently, rather than launch
an immediate major offensive they restricted themselves to a series of
raids against Israeli positions along the coastal plain near Tulkarm and
Qalqilya. Although the Iraqi attacks were inconclusive, they unnerved
the Israelis. To pin down the Iraqis and thereby forestall further assaults
in the vital area along the coastal plain, in late May the Israelis launched
an attack on Jenin in the Iraqi-held sector of the front about fifteen miles
north of Nablus. Initially the Israelis were successful; but the Iraqis
quickly counterattacked and in fierce fighting drove the Israelis from the
town, in the process inflicting heavy casualties. But the Iraqis did not follow up their victory, and so the battle did not have a decisive result.[29]

For the British the fighting that broke out in Palestine after 15 May 1948 was extremely unwelcome. Much of the problem lay in the fact that, because of their treaty commitments and their strategic interests, they felt obliged to continue to deliver arms to Iraq, Jordan, and Egypt. The United States, on the other hand, maintained a strict arms embargo on both sides in the conflict. But public and congressional opinion in the United States was generally pro-Zionist, and so the administration's policy was unpopular. Thus it appeared that if the war continued the United States would soon lift its arms embargo, and the two Western powers would then be supplying opposite sides in the conflict. Clearly such a situation would have very unfortunate consequences for Anglo-American relations.[30]

The British were eager to halt the fighting also because they believed that if the war continued the Arabs would probably suffer serious reverses. When this factor was combined with the deterioration in economic conditions that almost invariably accompanies military hostilities, they feared that their friends in Iraq and elsewhere in the Middle East would be ousted from power and replaced by anti-British and possibly even pro-Soviet elements.[31]

In addition, the British wanted to halt the fighting to end the criticism that they were receiving from the Iraqis for not supporting them in the conflict, although the Treaty of 1930 stipulated that if either party became engaged in war the other would "immediately come to his aid in the capacity of an ally." In justification, the British maintained that their obligations under the United Nations Charter took precedence over their obligations to Iraq, and that consequently they could not assist Iraq unless it was attacked by Israel and was thus exercising its right of self-defense. But to the Iraqis this argument sounded like the legal quibbling of an unreliable partner determined to evade its clear-cut responsibilities.[32]

With British support, on 29 May 1948 the United Nations Security Council passed a resolution calling for a four-week truce and an arms embargo on all parties to the conflict.[33] The British now pressed Iraqi and other Arab leaders to accept the resolution. They emphasized that international opinion was set on peace and would turn against the Arabs if they continued to pursue the war. They also pointed out that reverses on the battlefield, which were not improbable, would turn public opinion at home against them.[34]

After several weeks of hard campaigning in Palestine, by the beginning of June Iraqi and other Arab leaders were no longer as confident of victory as they had been at the outset. Combined with British pressure, this factor induced them to accept the Security Council resolution. Accordingly, on 11 June 1948 the truce entered into effect.[35]

Two weeks later, on 26 June 1948 Muzahim al-Pachachi succeeded Sadr as prime minister of Iraq. Muzahim, a Sunni Arab, had been an important politician during the mandate period but since 1934 had spent most of his time in Europe. He was appointed in part because his lengthy residence abroad and lack of recent government experience meant that he could not be held accountable for Iraq's current problems.[36]

Muzahim was generally well-disposed toward Britain.[37] In November 1948 he even defended the Treaty of Portsmouth in a speech in the Chamber of Deputies.[38] However, on Palestine he was as militant and uncompromising as most of the leading politicians in the country. For example, in August 1948 in a statement to an Iraqi newspaper he maintained that "the Palestine problem cannot be solved through political channels. Force alone will have to be relied on. . . . We must be ready for all sacrifices, and nothing should deter us from the liberation of Palestine."[39] And in November 1948 he declared to a joint session of both houses of the Iraqi Parliament that the aim of the Arabs was to exterminate the Zionist menace.[40] Thus the transition from Jabr to Sadr to Muzahim had little effect on Iraqi policy in Palestine.

On 27 June 1948 Count Folke Bernadotte, the United Nations mediator, proposed a settlement granting the Jews an independent state, although with significantly different borders than those recommended by the General Assembly in November 1947. Specifically, Bernadotte's changes were that the Negev and Jerusalem should go to the Arabs and be united with Jordan, while in return the western Galilee should be allocated to Israel. From the point of view of the amount and importance of the territory that they received, generally these changes favored the Arabs.[41]

Eager to prevent a resumption of hostilities and pleased about the prospect of an enlargement of their ally Jordan, the British pressed Iraq and the other Arab countries to negotiate on the basis of Bernadotte's proposals. They maintained that Israel was now a fait accompli recognized by the United States, the Soviet Union, and numerous other countries, and that the Arabs were not strong enough to destroy it. They also argued that if the Arabs resumed fighting the Security Council would probably act against them, and that in spite of its sympathies for the Arabs Britain would then feel unable to use its veto power to protect them. In addition, the British pointed out that if the Arabs resumed fighting the United States would probably lift its arms embargo with the result that large quantities of modern American weapons would flow to Israel. On the other hand, they said that if the Arabs agreed to negotiate they might be able to improve on the mediator's proposals, and that Britain would assist in this endeavor. Finally, to allow more time for negotiations the British advised the Arabs to accept the mediator's suggestion to extend the truce.[42]

Jordan was willing to negotiate on the basis of Bernadotte's proposals and extend the truce because it was the Arab country under the most British influence. Moreover, alone among the Arab nations it stood to gain a substantial amount of territory from a settlement along the lines of his proposals.[43]

However, in spite of Britain's repeated requests, Iraqi and other Arab leaders would not agree to negotiate on the basis of Bernadotte's proposals because this action would entail recognition of a Jewish state. For Egypt, Syria, and Saudi Arabia his proposals had the additional disadvantage of leading to the territorial aggrandizement of the pro-British regime in Jordan, while giving them nothing for their military exertions. Nor would Arab leaders accept a continuation of the truce, although by now most of them probably realized that the balance of power had turned against them and that a renewal of hostilities was unlikely to lead to favorable results. But public opinion in the Arab countries was militantly pro-war, and Arab leaders feared opposing it. Moreover, they had led their peoples to believe that the Arabs were winning and that only the cease-fire mandated by the Security Council had denied them final victory. Consequently, they now did not know how publicly to justify a continuation of the truce.[44]

Before the cease-fire the Arabs had generally held the initiative and almost everywhere forced the Israelis onto the defensive. For example, they had captured the Jewish quarter of the old city of Jerusalem and all of the Israeli settlements north, south, and east of Jerusalem; and repeatedly foiled Israeli efforts to seize the Arab Legion position at Latrun that blocked the only road from Tel Aviv to Jerusalem. They had also inflicted about 1,200 fatalities, and of course for the Jews this loss came on top of what they had already suffered in the fighting against the irregular Arab units before 15 May 1948. Indeed, by the time of the truce the Israelis were exhausted and virtually at the end of their tether. In the words of one of their commanders, "it came to us as dew from heaven."[45]

The Israelis utilized the four-week cease-fire to rest and reorganize their weary and inchoate forces. They also replenished their depleted manpower by bringing in substantial numbers of immigrants and volunteers, in the process increasing their forces by over 10,000. In addition, they imported from a variety of sources large quantities of badly needed arms and ammunition. Finally, they significantly improved a vital bypass on the road from Tel Aviv to Jerusalem, thereby giving themselves for the first time in the war a reasonably secure communications link between their two major population centers.[46]

Like Israel, Iraq and the other Arab countries used the truce to improve their military positions. For example, Iraq increased the number of its troops in Palestine to approximately 10,000, and brought into Palestine eleven large truck convoys full of arms and ammunition.[47]

In spite of these Arab efforts, it is clear that the Israelis used the cease-fire to greater advantage. As a result, immediately after the resumption of fighting on 9 July 1948[48] they were able to take the initiative and score impressive gains. For example, they promptly seized the large Arab-inhabited towns of Lydda and Ramla. These towns were situated close together about twelve miles southeast of Tel Aviv in a section of Palestine that in November 1947 the United Nations had allocated to the Arabs. Together they contained between 50,000 and 60,000 people and were garrisoned by about 130 Arab Legion personnel. However, these troops withdrew rather than combat a considerably superior Israeli force, and the Israelis captured the towns relatively easily. The Israelis then proceeded immediately to expel virtually all of the inhabitants.[49]

Alone among the Arab armies, the Iraqis gained territory in the military operations following the expiry of the truce. This land, which the Iraqis captured only after heavy fighting, lay north of Jenin.[50]

On 15 July 1948, a week after the resumption of hostilities, the United Nations Security Council ordered a second truce to commence in three days time and be of indefinite duration.[51] As eager as ever to halt the fighting, Britain pressed the Arabs to accept the resolution. Since the tide of war had clearly turned against them, most of the Arab countries did not require much persuasion to agree to the cease-fire. However, the Iraqis were different because they had done well in the recent fighting and were on the offensive. Moreover, public opinion in Iraq was strongly opposed to the cease-fire, and Iraqi leaders were afraid to have again to justify the acceptance of a truce. But they could not very well continue the struggle against Israel alone and in defiance of the United Nations. Consequently, without formally accepting the cease-fire, on 18 July, in conjunction with the other Arab armies, they halted all military operations against Israel.[52]

On 16 September 1948 Count Bernadotte, who was still functioning as the United Nations mediator, revealed his plan for a settlement of the

Palestinian conflict. Like his more tentative proposal in June, Bernadotte essentially recommended that the Jews have an independent state comprising the central plain and the Galilee, and that the remainder of Palestine be allocated to the Arabs and then merged with Jordan. However, this time he recommended that Jerusalem should be internationalized, as it had been in the General Assembly partition plan in November 1947, rather than placed under Arab administration.[53]

Eager to resolve the conflict that was straining their relations with the United States, jeopardizing world peace, and weakening their friends in the Arab world, the British supported the Bernadotte Plan. As in June, they were especially pleased that Bernadotte had recommended that the Arab section of Palestine be merged with Jordan because Jordan was very much under their influence. Moreover, this solution would mean that their enemy, the mufti of Jerusalem, would be frozen out of power.[54]

However, as they had been in June, Egypt, Syria, and Saudi Arabia were strongly opposed to the Bernadotte Plan because it entailed recognition of a Jewish state; and because it meant that they would have fought merely to secure for Jordan those sections of Palestine that the Arab nations, acting in concert, had seized. Consequently, on 20 September 1948 these countries established a pro-mufti Palestinian government with headquarters in Egyptian-occupied Gaza.[55]

The British now pressed Iraq hard to support the Bernadotte Plan and not recognize the Palestinian government in Gaza. They maintained that a strong and enlarged Jordan would be in Iraq's interests, while the extension of the mufti's influence would be dangerous to the Hashemite house both in Jordan and Iraq.[56]

But Britain's efforts were unavailing. Although privately conceding that Israel had come to stay and that a settlement would be desirable, Muzahim was unwilling publicly to recognize Israel, which acceptance of the Bernadotte Plan entailed, for fear of igniting a revolt at home. As a strong believer in Arab unity, he was also eager to avoid a split in the Arab world. In particular, he was concerned about maintaining good relations with Egypt because he hoped to get a sizable loan from that country. Consequently, on 11 October 1948 Iraq officially recognized the Palestinian government in Gaza.[57]

In spite of the second truce, between October 1948 and January 1949 Israel inflicted major defeats upon Egypt in serious fighting in the southern part of Palestine. During this combat the Iraqis did not assist Egypt by taking the offensive in their sector because, as a result of the United Nations arms embargo, they were very short of ammunition and spare parts for their weapons. In fact, in the event of an Israeli attack they did not even believe that they could hold their current positions, and so they did not want to do anything provocative. In reaching this decision the Iraqis were fully supported by the British government, which did not want the fighting to spread to other sectors of the front.[58]

In January 1949 Nuri al-Said replaced Muzahim as prime minister.[59] Nuri was more realistic or moderate about the Palestinian question than most Iraqi politicians. For example, in November 1944 he was willing seriously to consider allowing the Jews to establish an independent state in a portion of Palestine.[60] In June 1948, before the first truce, when the Arab military forces generally held the initiative, he said privately that the conflict would end with the creation of a Jewish state.[61] In July 1948, after the second truce, he said privately that it was clear that a Jewish state was in existence and that he approved of Count Bernadotte's compromise proposals.[62] And in November 1948, in a speech to a joint session of both houses of the Iraqi Parliament, he declared that Iraq should not rely on force alone for a settlement of the Palestinian question, and that it should "try to seek a solution based on reality, not on imagination."[63]

But like all Iraqi politicians, Nuri was constrained by public opinion which was militantly anti-Zionist. Consequently, he was determined not to sign an armistice agreement with Israel because he knew that in Iraq this decision would be widely interpreted as recognition of a Jewish state and formal acknowledgment of Arab defeat.[64] To avoid being pressured into such a measure through military setbacks as Egypt had been in February 1949, the following month Nuri withdrew the Iraqi army from its forward positions facing the Israelis and handed them over to the Arab Legion.[65] And in April, after the conclusion of an armistice agreement between Israel and Jordan, he withdrew all Iraqi forces from Palestine.[66]

And so ended Iraq's involvement in the first Arab-Israeli war.[67] Iraq and the other Arab countries had invested great effort but still had not achieved their objective of preventing the establishment of a Jewish state. Indeed, the Israel that emerged from the fighting was considerably larger than the one recommended by the United Nations in November 1947. It also had far fewer Arab inhabitants because the intervention of the Arab states gave Israel the opportunity to expel large numbers of them from their homes. In the final analysis it was they, whom Arab leaders were ostensibly attempting to protect, who paid the heaviest price for the determination of the Arab countries forcibly to oppose the recommendation of the United Nations to partition Palestine.

In Iraq and elsewhere in the Arab world the events in Palestine created great resentment against Britain. Britain was widely blamed for permitting the Jews to settle there in large numbers and arm themselves to the point where they were much stronger than the Arab inhabitants;[68] for adopting a neutral position in November 1947 when the United Nations voted to recommend the creation of a Jewish state in Palestine;[69] for pressing the Arabs to accept the first truce in June 1948 and thereby allowing the initiative in the fighting to pass to Israel;[70] for strictly adhering to the United Nations arms embargo while Israel was flagrantly violating it;[71] for failing to prevent the withdrawal of the Arab Legion (over which Britain had much influence because it was commanded by an Englishman and paid for by Britain) from Lydda and Ramla in July 1948;[72] and for accepting Bernadotte's proposal for the creation of a Jewish state in Palestine in September 1948.[73]

Many of these criticisms were unjust. For example, Britain was bound by the terms of the League of Nations mandate for Palestine to promote the establishment of a national home for the Jews; Britain did not tell the Arab states to attack Israel or promise them assistance if they did so; Britain worked hard at the United Nations to prevent the Security Council from labelling the Arab countries as aggressors and imposing an arms embargo exclusively upon them; Britain was bound by the terms of the United Nations Charter to obey the Security Council decision to suspend arms deliveries to all of the states engaged in the conflict; given their geographic position and the strength of the contending parties at the time, Lydda and Ramla were indefensible, and in any event probably never would have been attacked if the Arab states had followed Britain's advice and agreed to extend the first truce; and the Bernadotte Plan allotted considerably less territory to Israel than Israel secured in the next few months by its military victories against Egypt and its armistice agreement with Jordan, both of which were made possible or at least easier by the Arab states' rejection of the Bernadotte Plan.[74]

It was also incorrect of Iraq and the other Arab countries not to attribute greater responsibility for their failure to some of their own mistakes. For example, they undoubtedly would have achieved more if they had coordinated their activities better, committed their full troop strength at the outset rather than later in dribs and drabs, used their initial superiority in artillery and aircraft to greater advantage, and undertaken an immediate major offensive against the central plain with the objective of cutting Israel in two at its most vulnerable point.

But these arguments are only of academic interest. The important point is that by arousing so much ill-will against Britain, the Palestinian crisis contributed substantially to the decline in British influence in Iraq. In the short run this decline was manifested in 1948 when Britain was unable to prevail upon Iraq to abstain from sending volunteers to Palestine while Britain still held the mandate, to extend the first truce, to negotiate on the basis of Bernadotte's compromise proposals, to refrain from recognizing the pro-mufti government in Gaza, or to reopen the oil pipeline to Haifa.[75] In the long term it was manifested by Iraq's final break with Britain in 1958.

.13.

The United Nations
Arms Embargo

The Treaty of 1930, which governed Anglo-Iraqi relations, stipulated that the weapons used by the Iraqi armed forces "shall not differ in type from those of the forces of His Britannic Majesty." In other words, technically Iraq was permitted to buy weapons from any country, but in reality it was obliged to purchase virtually all of its military equipment from Britain. In 1930 the British had insisted upon including this provision in the treaty because they believed that similar military equipment would make it easier for the two armies to cooperate with each other in wartime, because Iraq would then be dependent upon Britain for a reliable and abundant supply of spare parts and ammunition, because the importation of non-British weapons might lead to the growth of foreign political influence, and because certain British arms manufacturers would benefit commercially from the exclusion of foreign companies from this valuable market.[1]

As a result of this provision, in late 1947, when Iraq was seriously contemplating military intervention in Palestine to prevent the establishment of a Jewish state, its arms were almost entirely of British manufacture, and it was extremely dependent upon Britain for spare parts and ammunition. Clearly a cutoff of British supplies would have a very detrimental effect on Iraq's military capabilities. Indeed, it would probably doom to failure any Iraqi intervention in Palestine.[2]

But at this time the British had no intention of halting the shipment of arms to Iraq. To begin with, they were under a firm legal obligation because the Treaty of 1930 clearly stated that upon Iraqi request Britain was required to sell to Iraq "arms, ammunition, equipment, ships and aeroplanes of the latest available pattern." In the Treaty of Portsmouth of January 1948, which was supposed to replace the Treaty of 1930 but was never ratified by Iraq and thus had no legal validity, but which indicates the thinking and intentions of the parties at the time, Britain's obligation in this area was repeated with even more emphasis: "His Britannic Majesty undertakes to grant whenever they may be required by His Majesty the King of Iraq . . . arms, ammunition, ships and aeroplanes of a modern pattern such as are in current use by the forces of His Britannic Majesty on a priority which, having regard to the relative needs of each force, shall treat both forces equally."[3]

Aside from their legal obligation, the British viewed the provision of arms as a key method of convincing Iraq of the value of maintaining close ties to Britain and in particular of concluding and ratifying a new treaty of alliance. Moreover, by providing weapons they hoped to keep Iraqi army officers loyal to the pro-British regime in Baghdad and thereby prevent an anti-British military uprising like the one that had occurred in 1941. They also wanted the Iraqi army to be strong enough to fight a reasonably effective delaying action in the event of a Soviet invasion of the country. Even if this were not possible, they wanted the Iraqi army to be strong enough to maintain domestic order, especially against Kurdish insurrectionary activities in the north, and thereby secure vital British strategic and economic interests in Iraq such as the oil fields near Kirkuk and the oil pipelines to the Mediterranean Sea. Finally, they wanted to discourage Iraq from going elsewhere for weapons because such a move would, at least to some extent, reduce British influence in the country.[4]

To prevent American weapons from being used in the struggle between the Arabs and Jews in Palestine, in November 1947 the United States imposed an embargo on the shipment of all arms to Palestine and its Arab neighbors. This embargo was quite strict and included arms already contracted for.[5]

Soon, however, the Truman administration came under strong pressure from the Jewish authorities in Palestine, Zionist organizations in the United States, pro-Zionist members of Congress, and distinguished public figures to lift the embargo. These groups pointed out that the embargo operated to the detriment of the Jews in Palestine because they were prohibited from importing American weapons at a time when Britain was continuing to supply weapons to the Arab countries who, in turn, undoubtedly delivered some of them to the Arab combatants in Palestine.[6]

The State Department did not want to lift the arms embargo because it feared that by enabling the Jews in Palestine to purchase American weapons, this action would alienate the Arab countries and thereby jeopardize important American strategic, economic, and philanthropic interests in the Middle East. It was also concerned about the possibility that if it raised the embargo the United States would come into conflict with Britain, its chief ally in the international struggle against the Soviet Union, because each nation would then be arming a different side in the Middle East conflict. Consequently, to enable it more effectively to resist Zionist and congressional pressure to lift the embargo, on 26 January 1948 the State Department appealed to the British government temporarily to suspend all arms shipments to the Arab countries.[7]

In response to this plea, on 29 January 1948 the British government implored the State Department to remain firm and not lift the American arms embargo. It pointed out that if the United States relented the Jews might purchase American weapons and use them against British soldiers in Palestine. It also explained that its regulations prohibited the import of arms into Palestine except for official purposes, and that consequently if the United States lifted the embargo Britain would have a terrible dilemma about whether to allow American ships carrying weapons for the Jews to dock and unload in Palestine. To assist the State Department in resisting Zionist and congressional pressure to lift the embargo, the British government said that it was only supplying military equipment to the Arab countries to fulfill orders for items that it considered necessary for internal security purposes, and that it was refusing to export military equipment wherever it thought that the arms might ultimately be destined for use in Palestine. But unlike the United States, the British government was not willing to impose a complete arms embargo on the Middle East because, it pointed out, it was bound by treaties with Iraq, Jordan, and Egypt to assist these countries to equip their armed forces, and it had long since entered into contracts for this purpose that it could not in good faith break. Moreover, it maintained that the good relations between Britain and the Arab countries that resulted from its fulfillment of these contracts was in America's interest as well as Britain's.[8]

In this message the British government did not actually undertake any new commitments. Rather, it simply informed the United States of its existing policy of continuing to supply arms to its Arab allies, and to assuage the State Department essentially said that regardless of their types all of these arms were for internal security purposes.

But the State Department was not assuaged, and it continued to press the British government for some form of arms embargo on the Arab countries.[9] Consequently, on 4 February 1948, and again two weeks later, Albert Alexander, the British minister of defense, publicly enunciated a new policy. Speaking in the House of Commons, he stated that while continuing to honor existing arms contracts with the Arab countries the government would not conclude any new agreements for war matériel and would even reconsider existing contracts if it appeared that those weapons were being diverted for use in Palestine.[10] In this manner the British government attempted to balance its treaty obligations and strategic interests in the Middle East with its political imperatives in the United States.

While the British government informed the United States in January 1948 that it was only supplying weapons to the Arab countries for internal security purposes, it interpreted this restriction loosely. Indeed, it did not use this restriction to withhold any military equipment that Iraq had already ordered, even though some of these items would normally be considered more appropriate for combat against the military forces of another country than for internal security purposes.[11] For example, between February and May 1948 the British government shipped to Iraq thirteen Sea Fury fighter-bombers,[12] in March thirty 25-pounder field guns[13] and thirty armored cars,[14] and in April six antitank guns.[15] It is interesting to observe that when Alexander spoke in Parliament in February 1948 he did not say anything about arms being sold to the Middle East exclusively for internal security purposes, probably because he realized that the government could not easily defend this position in public in view of the type of weapons that it was sending to Iraq.

Although in the period between January and May 1948 the British government did not withhold any weapons that Iraq had already ordered even if these types were not generally used for internal security purposes, it did observe its declaration in Parliament in February not to conclude any new arms contracts. For example, in March the Foreign Office rejected an Iraqi request for fifteen Tiger Moths, an unarmed training aircraft. To justify this refusal, the Foreign Office suggested that the Air Ministry inform Iraqi officers that Britain could not deliver any Tiger Moths because the aircraft was no longer being manufactured. While it was true that the aircraft was no longer being manufactured, British production for the RAF had exceeded 5,200 in order to meet very great wartime needs for pilot training. Now that the war was over the RAF was qualifying far fewer pilots, and thus undoubtedly had at least fifteen of its substantial holdings available for export to Iraq, especially since it was currently phasing the aircraft out of its inventory in favor of a more modern successor. Certainly the Air Ministry believed that fifteen were available because it wanted to deliver the planes in order to preserve its good relations with the Iraqi air force.[16] It is important to note, incidentally, that the British government's refusal to provide the Tiger Moths or comparable aircraft, and its entire policy of refusing to conclude new arms contracts, was a violation of its treaty obligation to provide weapons upon Iraq's request.

In an effort to halt the fighting between the Jews and the Arabs in Palestine, on 17 April 1948 the United Nations Security Council passed a resolution that called upon all governments "to take all possible steps" to oppose "the entry into Palestine of armed bands and fighting personnel, groups and individuals, and weapons and war materials."[17] The State Department was pleased with this resolution because it was now in a much stronger position to resist domestic pressure to lift its arms embargo. The British government was also pleased because the resolution said nothing about the delivery of arms to any nation other than Palestine. Thus while it prohibited the United States and other countries from shipping weapons to the Jews in Palestine, it enabled Britain to continue its policy of fulfilling existing arms contracts with the Arab states.[18]

On 14 May 1948 the Jews in Palestine proclaimed the independent state of Israel, and on the following day the British mandate was officially terminated. Iraq and the Arab nations bordering Israel thereupon sent their armies into the territory of what had been mandatory Palestine with the objective of destroying Israel or, at a minimum, limiting its size as much as possible. Of the combined Arab force, the Iraqi contribution was about 4,500 men.[19]

In its commitment to the United States in January 1948 the British government had said that it would not export military equipment to the Arab countries when it thought that the arms might be ultimately destined for use in Palestine. In its public statements in Parliament the following month it had said that it would even reconsider existing arms contracts if it appeared that those weapons were being diverted for use in Palestine. However, after 15 May 1948, when Iraq and the other Arab states used British-supplied military equipment in their invasion of Palestine, the British government did not suspend arms deliveries because it did not want to alienate the Arabs and thereby jeopardize its dominant position in the Middle East. It justified this decision with the argument that its previous statements were made because of the risk that the arms would be used against British troops in Palestine and thus only applied while Britain still retained the mandate. The British government further justified its position with the argument that until the United Nations decided that the Arab countries were acting contrary to the United Nations Charter or took some restrictive action against them, it was not necessary for Britain to depart from its treaty obligations to supply weapons to Iraq, Jordan, and Egypt.[20]

Although the British government did not suspend arms deliveries to the Arab states after they invaded Palestine on 15 May 1948, it did continue its policy of not concluding new contracts for war matériel. For example, on 19 May, four days after the outbreak of hostilities, the Iraqi government, which was now using up its munitions at a prodigious rate, requested that Britain sell 12,000 bombs that had not been included in any previous order for armaments. The British government refused this request, not from lack of sympathy for Iraq, but rather because it was publicly committed on this question and feared serious trouble in Parliament if it violated its pledge. Moreover, it believed that if it concluded new contracts for war matériel with the Arab countries the United States would lift its arms embargo. Such a situation, the British informed Iraq, would probably benefit Israel because, unlike Iraq, it had a relatively large quantity of dollars as a result of successful fund-raising activities in the United States.[21] Regardless of the reason, however, Britain's refusal to sell the bombs was, as we noted earlier in our discussion of the Tiger Moths, a violation of its treaty obligation to provide arms upon Iraq's request.

In an effort to end the fighting in Palestine, on 29 May 1948 the United Nations Security Council passed a resolution that ordered a four-week cease-fire and that "Call[ed] upon all Governments and authorities concerned to refrain from importing or exporting war material into or to Palestine, Egypt, Iraq, Lebanon, Saudi Arabia, Syria, Transjordan or Yemen during the cease-fire."[22] This resolution obviously conflicted with Britain's obligation under article 5 of the annexure of the Treaty of 1930 to supply upon Iraqi request "arms, ammunition, equipment, ships and aeroplanes of the latest available pattern." However, article 9 of the treaty stated that "Nothing in the present treaty is intended to or shall in any way prejudice the rights and obligations which devolve, or may devolve, upon either of the high contracting parties under the Covenant of the League of Nations." Since the United Nations had succeeded the League of Nations as the representative of the international community, then logically the precedence that article 9 gave to Britain's obligations to the League of Nations was transferred to the United Nations. Moreover, article 25 of the United Nations Charter stated that "The

Members of the United Nations accept and carry out the decisions of the Security Council in accordance with the present Charter;"[23] and article 103 stated that "In the event of a conflict between the obligations of the Members of the United Nations under the present Charter and their obligations under any other international agreement, their obligations under the present Charter shall prevail."[24] Consequently, it is difficult to escape the conclusion that after 11 June, when the Security Council resolution of 29 May entered into effect, the British government was legally obliged to suspend completely all arms deliveries to Iraq and the other Arab states. Now, therefore, for the first time Britain could reasonably argue that its policy of refusing to conclude new arms contracts with Iraq, which it had initiated the previous February, was in accordance with international law.

Although the cease-fire did not come into effect until 11 June, the British government halted all weapon shipments to the Arab states immediately after the Security Council resolution was passed. It acted so precipitately because it was being severely criticized for its decision to retain on Cyprus between 7,000 and 8,000 Jewish men of military age who wanted to immigrate to Israel. The British government justified its decision on the immigration question by citing the provision of the Security Council resolution of 29 May that "Call[ed] upon all Governments and authorities concerned to undertake that they will not introduce fighting personnel into Palestine, Egypt, Iraq, Lebanon, Saudi Arabia, Syria, Transjordan and Yemen during the cease-fire." However, it was not obvious that untrained civilian immigrants constituted "fighting personnel." Indeed, the State Department believed that the resolution did "not preclude the admission of men of military age for exclusively civilian purposes." And Count Folke Bernadotte, the United Nations mediator, said that he would "exercise his discretion during the period of the truce in determining whether men of military age are represented among immigrants in such numbers as to give one side a military advantage." Consequently, to compensate for this anti-Israeli interpretation of the immigration provision of the resolution, and to reduce the pressure that it was under to alter its decision on this matter, the British government decided to begin observing the arms embargo provision of the resolution even before the cease-fire went into effect.[25]

The United Nations arms embargo hit Iraq particularly hard because, owing to an error by the War Office in London, Britain had not shipped a large quantity of ammunition to Iraq that had been scheduled for delivery in October 1947. On 20 May 1948 the War Office discovered this error and took immediate action to correct the mistake. However, nine days later the Security Council passed its arms embargo resolution, and as a result the ammunition was not in fact sent.[26]

Iraq's problem was compounded because the thirteen Sea Fury fighter-bombers that Britain had delivered between February and May 1948 as the first part of a consignment of thirty-four, and that were the most modern aircraft in the Iraqi inventory, were useless because they lacked spare parts and ammunition. The remaining twenty-one planes, which were scheduled for delivery by August 1948, plus all of the spare parts and ammunition for the aircraft, were caught up in the embargo. Adding to Iraq's frustration in this matter, Britain had originally promised to deliver all of the planes by March 1948, but shipment was delayed because the Hawker Aircraft Company, which manufactured the planes, encountered production difficulties.[27]

Because the Iraqis had used up much of their ammunition in the fighting in Palestine and had not received the supplies to which we have just referred, they continued to press Britain for munitions even after the beginning of the truce on 11 June 1948. To justify this request, they said that while they did not intend to resume hostilities after the expiration of the truce they nonetheless had to be prepared in case the Israelis did so. They also emphasized that they needed munitions to be able to combat possible outbreaks of internal unrest, particularly in Kurdistan.[28]

British leaders were sympathetic to these Iraqi concerns. While none suggested that Britain actually give weapons to Iraq during the truce and thereby clearly violate the Security Council resolution, on 11 June Alexander recommended that Britain dispatch the munitions that Iraq needed to Habbaniya. From this point, he reasoned, Britain would be in a position to meet Iraq's requirements promptly in the event of internal disorder.[29]

Alexander's recommendation was not adopted because Bevin thought that it would violate the spirit of the Security Council resolution. Still, Bevin believed that it would be permissible for Britain to select and pack military equipment that was in the United Kingdom, or which was already in British depots in the Middle East, for delivery to Iraq as soon as possible after the expiration of the embargo. With Alexander's support, these steps were taken.[30]

As we observed in the previous chapter, on 9 July 1948 the four-week truce expired, and the fighting in Palestine resumed. To halt the renewed fighting, on 15 July 1948 the Security Council passed a resolution demanding that both sides accept a cease-fire within three days.[31] Unlike the previous resolution, which called for a four-week cease-fire, this one stipulated that "the truce shall remain in force, in accordance with the present resolution and with resolution 50 (1948) of 29 May 1948, until a peaceful adjustment of the future situation of Palestine is reached." The resolution also "Call[ed] upon all Governments and authorities concerned to continue to co-operate with the [United Nations] Mediator with a view to the maintenance of peace in Palestine in conformity with resolution 50 (1948) adopted by the Security Council on 29 May 1948." These two references to conformity with the Security Council resolution of 29 May 1948 meant that, contrary to its belief in May, Britain was now obliged to continue it arms embargo for an indeterminate though probably considerable period of time. For Iraq, whose army and air force were in a bad condition because of an acute shortage of spare parts and ammunition, and that had large quantities of arms on order from Britain, this development was unwelcome.

With the exception of some serious fighting between Israel and Egypt between October 1948 and January 1949, the second truce, which began on 18 July 1948, ended all major combat between Israel and the Arab states. But at the time the Iraqis did not know this and, as their army remained on the frontlines in Palestine until March 1949, they were concerned about the possibility of a renewed outbreak of hostilities. They were especially worried because it was common knowledge that Israel had violated the United Nations embargo by importing substantial quantities of arms and fighting personnel.[32]

Like Israel, in 1948-49 Iraq attempted to purchase arms in contravention of the United Nations embargo. However, it was unsuccessful because, unlike Israel, it was only able to offer sterling while arms dealers invariably insisted upon payment in dollars. In addition, Iraq lacked the intricate network of dedicated agents and sympathizers in the United States and Europe that Israel possessed.[33]

Aside from the immediate danger of renewed hostilities with Israel, during the summer and autumn of 1948 Iraqi leaders had other important security concerns. To begin with, they were alarmed about the possibility of internal disturbances when it became apparent that after all of their optimistic predictions and favorable reports they had failed to prevent the establishment of a Jewish state in Palestine. They were also worried that as international tension grew because of the Soviet blockade of Berlin in June 1948, the Soviet Union would foment insurrectionary activities in the Kurdish districts of northern Iraq in an effort to weaken Britain's position in the Middle East and distract its attention from the crisis in Europe. In addition, they feared that the army, upon which in the final analysis they depended to suppress their domestic opponents, was becoming increasingly alienated from the regime for having failed to provide it with sufficient arms to triumph in the fighting in Palestine. Even if the army remained loyal, Iraqi leaders were concerned about its ability to crush internal upheavals because it suffered from an acute lack of ammunition and spare parts.[34] Making matters worse, the police too were very short of ammunition,[35] and by the end of 1948 all of the planes in the air force were grounded for lack of spare parts.[36]

For these reasons, even after the second truce entered into effect on 18 July 1948 the Iraqis continued to press Britain for weapons. In order to make a resumption of deliveries more palatable for Britain, the Iraqis promised to earmark all of the arms for internal disturbances and training, and not ship any of them to their forces in Palestine.[37]

Sir Henry Mack, the British ambassador in Iraq, and J. C. B. Richmond, the counsellor at the embassy, were sympathetic to Iraq's problems.[38] So too were Bevin and the Foreign Office officials who dealt with this matter,[39] as well as Alexander and his military advisors.[40] These men were alarmed about the increase in anti-British sentiment in Iraq as a result of the arms embargo. They feared that if they did not show any appreciation for Iraq's concerns in this matter, Britain's friends in the country would become discredited and an extreme nationalist and anti-British government would come to power. Such a government, they believed, might attribute Iraq's defeat in Palestine to Britain's failure to deliver weapons and then retaliate by repudiating the Treaty of 1930, expelling Britain from its air bases, and possibly even turning to the Soviet Union for assistance. British officials were also conscious of the fact that Iraq had suffered in the war in Palestine because they had scrupulously observed the United Nations arms embargo while Israel had clearly benefited by engaging in wholesale violations. For them this consideration was particularly worrisome because at this time Iraq was assisting in the defense of Jordan, whose borders in the final analysis they were obliged to defend. Finally, they were annoyed by the fact that when the embargo was adopted they had not foreseen and certainly had not intended that it would last so long and have such a deleterious effect on the Iraqi military establishment.

For these reasons, in considerable secrecy in the autumn of 1948 the British decided to adopt a less strict interpretation of the arms embargo provision of the Security Council resolution of 29 May 1948. For example, in October they began to move many of the arms and much of the ammunition that Iraq had ordered, and that were currently in Britain awaiting shipment, to the British military bases in the Canal Zone in Egypt.[41] In November they sent spare parts for Iraqi aircraft to Habbaniya.[42] And in January 1949 they sent bombs and ammunition for Iraqi planes to Habbaniya,[43] and transferred 115 tons of ammunition that Iraq had ordered to the British air base at Amman in Jordan from which point in case of need it could be rapidly distributed to the Iraqi army in Palestine.[44]

The British dispatched these arms to the Canal Zone, Habbaniya, and Amman without informing Ralph Bunche, the United Nations acting mediator, because they were unsure of the legality of their action. For this reason initially they even hesitated to tell the Iraqis. The British also feared that if the Iraqis knew about the ready availability of munitions they might launch an attack against the Israelis or, in extreme desperation, even attempt to seize the supplies at Habbaniya. However, since the main purpose of moving these arms to forward positions was to improve Britain's standing in Iraq, and since this objective could not be achieved without giving the Iraqis at least some information, soon they relented. Accordingly, in November 1948 the British told the director-general of the Iraqi police, in strict confidence and without providing details, that in the event of large-scale internal disturbances with which he had difficulty coping he could depend upon quickly receiving a substantial additional quantity of small arms ammunition.[45] And in February 1949 they informed the regent and the prime minister in detail, but again in strict confidence, about the movement to Amman of large quantities of ammunition that Iraq had ordered.[46]

The Iraqis were pleased that Britain was now adopting a looser interpretation of its obligations under the terms of the United Nations arms embargo but, understandably enough, they still wanted actual deliveries. In addition to reiterating the arguments that they had used in their previous discussions with Britain, in 1949 they were able to cite some relevant new factors. For example, with Bunche's permission in January France gave Syria a quantity of arms for internal security purposes, even though France was not under any treaty obligation to supply arms to Syria and Syria had not signed an armistice agreement with Israel. Also in January Britain began allowing Jews of military age to leave Cyprus for Palestine, thereby interpreting in favor of Israel the fighting personnel provision of the Security Council resolution of 29 May 1948. And, as we observed in the previous chapter, in March the Iraqis withdrew their army from its forward positions facing the Israelis, and in April withdrew it entirely from Palestine. Consequently, for the Iraqis Britain's continued unwillingness to provide weapons became even more incomprehensible and infuriating. Indeed, the issue seriously embittered relations between the two countries.[47]

In spite of a strong desire to improve British standing in Iraq and the other Arab countries, Bevin was unwilling to raise the arms embargo until the Arabs had concluded armistice agreements with Israel lest he be accused of enabling them to renew hostilities. As a strong upholder of the United Nations, he was also reluctant to violate blatantly the Security Council resolution. In addition, he was fearful of alienating the United States, which supported the embargo, at a time when he needed American goodwill to bring the negotiations for the Atlantic Alliance to a successful conclusion. Consequently, in spite of considerable pressure from Alexander and British military leaders, during the first three and one-half months of 1949 the British government did not alter its policy on this question.[48]

However, in late April 1949 Bevin changed his mind and decided to resume the shipment of arms to the Arabs. In reaching this decision he was influenced by the arguments used by the Iraqis, plus the fact that in February, March, and April 1949 Egypt, Lebanon, and Jordan respectively had signed armistice agreements with Israel. (But Syria had still not signed an armistice agreement.) Moreover, on 4 April the agreement for the Atlantic Alliance had been concluded, thereby placing Britain's relations with the United States on firmer ground. Consequently, acting on instructions from the Foreign Office, on 29 April Sir Oliver Franks, the British ambassador in Washington, approached United States Secretary of State Dean Acheson in an effort to secure American support for a resumption of British arms shipments to the Arabs. Franks argued that the situation in the Middle East was now radically different from when the United Nations had imposed the embargo in May 1948 because hostilities in Palestine had ceased and the recently concluded armistice agreements had greatly reduced the prospect of a resumption of fighting in the near future. He also emphasized that Britain would demand firm guarantees that the arms that it was planning to provide to the Arabs would be used exclusively for training and internal security purposes rather than to facilitate offensive military action in Palestine. Along this line he pointed out that Iraq needed weapons because it had a serious internal security problem with the Kurds in the north that it had certainly not been the intention of the United Nations to exacerbate. In addition, he said that King Abdullah of Jordan, who was Britain's closest ally in the Arab world and who now controlled a large section of central Palestine, needed arms because of the possibility of subversive activities from the followers of Haj Amin al-Husayni, the ex-mufti of Jerusalem and his chief rival for the loyalty of the Palestinian Arabs. Nor did Franks fail to mention Egypt, which was demanding weapons as part of the price for the successful conclusion of negotiations with Britain for a new treaty of alliance. He then cited the precedent of France giving arms to Syria and, to alleviate American concerns that Israel's security might be jeopardized, said that Britain would not object if the United States gave arms to Israel for internal security purposes. Finally, Franks indicated that if Britain had American support on this matter it would proceed without reference to the United Nations.[49]

Acheson was sympathetic to Britain's request but he said that he could not commit himself until he had considered the matter further. He did, however, indicate concern over the possibility that if the British government went ahead in this matter the Truman administration would be vulnerable to the criticism that Britain was diverting to the Arabs arms that the United States had provided for NATO purposes, or British-manufactured arms that were currently being replaced or supplemented in British arsenals by American-made equipment.[50]

Possibly because he preferred to avoid this contentious subject, Acheson did not respond to the British inquiry. Consequently, one month later, on 26 May 1949 Bevin personally approached Acheson while the two were in Paris for a conference on an unrelated matter. After listening to Bevin repeat all of the by now familiar British arguments in favor of a resumption of arms supplies to the Arab states, Acheson suggested that the British government seek Bunche's permission. As long as the weapons were reserved for internal security purposes, he believed that Bunche would approve. In this manner, Acheson said, Britain could achieve its purpose without being accused of having violated the Security Council resolution. Although Acheson did not say so, he probably hoped that when the matter eventually became public Bunche's approval would enable the Truman administration to avoid blame for having sanctioned a resumption of British arms deliveries to the Arabs at a time when the United Nations embargo was still in effect and Syria had not yet signed an armistice agreement with Israel.[51]

Acting on Bevin's instructions, two days later, on 28 May 1949 Sir Alexander Cadogan, Britain's representative at the United Nations, raised the question with Bunche. The latter replied that he would permit a resumption of arms shipments to the Arab states but only for police forces. Except to this small degree, he said that he could not authorize any action contrary to the Security Council decision. Why Bunche felt able to authorize even this exception, he did not indicate.[52]

While Bevin was willing to restrict British arms deliveries to the Arabs to those that he felt were required for internal security purposes, he was unwilling to provide weapons only for the police. Consequently, on 1 June 1949, when Bevin again spoke with Acheson in Paris, he informed him that Bunche had consented to arms shipments to the Arab states for internal security purposes without mentioning that Bunche had specified that the deliveries must be restricted to police forces. Perhaps because of this important omission, and because Bevin said that for the time being Britain would not send major equipment such as heavy guns or fighter planes, Acheson did not oppose Bevin's plan.[53]

Now that Bevin had secured Acheson's acquiescence, on 9 June 1949, after one year of maintaining a strict embargo in conformity with the Security Council resolution, the British government authorized the release to Iraq of a substantial amount of military hardware. This release included 512 machine guns, 110 mortars, 3.1 million rounds of small arms ammunition, much other ammunition, and large quantities of spare parts for vehicles, planes, and weapons in the Iraqi inventory.[54]

On 20 July 1949 Syria became the last of the Arab states bordering Israel to conclude an armistice agreement. Largely as a result of this development, which signified the return to relative normalcy in the Middle East, on 11 August the Security Council voted to repeal the arms embargo.[55] Freed from all legal restraints for the first time in fourteen months, on 23 August the British government authorized the release of all of the remaining military equipment that Iraq had ordered prior to the imposition of the embargo. The items on this list included twelve 17-pounder guns, eighteen 40mm. guns, 120 light antitank weapons, twenty-one Sea Fury aircraft, and large quantities of spare parts, rockets, bombs, and ammunition.[56]

In spite of the serious fighting that broke out between the Arabs and the Jews in Palestine after the General Assembly partition resolution in late November 1947, until the end of May 1948 Britain continued to deliver arms to the Arab states under the terms of existing contracts while both Britain and the United States refused to permit the export of any weapons to the Jews in Palestine. As a result of these arms export policies, by the spring of 1948 the military situation in the Middle East was favorable for the Arab countries and unfavorable for the Jews in Palestine. It is, therefore, not unreasonable to assume that these policies were, inadvertently of course, a major factor in encouraging Iraq and the other Arab nations to attack the fledgling state of Israel immediately after the termination of the mandate and thereby initiate the first of the Arab-Israeli wars.

Until the end of May 1948 Britain's policy on the question of arms exports was motivated by the desire to ingratiate itself with Iraq and the other Arab countries and thereby protect its vital strategic and economic interests in the Middle East. However, it is unlikely that Britain won much goodwill in the Arab world because it combined its policy of fulfilling existing arms contracts, which favored the Arabs, with a policy of refusing to conclude new arms contracts, which favored the Jews and violated its treaties with the Arabs.

After the passage of the Security Council arms embargo resolution on 29 May 1948 Britain refused to send any arms to the Arabs. In this manner it gravely damaged the Arab military forces and significantly facilitated Israel's victory in the war.

Britain's policy of strictly adhering to the arms embargo resolution was motivated by the desire to dampen the flames of war in the Middle East, protect its relations with the United States, and uphold the concept of international law as represented by Security Council decisions. However, in Iraq and elsewhere in the Arab world the result of this policy was to acquire a reputation, if not for pro-Zionism, then at least for unreliability. And for many Iraqis the usefulness of a military alliance with such a country—a nation that seemingly without hesitation would leave its ally in the lurch at a moment of great need in the middle of a serious conflict—became increasingly problematic.

.14.

The Economic Crisis

In 1948-49 Iraq suffered a severe financial crisis because of a significant increase in expenditure and decrease in revenue. Much of the increase in expenditure resulted from Iraq's involvement in the war in Palestine that broke out after the creation of the state of Israel on 14 May 1948. As we observed in chapter 12, to assist the Arab cause Iraq immediately dispatched about 4,500 troops to Palestine and then gradually increased this number until by January 1949 it stood at approximately 20,000. By the autumn of 1948 this military commitment was costing Iraq ID 1.5 million per year, which was 5 percent of total government expenditure.[1]

In addition to a serious rise in expenditure, for Iraq the war in Palestine resulted in a considerable drop in revenue because in May 1948 the government halted the flow of oil through the 12-inch pipeline from Kirkuk to Haifa to prevent any of it from falling into the hands of the Jews. This action immediately reduced Iraqi oil exports from, in round figures, 4 million tons per year to 2 million tons per year, and deprived Iraq of £1 million per year in royalties.[2]

For Iraq the war in Palestine resulted in an even greater loss of revenue from oil than this figure indicates because by the spring of 1948 the Iraq Petroleum Company had nearly completed a 16-inch pipeline from Kirkuk to Haifa. This pipeline would have had a capacity of more than 4 million tons per year, but the IPC never finished it because Iraq would not permit any oil to be exported via this route. Thus Iraq lost not merely £1 million per year from the closure of the 12-inch pipeline to Haifa but also £2 million per year from the noncompletion of the 16-inch pipeline to Haifa. This combined loss of £3 million per year was 12 percent of total government revenue.[3]

After the outbreak of the Arab-Israeli war in May 1948 there was much animosity toward the Jewish community in Iraq because it was widely assumed that it was pro-Israeli and possibly even a fifth column. Consequently, the Iraqi government now took a variety of repressive measures against the Jews. For example, it imposed restrictions on Jewish businesses and arrested many wealthy Jews, ostensibly for Zionist activities but in reality to extort money from them. Because the Jews played a major role in Iraq's business affairs, these measures upset commercial life and had a detrimental effect on the economy. In particular, they reduced the government's custom revenues because the Jews had done much of the country's importing, and they reduced the amount of credit available because the Jews had done much of the country's lending. They also led to a capital flight because the Jews now transferred much of their wealth to securer locations. Thus the anti-Jewish campaign contributed significantly to the government's financial crisis.[4]

Aside from losses related to the war in Palestine, the economy suffered from a reduction in British military expenditure because in October 1947 the last British ground troops left Iraq. The amounts involved are indicated by the fact that in 1947 British military expenditure in Iraq was ID 2.6 million, while in 1948 it was negligible.[5]

In 1947 and 1948 an infestation of locusts and a severe drought in Iraq caused extremely bad wheat harvests. The dimensions of the problem are indicated by the fact that in 1946 the wheat harvest had been 370,000 tons, while in 1947 it fell to 235,000 tons. Measured differently but still showing the great decline in production during this period, between 1935 and 1939 the average annual wheat harvest had been 18.1 million bushels, while in 1948 it fell to 12 million bushels. The bad harvests, in turn, increased the price of wheat. Because the government felt obliged to purchase wheat from the country's agricultural interests and from abroad to provide sufficient quantities of inexpensive bread for the urban poor, its costs rose considerably. An idea of the sums involved can be seen from the fact that between 1941 and 1946 the government spent a total of ID 750,000 on this program, while in the first ten months of 1947 alone it spent ID 1.25 million.[6]

Still another cause of the financial crisis was the great rise in the number of government employees. For example, between 1939 and 1947 the number of government officials including school teachers rose from 10,000 to 18,000, and between 1930 and 1948 the number of police officers rose from 7,000 to 25,000. Much of this increase was due to nepotism, though of course more teachers were necessary to educate the largely illiterate population, and more police were necessary to protect the regime from its increasing number of enemies. But regardless of the question of need, the fact remains that these added employees cost money that the government could not easily afford. The expense involved is indicated by the fact that in the autumn of 1948 the government was spending ID 15 million per year on salaries, which was 50 percent of total government expenditure.[7]

Exacerbating the situation, the government was unable to collect much of the tax revenue due to it. This failure was the result of general inefficiency, accentuated by the chaos and upheaval following the conclusion and repudiation of the Treaty of Portsmouth in January 1948. It was also caused by widespread corruption among the civil servants in charge of tax collection who, desperate to supplement their inflation-eroded salaries, often pocketed money due to the state or accepted bribes in lieu of tax payments.[8] Indeed, corruption was so extensive that in December 1948 the counsellor at the British embassy in Baghdad maintained that there were countless examples of influential Iraqis who only paid about 10 percent of their chargeable taxes.[9] In July 1949 the Iraqi minister of finance estimated that in the province of Amara in southern Iraq the government had only been able to collect ID 1,000 out of a total of ID 750,000 due for various taxes.[10] And the following month the Iraqi prime minister calculated that nationwide the government regularly failed to collect about 30 percent of the consumption (sales) tax from storekeepers.[11]

In spite of the problem of tax evasion, the government could have raised more revenue by imposing additional levies on the wealthy, who were notoriously under-taxed. However, it refused to do so because most ministers and other members of Parliament, together with their chief supporters in the country, were wealthy, and no matter how necessary for the country were unwilling to take measures inimical to their immediate interests.[12]

In theory the government could also have raised more revenue by resorting to an internal loan. However, this option was not viable because in 1948 and 1949 its solvency was not sufficiently respected, even by the affluent Muslim and Christian members of society who presumably were its strongest supporters. And the Jews, many of whom were prosperous, were disinclined to lend money to a regime that was persecuting them and causing them increasingly to contemplate emigration.[13]

Consequently, to deal with the financial crisis, in April 1948 Iraqi leaders asked Britain for a loan of £2 million. Emphasizing the urgency of the situation, they maintained that they did not even have enough money to pay the salaries of government employees. They also said that they wanted to use some of the money for public works and thereby reduce unemployment and alleviate social discontent.[14]

Supporting this request, in April and May 1948 the British ambassador in Iraq, Sir Henry Mack, informed the Foreign Office that Iraq's financial situation was now quite desperate. He feared that if Britain did not immediately grant £500,000 the Iraqi government, which had more than £1.7 million in (disputed) claims against Britain dating back to the Second World War, would seize some of this money from the British-owned Eastern Bank in Baghdad, which functioned as the British government's agent. Alternatively, he was concerned that the Iraqi government would turn public opinion against Britain by maintaining that it could not pay its employees because Britain did not pay its debts. In either case, Mack believed that British prestige in Iraq would be damaged and the position of the pro-British elements in Iraqi society weakened.[15]

In chapter 11 we observed that the government of Muhammad al-Sadr came to power in January 1948 as a result of a popular uprising against the government of Salih Jabr, with which Britain had enjoyed particularly good relations. We also observed that the leading members of the Sadr government were at least partly responsible for engineering Jabr's ouster, and that immediately upon assuming office they repudiated the Treaty of Portsmouth. For these reasons, initially Foreign Office officials were not well-disposed toward the Sadr government. And soon they became even less well-disposed because the government quickly showed an unwillingness or inability to halt the continuing series of demonstrations and protests, many of which had an anti-British theme, or to put its financial house in order. Consequently, at first Foreign Office officials did not support the extension of financial assistance to Iraq. Their attitude was illustrated on 10 May 1948 by Michael Wright, the assistant undersecretary of state supervising Middle Eastern policy, when he wrote that

> it would be financially disastrous for the Iraqis to think they can balance their budgets by crying to His Majesty's Government instead of imposing and collecting taxes from their own wealthy citizens. . . . We are doubtful also of the political wisdom of assisting the present Iraqi Government. It has done nothing whatever either to improve relations with us or to restore order in Iraq and we feel most reluctant to help it in any way.[16]

However, influenced by a particularly alarmist report from Mack, by 14 May 1948 Foreign Office officials had become more amenable to the

idea of extending financial assistance to Iraq. Illustrating their new attitude, Wright now maintained that "Iraq was very important to us and
we could not contemplate letting her sink without a struggle"; and B. A.
B. Burrows, the head of the Eastern Department, argued that it was "better to help than to let the situation in Iraq get entirely out of hand and
to run the risk of the Iraqis helping themselves at our expense while
embarking on a virulent propaganda campaign against us."[17]

But the Treasury was firmly opposed to financial assistance to Iraq
because of Britain's generally weak financial position in the aftermath of
the Second World War; the possibility of encouraging claims for assistance from other at least equally deserving countries that Britain perforce
would have to reject; the probability that Britain would not be repaid;
and the likelihood that Iraq would then request financial help again and
again, and that the arguments in favor of granting it would be just as
compelling and perhaps even more so if a more accommodating government came to power.[18]

Stymied by the opposition of the Treasury, on 18 May 1948 Foreign
Office officials suggested that the Anglo-Iranian Oil Company and the
Iraq Petroleum Company extend financial assistance to Iraq. The former
was a British-owned oil company that operated in Iran and Kuwait and
owned nearly one-quarter of the IPC. Independent of the IPC, it also held
the entire concession for a small part of Iraq near the Iranian border
known as the transferred territories. From this area it extracted about
350,000 tons of oil per year, and paid annual royalties of approximately
£120,000. In April 1948 Iraqi leaders had already asked the AIOC for a
loan of £5 million. To reinforce this request, they had informed the
company that unless it granted this loan it would not be permitted to construct a pipeline from its rich oil fields in Iran and Kuwait across Iraqi territory to the Mediterranean Sea. Although AIOC officials wanted to
proceed with the pipeline, they did not believe that their company had
sufficient interests in Iraq or in the pipeline to warrant such a large outlay. Consequently, they had rejected Iraq's request, and now refused the
Foreign Office's invitation to reconsider the matter.[19]

In April 1948, at the same time as they had approached the AIOC,
Iraqi leaders had requested a £2 million loan from the IPC. IPC officials
had rejected the request because Iraq already owed the company most
of the money from a £3 million loan made in 1939 and a £1.5 million
loan made in 1943. Moreover, they were aggrieved because the Iraqi government had just halted the flow of oil through the pipeline to Haifa and
thereby greatly reduced the company's profits. However, to appease

the Iraqis and accommodate the Foreign Office, IPC officials were willing to pay their royalties at the end of each quarter rather than at the end of the year as was currently the case. This new procedure meant that Iraq would immediately receive a payment of £420,000 for the first quarter of 1948. Thus with the cooperation of the IPC, in May 1948 the Foreign Office was able to alleviate Iraq's most pressing financial needs.[20]

It should be recalled that on 15 May 1948, just three days before the Foreign Office approached the oil companies for aid to Iraq, Iraq had embarked upon its military campaign in Palestine to prevent the establishment of a Jewish state. Although it does not appear that the Foreign Office tried to improve Iraq's finances for the purpose of facilitating this campaign, its action did have this result.

As we observed in chapter 12, in June 1948 the Sadr government resigned and was replaced by an administration under Muzahim al-Pachachi. The minister of finance in the new government was Ali Mumtaz al-Daftari. Having served as director-general of revenues and several previous times as minister of finance, Mumtaz was well-qualified for the position. The British officials with whom he dealt generally regarded him highly and believed that he was sincerely attempting to place Iraq's finances on a sound footing.[21]

Mumtaz quickly took several important measures. For example, in July 1948 he increased various taxes and custom duties, and cut the cost of living allowances for many government employees. And the following September he introduced considerably tighter controls on imports.[22]

But these measures were insufficient to cope with Iraq's budgetary problems, and so in August 1948 Mumtaz requested British assistance. In order to ensure an adequate supply of inexpensive bread for the urban poor, he said that he needed an immediate British government loan of £3 million to purchase the necessary quantities of wheat and barley. And in order to avoid significant unemployment, he said that he needed the British government's permission to float a £5 million loan in London to raise private capital for the purchase of materials necessary for the completion of several railway construction projects that were already underway.[23]

J. C. B. Richmond, the chargé d'affaires at the British embassy in Baghdad, supported Mumtaz's request. He believed that the effects of a breakdown in the government's scheme for distributing inexpensive bread to the urban poor would be extremely serious and possibly lead to an administrative collapse and the emergence of a militantly anti-British government in Iraq.[24]

Ambassador Mack too recommended that Britain extend financial aid to Iraq. He emphasized that Muzahim's government deserved support because it was friendly and trying to improve the financial situation. He also pointed out that the government was now in considerable danger because the food crisis coincided with the imminent return of the defeated army from Palestine. In addition, Mack believed that financial aid was necessary to combat anti-British sentiment in Iraq that currently was unusually pronounced because Britain's arms embargo and support for the Bernadotte Plan for the partition of Palestine had convinced many Iraqis that Britain bore much of the responsibility for the establishment of the state of Israel.[25]

As they had done the previous May, in August and September 1948 Foreign Office officials supported the extension of financial assistance to Iraq. They feared that without an infusion of revenue to enable the government to provide an adequate supply of inexpensive bread for the urban poor and to keep men employed on railway construction, there would be serious social unrest that might spread to the oil producing areas and interrupt production there. They were also concerned that without aid Muzahim's pro-British government would fall and be replaced by an anti-British government that would make Britain's position at Habbaniya and Shaiba untenable, cancel the IPC's oil concession, and dismiss the British personnel in charge of the Basra Port Directorate and the Fao Dredging Service with the result that navigation on the Shatt al-Arab would become difficult and the export of oil from the AIOC's facilities at Abadan would be endangered. On the other hand, Foreign Office officials thought that if only Iraq could survive this difficult period without upheaval, its long-range economic prospects were quite favorable. They pointed out that during the next few years Iraqi oil production was scheduled to rise from its current level of about 2 million tons per year to approximately 25 million tons per year, with a proportionate increase in royalties. Since the IPC was nearly half-owned by British interests (the AIOC and Shell), and since Iraq was a member of the sterling area and spent much of its income on British goods, they believed that this prospective development promised much benefit for the British economy, provided of course that Iraq remained friendly to Britain.[26]

However, in October 1948 the Treasury again refused to agree to provide financial assistance to Iraq. It repeated the arguments that it had used the previous May about Britain's weak financial position, the possibility of encouraging appeals for assistance from other countries, and the unlikelihood that Iraq would either repay the loan or cease to make further requests for money. The Treasury now also maintained that if Iraqi leaders realized that they could turn to Britain for assistance they would never take the drastic steps necessary to remedy their financial problems, that there were large sums of money in private hands in Iraq that the government should tap before turning to Britain for help, and that by providing assistance Britain would in effect be subsidizing Iraq's war effort in Palestine. In addition, the Treasury noted that Iraq already owed Britain £2 million for military equipment, that £2.5 million of the money that Iraq wanted to borrow for railway construction was scheduled to go for a single station in Baghdad that would be quite unproductive and serve primarily to enhance the prestige of the railway administration, and that there was already a long line of colonies waiting for loans for railway construction whose claims the British government could not reasonably subordinate to those of Iraq. Finally, the Treasury pointed out that a government loan would require parliamentary approval that it believed would be difficult to obtain because of Iraq's rejection of the Treaty of Portsmouth, closure of the Haifa pipeline, participation in the war in Palestine, and unwillingness adequately to tap domestic sources of revenue.[27]

Stymied once more by the opposition of the Treasury, in October 1948 the Foreign Office again requested that the oil companies extend financial assistance to Iraq. Just as in May, however, both the AIOC and the IPC refused to lend money to Iraq. In justification, AIOC officials repeated their previous argument about their company's relatively small direct interests in Iraq. They also said that they were concerned that if they granted a loan to Iraq, Iran, where they had much greater interests, would immediately demand similar consideration.[28]

IPC officials too repeated their previous arguments about their company's outstanding loans to Iraq and the closure of the Haifa pipeline. They also pointed out that they would soon have to begin negotiations with Iraq for a revision of their concession, and they wanted to be able to hold out the possibility of a loan as a means of gaining a favorable agreement. In addition, they said that they were concerned that if they granted a loan to Iraq, Syria, through which valuable IPC pipelines ran, would immediately demand similar consideration. However, the IPC was willing to help by paying in advance £1 million that it was due to give Iraq in January 1949. This sum consisted of £200,000 in royalties for the last quarter of 1948 plus £800,000 in dead rent payments for the company's Mosul and Basra concessions that were not yet producing oil. Thus in October 1948, when Iraq was maintaining a large and costly military force in Palestine, the Foreign Office was again able to use a third party to provide valuable financial assistance.[29]

In October 1948 the Foreign Office gave further assistance by informing Iraqi leaders that it would not object if they withdrew some of the sterling that they kept in the British-managed Iraq Currency Board in London as cover and support for the dinar, their own currency. In order to keep confidence in the dinar, the board preferred to maintain sterling assets at least equal to the amount of dinars in circulation. However, after receiving this information from the Foreign Office, Iraqi leaders, desperate for revenue, took £1.5 million from the board and thereby reduced their note cover to below 100 percent. Fortunately for them, this move did not cause a run on the dinar because in Iraq it was not widely known.[30]

In November 1948 Mumtaz resigned because Muzahim's government would not adopt his proposals to implement further substantial cuts in expenditure and raise additional large quantities of revenue by means of a land tax. Probably the government's refusal to adopt Mumtaz's proposals was due in considerable measure to the opposition of Iraq's powerful landed interests who objected to paying more taxes no matter how great the country's need.[31]

Unable to solve Iraq's financial crisis or achieve success in the military campaign in Palestine, in early January 1949 Muzahim resigned. He was replaced by Nuri al-Said, the many time former prime minister.[32]

The minister of finance in Nuri's government was Khalil Ismail. Ismail had held numerous government positions but had never served in the cabinet and thus lacked the experience and stature of Mumtaz.[33] Nonetheless, he made a serious effort to improve the financial situation. For example, he reduced the amount of money allocated to all government departments by an average of 15 percent, reduced the number of civil servants by not filling vacancies as they occurred, and reduced the cost of living allowances for civil servants. Nuri assisted Ismail in cutting costs by withdrawing the Iraqi army from Palestine. While these measures helped, Iraq's financial situation was so serious that by themselves they were insufficient, and the government still needed more money.[34]

However, the government was unable to raise much more revenue because most of its proposals for tax increases were blocked by Parliament, and Nuri was not inclined to press the deputies on this issue because he did not want to lose their support and thereby jeopardize his political position. Moreover, he believed that if he could only get by the next few years, increased oil revenues would eliminate the need for new taxes.[35]

Of course, the obvious way for the government to raise more revenue was to reopen the Haifa pipeline. But Nuri consistently rejected this alternative for fear of alienating public opinion at home and incurring criticism from other Arab countries.[36]

To raise more revenue in a politically palatable manner, in January 1949 Nuri requested a loan totalling £300,000 from the three British-owned banks in Iraq, and a loan of £3 million from the IPC. Acting at the behest of the Foreign Office, all three banks lent their full share.[37] As usual, the IPC refused to make a loan, but it did advance £1 million consisting of royalty and dead rent payments that were due in January 1950.[38] Thus without using British government funds, the Foreign Office was again able to help Iraq.

To provide further assistance, in June 1949 the British government agreed to allow Iraq to raise a £3 million loan in London for railway equipment that it had already ordered from British manufacturers. It will be recalled that Iraq had originally requested permission to do this in August 1948, but in spite of support for the proposal from the Foreign Office the Treasury had refused. Now, however, the Treasury was amenable because it believed that Iraq was finally making a serious effort to put its financial house in order. The Treasury was also under pressure from the Board of Trade, which was concerned about Iraq's inability to pay for the railway equipment. In addition, the Treasury was influenced by the Foreign Office's argument that Britain should strengthen Nuri because he was Britain's closest friend among the leading politicians.[39]

Barings, the large well-established investment firm, was willing to act as Iraq's agent in placing the £3 million loan. However, to attract investors, in June 1949 Barings maintained that Iraq would have to pay an interest rate of 4 percent, and as security offer a first charge upon its oil royalties supplemented by a first charge upon the sterling balances that it held in London as cover for its currency.[40]

Iraqi leaders were not satisfied with this offer because they believed that an interest rate of 4 percent was excessive. In support of their contention, they pointed out that Northern Rhodesia had just raised a loan in London at 3 percent, and they maintained that at this time the World Bank was lending money at 2.5 percent. Aside from the matter of the interest rate, they did not believe that they should have to offer any part of their sterling balances as security.[41]

In response, Foreign Office officials pointed out that Northern Rhodesia was able to raise a loan at only 3 percent because unlike Iraq it was located in a politically stable area far from the Soviet Union, and because its status as a British colony led investors to believe that the British government would not permit it to default. They also noted that recently Iceland had had to pay 4.5 percent for a loan that it had raised in London. In addition, they maintained that the World Bank would not now lend money at 2.5 percent; the true figure, they believed, was 4.5 percent. Finally, they said that investors would insist that Iraq offer its sterling balances as security because under certain circumstances, such as a Soviet invasion, an internal upheaval, a dispute with the IPC, or a problem with Syria through which Iraq's pipelines ran, Iraq's oil exports might be cut off.[42]

However, to accommodate the Iraqis, in November 1949 the Foreign Office offered them a £3 million British government loan under the terms of a recently enacted law that in certain circumstances enabled the government to avoid seeking parliamentary approval. As in the case of the Barings proposal, the interest rate was specified at 4 percent, and Iraq would have to use all of the proceeds from the loan to pay for railway equipment from British manufacturers. But from Iraq's perspective the British government loan was better than the Barings proposal because as security Iraq would only have to agree to a first charge upon its oil royalties and not also upon its sterling deposits in London, and Iraq could avoid paying the 3 percent commission that Barings was planning to charge.[43]

Iraqi leaders were definitely interested in this offer, but they maintained that since Barings was planning to charge 4 percent the British government loan should cost less. Specifically, they requested that the interest rate be reduced to 2.5 percent, which they said was the rate at which the British government could itself borrow money in the home market. They also asked that the Iraqi State Railways, a quasi-independent state-owned corporation that had its own budget, should be permitted to use £652,000 from the loan to repay money that it owed to the Iraqi Treasury. Finally, they pointed out that they were currently negotiating with the World Bank for a loan and to receive the money might have to offer that institution a first charge upon their oil royalties. Consequently, they requested that the British government should agree that its loan, and the prospective World Bank loan, would share a first charge upon Iraq's oil royalties on a basis of equality.[44]

To accommodate the Iraqis, the British agreed that the Iraqi State Railways could use £652,000 from the loan to repay money that it owed to the Iraqi Treasury and that the British government would share a first charge upon Iraq's oil royalties with the World Bank on a basis of equality. However, for various reasons the British Treasury would not agree to reduce the interest rate on the loan below 4 percent. To begin with, and contrary to Iraq's contention, it did not believe that the British government could now borrow money in the home market for a time period of six years (the duration of the proposed Iraqi loan) at an interest rate as low as 2.5 percent. But even if the British government could do so, the Treasury did not see any reason why it should lend money to a foreign country on the same terms that it could borrow itself. On the contrary, the Treasury pointed out that for loans of this type it had always been standard practice to charge a premium, in the form of an addition to the rate of interest at which the British government could itself borrow, to cover against the risk of default and for administrative expenses. The Treasury also maintained that the mere fact that the British government was offering to lend money to Iraq was a considerable favor because by lending it was reducing the amount of capital available to itself and to British industry. In addition, the Treasury pointed out that Iraq would now have to pay more than 4 percent on a commercial loan in the City of London because interest rates had risen since Barings had quoted that figure nearly six months ago. Finally, the Treasury was concerned that a loan to Iraq at an exceptionally low rate of interest would establish an undesirable precedent for other countries.[45]

Observing that they could not make any headway on this point, Iraqi leaders finally accepted the British proposal. Accordingly, on 2 December 1949 in London the loan agreement was officially concluded.[46]

In 1948 and 1949 the British government had important differences with Iraq. For example, it opposed Iraq's refusal to ratify the Treaty of Portsmouth, unwillingness adequately to tap domestic sources of revenue or sufficiently reduce government expenditure, closure of the Haifa pipeline, refusal to extend the first truce in the war in Palestine or support the Bernadotte Plan, and recognition of the pro-mufti government in Gaza.

In spite of these differences, during this period the British government provided valuable assistance to help Iraq through its severe financial crisis. Initially it aided Iraq indirectly by encouraging the IPC to make its royalty payments in advance, suggesting that Iraq withdraw funds that it held in London as cover for its currency, pressing the British-owned banks in Baghdad to lend money to Iraq, and permitting Iraq to float a sizable loan in London. Eventually, however, it granted Iraq a substantial loan on favorable terms.

The British government provided this assistance because it wanted to prevent an administrative collapse and the possible rise to power of strongly anti-British elements like the extreme nationalist Istiqlal party or the pro-Soviet Communist party. Only by keeping its friends in power could the British government be confident of preserving its important air bases in Iraq, its predominant share of Iraq's growing import market, its control over vital dredging operations in the Shatt al-Arab, and the IPC's increasingly valuable oil concession.

However, it is unlikely that Britain won much goodwill in Iraq for these efforts. To begin with, the advance payments from the IPC that the Foreign Office arranged were sums that Iraq was entitled to receive soon anyway. And all of the money that Iraq withdrew from the Currency Board was actually owned by Iraq and was not a gift from Britain. What Iraq really wanted during this period, and what it did not get until the end of 1949 and even then only after much haggling, were sizable loans from the British government or private British interests. Accounting for the British government's unwillingness to grant these loans or permit them to be raised in Britain, Iraqis generally gave little credence to Britain's economic problems. Rather, they believed that the British government was attempting to pressure them to change their Palestinian policy, and in particular to reopen the Haifa pipeline. In other words, in Iraq Britain's behavior was widely perceived as an effort to induce the country to abandon the principled policy that at considerable cost it had adopted on a matter of great importance. And for this Britain incurred a great deal of criticism in Iraq. The fact that for much of this time Britain was also imposing an embargo on the shipment of much needed weapons simply intensified the criticism. And thus did the events of 1948-49 embitter the Anglo-Iraqi relationship and weaken the position of Britain's friends in Iraq.[47]

By 1950 Iraq's financial situation had improved substantially because of better harvests,[48] a large loan from the World Bank,[49] greatly increased oil production following the opening of a 16-inch pipeline to Tripoli,[50] and a significantly altered concession agreement with the IPC.[51] The extent of the improvement can be seen in the fact that in 1948 Iraq's oil revenue was £2.3 million, while in 1950 it was £6.9 million.[52]

After 1950 Iraq's financial situation continued to improve because of even more oil production and pipeline construction and a second significantly altered concession agreement with the IPC.[53] The extent of this further improvement can be seen in the fact that in 1958 Iraq's oil revenue was £84.4 million.[54]

By helping the regime to weather the severe crisis of 1948-49, Britain succeeded in preserving its dominant position in Iraq. But the regime did not use the time that it had gained wisely. Indeed, a decade later it still lacked a wide base of support in the country. As a result, in 1958 it was easily overthrown, and with its demise the British ascendancy in Iraq came to an end.

.15.

The Syrian Imbroglio

During the 1940s most of the Sunni Arab elite that dominated Iraqi politics supported the cause of Arab unity. Many of these men had served the Ottoman Empire and therefore remembered a government that had administered most of the Middle East as a single unit. Some of them, such as Nuri al-Said, Jamil al-Midfai, and Ali Jawdat al-Ayyubi, had long experience with the cause of Arab nationalism because they had participated in the Arab revolt in the Hijaz during the First World War and immediately afterward served in Faysal's Arab government in Damascus. And nearly all of them resented the fact that after the First World War the victorious Allied powers had divided the Arab lands of the Middle East into numerous different countries.[1]

Aside from these emotional or ideological considerations, most of the Sunni Arab elite supported Arab unity because they believed that it would be in Iraq's interests. For example, it would strengthen Iraq's ability to resist pressure from Turkey, which many Iraqis suspected of harboring territorial designs on oil-rich areas in northern Iraq. It would also strengthen Iraq's ability to resist pressure from Iran, with which Iraq had important differences concerning navigation on the Shatt al-Arab. In addition, Arab unity would provide Iraq with securer access to the Mediterranean Sea. For Iraq access to the Mediterranean was vital because all of its oil exports traveled by pipeline to Tripoli in Lebanon and Haifa in Palestine, and Basra, its only port, was located dangerously near the Iranian border. If Arab unity were restricted to the Fertile Crescent, which Iraqi leaders generally preferred, it would have the further benefit of excluding Egyptian influence from an area that they considered to be rightfully their sphere of influence. Ultimately it might even strengthen Iraq sufficiently to enable the country to dispense with British support and protection.[2]

For Iraq's Sunni Arab elite, ethnic and sectarian interests were also involved because unity with the predominantly Sunni Arab-inhabited lands of the Fertile Crescent would eliminate the numerical preponderance of Iraq's Kurdish and Shiite population. Although this goal naturally had no appeal for Iraq's Kurdish and Shiite communities, in Iraqi politics these groups usually counted for less than the Sunni Arabs, and in any event their leaders generally did not oppose Arab unity because within Iraq the movement had the status of a credo and they did not wish to appear unpatriotic.[3]

In 1945 Iraq cooperated with the other Arab states to form the Arab League. But this organization was only a loose grouping of sovereign countries with no coercive powers. Consequently, it did little to satisfy the widely felt desire in Iraq for a more concrete form of unity.[4]

In 1948, when Israel was created with full control over the port of Haifa, Iraq was deprived of one of its two outlets on the Mediterranean for oil exports. As a result, Iraqi leaders became particularly concerned about union with Syria because it would safeguard their remaining route to the Mediterranean. Moreover, the fighting in Palestine had revealed that disunity was a major factor in the Arab defeat, and consequently sentiment in Iraq for some form of unity was now unusually strong.[5]

The regent was particularly eager for unity with Syria because he could then go to that country as viceroy in 1953 when the boy king of Iraq reached the age of majority. Moreover, the Hashemites had a previous connection with Syria because Faysal, the regent's uncle and the king of Iraq from 1921 to 1933, had ruled in Damascus from the end of the First World War in 1918 until he was evicted by the French in 1920.[6]

Nuri al-Said was prime minister of Iraq during 1949 when the Syrian question was at the forefront of Iraqi politics. Now sixty-one years old, he had struggled for Arab unity for most of his life and was eager to cap his career by finally achieving some success.[7]

Nuri's foreign minister was Fadhil al-Jamali. Jamali was a Shiite but he was very much a part of the Iraqi establishment. Indeed, on the question of union with Syria he was as militant as any of the leading Sunni Arab politicians. His feelings on this subject are illustrated in an interview with an Egyptian newspaper in July 1949 when he maintained that the Iraqi-Syrian boundaries were

> artificial and that there is nothing natural about them. Nature
> refuses to separate Syria and Iraq; they are one land and watered
> by the same rivers, closed in by common boundaries, and their

two peoples are tied together by intertwined relations and interests. . . . Why should not these artificial boundaries be erased? They are just ink on paper traced by the hand of partition and occupation which unity and independence should wipe out. They will disappear if not to-day, then tomorrow.[8]

In Iraq it was not only the ruling class that sought union with Syria. On the contrary, in 1949 all Iraqi newspapers, irrespective of their attitude toward the current government, favored this objective because they believed that it would strengthen Syria's position vis-à-vis Israel and be a step toward the realization of the widely held aspiration for complete Arab unity.[9] For example, in October *Liwa al-Istiqlal,* the newspaper of the Istiqlal party, argued that "we must take advantage of present historic opportunity and finally establish union."[10] Also in October, *Sada al-Ahali* (formerly *Sawt al-Ahali,* now temporarily suspended), the newspaper of the National Democratic party, maintained that every Iraqi concerned with the future of his country "has not hesitated to accept the plan in principle regardless of the causes and factors which have made the ruling class strive for it."[11] And in November *Al-Yaqazah,* an ultranationalist newspaper close to the Istiqlal party, wrote that "if a union of two Arab states threatens the well being of the [Arab] League, then down with the League and long live unity."[12]

It is interesting to observe that on this issue the attitude of the Istiqlal and other nationalists in Iraq was at variance with that of most nationalists in Egypt and Syria. In the latter countries nationalists generally regarded the unity of the Fertile Crescent as a British scheme to expand their influence in the region. In Iraq, however, the Istiqlal maintained that the history of the Middle East since the First World War demonstrated that the imperialist powers worked by division, and that therefore any step toward Arab unity would strengthen the Arabs and make them less susceptible to foreign domination. They also pointed out that before Saladin won his great victories over the crusaders in the twelfth century (and by implication before the Arabs could triumph over the Israelis), he first united most of the Fertile Crescent under his control.[13]

At the beginning of 1949 Syria, like Iraq, was ruled by a relatively small group of wealthy landowners and businessmen through the medium of a parliamentary regime. These men had done little to promote the cause of union with Iraq because until 1946 they were busy trying to get the French out of Syria, and after 1947 they were preoccupied with the Palestinian crisis. Moreover, most of them had grown attached to the idea of an independent Syria with a republican regime and were not enamored of the prospect of sharing power with a monarchical Iraq in intimate treaty relationship with Britain.[14]

In early 1949 in the Syrian army there was much dissatisfaction with the parliamentary regime for its inept conduct of the Arab-Israeli War. For example, the army criticized the government for not securing a united Arab command; for sending the army into battle with defective and insufficient quantities of arms, ammunition, and medical supplies; and for attempting to terminate the campaign by concluding an armistice agreement with Israel. Because of these grievances, on 30 March 1949 the army, under the direction of Colonel Husni al-Zaim, overthrew the parliamentary regime. Zaim then dissolved the Parliament, proscribed all political parties, arrested political leaders who dared to oppose him, and generally set himself up as a dictator.[15]

Like his predecessors in office, Zaim did not seek union with Iraq because he was unwilling to abandon Syria's independence, its republican form of government, and his personal power. However, Zaim was worried about an Israeli attack because Syria had not yet concluded an armistice agreement. Consequently, in early April 1949 he proposed that Syria and Iraq conclude a military agreement pledging each country to assist the other in the event of an attack.[16]

But Nuri had no intention of concluding a military agreement with Zaim. He strongly disliked Zaim because he feared that his military coup might encourage some Iraqi army officers to attempt a similar move. On this question Nuri was particularly sensitive because during the 1936-41 period Iraq had experienced a series of military coups, one of which resulted in the death of his brother-in-law. Nuri disliked Zaim also because the latter quickly indicated that he was ill-disposed toward the idea of union with Iraq. Indeed, within three weeks of coming to power it was apparent that Zaim had definitely gravitated toward Egypt and Saudi Arabia, both of which were firmly opposed to Iraqi-Syrian union because it would reduce their own influence in the Arab world.[17]

Rather than conclude an agreement with Zaim, Nuri contemplated military intervention to remove him from power. As an excuse, he hoped to use a breakdown of order in Syria or an invitation from some leading Syrian politicians. Aside from removing Zaim, for Nuri military intervention would have the advantage of placing him in a favorable position to achieve union. It would also have occupied the attention and energy of the Iraqi army, which was discontented and aggrieved after its defeat in Palestine. In addition, it would have given Nuri a major foreign policy success and thereby helped compensate for his withdrawal of the Iraqi army from Palestine.[18]

But Nuri wanted British support before he moved, especially to keep Turkey and Israel in check. After all, there was the possibility that either or both of those countries would attempt to prevent the emergence of a large united Arab state that might one day threaten their interests. Alternatively, either or both of them might take advantage of the upheaval to grab pieces of Syrian territory for themselves. In an effort to gain British support, in the spring of 1949 Nuri argued that most Syrian political leaders were opposed to Zaim and wanted Iraq to intervene to restore constitutional rule and political freedom. He also maintained that Britain had a moral obligation to support Iraq in this endeavor because of the major role that it had played in establishing Syrian independence. To reduce Britain's apprehension, he said that the military operation itself would not be difficult and would in fact be over in forty-eight hours. After the completion of the operation he promised to withdraw the Iraqi troops immediately and leave the question of union to the free decision of the Syrian people. Finally, to turn Britain against Zaim Nuri spoke about him in the most scathing terms, describing him as "tricky, untrustworthy, mad and a fool."[19]

But the British were not persuaded, and they argued repeatedly and strongly against Iraq's use of military force.[20] To begin with, they were alarmed about the effect of such an operation on their relations with France. The French, it must be recalled, had held a League of Nations mandate for Syria. Indeed, it was only in 1946, under British compulsion, that they had finally withdrawn all of their troops from the country. After their withdrawal, however, they still wanted to retain at least some influence, and when Zaim came to power they viewed him as the perfect instrument. After all, he was well-disposed toward them, needed their arms, and wanted their assistance to help preserve Syrian independence against Iraqi encroachments. Consequently, if Nuri marched into Syria to overthrow Zaim, the French, who always suspected that Britain was attempting to oust them entirely from the Middle East, would undoubtedly believe that Britain had instigated or at least connived in the operation in an effort to bring Syria into the British orbit.[21]

The French would be especially upset because it would appear that Britain had violated a series of pledges and agreements recognizing French primacy in Syria. For example, in August 1941 Oliver Lyttelton, the British minister of state in the Middle East, wrote to General Charles de Gaulle, the Free French leader, that

> I am happy to repeat to you the assurance that Great Britain has
> no interest in Syria or the Lebanon, except to win the war. We
> have no desire to encroach in any way upon the position of
> France. Both Free France and Great Britain are pledged to the
> independence of Syria and the Lebanon. When this essential
> step has been taken, and without prejudice to it, we freely
> admit that France should have the predominant position in
> Syria and the Lebanon over any other European Power.

In September 1941 British Prime Minister Winston Churchill stated in
the House of Commons that

> we have no ambitions in Syria. We do not seek to replace or
> supplant France, or substitute British for French interests in any
> part of Syria. . . . We recognize that among all the nations of
> Europe the position of France in Syria is one of special privi-
> lege,—and that in so far as any European countries have influ-
> ence in Syria, that of France will be pre-eminent.

And in December 1945 Britain agreed with France that

> each Government affirms its intention of doing nothing to sup-
> plant the interests or responsibilities of the other in the Middle
> East.[22]

The Turks also opposed Iraqi-Syrian unity because they preferred to
have two relatively small and weak states along their southern border.
For them the question of strengthening the Arabs was especially important because Syria had territorial claims against the Turkish province of
Hatay along the Mediterranean Sea.[23]

Aside from concern about relations with France and Turkey, the
British opposed Nuri's plan to march into Syria because they did not
want to alienate Egypt. As we have observed, Egypt opposed any
increase in Iraqi strength because it would diminish its own influence in
the Middle East. And for the British Egypt was important because they
needed an agreement with that country to ensure the continued presence of their military bases along the Suez Canal. In March 1949 Sir
John Troutbeck, the head of the British Middle East Office in Cairo, indicated the high priority that they placed on this consideration when he
maintained that "whereas good relations with Egypt are a necessity of the
first degree, good relations with Transjordan and indeed with any other
Arab state must come in comparison rather within the second degree."[24]

In July 1949 Sir William Strang, the permanent undersecretary of state for foreign affairs, also argued that Egypt was "strategically more important than any of the others [that is, the other Arab states], and we have perforce to rely on her."[25] And in a similar vein, in October 1949 B. A. B. Burrows, the head of the Eastern Department of the Foreign Office, warned that "we must be most careful not to do anything which would make more difficult the defense discussions with Egypt which are our primary strategic concern at present."[26]

The British opposed Nuri's plan too because they did not want to alienate Saudi Arabia. Like Egypt, Saudi Arabia opposed any increase in Iraqi strength because it would diminish its own influence in the Middle East. The Saudis were also concerned that an Iraqi attack on Syria might be a precursor to an Iraqi attack on themselves. After all, the regent was the son of Ali, the Hashemite king of the Hijaz whom the Saudis had evicted when they took over that territory in 1925. And for the British Saudi Arabia was important because it could undermine their dominant position in Kuwait and the other small British-protected principalities along the Persian Gulf.[27]

Moreover, Nuri's plan would upset King Abdullah of Jordan, Britain's loyal ally, because he wanted to take over Syria for himself. Indeed, in October 1949 he actually threatened military action to prevent Syria from uniting with Iraq.[28]

For the British another concern was that if Nuri marched into Syria Israel might maintain that its vital interests were threatened and respond by seizing the Jordanian-occupied section of Palestine known as the West Bank. Because Britain was in close treaty relationship with Jordan, this consideration was important.[29]

The British were also influenced by the fact that the United States was well-disposed toward Zaim because he quickly banned the Communist party and arrested over 400 party members; ratified an agreement with the Arabian-American Oil Company, which was owned by American interests, to construct an important oil pipeline from Saudi Arabia across Syria to the Mediterranean; withdrew Syrian territorial claims against Turkey; and concluded an armistice agreement with Israel.[30]

For the British a further consideration was the fact that Zaim was not unfriendly toward them. Indeed, in June 1949 he even expressed a willingness to conclude a treaty of alliance with Britain, and the following month his prime minister said that in the event of a major war Syria would put all necessary facilities at Britain's disposal. Zaim also indicated a willingness to accommodate Britain by settling a sizable number of

Palestinian refugees in Syria. And in the domestic area he appeared to be attempting to improve economic and social conditions, which pleased British officials. Thus they lacked an incentive to oust him.[31]

In addition to all of these concerns, the British believed that Nuri's proposed action would be a violation of the United Nations Charter, and that therefore considerations of international law would oblige them publicly to oppose it. But clearly such condemnation would severely damage their relations with Iraq.[32]

Finally, the British doubted that an Iraqi military operation would be as simple or quick as Nuri predicted because they did not believe that there was much sentiment in Syria for union with Iraq. They were also concerned that Egypt would intervene on the side of Syria, and that the Kurds in northern Iraq would take advantage of the turmoil to revolt against the central government in Baghdad. And we have already mentioned their apprehension that Israel would respond by seizing the West Bank. In other words, the British feared that Nuri's proposed action would plunge the entire region into a conflagration with unpredictable though probably detrimental consequences for Britain's position and influence.[33]

Rather than support Nuri's proposed attack, in the spring of 1949 the British constantly reiterated their long-established policy that they were not opposed to Arab unity but that it must be carried out peacefully by the free decision of the peoples involved. In this manner they hoped to cause the minimum possible offense to the maximum number of governments.[34]

Nuri was disappointed by Britain's attitude but he did not abandon his goal of ousting Zaim. However, he did change his tactics and now, instead of a military assault, used subterfuge and bribery. Although details are lacking, it appears that his efforts in this area were a factor in the military coup which overthrew Zaim on 14 August 1949.[35]

Immediately after the coup the military conspirators, led by Colonel Sami al-Hinnawi, turned power over to a group of prominent politicians. These politicians then formed a provisional government with the mission of restoring constitutional rule. This government was led by members of the People's party, which represented business interests in Aleppo and elsewhere in northern Syria. This area had traditionally had close commercial links with Iraq and had suffered from the partition of the Arab lands of the Ottoman Empire after the First World War. Consequently, for economic reasons the People's party was well-disposed toward the idea of union with Iraq.[36]

The People's party, and many other leading Syrian politicians, supported union with Iraq also because after two military coups within five months they wanted Iraqi assistance to keep the Syrian army in check. In addition, they feared an Israeli attack and wanted Iraqi help to combat it. Finally, to a certain extent they reacted against Zaim's policy of close relations with Egypt and strong opposition to union with Iraq.[37]

Thus it appeared that the stage was finally set for Iraqi-Syrian union. And indeed in the late summer and autumn of 1949 serious negotiations did occur. But for a variety of reasons these negotiations foundered, and no unity agreement was ever concluded. One of the problems was, ironically, Nuri himself. Although a strong proponent of Arab unity, Syrian leaders disliked dealing with him on this subject because he was so closely tied to Britain. Indeed, on several occasions they indicated that the unity negotiations would be facilitated by his removal. Heeding these signs, in early November the Istiqlal party newspaper maintained that if Nuri stayed in power he would be "jeopardizing Syria-Iraq federation." Probably because he shared this view, on 10 December the regent replaced Nuri with Ali Jawdat al-Ayyubi. But this move proved ineffectual because nine days later a military coup, led by Colonel Adib al-Shishakli and other strongly antiunity Syrian officers, put an end to the negotiations.[38]

Another and more important problem was the Anglo-Iraqi treaty. Syrian leaders, who had just freed their country from French control, were reluctant to unite with a country that was still closely bound to a European power. They were particularly concerned that a unity agreement might enable Britain to extend its influence to Syria.[39] Since Britain was unwilling to terminate the treaty before a replacement was concluded and ratified, this obstacle was formidable.[40] But Syrian leaders wanted unity, and so they tried to compromise. For example, they suggested that a clause be written into the act of federation providing for the maintenance within the territorial limits of Syria and Iraq of their previous international obligations, and an additional clause to the effect that the federal government would be responsible for upholding these obligations.[41]

The British were willing to negotiate along these lines because such an arrangement would enable them to maintain their air bases and other privileges in Iraq. Moreover, they did not want to alienate Syria and Iraq by appearing to obstruct their unity movement.[42]

But the bulk of the Syrian army officers would not compromise on the question of the Anglo-Iraqi treaty. They also opposed unity because they did not want to take second place in, or to, a stronger Iraqi army. To understand their attitude more fully, it must be recalled that many of these men were from minority groups that traditionally had been less interested in Arab unity than the Sunni Muslim sect from which most of the political leaders came. A considerable number of them had also served in the French military forces and were still amenable to the pressure that France was now exerting against unity. Some of them too were probably impressed by the prospect of a military alliance among all of the Arab states that Egypt had recently proposed as an alternative means of satisfying Syria's need for security against Israel. And no doubt some of them succumbed to bribes from Saudi Arabia that, like France and Egypt, worked hard to prevent unity. Because the Syrian officers were the ultimate arbiter of the country's destiny, in the final analysis their view on this question prevailed.[43]

To reduce the ability of the Syrian officers to prevent union, in September 1949 Nuri tried to introduce Iraqi troops into Syria. Initially he proposed that Iraq and Syria exchange assurances of military assistance in the event of internal trouble in either country. Alternatively, he suggested that the two countries exchange certain military formations, ostensibly for the purpose of training and goodwill. Nuri apparently believed that Syrian political leaders would accept some such arrangement; and Colonel Hinnawi, who led the coup against Zaim and unusually for a Syrian officer was a firm proponent of unity, appeared amenable. But without British approval Nuri did not believe that he could move because the risk of Turkish, Israeli, or Egyptian opposition was just too great. To gain this approval, Nuri maintained that Britain was largely responsible for the division of the Arab world after the First World War, and that therefore it now had a moral obligation to promote its unity. He also emphasized how important the scheme was to him and the consequences of failure:

> If His Majesty's Government prevented him from responding to an appeal for help from the Syrian Government his own career would be finished; but in that case he could not prevent large numbers of volunteers from Iraq responding to Syrian appeal. It was a cause near to his heart and he would go himself as a private individual.[44]

But the British did not approve. On the contrary, they opposed the movement of Iraqi troops to Syria under any pretext because they believed that they would be generally viewed as the instigators, and therefore their relations with France and most of the countries of the Middle East would be damaged. Consequently, rather than support Nuri on this question, they simply reiterated their long-established policy that all steps toward Arab unity should be carried out peacefully and with the full consent of the peoples concerned. And so Nuri's proposal to introduce Iraqi troops into Syria, and thereby thwart the opposition of the Syrian officers to the conclusion of a unity agreement, came to naught.[45]

During 1949 Iraqi leaders made serious efforts to realize their long-held goal of union with Syria. All of these efforts failed, not least because of a lack of British support. As we have observed, the British had cogent reasons for reticence. For example, all of the other Arab countries in the region opposed Iraqi-Syrian unity. France, Turkey, and Israel also opposed, and the United States was not enthusiastic. But Iraqi leaders could not be expected to view the situation from the perspective of Whitehall. Among them there was a sense of grievance, a feeling that Britain had failed to put right the injustice that it had perpetrated upon the Arabs at the end of the First World War when it had divided their lands, and a belief that in the crunch their intimate links with Britain had once more proven less useful than they had had reason to expect.

It is not obvious that Britain gained by impeding Iraqi-Syrian union in 1949. In the next few years Syria drifted increasingly toward the Soviet Union and the militantly anti-British regime that emerged in Egypt in 1952. In 1956 it even cut the oil pipelines from Iraq to the Mediterranean, thereby depriving Iraq of much needed revenue and helping to cause an acute shortage of oil in Britain and elsewhere in western Europe. Thus from Britain's perspective the preservation of Syria's independence in 1949, at the expense of alienating Iraq, proved of doubtful utility.

.16.

The Oil Pipelines

As a result of a series of agreements concluded in the 1920s and 1930s, during the 1940s the Iraq Petroleum Company and its two wholly owned subsidiaries, the Mosul Petroleum Company and the Basra Petroleum Company, held concessions to develop and export virtually all of the oil in Iraq. The only part of the country for which they did not hold concessions was a small area near Khanaqin along the border with Iran known as the transferred territories for which the concession was held by the Anglo-Iranian Oil Company. Except for the 5 percent that was held by a wealthy Armenian investor named C. S. Gulbenkian, the IPC was owned in equal amounts of 23.75 percent by four different groups representing four separate nations acting together as a conglomerate. These groups were the AIOC (British), Royal Dutch-Shell (British and Dutch), Compagnie Française des Pétroles (French), and the Near East Development Corporation (an American consortium held in equal shares by Standard Oil of New Jersey and Socony-Vacuum). However, at the insistence of the British government, which held the mandate for Iraq when the original seventy-five-year concession was granted in 1925, the IPC was registered in Britain and always had a British chairman. These provisions, combined with the substantial degree of British ownership, enabled the British government to exert a considerable degree of influence over the company.[1]

Since 1934 the IPC had exported all of Iraq's oil through a pipeline system to the Mediterranean Sea. The system consisted of two parallel lines, each twelve inches in diameter, from Kirkuk in northeastern Iraq to Haditha on the Euphrates River in northwestern Iraq. At that point one line extended through Jordan to Haifa in Palestine (620 miles in all) and the other through Syria to Tripoli in Lebanon (532 miles in all). Each of these lines was capable of carrying more than 2 million tons of oil per year.[2]

In the middle and late 1940s Iraqi leaders were acutely conscious of the fact that in recent years oil production in neighboring countries such as Iran, Kuwait, and Saudi Arabia had increased dramatically. For example, between 1934 and 1948 Iranian production had increased from 7.5 million tons to nearly 25 million tons. Between 1945 and 1948 Kuwaiti production had increased from zero to more than 6 million tons. And between 1938 and 1948 Saudi Arabian production had increased from zero to nearly 19 million tons. However, to the consternation of Iraqi leaders, who desperately wanted to increase their country's income from oil, since the mid-1930s Iraqi production had remained essentially constant at little more than 4 million tons per year. Because of this lack of development, many Iraqis concluded that the IPC was deliberately holding down production in Iraq to avoid flooding the market or because several of its constituent elements had extensive oil interests elsewhere that for various reasons they preferred to develop first. Since most Iraqis believed that the British government exerted or could exert considerable influence over the activities of the IPC, the widespread displeasure in which the company was held in Iraq could not fail to reflect also upon the British government.[3]

Iraqi complaints against the IPC on this issue were not entirely just. True, for various reasons for the first five years after oil exports began in 1934 the IPC deliberately refused to expand the pipeline system to the Mediterranean, which would have been necessary for a serious increase in production. However, in July 1939, on the eve of the Second World War, the IPC decided to construct a pipeline with a capacity of 3 million tons per year from Kirkuk to Tripoli that would run parallel to the existing pipeline between those two places. By undertaking various improvements, the company also planned to increase the capacity of the existing pipeline from Kirkuk to Haifa by 1 million tons per year. The implementation of this scheme would have doubled Iraqi oil exports from 4 million tons per year to 8 million tons per year. However, the outbreak of the Second World War in September 1939, with all of the attendant problems of transport through the Mediterranean, steel shortages due to the construction of armaments, and dollar shortages inhibiting the purchase of materials in the United States, induced the British government to shelve the project.[4]

At the end of the war the Iraqi government resumed its pressure on the IPC to expand oil production. The IPC was amenable because in 1939 and 1943 it had agreed to loan Iraq a total of £4.5 million that Iraq was not obliged to repay until the company had increased oil exports.[5]

Moreover, with the postwar economic recovery in Europe and the United States, the constituent groups in the organization believed that they could market the additional quantities of oil. Consequently, in October 1946 the IPC began construction of 16-inch pipelines paralleling the existing 12-inch pipelines from Kirkuk to Tripoli and Haifa. The capacity of the 16-inch system was scheduled to be more than 8 million tons per year with each of the 16-inch lines having about twice the capacity of each of the 12-inch lines. Thus the completion of the 16-inch lines would have enabled Iraq to increase production from a little more than 4 million tons per year to 13 million tons per year.[6]

Although the Iraqis were pleased that the IPC was finally making a serious effort to raise production, they were aggrieved that the new pipelines were only 16-inches and therefore, from their perspective, the increase in production would be relatively small. As the Iraqis knew, the pipelines were only 16-inches because this size was the maximum that British companies were able to manufacture, and the British government refused to provide dollars for the purchase of larger pipe from the United States.[7] The different industrial capacities of the two countries in this area and the consequent impact on the development of oil in the Middle East are illustrated by the fact that in November 1947 the American-owned Arabian-American Oil Company, which held the concession for Saudi Arabia, began construction of a 30-inch American-manufactured pipeline from the eastern part of Saudi Arabia to Sidon in Lebanon. In contrast to the 4 million tons per year capacity of each of Iraq's 16-inch pipelines, Saudi Arabia's 30-inch pipeline had a capacity of 15 million tons per year.[8]

But even Iraq's 16-inch pipeline system was not completed. Because of the outbreak of fighting between the Jews and the Arabs in Palestine, in the spring of 1948 the IPC halted construction work on the southern branch, which had progressed all of the way from Kirkuk to the Jordan River, just forty-two miles from the sea. At this time the Iraqi government also stopped the flow of oil through the 12-inch pipeline to Haifa to prevent the Jews in Palestine from using any of it to increase their military power and economic strength.[9]

The noncompletion of the 16-inch pipeline to Haifa and the halting of the flow of oil through the 12-inch pipeline to Haifa reduced Iraq's oil exports by more than 6 million tons per year. In financial terms this self-inflicted wound cost Iraq £3 million per year in royalties.[10]

Iraq was not the only loser in this affair. The constituent groups in the IPC lost a considerable amount of money because they were deprived of a substantial quantity of crude oil. Of these groups, the AIOC and Shell, the two British companies in the IPC, lost the most because they also owned a large refinery at Haifa, valued at £40 million, that was now standing idle for want of crude from Iraq.[11]

Aside from Iraq and the oil companies, Britain and the rest of Europe suffered from the closure of the Haifa pipeline because the Marshall Plan for recovery from the ravages of the war was dependent upon a substantially increased flow of oil from the Middle East. The large amounts involved are indicated by the State Department's calculation in January 1948 that to fulfill the goals of the plan Middle Eastern production would have to be raised from its current level of 800,000 barrels a day to 2 million barrels a day.[12]

To some extent the loss of Iraqi production could be made up by using tankers to bring more oil from the Persian Gulf to Europe. But this expedient had its limitations because at this time there was a general shortage of tankers. Moreover, by increasing the demand for the inadequate number of tankers, the closure of the Haifa pipeline raised tanker rates and thereby raised the price of oil to the European countries. The fact that the United States owned most of the world's tankers (in 1946, 59 percent of the tonnage) compounded the problem because it meant that for Britain and the rest of Europe chartering more tankers usually involved an increased outlay of precious dollars.[13]

In addition to the problem resulting from the loss of Iraqi crude, Britain and the rest of Europe suffered from the closure of the Haifa refinery because at this time there was a general shortage of refining capacity.[14] The importance of the Haifa refinery in this regard is indicated by the fact that it was capable of processing 4 million tons of oil per year and was being expanded to enable it to process 7.5 million tons per year.[15] By contrast, in 1947 the total amount of crude oil refined in the entire United Kingdom was only 2.6 million tons.[16]

For Britain the loss of Iraqi crude oil and refined oil products was especially damaging because this was oil that it and other countries in the sterling area could have purchased in sterling rather than dollars. The importance of this consideration is indicated by the fact that during the twelve-month period between 1 July 1948 and 30 June 1949 Britain was obliged to import 38 percent of its petroleum from the dollar area.[17] In monetary terms, for Britain the loss of Iraqi oil amounted to as much as $50 million a year.[18] Moreover, the British government was deprived of tax revenues of about £5 million a year from the profits that the AIOC and Shell would have made if Iraq had not halted the flow of oil to Haifa.[19]

Israel also lost because it had to pay more to import oil products from the Western Hemisphere than it would have had to pay if the products could have been refined locally. Israel lost too in the form of payments from the oil companies in lieu of local taxes, port dues for the loading of tankers in Haifa harbor, wages to Israeli workers, and purchases from Israeli shops and companies. In all, the direct cost to Israel may have been as high as £1.6 million per year. In addition, Israel's economic development was hindered because it could not proceed with its plans to develop a petrochemical industry.[20] It was precisely this damage to Israel's economy, combined with pressure from public opinion within Iraq and from neighboring Arab states, that induced Iraqi leaders to halt the flow of oil to Haifa in spite of the cost to their own economy.[21]

Upset by the closure of the pipeline and the refinery, the British pressed Iraq to resume the flow of oil to Haifa. They pointed out that the royalties that Iraq was forfeiting would mean a great deal to the Iraqi economy. They also emphasized that loans that Iraq was attempting to procure from the IPC, plus a revision of the oil concession to provide more revenue for Iraq, would probably be dependent upon the resumption of the flow of oil.[22] To assist Iraq in reopening the pipeline, between June and September 1948, while Count Bernadotte was attempting to arrange a settlement of the Palestinian problem, the British recommended placing Haifa's port and refinery under United Nations administration. Because this scheme would deprive Israel of any control over Iraqi oil, the British believed that Iraq would then be willing to reopen the pipeline and tolerate the reopening of the refinery.[23] However, the Bernadotte Plan of September 1948, while recommending the creation of a free port at Haifa, did not provide for any United Nations role in administering it. In other words, the Bernadotte Plan left all of Haifa, including the port and the refinery, entirely under Israeli administration.[24] Predictably, Iraq refused to negotiate on this basis, and so Britain's scheme failed.[25]

As another method of assisting Iraq in reopening the pipeline, in November 1948 the British government, in conjunction with the French and American governments, proposed that Iraq resume the flow of oil through the pipeline on the condition that none of the oil would go into the refinery at Haifa or reach the Israelis in any other way. Instead, all of the oil would be immediately loaded aboard ships and dispatched to overseas destinations.[26]

Initially Iraqi leaders were willing to consider this proposal if the IPC disconnected the spur running into the refinery to ensure that no oil reached that installation, and if they could station their own representatives in Haifa to observe the operation.[27] However, in January 1949 Nuri al-Said, who had just reassumed the office of prime minister, stiffened Iraq's terms by also insisting upon the internationalization of Haifa.[28]

The IPC did not like the Anglo-French-American proposal much more than the Iraqis. To begin with, the company emphasized the practical difficulties of disconnecting the spur running into the refinery. But more importantly, the AIOC and Shell were unamenable because it would not have led to the reopening of the refinery from whose products they derived considerable profit.[29]

The Israelis too refused to agree to any proposal to ship crude oil through Haifa while the refinery, which meant so much to their economy, remained closed. And, of course, they would not even consider the Iraqi demand for the internationalization of Haifa. Consequently, the Anglo-French-American proposal to resume the flow of oil through the pipeline while bypassing the Haifa refinery was not adopted.[30]

As an alternative to this proposal, in January 1949 Nuri suggested that the IPC divert the nearly completed southern branch of the 16-inch pipeline system from a pumping station in Jordan to a terminal in Lebanon, thereby bypassing Israeli territory. The French group in the IPC was amenable to the idea of diversion because, as we shall observe presently, it was especially eager to acquire more nondollar crude oil. However, the other groups in the IPC refused because it would have taken considerable time and cost an appreciable amount, especially for the construction of a deep-water harbor; because it would have meant the loss of valuable terminal facilities at Haifa; because it would have meant conceding the principle that Iraq had the right to control the destination of its oil once that oil had become company property; and because it would not have resulted in the reopening of the Haifa refinery, which for the AIOC and Shell was the primary consideration.[31]

Stymied, in May 1949 Nuri modified his terms for reopening the Haifa pipeline. Whereas previously he had insisted upon the internationalization of Haifa, he now said that he would do so if Israel would accept one of the following four conditions: take back the Arab refugees from the fighting in Palestine in 1948; agree to the borders established by the United Nations partition resolution in November 1947 or the borders established by the Bernadotte Plan in September 1948, both of which would have involved the surrender of an appreciable amount of territory; or agree to the internationalization of Haifa. But Israel would not accept any of these conditions because it was not so desperate for Iraqi oil that it would compromise its security.[32]

In 1949 Nuri probably wanted to reopen the Haifa pipeline to acquire additional revenue and accommodate Britain, but he was constrained by public opinion. The strength of sentiment in Iraq on this question is indicated by an article in the newspaper of the Istiqlal party that maintained that "no Iraqi leader can bear the historic responsibility of allowing the pumping of oil to Haifa or face the indignation of the people if he decides to do so."[33] And in another newspaper a member of Parliament wrote that he did not believe that there was a single Arab statesman who would agree to the pumping of oil to Haifa but that if one did so the action would be regarded as high treason.[34]

With the pipeline still closed, in March 1949 representatives of the AIOC raised with British officials the possibility of bringing crude oil from the Persian Gulf by tanker through the Suez Canal to Haifa for refining.[35] However, this scheme foundered because Egypt was unwilling to allow Israeli-bound cargoes to pass through the Suez Canal and the Foreign Office, fearful of jeopardizing its relations with Egypt and uncertain of the strength of its legal case, was unwilling to press hard for permission.[36]

In July 1949 the financial pressure on Iraq caused by the closure of the pipeline to Haifa was considerably reduced when the northern or Tripoli branch of the 16-inch pipeline system from Kirkuk was opened. Together with the old 12-inch pipeline to Tripoli, Iraq was now able to export more than 6 million tons of oil per year. This figure was about 50 percent more than it had been able to export before the closure of the pipeline to Haifa.[37]

With all of this oil flowing to Tripoli, in August 1949 representatives of the AIOC raised with British officials the possibility of bringing some of it to Haifa by tanker for refining.[38] However, this scheme foundered because Lebanon would not agree for fear of being accused of breaking the Arab boycott of Israel.[39]

By June 1950 the AIOC and Shell had finally lost hope of inducing Iraq to reopen the Haifa pipeline, of inducing Egypt to permit Israeli-bound tankers from the Persian Gulf to transit through the Suez Canal, or of inducing Lebanon to permit the shipment of oil from Tripoli to Haifa. They were also concerned that Israel might nationalize the idle refinery at Haifa and operate it with oil imported entirely independent of any of the companies in the IPC. Consequently, with the support of the Israeli government, the AIOC and Shell now decided to reopen the Haifa refinery with oil that they would import from Qatar (for which country the

IPC held the concession) around the Cape of Good Hope and from Venezuela (where Shell had extensive interests). Although higher transportation costs would make oil obtained in this manner more expensive than oil obtained through the pipeline from Kirkuk, the AIOC and Shell believed that they could still operate the refinery profitably. The British government, which for economic reasons we have already discussed had long sought the reopening of the Haifa refinery, supported this scheme. Thus the frequent and bitter Israeli accusations against Britain two years earlier for favoring the Arabs during the fighting in Palestine quickly gave way to an elaborate and successful scheme of collusion to reopen the Haifa refinery, Israel's most valuable economic asset, and thereby help to frustrate Arab efforts to weaken Israel's economy.[40]

The revenue that the Iraqis derived from the 12-inch and 16-inch pipelines was not nearly sufficient to pay for all of their development projects, social welfare measures, and military expenditures. Consequently, throughout 1949 they pressed the IPC to begin construction of a 30-inch pipeline from Kirkuk to Banias in Syria with a capacity of 13 million tons per year.[41]

Initially the AIOC and Shell did not favor proceeding with the Banias pipeline because they were concerned about the high cost, which they estimated at £50 million. They were also not pleased with the idea of embarking upon this large and expensive project while their negotiations with Iraq for a revision of the terms of their concession were still unresolved, and consequently they did not know what their royalty payments would be. In fact, to some extent they viewed their refusal to agree to the construction of the Banias pipeline as a bargaining chip in these negotiations. Moreover, they were still upset about the continued closure of the Haifa pipeline and reluctant to accommodate Iraq on other matters until this issue was settled to their satisfaction. Finally, the AIOC and Shell were in the process of greatly increasing the amount of oil that they received from Kuwait, and were concerned about the possibility that with the Banias pipeline they might be producing more oil in the Middle East than they could easily and profitably market.[42]

The Compagnie Française des Pétroles, however, was eager to proceed with the construction of the Banias pipeline because for France it would make accessible a substantial additional amount of conveniently located oil that it could purchase at cost and pay for in its own currency. The importance of this consideration is indicated by the fact that in 1949 France had to pay for more than half of its oil imports in dollars. Moreover, since the IPC was the only French interest in Middle Eastern oil production, the CFP, unlike the AIOC and Shell, did not have to worry about having excessive quantities of Middle Eastern oil on its hands. Again, unlike the AIOC and Shell, the CFP was not concerned about the reopening of the Haifa refinery because, having no equity in that installation, its interests lay in obtaining crude oil for refining in France. Consequently, within the IPC the CFP, fully supported by representations by the French government to the Foreign Office, pressed hard for the construction of the Banias pipeline. It flatly rejected a substitute offer by the AIOC to supply French refineries with adequate amounts of crude oil at attractive prices. And it even threatened to take legal action against the other groups in the consortium on the grounds that without the Banias pipeline the IPC would not be able to provide it with the amount of oil to which, by the terms of an earlier agreement among the partners, it was entitled. It is interesting to note, parenthetically, that even though Iraq had long been hostile toward France because of that country's efforts to preserve its influence in Syria and Lebanon and refusal to withdraw from North Africa, on this important question Iraqi and French interests coincided.[43]

To accommodate the French, provide more revenue for Iraq for economic development and social welfare, and make more sterling oil available, the British government supported the construction of the Banias pipeline. As an indication of the degree of its commitment and in contrast to its position in 1946, it was now willing to provide the IPC with the dollars required for the purchase of large-diameter pipe in the United States. Although the United States government had less interest than the British government in making more sterling oil available, it too wanted to accommodate the French and improve conditions in Iraq. In addition, it generally favored an increase in oil production in the Middle East in order to conserve reserves in the Western Hemisphere. Consequently, like the British government it supported the construction of the Banias pipeline and thereby helped sway the American groups in the IPC, which initially had sided with the British companies. By December 1949 this confluence, combined with fear of legal action by the CFP and fear of nationalization of the concession by the Iraqis, induced the AIOC and Shell to abandon their opposition to the project.[44]

We have observed that in the 1945-50 period Iraq failed to secure the use of large-diameter pipe on the new lines to Haifa and Tripoli, failed to secure the completion of the 16-inch line to Haifa through an Arab-ruled Palestine, failed to obtain the diversion of the southern branch of the 16-inch pipeline system to a terminal in Lebanon, and failed to shut permanently the Haifa refinery. These setbacks, in areas where the British government could have been of assistance, strengthened the anti-British elements in Iraq and contributed to the general deterioration of Anglo-Iraqi relations resulting from the Arab-Israeli War of 1948.

In spite of these setbacks, however, in the matter of pipeline construction and production totals Iraq did not do badly. While at the end of the Second World War in 1945 Iraq only had 12-inch pipelines to Tripoli and Haifa with a combined throughput of a little more than 4 million tons per year, in July 1949 it added the 16-inch pipeline to Tripoli with a capacity of over 4 million tons per year and in April 1952 the 30-inch pipeline to Banias with a throughput of 13 million tons per year. And while we have not focused on this question in our discussion, in October 1951 and March 1953 Iraq also added a 12-inch pipeline and a 24-inch pipeline from its newly developed oil field near Zubair in southern Iraq to the port of Fao near the mouth of the Shatt al-Arab.[45]

This pipeline construction, which resulted from Iraq's successful management of its relations with the IPC and the British government, enabled Iraq in 1953 to produce nearly 28 million tons of oil. By contrast, in that year Iran, which was locked in a bitter concession dispute with the AIOC and the British government, produced less than 1 million tons of oil.[46]

True, in 1953 Kuwait and Saudi Arabia produced 43 million and 41 million tons of oil respectively. However, in these two countries the oil fields were situated much nearer to the sea than the Kirkuk field in Iraq, and consequently their development required less expensive and time-consuming pipeline construction.[47]

It is important to note, finally, that in return for achieving this substantial increase in production Iraq did not have to make any political concessions. Indeed, on the crucial question of the Haifa pipeline it successfully resisted pressure from the IPC and the Western powers to resume the flow of oil, and in this manner did much to accommodate public opinion within Iraq, immunize itself from criticism from other Arab countries, and achieve a major policy goal in its struggle against Israel.

Like Iraq, Britain favored pipeline construction from Kirkuk to the Mediterranean and from Zubair to Fao. Thus in this area the interests of the two powers coincided, and the resulting increase in Iraqi production favored Britain too. However, in the matter of reopening the Haifa pipeline the interests of the two powers diverged, and in this matter Iraq triumphed.

Conclusion

In 1941 the British reestablished their dominant position in Iraq and, in spite of their weakened condition after the war, maintained it for the rest of the decade. That is to say, in 1950 in the military sphere Britain had complete control over two air bases; protected the bases with a locally recruited British-controlled force;[1] provided nearly all of the equipment for the Iraqi military establishment; trained many Iraqi officers in military academies in Britain; and, in spite of the withdrawal of the military mission in 1948, provided military personnel for in-country training of Iraqi soldiers.[2] In the political sphere the pro-British regent was head of state; politicians willing to work closely with Britain held office;[3] and the boy king was being educated in a British school.[4] And in the economic sphere Iraq was a member of the sterling area; the British-controlled and largely British-owned IPC and its subsidiaries held concessions for all of Iraq except a small section that was held by the entirely British-owned AIOC; and more than 200 British subjects were employed by the Iraqi government, thereby helping to steer important government contracts to British manufacturers.[5]

To an appreciable extent the British succeeded in maintaining their position in Iraq because the Iraqi ruling class felt threatened by the Soviet Union.[6] After all, in the immediate postwar period the Soviets had fostered pro-Soviet secessionist movements in the Azerbaijani and Kurdish sections of Iran near the Iraqi border; delayed the withdrawal of their troops from Iran beyond the permitted time; and put considerable pressure on Turkey for territorial concessions in the eastern part of the country and military bases at the Straits.

Aside from the foreign threat, Iraqi rulers wanted to maintain close ties with Britain because they feared domestic upheaval.[7] Nor were they without reason because between 1936 and 1941 there were a series of military coups; between 1943 and 1945 there were two Kurdish revolts; and in 1948 there was a large-scale urban uprising. The fact that the Soviet Union supported the illegal but strong Communist party in Iraq linked the foreign and domestic threats.

Iraqi rulers wanted to maintain close ties with Britain also because they did not have any other major power to turn to for assistance. Germany and Japan, of course, had been destroyed by the war. France was anathema because of its high-handed and even ruthless behavior in Lebanon and Syria between 1943 and 1945, combined with its determination to retain control of the Arab countries of North Africa. And the United States was problematic because of its pro-Zionist policies. Indeed, Iraqi anger at the United States was so great that in January 1948 Prime Minister Salih Jabr said "[I] will do my best, not only within Iraq but elsewhere, to paralyze American interests"; and the following August his successor, Muzahim al-Pachachi, pledged that he would never accept any financial aid from the United States or in any way assist the expansion of American interests in Iraq.[8]

Nor was the United States eager to become involved in Iraq because it considered Iraq part of the British sphere of influence and was displeased with Iraq's intervention in Palestine. Moreover, it was busy aiding other countries in the region such as Turkey, Israel, Iran, and Saudi Arabia, and did not want to dissipate its resources. American priorities are indicated by the fact that between 1946 and 1951 United States net aid (that is, the combined grant and credit figure less returns to the United States) to Turkey was $264 million, to Israel $68 million, to Iran $16 million, and to Saudi Arabia $14 million. By contrast, during this period the United States did not give any aid to Iraq.[9]

Although the British were still supreme in Iraq in 1950, their position was insecure because it was completely dependent upon their ties with a small ruling class. This ruling class, in turn, was unpopular because it was wealthy, corrupt, repressive, unrepresentative of the country's ethnic and sectarian balance, seemingly uninterested in economic or social programs designed to improve the lot of the vast majority of the population that lived in poverty, and so closely tied to Britain that it appeared unnationalist.

Immediately after the Second World War the British tried to reduce their dependence upon this ruling class by promoting liberalization and democratization in Iraq. However, they were soon forced to abandon the effort because all of the newspapers and political parties that blossomed during this period opposed the continuation of Britain's dominant position in Iraq. In other words, the British could not find any collaborators outside the ruling class and so they were quickly forced to fall back upon that class. Thus Bevin's policy of expanding the basis of support for Britain's position in Iraq failed because almost no one in the country wanted to see that position continue.

Since Britain was so dependent upon the existing regime, anything that discredited it weakened Britain's position in the country. And in

1948 the regime was discredited by the Treaty of Portsmouth because it now appeared that the British bases were going to remain in Iraq for the foreseeable future; by the creation of Israel because it now appeared that Iraq was aligning itself with a nation that had permitted, or at least not prevented, the usurpation of Arab rights and the implantation of an alien and aggressive people in a neighboring country that was of vital strategic interest to Iraq; and by Britain's arms embargo and failure to provide economic assistance because it now appeared that Iraq was tied to an unreliable and ungenerous power. Iraq's failure to defeat Israel in the fighting in Palestine in 1948 simply increased the regime's disgrace.

The regime was also discredited by its consistent failure to manage the economy successfully. Indeed, for the masses the greatly reduced living standards caused by the terrible inflation, and the hunger caused by the severe shortage of bread and poor quality of what was available, contrasted maddeningly with the conspicuous wealth and blatant corruption of a small number at the top.

In addition, the regime was discredited by the opposition of Egypt. During the postwar period Egyptian governments had strong nationalist credentials because they were struggling vigorously to compel Britain to withdraw all of its military forces from Egypt. Simultaneously, they were struggling against Iraq for a position of leadership and dominance in the Arab world, and to further this objective they continually depicted Iraq as a British tool trying to split the Arab League. This propaganda was effective because Egyptian newspapers and magazines were widely read in Iraq, and many Egyptians were employed there as teachers and technical personnel.[10]

The fact that the military was badly disaffected further weakened the regime. Partly this was due to resentment at the defeat that Britain inflicted upon the army in the fighting in May 1941. It was also attributable to the widely perceived belief that after 1941 the regime and the British conspired to weaken the army as punishment for its frequent uprisings after 1936 and its alignment with Germany in 1941. Even after Britain decided to strengthen the army in 1944, the army was upset over Britain's refusal to supply enough military equipment, and over the arms embargo that Britain imposed in 1948. Iraq's failure during the war in Palestine further alienated the army from Britain and the regime because the army held these parties ultimately responsible for the Arab defeat. And, of course, the army was not immune to the widespread criticism of the prevailing social injustices, or to the idea that it was humiliating for an independent Arab country to be so closely tied to a European power. Because in the final analysis the regime depended upon the army for security, its disaffection was of great importance.[11]

Long term social trends were also undermining the regime. For example, there was a rapid growth in the number of educated and politically conscious people. The extent of this development is indicated by the fact that in the ten-year period between 1946-47 and 1956-57 the number of secondary school students increased from 3,100 to 47,000.[12] And in the twelve years after 1932 2,500 students graduated from Iraqi colleges, while in the twelve years after 1945 this figure increased to 12,000.[13] But upon graduation many of these people were unemployed and discontented because the government bureaucracy and the private sector could not accommodate them. Having the time and incentive to seek radical change, they became ready recruits for the various political parties seeking to overthrow the regime.[14]

Another social trend undermining the regime was the increased urbanization of the country, and especially the growth of the population of Baghdad. The extent of the process is indicated by the fact that between 1947 and 1957 a total of about 200,000 people from rural areas migrated to Baghdad. Combined with natural increase, this led to a rise in population from 515,000 to 793,000. As in many countries, the migration was caused by poor economic conditions in the countryside and better job opportunities in the cities. But for the regime the migration resulted in the transformation of large numbers of dispersed, isolated, and politically impotent agricultural laborers under the control of conservative landowners and tribal leaders into a concentrated and dangerous mass of impoverished and discontented workers in the heart of the capital vulnerable to the appeal of radical agitators.[15]

Nor was the regime headed by a figure with sufficient popularity and strength to prevail over its numerous enemies. On the contrary, the regent was generally unpopular because, like most of the leading politicians, he was authoritarian, closely associated with the British, and unwilling to discomfort the wealthy and conservative elements in society by pressing for meaningful reforms. He also lacked self-confidence and determination, and was infected with a profound sense of pessimism. Indeed, he seemed to feel that regardless of his actions, in the final analysis he would not be able to hold back the inexorable tides of history that were destined soon to engulf the frail edifice that he headed. In 1945, for example, the British ambassador reported that "he felt he was bound to fail sooner or later in what he considered was too difficult a task for him," and that "he expected the King would be dethroned in due course 'with all these Communists about.'"[16] Possibly because of this sense of fatalism, in 1958, when a relatively small number of army troops came for him, he surrendered quickly and made little effort to resist or rally other forces to his side.[17]

Aside from its dependence upon a small, weak, unpopular, and increasingly discredited ruling class, Britain's position in Iraq was insecure because the Treaty of 1930, which was the legal underpinning of that position, was due to expire in 1957. In 1948 the British negotiated a new agreement that would have permitted them to continue to maintain their position for an additional extended period, but popular resistance prevented Iraqi leaders from accepting it. Thus in 1950 Britain's position in Iraq was only legally sanctioned for seven more years.

In addition, Britain's position was insecure because after the Second World War the country was too weak to give the sort of large-scale economic assistance that would have been necessary to develop Iraq and raise the standard of living of the people. It was not even able to provide many of the experts that Iraq wanted to employ in areas like agriculture, irrigation, forestry, and medicine.[18] And, of course, it was unable to give the sort of large-scale military assistance that might have ingratiated itself with the army. In other words, Britain lacked the resources to make the relationship sufficiently attractive to induce large numbers of Iraqis to subordinate nationalist passions to practical considerations.

And even when Britain did have the ability to assist Iraq, for example in the diplomatic sphere in 1949 when Iraq sought to take over Syria, it declined to do so for fear of jeopardizing its relations with other Middle Eastern countries. In other words, Britain's interests elsewhere in the region made it difficult for it to be overly responsive to Iraq's concerns. And thus Britain was trapped in a dilemma. It needed to maintain a dominant position in Iraq in order to maintain a dominant position in the Middle East as a whole, but its efforts to maintain a dominant position in the Middle East as a whole impeded its efforts to maintain a dominant position in Iraq.

Of course, by 1950 it was not only in Iraq that Britain was having difficulty maintaining its dominant position. In Egypt, for example, the movement to force Britain to withdraw all of its military forces was so strong that the following year the government repudiated the Anglo-Egyptian Treaty of 1936 and initiated a guerrilla war against the British troops in the Canal Zone.

Essentially Britain's problem was the same throughout the region. That is to say, Britain felt obliged to maintain military forces in the various Arab

countries to defend against Soviet aggression, protect the British oil concessions, and ensure the security of the communications link with the East.
But these military forces, combined with the oil concessions that they were
designed to protect, inflamed local nationalism. In the hostile environment
produced by this policy, in the long run neither Britain's traditional
reliance upon local elites, nor Bevin's alternative of promoting democracy
and encouraging economic and social reform, had much chance of success.

While in the immediate postwar period Britain succeeded in maintaining its dominant position in Iraq, it does not follow that Iraq lost from
this arrangement. On the contrary, because Britain was so eager to keep
its friends in control and prevent the accession to power of a hostile government, within the limits of its diminished capabilities it extended
meaningful assistance to Iraq. Some of this assistance came from its own
resources. For example, throughout this period Britain gave Iraq more
dollars from the sterling area's central pool than Iraq earned; in 1947 it
agreed to make generous releases from Iraq's sterling balances; and in
1949 it gave Iraq a sizable loan. Often, however, the British government
used its influence with other organizations to assist Iraq. For example,
in the 1948-50 period it prevailed upon the IPC to pay its royalties in
advance, proceed with the construction of the Banias pipeline, and
adopt a generous attitude in its negotiations with the Iraqi government
for a revision of its concession; in 1949 it prevailed upon the three
British banks in Baghdad to loan money to Iraq; and in 1950 it used its
influence with the World Bank to facilitate a large loan to Iraq.
Consequently, it is not obvious that Iraq would have done better if it had
adopted a more militant or confrontational posture toward Britain and
the IPC.

Indeed, when Iran adopted such a posture in 1951 by nationalizing the
AIOC's concession and refinery it paid a heavy price, because the AIOC
prevented it from exporting oil by taking legal action against the cargoes.
The extent of Iran's loss is indicated by the fact that in 1950 the country produced 32 million tons of oil, while in 1951 this figure declined to
17 million tons, and in 1952 and 1953 to less than 1 million tons each
year. Not until 1957, three years after the settlement of the dispute, did
Iran produce more oil than it had in 1950, and even then by only 3 million tons.[19]

On a comparative basis, in 1950 Iranian oil production exceeded Iraqi by 25 million tons. In 1951, however, this figure declined to 8 million tons, while in each year between 1952 and 1956 Iraqi oil production exceeded Iranian. Even by 1958 Iranian oil production exceeded Iraqi by less than 5 million tons.[20]

Nor did Iran emerge from its confrontation with Britain with an especially advantageous financial settlement. On the contrary, Zuhayr Mikdashi, a leading oil economist, calculated that in the 1954-64 period Iran received an average annual payment of 43.4 shillings per ton, while Iraq received 44.8 shillings per ton. And Mikdashi concluded that "the financial terms of the agreement negotiated by Persia late in 1954 are in no way more favorable than those already received by other Middle Eastern countries. In principle, they compare less favorably with terms obtained by Iraq three years earlier."[21] Thus after all of the loss of revenue that Iran endured as a result of the virtual shutdown of its oil industry for most of the 1951-54 period, it achieved less than Iraq had already secured without any disruption of its oil industry.

It is interesting to observe that Britain's success in 1954 in compelling Iran to accept a settlement not unfavorable to the AIOC was achieved primarily by means of economic sanctions. In other words, when an emergency arose Britain's panoply of expensive and invidious military bases in the Middle East proved useless. Even a British naval blockade of Iran was unnecessary. Thus the Iranian oil crisis suggests that by withdrawing from its bases Britain would not have reduced its ability to deal with troublesome nationalist movements threatening important British economic interests in the area.

As far as a Soviet military threat to the main oil-producing regions of the Middle East was concerned, it is difficult to imagine how the bases would have enabled Britain successfully to resist. After all, the Soviets were much nearer and more numerous than the British. Moreover, a Soviet threat to the Middle East would probably have occurred in conjunction with an even more dangerous Soviet threat to western Europe that would have demanded virtually all of Britain's energies and left few resources available for deployment to the Middle East.[22]

Nor were Iraqi bases necessary for an offensive air campaign against the southern part of the Soviet Union because Britain could have used bases in Cyprus for this purpose. Moreover, a Soviet attack on the Middle East would probably have brought Turkey into the war and thereby given Britain additional well-located bases.

And as far as the air route to the East was concerned, it seems likely that in exchange for a modest recompense the Iraqi government would have permitted British military aircraft to refuel in Iraq. After all, in 1950 it agreed to allow French military aircraft traveling to Indochina to refuel in Iraq.[23] In this context it is also worth noting that Britain did not retain any bases in India after that country became independent in 1947, but nonetheless the government of India permitted British military aircraft en route to the Far East to refuel in India.[24]

But even conceding the usefulness of the Iraqi bases in the event of local turmoil or a Soviet invasion, or for the air route to the East, it would have been wiser for Britain to accept a degree of military risk and logistical inconvenience in order to secure an important political advantage. In other words, by yielding the bases and not insisting upon a military alliance, Britain would have strengthened the position of its friends in Iraq by giving them a major foreign policy victory and thereby enabled them more easily to respond to their opponents' constant impugning of their nationalist credentials.

During the 1950s rising nationalism in the Middle East and continued economic weakness at home compelled the British to abandon their strategic positions in Egypt, Jordan, and Iraq. But it is not evident that Britain's security or prosperity was thereby reduced. After all, the Soviet Union did not attack the Middle East and probably never had any intention of doing so; Britain's decreased military burden probably led to increased prosperity at home; and the British oil companies, like the American ones, skillfully survived the inevitable nationalizations and today are not noticeably impecunious. Thus it would appear that Attlee was correct immediately after the war when he argued that Britain should abandon its leading role in the Middle East and withdraw gracefully from the region. Because Bevin and the Chiefs of Staff won the debate, for many years the British expended valuable resources clinging tenaciously to ultimately indefensible positions of questionable importance. And by remaining too long in places where they were not wanted, the British ensured that when their withdrawal came it would be ignominious.

Notes

NOTES TO THE INTRODUCTION

1. Doris G. Adams, "Current Population Trends in Iraq," *Middle East Journal*, vol. 10 (1956), pp. 152-54; Hanna Batatu, *The Old Social Classes and the Revolutionary Movements of Iraq: A Study of Iraq's Old Landed and Commercial Classes and of Its Communists, Bathists, and Free Officers* (Princeton, N.J., 1978), pp. 40, 1125. The census of 1947 counted 4.8 million inhabitants. However, this figure was a considerable underenumeration because many men avoided registration for fear of conscription.
2. Majid Khadduri, *Independent Iraq 1932-1958: A Study in Iraqi Politics*, 2nd ed. (London, 1960), pp. 20-21, 28, 259, 288, 364.
3. The remainder of the Introduction is based on Daniel Silverfarb, *Britain's Informal Empire in the Middle East: A Case Study of Iraq, 1929-1941* (New York, 1986), primarily chapter 12.
4. The text of this treaty, together with the annexure and all the published and unpublished letters that accompanied it, is in FO 371/27092, E1576/146/93. All of this material is reprinted in Mohammad A. Tarbush, *The Role of the Military in Politics: A Case Study of Iraq to 1941* (London, 1982), pp. 198-222. However, Tarbush inadvertently omitted article 4 of the annexure, and as a result incorrectly numbered the remaining articles. Thus in his account articles 5, 6, and 7 of the annexure are wrongly labeled as articles 4, 5, and 6.

NOTES TO CHAPTER 1

1. Report by Colonel H. L. Birks (Royal Tank Regiment), no date, in Lt.-Gen. E. P. Quinan (GOC BTI) to General Hdq. India, 23 July 1941, WO 201/1326.
2. Appreciation by General Staff and Air Staff India, 10 Sept. 1941, WO 201/1276.
3. Hdq. RAF Iraq to Hdq. Tenth Army, 4 Feb. 1942, WO 201/1325.
4. PAIC to WO, 26 Sept. 1942, AIR 20/2530.
5. WO to C-in-C PAIC, 12 Oct. 1942, AIR 20/2530.
6. IDC, 11 June 1940, Petroleum Dept. to IPC, 11 June 1940, IPC to Petroleum Dept., 12 June 1940, FO 371/24547, E2129/E2129/E2129/213/65; appreciation by CICI, 2 June 1941, WO 201/1257.
7. WO to C-in-C Middle East, 17 July 1941, FO 371/27104, E3973/1627/93; Hdq. RAF Iraq to Hdq. Tenth Army, 4 Feb. 1942, WO 201/1325; senior naval officer Persian Gulf to C-in-C East Indies, 14 June 1942, WO 201/1308.
8. WO to C-in-C Middle East, 17 July 1941, FO 371/27104, E3973/1627/93; plan by Air Hdq. RAF Iraq, 15 March 1942, AIR 23/5856.
9. Appreciation by CICI, 2 June 1941, WO 201/1257; WO to C-in-C Middle East, 17 July 1941, FO 371/27104, E3973/1627/93; report by General A. P. Wavell (C-in-C India), 18 Oct. 1942, FO 371/52341, E2219/2219/65; Lt.-Gen. H. Pownall (C-in-C PAIC) to secretary of state for war, 12 Oct. 1943, WO 32/10540.
10. Anthony Eden (foreign secretary) to Sir James Grigg (secretary of state for war), 25 April 1942, FO 371/31334, E2285/26/65; meeting in Baghdad of Transportation Priority Subcommittee, 5 May 1942, FO 371/31334, E3739/26/65; memorandum by General Sir H. Maitland Wilson (C-in-C PAIC), 17 Feb. 1943, FO 371/34968, E2804/1549/65; Pownall to secretary of state for war, 12 Oct. 1943, WO 32/10540; T. H. Vail Motter, *United States Army in World War II, The Middle East Theater: The Persian Corridor and Aid to Russia* (Washington, 1952), p. 35.

11. Pownall to secretary of state for war, 12 Oct. 1943, WO 32/10540; W. K. Hancock and M. M. Gowing, History of the Second World War, United Kingdom Civil Series: British War Economy, rev. ed. (London, 1975), p. 361.

12. Minute by P. M. Crosthwaite (Eastern Dept. of FO), 16 April 1942, FO 371/31334, E2285/26/65; meeting in Baghdad of Transportation Priority Subcommittee, 5 May 1942, FO 371/31334, E3739/26/65; Pownall to secretary of state for war, 12 Oct. 1943, WO 32/10540.

13. Appreciation by General Staff and Air Staff India, 10 Sept. 1941, WO 201/1276.

14. Wilson to R. G. Casey (minister of state in Cairo), 3 Dec. 1942, WO 32/10175. After the Anglo-Soviet occupation of Iran in August 1941 the British documents usually give troop figures for Iraq and Iran together without identifying the number in each country.

15. Memorandum by chief of the Air Staff, 17 March 1943, AIR 20/2531.

16. Appreciation by General Staff and Air Staff India, 10 Sept. 1941, WO 201/1276.

17. Hdq. BTI to Hdq. Eighth and Tenth Indian Divisions, 20 Oct. 1941, WO 201/1290.

18. Hdq. BTI to Hdq. Sixth, Eighth, and Tenth Indian Divisions and Fiftieth British Division, 17 Nov. 1941, WO 201/1291.

19. Brig.-Gen. P. L. Costeloe (financial adviser, Hdq. PAIC) to director of finance, WO, 12 Jan. 1945, FO 371/45325, E1171/903/93.

20. Air Hdq. Iraq to Sir Kinahan Cornwallis (British ambassador in Baghdad), 18 Oct. 1941, FO 624/23/345; FO to minister of state in Cairo, 26 May 1942, FO 624/29/630; Silverfarb, Informal Empire, chapter 5.

21. Thirty-two thousand was the approximate strength of the Iraqi army and the small Iraqi air force throughout 1942. As we observed in the Introduction, before the fighting in May 1941 this number had been considerably larger. Hdq. BTI to Hdq. MEF Cairo, 15 Jan. 1942, WO 201/1299; report by Maj.-Gen. D. G. Bromilow (head of the British military mission in Iraq), 31 Aug. 1942, FO 371/31366, E6144/101/93; report by Bromilow, 28 Feb. 1943, FO 371/34989, E2260/21/93.

For Britain's concern about the loyalty of the Iraqi army, see Cornwallis to Eden, 11 July 1941, FO 371/27078, E4231/1/93; memorandum by the commander of the Fifth Indian Division, 22 Sept. 1941, WO 201/1289; Brig.-Gen. A. W. S. Mallaby (WO) to Sir Horace Seymour (assistant undersecretary of state for foreign affairs), 22 Nov. 1941, FO 371/27120, E7742/7491/93; and Sir Maurice Peterson (assistant undersecretary of state for foreign affairs) to Mallaby, 31 March 1942, FO 371/31370, E1870/190/93.

The text of the armistice agreement of 31 May 1941 is in Major-General I. S. O. Playfair, History of the Second World War, United Kingdom Military Series: The Mediterranean and Middle East, vol. 2: The Germans Come to the Help of Their Ally (1941) (London, 1956), p. 332.

For the question of disbanding the Iraqi army, see minutes by Sir Orme Sargent (deputy undersecretary of state for foreign affairs), 13 March 1942, Crosthwaite, 16 March 1942, and H. A. Caccia (Eastern Dept. of FO), 16 March 1942, FO 371/31362, E1611/E1611/E1611/92/93; Peterson to Mallaby, 31 March 1942, Brig.-Gen. F. E. W. Simpson (WO) to Peterson, 14 April 1942, FO 371/31370, E1870/E2317/190/93; and G. H. Thompson (British chargé d'affaires in Baghdad) to Bromilow, 27 Jan. 1943, FO 624/32/334.

For details of a British plan to disarm the Iraqi troops at Kirkuk, see memorandum by the commander of the Fifth Indian Division, 24 Sept. 1941, WO 201/1534.

For British efforts to reduce the size of the Iraqi army, see Maj.-Gen. G. G. Waterhouse (head of the British military mission in Iraq) to Cornwallis, 7 July 1941, FO 371/27078,

E4233/1/93; A. Holman (British chargé d'affaires in Baghdad) to FO, 12 Sept. 1941, FO 371/27080, E5668/1/93; Bromilow to British embassy Baghdad, 28 Dec. 1943, FO 624/33/582.

The supply of arms to the Iraqi army is discussed briefly later in this chapter and in more detail in chapter 8.

For the deployment of the Iraqi army, see C-in-C India to WO, 17 Nov. 1941, FO 371/27120, E7680/7491/93; and C-in-C PAIC to WO, 10 Oct. 1942, AIR 20/2530.

22.   WO to C-in-C PAIC, 5 March 1943, AIR 20/2531.

23.   Note by WO, 2 Sept. 1945, AIR 20/2531.

24.   Comments by Cornwallis at a meeting of British officials at the embassy in Baghdad, no date but probably early June 1944, in memorandum by CICI, 15 June 1944, FO 624/66, part 5.

25.   Cornwallis to Eden, 9 Jan. 1945 and 30 March 1945, FO 371/45302, E608/E2431/195/93; review by Stewart Perowne (oriental counsellor, British embassy Baghdad), 6 Jan. 1947, FO 371/61588, E506/3/93; Khadduri, *Independent Iraq*, pp. 140-42; Gerald de Gaury, *Three Kings in Baghdad: 1921-1958* (London, 1961), pp. 112-14; Batatu, *Social Classes*, pp. 30, 345.

26.   Cornwallis to Eden, 12 Nov. 1943, FO 371/35013, E7407/489/93; Cornwallis to Eden, 30 March 1945, FO 371/45302, E2431/195/93; Khadduri, *Independent Iraq*, pp. 20-21, 28, 251, 272, 293-97, 364; Batatu, *Social Classes*, pp. 349-50.

The extent to which members of the Chamber of Deputies were really appointed by the government rather than elected by the people is indicated in Abd al-Karim al-Uzri's memoirs, where he reports that in 1943 he was surprised to learn that he had just been elected to the chamber, although he had not even declared himself a candidate. Abd al-Karim al-Uzri, *Tarikh fi Dhikrayat al-Iraq 1930-1958 (Iraqi Memoirs 1930-1958)* (Beirut, 1982), pp. 160-61.

27.   Khadduri, *Independent Iraq*, pp. 259, 308-9; Elie Kedourie, *The Chatham House Version and Other Middle-Eastern Studies* (New York, 1970), pp. 268-69, 303; Batatu, *Social Classes*, pp. 101, 319-20, 345, 352-53, 1115.

Indicating the extent to which a relatively small group dominated Iraqi cabinets, between 1920 and 1958 there were 59 different cabinets but only 177 men held the offices. David Pool, "The Politics of Patronage: Elites and Social Structure in Iraq" (Ph.D. dissertation at Princeton University, 1972), p. 141.

28.   Khadduri, *Independent Iraq*, p. 246.

29.   CICI to WO, 1 Sept. 1941, FO 371/27080, E5432/1/93.

30.   Cornwallis to FO, 12 Nov. 1941, FO 371/27120, E7491/7491/93; Bromilow to Hdq. BTI, 6 Feb. 1942, WO 201/1299.

Between 1941 and 1958 Nuri was the most powerful politician in Iraq. There is a biography of him by Lord Birdwood, *Nuri as-Said: A Study in Arab Leadership* (London, 1959); and an informative essay on him in Majid Khadduri, *Arab Contemporaries: The Role of Personalities in Politics* (Baltimore, 1973), pp. 19-42.

31.   Air Hdq. Iraq to Cornwallis, 18 October 1941, FO 624/23/345.

32.   Cornwallis to Eden, 11 Nov. 1941, FO 371/27082, E8023/1/93; Khadduri, *Independent Iraq*, pp. 146, 247, 249.

33.   Cornwallis to FO, 25 July 1941, FO 371/27078, E4194/1/93; memorandum by Bromilow, 14 May 1942, FO 371/31366, E3565/101/93; Khadduri, *Independent Iraq*, p. 246.

34.   Cornwallis to Eden, 11 Nov. 1941, FO 371/27082, E8023/1/93; report by Bromilow, 30 Nov. 1941, FO 371/31366, E1108/101/93; Cornwallis to Eden, 14 Dec. 1941, FO

371/31371, E258/204/93; Cornwallis to Eden, 22 Jan. 1943, FO 371/35010, E946/489/93; Khadduri, *Independent Iraq*, pp. 237-38, 249.

35. Waterhouse to British embassy Baghdad, 14 July 1941, FO 624/23/344.

36. Cornwallis to Eden, 14 Dec. 1941, FO 371/31371, E258/204/93.

37. Cornwallis to Sir Alexander Cadogan (permanent undersecretary of state for foreign affairs), 19 Feb. 1944, FO 371/40041, E1336/37/93; Cornwallis to Eden, 30 March 1945, FO 371/45302, E2431/195/93.

38. C. J. Edmonds (adviser to the Iraqi Ministry of Interior), to Cornwallis, 27 July 1941, Edmonds Papers, box 3, file 1; minute by Peterson, 10 Nov. 1943, FO 371/34992, E6990/44/93; Cornwallis to Eden, 19 March 1945, FO 371/45302, E2177/195/93.

39. Cornwallis to FO, 20 June 1941 and 20 June 1941, FO 371/27076, E3238/E3254/1/93; C. W. Baxter (head of the Eastern Dept. of FO) to J. Skliros (IPC), 8 July 1941, FO 371/27077, E3554/1/93; Cornwallis to Eden, 11 Nov. 1941, FO 371/27082, E8023/1/93. In 1944 there were sixteen British officials in the political advisory organization. These sixteen consisted of political advisers, assistant political advisers, and deputy assistant political advisers. Cornwallis to Nuri, 5 Jan. 1944, FO 624/35/1.

40. Edmonds to Cornwallis, 31 Oct. 1944, Edmonds Papers, box 3, file 1.

41. C-in-C Middle East to WO, 24 June 1941, FO 371/27076, E3342/1/93; Air Vice-Marshal J. H. D'Albiac (AOC Iraq) to Cornwallis, 2 Sept. 1941, FO 624/24/474.

42. Minute by Peterson, 16 Nov. 1942, FO 371/31370, E6664/190/93; Cornwallis to FO, 7 Jan. 1943, FO 371/34996, E183/103/93; Cornwallis to Eden, 8 Feb. 1944, FO 371/40041, E1143/37/93; Khadduri, *Independent Iraq*, pp. 333-34.

43. Cornwallis to FO, 9 Feb. 1943, FO 371/34997, E835/103/93.

44. Thompson to FO, 6 Sept. 1943 and 7 Sept. 1943, FO 371/34998, E5377/E5377/103/93.

45. For Britain's rejection of Nuri's February 1943 offer, see C-in-C PAIC to WO, 8 Feb. 1943 and 23 Feb. 1943, FO 371/34997, E821/E915/103/93; Cornwallis to FO, 9 Feb. 1943, WO to C-in-C PAIC, 12 Feb. 1943, FO 371/34997, E835/E915/103/93; WO to FO, 26 Feb. 1943, FO to British embassy Baghdad, 27 Feb. 1943, FO 371/34998, E1169/E1169/103/93.

For Britain's rejection of Nuri's September 1943 offer, see Thompson to FO, 6 Sept. 1943 and 7 Sept. 1943, FO 371/34998, E5377/E5377/103/93; R. M. A. Hankey (Eastern Dept. of FO) to Simpson, 11 Sept. 1943, FO 371/34998, E5377/103/93; C-in-C PAIC to WO, 20 Sept. 1943 and 23 Sept. 1943, FO 371/34998, E6061/E6061/103/93; T. J. Cowen (WO) to Hankey, 25 Sept. 1943, FO 371/34998, E5755/103/93.

NOTES TO CHAPTER 2

1. Stephen H. Longrigg, *Oil in the Middle East: Its Discovery and Development*, 3rd ed. (London, 1968), pp. 76-78; Benjamin Shwadran, *The Middle East, Oil and the Great Powers*, 3rd ed. (New York, 1973), pp. 240-42.

2. Longrigg, *Oil*, pp. 79-82; Shwadran, *Oil*, pp. 239, 250.

3. Longrigg, *Oil*, pp. 66-67; Shwadran, *Oil*, pp. 240, 242.

4. Silverfarb, *Informal Empire*, p. 103.

5. C-in-C Middle East to WO, 15 April 1941, AIR 8/497; Lindemann to Churchill, 28 April 1941, minute by Churchill, 29 April 1941, CAB 80/27, COS(41)270; minutes of COS, 30 April 1941, CAB 79/11, COS(41)153.

6. C-in-C Middle East to WO, 15 April 1941, report by JPS, 2 May 1941, WO to C-in-C Middle East, 2 May 1941, AIR 8/497; minutes of Defence Committee, 5 June 1941, CAB 69/2, DO(41)39.

7. Note by Maj.-Gen. H. L. Ismay, 22 May 1941, CAB 80/28, COS(41)323; minutes of COS, 23 May 1941, CAB 79/11, COS(41)18; COS to C-in-C Middle East, 24 May 1941, AIR 8/497.
8. C-in-C Middle East to WO, 28 May 1941, AIR 8/497.
9. Minutes of Defence Committee, 5 June 1941, CAB 69/2, DO(41)39; WO to C-in-C Middle East, 6 June 1941, WO 201/1519.
10. C-in-C Middle East to WO, 8 June 1941, AIR 8/497; Hdq. MEF to GOC British Forces in Palestine and Transjordan, 8 June 1941, memorandum by Lt.-Col. Jacques (RE Tenth Indian Division), 15 June 1941, WO 201/1431.
11. WO to C-in-C Middle East, 10 June 1941, AIR 8/497; memorandum by Jacques, 15 June 1941, WO 201/1431.
12. IPC to Maj.-Gen. RE Tenth Army, 25 July 1942, WO 201/1519; C-in-C India to WO, 26 Aug. 1941, AIR 8/497.
The British junking operations at Kirkuk were so thorough that after the war all of the junked wells were written off as possible sources of production. Memorandum by Victor von Lossberg (commercial attaché, U.S. embassy Baghdad), 28 May 1947, in George Wadsworth (U.S. ambassador in Baghdad) to secretary of state, 28 May 1947, 890G.6363/5-2847.
13. Meeting in Baghdad of leading British army officers, civilian officials, and oil company representatives, 2 July 1941, WO 201/1519; C-in-C India to WO, 29 July 1941 and 26 Aug. 1941, AIR 8/497.
14. Sir Leslie Hollis (Office of the War Cabinet) to the chief of the Air Staff, 10 May 1941, AIR 8/549.
15. Meeting in Baghdad of leading British army officers, civilian officials, and oil company representatives, 2 July 1941, WO 201/1519.
16. Reports by Hdq. Tenth Army, 8 April 1942, 6 May 1942, and 4 June 1942, WO 201/1340.
17. Hdq. MEF to commander Tenth Army, 9 March 1942, WO 201/1520.
18. Hdq. Tenth Army to G (Ops.), 6 July 1942, commander Tenth Army to British embassy Baghdad, 8 Aug. 1942, WO 201/1340.
19. Instructions to demolition parties by Hdq. MEF, 6 Sept. 1942, WO 201/1466.
20. Hdq. Tenth Army to Major A. E. L. Crosthwait (RE), 4 July 1942, WO 201/1340; The Petroleum Times, 22 May 1948, p. 521.
21. Note by Lt.-Col. C. Hubert (Hdq. MEF), 16 Nov. 1941, WO 201/2113; Tenth Army Operation Instructions, 27 June 1942 and 28 July 1942, WO 201/1450.
22. Meeting in Baghdad of leading British officers from the Tenth Army, 6 March 1942, Tenth Army Operation Instruction, 27 June 1942, WO 201/1450; Hdq. PAIC Operation Instruction, 6 Jan. 1943, WO 201/1532.
23. Carson to Second Indian Division, 27 Aug. 1942, WO 201/1514.
24. Meeting in Baghdad of leading British officers from the Tenth Army, 6 March 1942, WO 201/1450; Hdq. Tenth Army to British embassy Baghdad, 21 June 1942, WO 201/1514; Tenth Army Operation Instruction, 27 June 1942, commander Tenth Army to Cornwallis, 3 July 1942, Tenth Army Operation Instruction, 28 July 1942, WO 201/1450; Hdq. PAIC Operation Instruction, 6 Jan. 1943, WO 201/1532.
25. Tenth Army Operation Instruction, 27 June 1942, meeting in Cairo of leading British army officers, 16 July 1942, WO 201/1450.
26. Hdq. BTI to Hdq. Eighth and Tenth Indian Divisions, 3 October 1941, WO 201/1289; Hdq. BTI to commanders Sixth, Eighth, and Tenth Indian Divisions, 28 Oct. 1941, WO

201/1291; appreciation by chief RE Tenth Indian Division, 5 Nov. 1941, WO 201/1287; Hdq. BTI to Tenth Indian Division, 28 Nov. 1941, WO 201/1291.

27.   Hdq. MEF to Tenth Army, 4 June 1942, WO 201/2113; Hdq. Tenth Army to British embassy Baghdad, 21 June 1942, WO 201/1514; meeting in Cairo of leading British army officers, 16 July 1942, WO 201/1450; Hdq. PAIC Operation Instruction, 6 Jan. 1943, WO 201/1532.

28.   Hdq. MEF to Tenth Army, 4 June 1942, WO 201/2113; Hdq. Tenth Army to British embassy Baghdad, 21 June 1942, Tenth Army Operation Instruction, 27 June 1942, meeting in Cairo of leading British army officers, 16 July 1942, WO 201/1450.
The famine in Lebanon and elsewhere in greater Syria during the First World War is discussed in George Antonius, *The Arab Awakening: The Story of the Arab National Movement* (London, 1938), pp. 240-42; and L. Schatkowski Schilcher, "The Famine of 1915-1918 in Greater Syria," in John P. Spagnolo (ed.), *Problems of the Modern Middle East in Historical Perspective: Essays in Honour of Albert Hourani* (Reading, 1992), pp. 229-58.

29.   Hdq. BTI to Tenth Indian Division, 22 June 1941, WO 201/1431; FO to Cornwallis, 18 Feb. 1942, WO 201/1432; meeting in Baghdad of leading British officers from the Tenth Army, 6 March 1942, WO 201/1450; commander Tenth Army to M. M. Stuckey (general manager IPC), 11 Aug. 1942, WO 201/1340; Hdq. PAIC to Tenth Army, 19 Nov. 1942, WO 201/1369.

30.   Commander Tenth Army to Cornwallis, 3 July 1942, WO 201/1450.

31.   Memorandum by Bill Orgill (IPC), 23 June 1941, WO 201/1519; FO to Cornwallis, 18 Feb. 1942, WO 201/1432; meeting in Baghdad of leading British army officers, civilian officials, and oil company representatives, 11 July 1942, WO 201/1340.

32.   For Lebanon, Syria, and the Free French, see meeting in Cairo of leading British army officers, 16 July 1942, WO 201/1450. For Iran, see meeting in Baghdad of leading British army officers, civilian officials, and oil company representatives, 11 July 1942, WO 201/1340. There is also information about oil denial in Iran in WO 201/1354 and L/P&S/12/3949. For Saudi Arabia, see Daniel Silverfarb, "Britain, the United States, and the Security of the Saudi Arabian Oilfields in 1942," *The Historical Journal,* vol. 26 (1983), pp. 719-26. In Saudi Arabia the British were handicapped because they did not have any troops stationed in the country, and the American-owned oil company that held the concession was uncooperative. For Kuwait, see WO 201/1327, WO 201/2108, L/P&S/12/3949, and L/P&S/12/3960. For Bahrain, see L/P&S/12/3949, L/P&S/12/3960, and R/15/2/662. For Qatar, see L/P&S/12/3949, L/P&S/12/3959, and R/15/2/729.

33.   Minister of state in Cairo to FO, 5 July 1942, WO 201/2107.

34.   Commander Second Indian Division to Hdq. PAIC, 31 March 1943, WO 201/1531.

NOTES TO CHAPTER 3

1.   Paper by the secretariat of the MEFC in Cairo, "Notes and Statistics Relating to Inflation in the Middle East" (hereafter referred to as "Notes"), no date but probably May 1944, FO 921/235.

2.   Ibid.

3.   Paper by C. E. Loombe (commercial counsellor, British embassy Baghdad) for the MEFC, "Currency and Banking Iraq, part 1: Currency" (hereafter referred to as "Currency"), no date but probably May 1944, FO 371/40053, E3383/79/93; Carl Iversen, *A Report on Monetary Policy in Iraq* (Copenhagen, 1954), p. 5.

4.   Loombe, "Currency."

5.   MEFC, "Notes"; Cornwallis to Eden, 9 Jan. 1945, FO 371/45302, E608/195/93.

6. MEFC, "Notes"; Loombe, "Currency"; memorandum by E. R. Lingeman (commercial counsellor, British embassy Baghdad), 26 Oct. 1944, FO 624/39/574.

7. Report by Loombe on economic conditions in Iraq, 23 July 1943, FO 371/35022, E4622/313/93; Thompson to Eden, 12 Sept. 1943, FO 371/35012, E5797/489/93; MEFC, "Notes."

8. Note by the Iraqi Ministry of Finance on Iraq's requirements from its sterling balances, no date but probably about 30 June 1947, T 236/1190.

9. Comments by the British embassy in Baghdad on the Iraqi Inflation Committee report of 11 Nov. 1942, no date, in Cornwallis to Eden, 19 Jan. 1943, FO 624/32/297; Cornwallis to Abdul Illah Hafidh (Iraqi foreign minister), 4 March 1943, FO 624/33/534; memorandum by G. C. Pelham (commercial counsellor, British embassy Baghdad) on the standard of living in Iraq, no date, in Sir Hugh Stonehewer-Bird (British ambassador in Baghdad) to Ernest Bevin (foreign secretary), 13 March 1947, FO 371/61648, E2466/453/93.

10. Cornwallis to Eden, 23 June 1944, FO 371/40057, E3823/193/93. See also Cornwallis to FO, 5 March 1943, FO 371/35006, E1313/430/93; and Cornwallis to Eden, 5 June 1943, FO 371/35010, E3585/489/93.

11. A. R. Prest, War Economies of Primary Producing Countries (Cambridge, 1948), p. 213.

12. Comments by the British embassy in Baghdad on the Iraqi Inflation Committee report of 11 Nov. 1942, no date, in Cornwallis to Eden, 19 Jan. 1943, FO 624/32/297; Alexander Cadogan (permanent undersecretary of state for foreign affairs) to Cornwallis, 24 Jan. 1944, FO 371/40041, E345/37/93; paper by L. M. Swan (adviser to the Iraqi Ministry of Finance) for the MEFC, "Taxation Iraq," no date but probably May 1944, FO 371/40053, E3383/79/93; MEFC, "Notes."

13. Report of the Iraqi Inflation Committee, 11 Nov. 1942, comments by the British embassy in Baghdad on this report, no date, in Cornwallis to Eden, 19 Jan. 1943, FO 624/32/297; Stonehewer-Bird to Bevin, 4 March 1946, FO 371/52423, E2469/652/93; Prest, War Economies, pp. 214, 219; Joseph Sassoon, Economic Policy in Iraq: 1932-1950 (London, 1987), p. 95.

14. Cornwallis to Eden, 13 Jan. 1944, FO 371/40041, E519/37/93; Office of the Minister of State in Cairo, "Middle East Economic and Statistical Bulletin" (hereafter referred to as "Bulletin"), Jan. 1944, FO 921/235; paper by Col. Bayliss (director general of imports in Iraq) for the MEFC, "Prices and Distribution Iraq" (hereafter referred to as "Prices"), no date but probably May 1944, FO 371/40053, E3818/79/93.

15. Cornwallis to Eden, 23 March 1944, FO 371/40041, E2113/37/93; Bayliss, "Prices"; paper by Loombe for the MEFC, "General Economic Position Iraq" (hereafter referred to as "Position"), no date but probably May 1944, FO 371/40053, E3383/79/93; E. M. H. Lloyd, Food and Inflation in the Middle East: 1940-45 (Stanford, Calif., 1956), pp. 237-38.

16. Cornwallis to Eden, 13 Jan. 1944 and 8 Feb. 1944, FO 371/40041, E519/E1143/37/93.

17. Cornwallis to Eden, 13 Jan. 1944, Cornwallis to FO, 27 Jan. 1944, FO 371/40041, E519/E649/37/93; memorandum by Chaplin, 12 Jan. 1944, FO 371/40041, E345/37/93.

18. Thompson to Eden, 12 Sept. 1943, FO 371/35012, E5797/489/93; Cornwallis to Eden, 13 Jan. 1944, FO 371/40041, E519/37/93; Bayliss, "Prices"; Loombe, "Position."

19. Office of the Minister of State, "Bulletin"; Cornwallis to Eden, 23 March 1944, FO 371/40041, E2113/37/93; Loombe, "Position"; Cornwallis to Eden, 8 June 1944, FO 371/40042, E3640/37/93.

20. Cornwallis to Eden, 2 Aug. 1942, Thompson to FO, 24 Nov. 1942, Cornwallis to FO, 17 Dec. 1942, FO 371/31371, E4722/E6975/E7414/204/93; Cornwallis to Eden, 6 Nov. 1943, FO 371/35013, E7266/489/93.

21. Report of the Iraqi Inflation Committee, 11 Nov. 1942, FO 624/32/297; Cornwallis to Eden, 9 Jan. 1945, FO 371/45302, E608/195/93; Iraqi Ministry of Economics calculation of the laborers cost of living index, no date but probably March 1947, FO 371/61648; E2466/453/93; statement by Salih Haidar (Iraqi Ministry of Finance) at a meeting of British and Iraqi officials in London, 27 June 1947, T 236/1190.
22. Thompson to Eden, 26 July 1943, FO 371/35011, E4699/489/93.
23. Thompson to Eden, 27 July 1944, FO 371/40058, E4877/193/93.
24. Review by P. F. Hancock (second secretary, British embassy Baghdad), no date, in Cornwallis to Eden, 9 Jan. 1945, FO 371/45302, E608/195/93.
25. Thompson to Eden, 26 July 1943, FO 371/35011, E4699/489/93; Loombe, "Position"; Stonehewer-Bird to Eden, 2 June 1945, FO 371/45302, E4269/195/93.
26. Report of the Iraqi Inflation Committee, 11 Nov. 1942, FO 624/32/297; Cornwallis to Eden, 21 Feb. 1943, FO 371/35010, E1667/489/93; Loombe, "Position."
27. Cornwallis to Eden, 6 Nov. 1943, FO 371/35013, E7266/489/93.
28. Cornwallis to Eden, 19 Jan. 1943, FO 624/32/297; Lord Moyne (minister of state in Cairo) to Cornwallis, 17 May 1944, FO 624/37/429.
29. Report of the Iraqi Inflation Committee, 11 Nov. 1942, FO 624/32/297.
30. I have treated the entire question of the production and export of Iraqi barley during the Second World War in a forthcoming article in *Middle Eastern Studies.*
31. Cornwallis to Eden, 8 Feb. 1944, FO 371/40041, E1143/37/93; report by the Minister of State's Office in Cairo on gold sales in the Middle East, 20 March 1944, FO 921/254; MEFC, "Notes"; Thompson to Eden, 14 Aug. 1944, FO 371/40042, E5285/37/93; Sassoon, *Economic Policy,* pp. 120-22.
   Incidentally, the British made a profit on these sales because they bought the gold in South Africa at the official price and sold it in Iraq at the free market price, which was more than twice as high. Report by John Walker (commercial counsellor, British embassy Baghdad), 7 Feb. 1944, British high commissioner in South Africa to Dominions Office, 31 March 1944, FO 921/254; H. A. Shannon, "The Sterling Balances of the Sterling Area 1939-49," *The Economic Journal,* vol. 60 (1950), p. 536.
32. Paper by Loombe for the MEFC, "Loans and Savings Iraq," no date but probably May 1944, FO 371/40053, E3383/79/93; memorandum by Loombe, 27 March 1945, T 236/1178.
33. Cornwallis to Eden, 28 March 1943, FO 371/35010, E2239/489/93; Cornwallis to FO, 2 Nov. 1943, FO 371/35012, E6698/489/93; Thompson to Eden, 27 July 1944, FO 371/40058, E4877/193/93.
34. In January 1944, in Iraq the wholesale price index stood at 614 (100 being the prewar level), while in Egypt it was 295.4 and in Palestine it was 341. MEFC, "Notes."

NOTES TO CHAPTER 4

1. Batatu, *Social Classes,* p. 40.
2. The Kurds are discussed in Wadie Jwaideh, "The Kurdish Nationalist Movement: Its Origins and Development" (Ph.D. dissertation at Syracuse University, 1960); Hassan Arfa, *The Kurds: An Historical and Political Study* (London, 1966); Martin van Bruinessen, *Agha, Shaikh and State: On the Social and Political Organization of Kurdistan* (Utrecht, 1978); and Mehrdad R. Izady, *The Kurds: A Concise Handbook* (Washington, 1992).
3. C. J. Edmonds (adviser to the Iraqi Ministry of Interior) to Cornwallis, 24 Nov. 1943 and 14 March 1944, Edmonds Papers, box 3, file 1; Stephen H. Longrigg, *Iraq, 1900 to 1950: A Political, Social, and Economic History* (London, 1953), p. 326.

According to the United States minister in Baghdad, one of the members of this group, Ahmad Mukhtar Baban, could not even speak Kurdish. Thomas M. Wilson to secretary of state, 17 Feb. 1943, 890G.00/655.

4. Note by Edmonds, 27 July 1941, FO 624/60, part 2.

5. Lt.-Col. W. A. Lyon (political adviser, northern area) to Cornwallis, 4 Jan. 1944, FO 624/66, part 1; Longrigg, *Iraq*, p. 326.

6. Note by Edmonds, 24 June 1941, Edmonds Papers, box 3, file 2; Lyon to Cornwallis, 19 June 1942, FO 624/27/42; Edmonds to Cornwallis, 23 Dec. 1944, Edmonds Papers, box 3, file 1.

7. Loy W. Henderson (U.S. minister in Baghdad) to secretary of state, 4 Feb. 1944, 890G.4016 KURDS/23.

8. Report by CICI, "A Review of the Economic situation in the Frontier Districts of Kurdistan, May-June 1943," no date but probably July 1943, in Daniel Gaudin (U.S. chargé d'affaires in Baghdad) to secretary of state, 23 July 1943, 890G.00/664.

9. Cornwallis to Eden, 23 March 1944, FO 371/40041, E2113/37/93; memorandum by *mutasarrif* of Mosul, 15 May 1944, FO 624/66, part 4; Cornwallis to Eden, 8 June 1944, FO 371/40042, E3640/37/93.

10. Lyon to Cornwallis, 19 June 1942, FO 624/27/42.

11. Report by CICI, "A Review of the Economic Situation in the Frontier Districts of Kurdistan, May-June 1943," no date but probably July 1943, in Gaudin to secretary of state, 23 July 1943, 890G.00/664.

12. Cornwallis to Eden, 16 Oct. 1943, FO 371/35012, E6499/489/93.

13. K. J. Ritchie (adviser to the Iraqi Ministry of Education) to V. Holt (oriental counsellor, British embassy Baghdad), 16 May 1944, FO 624/39/561, part 1.

14. James S. Moose (U.S. chargé d'affaires in Baghdad) to secretary of state, 26 Nov. 1945, 890G.50/11-2645.

15. Lyon to Cornwallis, 4 Jan. 1944, FO 624/66, part 1.

16. Ritchie to Holt, 16 May 1944, FO 624/39/561, part 1.

17. Edmonds to Cornwallis, 5 Dec. 1944, Edmonds Papers, box 3, file 1.

18. Pool, "Politics of Patronage," pp. 237-38.

19. Adams, "Population Trends," p. 165.

20. Pool, "Politics of Patronage," p. 237.

21. Note by Edmonds, 24 June 1941, Edmonds Papers, box 3, file 2.

22. Minute by Perowne, 20 June 1945, FO 624/71, part 5.

23. Ritchie to the Iraqi minister of education, 14 March 1944, FO 624/39/561, part 1.

24. Ritchie to Holt, 16 May 1944, FO 624/39/561, part 1; Edmonds to Cornwallis, 5 Dec. 1944, Edmonds Papers, box 3, file 1; Yitzhak Nakash, *The Shiis of Iraq* (Princeton, N.J., 1994), pp. 125-26.

25. Minute by Perowne, 20 June 1945, FO 624/71, part 5.

26. Lyon to Holt, 12 Feb. 1943, FO 624/33/411.

27. Major John Stebbing (area liaison officer) to Captain C. Hohler (CICI), 8 Nov. 1944, in Lyon to Perowne, 13 Nov. 1944, FO 624/66, part 9.

28. Sir Francis Humphrys (British ambassador in Baghdad) to Sir John Simon (foreign secretary), 9 Feb. 1933, FO 371/16913, E968/502/93; Jwaideh, "Kurdish Nationalist Movement," pp. 641-88.

29. Cornwallis to Eden, 8 Feb. 1944, FO 371/40041, E1143/37/93; report by Maj.-Gen. D. G. Bromilow (head of the British military mission in Iraq), 31 March 1944, FO 371/40044, E2580/42/93; Jwaideh, "Kurdish Nationalist Movement," pp. 671-76.

30. Note by WO, 4 Nov. 1943, WO 106/5708; Cornwallis to Eden, 13 Jan. 1944 and 8 Feb. 1944, FO 371/40041, E519/E1143/37/93; report by Bromilow, 31 March 1944, FO 371/40044, E2580/42/93.
31. Note by WO, 4 Nov. 1943, WO 106/5708; Cornwallis to Eden, 12 Nov. 1943, FO 371/35013, E7407/489/93; report by Bromilow, 31 March 1944, FO 371/40044, E2580/42/93.
32. Edmonds to Cornwallis, 10 Dec. 1943, Edmonds Papers, box 3, file 1; Cornwallis to Eden, 13 Jan. 1944, FO 371/40041, E519/37/93.
33. Cornwallis to Eden, 13 Jan. 1944, FO 371/40041, E519/37/93.
34. Cornwallis to FO, 28 June 1941, FO 371/27077, E3422/1/93; Cornwallis to Eden, 16 Oct. 1943, FO 371/35012, E6499/489/93; Edmonds to Cornwallis, 10 Dec. 1943, Edmonds Papers, box 3, file 1.
35. Cornwallis to FO, 13 Dec. 1943 and 16 Dec. 1943, FO 371/35013, E7823/E7889/489/93; Cornwallis to FO, 31 Dec. 1943, FO 371/40038, E26/26/93.
36. Report by Bromilow, 31 March 1944, FO 371/40044, E2580/42/93; Gaudin to secretary of state, 19 Oct. 1943, 890G.00/671.
37. FO to Baghdad, 13 Dec. 1943, FO 371/35013, E7769/489/93; Cornwallis to Eden, 13 Jan. 1944 and 8 Feb. 1944, FO 371/40041, E519/E1143/37/93.
38. Cornwallis to Eden, 8 Feb. 1944, FO 371/40041, E1143/37/93; report by CICI, 22 Feb. 1944, AIR 24/851.
39. Report by CICI, 23 Oct. 1944, FO 624/66, part 8; Jwaideh, "Kurdish Nationalist Movement," p. 680.
40. Edmonds to Cornwallis, 10 Nov. 1943, Edmonds Papers, box 3, file 1; Cornwallis to Eden, 8 Feb. 1944, FO 371/40041, E1143/37/93; Major E. A. Kinch (officiating political adviser, northern area) to Cornwallis, 6 March 1944, FO 624/66, part 1; report by CICI, 23 Oct. 1944, FO 624/66, part 8.
41. Cornwallis to Eden, 8 Feb. 1944 and 23 March 1944, FO 371/40041, E1143/E2113/37/93; report by CICI, 22 Feb. 1944, AIR 24/851.
42. Cornwallis to Eden, 23 March 1944, FO 371/40041, E2113/37/93; report by CICI, 23 Oct. 1944, FO 624/66, part 8.
43. Report by CICI, 23 Oct. 1944, FO 624/66, part 8.
44. Ibid.
45. Ibid.
46. Intelligence summary by CICI, 29 Feb. 1944, AIR 24/851; Holt to Cornwallis, 9 March 1944, FO 624/67, part 3; Cornwallis to Eden, 8 June 1944, FO 371/40042, E3640/37/93; report by CICI, 23 Oct. 1944, FO 624/66, part 8.
47. Edmonds to Cornwallis, 14 March 1944, Edmonds Papers, box 3, file 1; report by CICI, 23 Oct. 1944, FO 624/66, part 8.
48. Cornwallis to FO, 13 Feb. 1944, Cornwallis to Eden, 23 March 1944, FO 371/40041, E1013/E2113/37/93; Edmonds to Cornwallis, 14 March 1944, Edmonds Papers, box 3, file 1.
49. Cornwallis to Eden, 8 June 1944, FO 371/40042, E3640/37/93; report by CICI, 23 Oct. 1944, FO 624/66, part 8.
50. Cornwallis to Eden, 8 June 1944, FO 371/40042, E3640/37/93; report by CICI, 23 Oct. 1944, FO 624/66, part 8; Edmonds to British embassy Baghdad, 10 Dec. 1944, FO 624/66, part 10.
51. Cornwallis to Eden, 8 June 1944, FO 371/44042, E3640/37/93; report by CICI, 23 Oct. 1944, FO 624/66, part 8.

52. Edmonds to Cornwallis, 27 June 1944, Edmonds Papers, box 3, file 1; Kinch to Thompson, 28 July 1944, FO 624/66, part 5; Lyon to Holt, 29 Aug. 1944, Edmonds Papers, box 3, file 1; report by CICI, 23 Oct. 1944, FO 624/66, part 8.

53. Intelligence summary by CICI, 3 Oct. 1944, AIR 24/855; report by CICI, 23 Oct. 1944, FO 624/66, part 8.

54. Renton to Tahsin Ali, 8 July 1944, FO 371/40044, E4439/42/93.

55. Memorandum by CICI, 15 June 1944, FO 624/66, part 5; Thompson to Eden, 14 Aug. 1944, Cornwallis to Eden, 31 Oct. 1944, FO 371/40042, E5285/E7011/37/93.

56. Thompson to Eden, 14 Aug. 1944, FO 371/40042, E5285/37/93; report by CICI, 23 Oct. 1944, FO 624/66, part 8; Moore (assistant political adviser, northern area) to Major R. Wilson (officiating political adviser, northern area), 29 April 1945, FO 624/71, part 4.

57. Report by CICI, 23 Oct. 1944, FO 624/66, part 8; Cornwallis to Eden, 31 Oct. 1944, FO 371/40042, E7011/37/93; Lyon to Perowne, 13 Nov. 1944, FO 624/66, part 9; Lyon to Holt, 19 Dec. 1944, FO 624/66, part 11; Moore to Wilson, 29 April 1945, FO 624/71, part 4; Lt.-Col. R. Mead (political adviser, northern area) to Perowne, 24 May 1945, FO 624/71, part 5.

58. Cornwallis to Eden, 9 Jan. 1945, FO 371/45302, E608/195/93; Moore to Wilson, 29 April 1945, FO 624/71, part 4; Mead to Perowne, 24 May 1945, FO 624/71, part 5; Said Qazzaz (*mutasarrif* of Arbil) to Iraqi Ministry of Interior, 31 July 1945, FO 624/71, part 6.

59. Conference in Baghdad of the regent, four leading Iraqi ministers, the chief of the Iraqi General Staff, and the head of the British military mission, 7 Dec. 1944, FO 624/66, part 11; Wilson to British embassy Baghdad, 8 March 1945, FO 624/71, part 2; Mead to Perowne, 11 June 1945, FO 624/71, part 5.

60. Captain F. Stoakes (deputy assistant political adviser, northern area) to Wilson, 17 March 1945, FO 624/71, part 2; A. H. Ditchburn (adviser to the Iraqi Ministry of Interior) to British embassy Baghdad, 6 Aug. 1945, FO 624/71, part 6; conversation between Ismail Namiq (Iraqi minister of defense) and Major P. A. Uniacke (British military mission), 11 Aug. 1945, FO 624/71, part 6; review by CICI, 15 Aug. 1945, FO 624/71, part 7.

61. Meeting in Baghdad of Salih Jabr (acting prime minister), Ismail Namiq, the chief of the Iraqi General Staff, and leading British officials in Iraq, 10 Aug. 1945, FO 624/71, part 6; conversation between Ismail Namiq and Uniacke, 11 Aug. 1945, FO 624/71, part 6; memorandum by Renton, 14 Aug. 1945, FO 624/71, part 7; meeting of leading Iraqi ministers and army officers, 23 Sept. 1945, FO 624/84, part 2.

62. Renton to British embassy Baghdad, 3 Sept. 1945, FO 624/71, part 8; Thompson to FO, 4 Sept. 1945, FO 624/71, part 9; report by Renton, 31 March 1946, FO 371/52422, E4145/649/93.

63. Report by CICI, 19 Aug. 1945, FO 624/71, part 7; C-in-C PAIC to C-in-C MEF, 23 Aug. 1945, FO 371/45340, E6013/2199/93; report by Renton, 31 March 1946, FO 371/52422, E4145/649/93.

64. Memorandum by Renton, 22 Sept. 1945, FO 624/84, part 2; report by Renton, 30 Sept. 1945, FO 371/45342, E7939/2435/93; report by Renton, 31 March 1946, FO 371/52422, E4145/649/93.

65. Report by Renton, 30 Sept. 1945, FO 371/45342, E7939/2435/93.

66. Ibid.

67. Ibid.

68. Ibid.; Stonehewer-Bird to FO, 10 Oct. 1945, FO 371/45342, E7939/2435/93; Stonehewer-Bird to Bevin, 4 March 1946, FO 371/52423, E2469/652/93; report by Renton, 31 March 1946, FO 371/52422, E4145/649/93; Archie Roosevelt Jr., "The

Kurdish Republic of Mahabad," *The Middle East Journal*, vol. I (1947), p. 256. The quotation is in Stonehewer-Bird to FO, 10 Oct. 1945.

69. Renton to Ismail Namiq, 7 Sept. 1945, FO 624/84, part 2; report by Renton, 30 Sept. 1945, FO 371/45342, E7939/2435/93; report by Wing-Commander R. M. Bradley (inspector of the Iraqi air force), 30 Sept. 1945, FO 371/45330, E9531/1393/93; report by Renton, 31 March 1946, FO 371/52422, E4145/649/93. The figures for Iraqi air force activity, which are in Bradley's report, are understatements because they only cover the period until 19 September while hostilities lasted until 10 October. I do not have figures for the period after 19 September.
70. Thompson to FO, 1 Aug. 1945, FO 371/45340, E5687/2199/93.
71. Cornwallis to Eden, 15 Jan. 1945, FO 371/45302, E627/195/93.
72. Stonehewer-Bird to FO, 10 Oct. 1945, FO 371/45342, E7939/2435/93.
73. Thompson to FO, 7 Aug. 1945, FO 371/45340, E5787/2199/93.
74. Perowne to Stonehewer-Bird, 8 April 1945, FO 624/71, part 3.
75. This quotation is in Moose to secretary of state, 23 Aug. 1945, 890G.4016 KURDS/8-2345.
76. Ditchburn to British embassy Baghdad, 6 Aug. 1945, FO 624/71, part 6.
77. FO to Clement Attlee (prime minister), 16 Aug. 1945, FO 371/45340, E5942/2199/93.
78. Wing-Commander H. Dawson-Shephard (head of CICI) to area liaison officers Mosul, Arbil, and Sulaimaniya, 13 Aug. 1945, FO 624/71, part 9; Thompson to Mead, 20 Aug. 1945, FO 624/71, part 7; Lt.-Gen. Sir Arthur Smith (C-in-C PAIC) to WO, 25 Aug. 1945, FO 624/71, part 8; report by Renton, 30 Sept. 1945, FO 371/45342, E7939/2435/93.
79. Dawson-Shephard to area liaison officers Mosul, Arbil, and Sulaimaniya, 13 Aug. 1945, FO 624/71, part 9; Major R. Wilson (assistant political adviser, northern area) to Mead, 13 Aug. 1945, FO 624/71, part 7; Thompson to Mead, 20 Aug. 1945, FO 624/71, part 7; Mead to Perowne, 27 Sept. 1945, FO 624/71, part 11.
80. Smith to WO, 25 Aug. 1945, FO 624/71, part 8; Renton to British embassy Baghdad, 3 Sept. 1945, FO 624/71, part 8; report by Renton, 30 Sept. 1945, FO 371/45342, E7939/2435/93.
81. Report by Bradley, 30 Sept. 1945, FO 371/45330, E9531/1393/93.
82. Memorandum by Renton, 4 Aug. 1947, FO 371/61593, E7401/3/93.
83. Thompson to FO, 12 Sept. 1945, FO 371/45341, E6786/2199/93.
84. Silverfarb, *Informal Empire*, pp. 42-44.
85. Ibid., pp. 81-83.
86. I am treating this question in a separate article.
87. Cornwallis to FO, 13 Dec. 1943, FO 371/35013, E7823/489/93; intelligence summary by CICI, 29 Feb. 1944, AIR 24/851; Cornwallis to FO, 6 March 1944, FO 371/40041, E1495/37/93; report by CICI, 23 Oct. 1944, FO 624/66, part 8; Edmonds to Cornwallis, 5 Dec. 1944 and 23 Dec. 1944, Edmonds Papers, box 3, file 1; Stonehewer-Bird to Eden, 3 May 1945, FO 371/45346, E3229/3229/93.
88. Cornwallis to Eden, 2 July 1944, FO 371/40038, E4117/26/93; Thompson to Eden, 10 Sept. 1944, FO 371/40039, E5841/26/93; R. A. Beaumont (British consul, Mosul) to J. C. B. Richmond (oriental counsellor, British embassy Baghdad), 7 July 1947, minute by Richmond, 19 July 1947, minute by M. T. Walker (Eastern Dept. of FO), 17 July 1947, FO 624/114, part 2.
89. For the turning of the Kurds against Britain and toward the Soviet Union, see Mead to Perowne, 23 Nov. 1945, FO 624/71, part 12; Stonehewer-Bird to Bevin, 4 March 1946, FO 371/52423, E2469/652/93; and Longrigg, *Iraq*, p. 353. For the Iraqi Communist

party's opposition to the government's attack on Mulla Mustapha in September 1945, see their leaflet, no date but probably about 14 Sept. 1945, in CICI to British embassy Baghdad, 15 Sept. 1945, FO 624/71, part 9. For the Soviet Union's facilitating the creation of an independent Kurdish state in northwestern Iran, see Roosevelt, "Kurdish Republic," pp. 247-69; and William Eagleton Jr., *The Kurdish Republic of 1946* (London, 1963).

NOTES TO CHAPTER 5

1. Memorandum by John W. Field (FO), "British Political Relations with Koweit," 29 March 1922, L/P&S/18/B 391; memorandum by J. G. Laithwaite (IO), "Koweit 1908-1928," 1 Oct. 1928, L/P&S/18/B 395; IDC (including appendices and enclosures), 5 Oct. 1933, L/P&S/12/3732, PZ 1384/34; Great Britain, Admiralty, Naval Intelligence Division, *Iraq and the Persian Gulf* (London, 1944), p. 149; Briton Cooper Busch, *Britain and the Persian Gulf, 1894-1914* (Berkeley, Calif., 1967), pp. 108-10, 346-47; Husain M. Albaharna, *The Legal Status of the Arabian Gulf States: A Study of Their Treaty Relations and Their International Problems* (Manchester, 1968), pp. 40-46.
   To provide the necessary background, in this chapter I have begun my account in the late 1930s.
   I have derived much of the material in this chapter from my previous accounts of this subject in "The British Government and the Question of Umm Qasr 1938-1945," *Asian and African Studies*, vol. 16 (1982), pp. 215-38; and *Informal Empire*, pp. 65-73.

2. Memorandum by J. G. Ward (Eastern Dept. of FO), 10 May 1935, L/P&S/12/2878, PZ 3346/35; W. E. Houstoun-Boswall (British chargé d'affaires in Baghdad) to H. L. Baggallay (Eastern Dept. of FO), 10 Sept. 1938, FO 371/21813, E5348/75/91; Tawfiq al-Suwaydi (Iraqi foreign minister) to R. A. Butler (parliamentary undersecretary of state for foreign affairs), 28 Sept. 1938, FO 371/21858, E5688/1982/93; meeting in London between Tawfiq al-Suwaydi and FO officials, 4 Oct. 1938, FO 371/21859, E5841/1982/93; J. C. Hurewitz (ed.), *The Middle East and North Africa in World Politics: A Documentary Record*, 2nd ed., vol. 2: *British-French Supremacy, 1914-1945* (New Haven, Conn., 1979), pp. 477-79; Richard Schofield, *Kuwait and Iraq: Historical Claims and Territorial Disputes* (London, 1991), pp. 68-71.

3. Sir Maurice Peterson (British ambassador in Baghdad) to Lord Halifax (foreign secretary), 30 March 1938, R/15/1/541; Tawfiq al-Suwaydi to Butler, 28 Sept. 1938, FO 371/21858, E5688/1982/93; meeting in London between Tawfiq al-Suwaydi and FO officials, 4 Oct. 1938, FO 371/21859, E5841/1982/93; Admiralty, *Iraq and the Persian Gulf*, pp. 150-51; Khadduri, *Independent Iraq*, pp. 324-30.

4. Iraq's justification of its claim to Kuwait is in Peterson to Halifax, 19 April 1938, R/15/1/541; Tawfiq al-Suwaydi to Butler, 28 Sept. 1938, FO 371/21858, E5688/1982/93; and David H. Finnie, *Shifting Lines in the Sand: Kuwait's Elusive Frontier with Iraq* (Cambridge, Mass., 1992), pp. 99-100, 114. This claim is critically analysed in Albaharna, *Legal Status*, pp. 250-58. The Anglo-Ottoman Convention of 1913 is discussed in Busch, *Persian Gulf*, pp. 336-40; and John C. Wilkinson, *Arabia's Frontiers: The Story of Britain's Boundary Drawing in the Desert* (London, 1991), pp. 61-99. The Kuwaiti section of the original French language version of the agreement is printed in Schofield, *Kuwait and Iraq*, pp. 136-37. There is an English translation in J. C. Hurewitz (ed.), *The Middle East and North Africa in World Politics: A Documentary Record*, 2nd ed., vol. 1: *European Expansion, 1535-1914* (New Haven, Conn., 1975), pp. 568-69.

5. Peterson to Halifax, 19 April 1938, memorandum by C. H. Fone (FO Library), 21 May 1938, R/15/1/541; note by W. E. Beckett (legal adviser at FO), 30 May 1938, R/15/5/207; Finnie, *Shifting Lines*, pp. 100-106.

6. IDC, 5 Oct. 1933, L/P&S/12/3732, PZ 1384/34; memorandum by G. W. Rendel (head of the Eastern Dept. of FO), 10 May 1937, IDC, 18 May 1937, L/P&S/12/3784, PZ 3212/3470/37; Lord Linlithgow (viceroy of India) to Lord Zetland (SSI), 19 May 1938, L/P&S/12/2892, PZ 3836/38; Lt.-Col. T. C. Fowle (political resident in the Persian Gulf) to IO, 31 Oct. 1938, L/P&S/12/3864, PZ 7742/38; Gerald de Gaury (political agent in Kuwait) to PR, 20 Nov. 1938, R/15/1/541.
7. RAF Intelligence Summary for Iraq for May 1938, FO 371/21832, E4042/1642/91; RAF Intelligence Summary for Iraq for Feb. 1939, R/15/1/549; de Gaury Intelligence Summary for Kuwait for 16-28 Feb. 1939, L/P&S/12/2864, PZ 1744/39; Schofield, *Kuwait and Iraq*, pp. 74-76; Kamal Osman Salih, "The 1938 Kuwait Legislative Council," *Middle Eastern Studies*, vol. 28 (1992), pp. 71-75.
8. PR to British embassy Baghdad, 21 March 1939, Houstoun-Boswall to Nuri al-Said (Iraqi foreign minister), 25 March 1939, L/P&S/12/2884, PZ 1807/2381/39; Houstoun-Boswall to FO, 20 April 1939, R/15/5/127; Jill Crystal, *Oil and Politics in the Gulf: Rulers and Merchants in Kuwait and Qatar* (Cambridge, 1990), p. 53; Schofield, *Kuwait and Iraq*, p. 83.
9. Peterson to Halifax, 30 March 1938, R/15/1/541; Tawfiq al-Suwaydi to Butler, 28 Sept. 1938, FO 371/21858, E5688/1982/93; Houstoun-Boswall to FO, 25 March 1939, L/P&S/12/2864, PZ 1951/39; Schofield, *Kuwait and Iraq*, pp. 78-80.
10. Baggallay to Houstoun-Boswall, 15 Aug. 1938, Houstoun-Boswall to FO, 7 Sept. 1938, R/15/1/541; meeting in London between Tawfiq al-Suwaydi and FO officials, 4 Oct. 1938, FO 371/21859, E5841/1982/93; Houstoun-Boswall to FO, 25 March 1939, R/15/5/127. After the death of King Ghazi in April 1939, Iraq pursued its claim to Kuwait less vigorously. Houstoun-Boswall to Halifax, 20 April 1939, R/15/5/127; Schofield, *Kuwait and Iraq*, p. 77.
11. C. W. Baxter (head of the Eastern Dept. of FO) to undersecretary of state for India, 2 May 1938, Baggallay to R. T. Peel (head of the External Division of the Political Dept. of IO), 26 Aug. 1938, R/15/1/541; minutes of ME(O), 28 Sept. 1938, L/P&S/12/2892, PZ 7136/38; meeting in London between Tawfiq al-Suwaydi and FO officials, 4 Oct. 1938, FO 371/21859, E5841/1982/93; Baggallay to C. G. Jarrett (Admiralty), 5 Aug. 1939, R/15/1/541; J. G. Lorimer, *Gazetteer of the Persian Gulf, Oman, and Central Arabia*, vol. 2: *Geographical and Statistical* (Calcutta, 1908; reprint, Farnborough, 1970), pp. 15-16; Schofield, *Kuwait and Iraq*, p. 80.
12. Baggallay to Jarrett, 5 Aug. 1939, Houstoun-Boswall to Halifax, 14 Nov. 1939, R/15/1/541; Lorimer, *Gazetteer*, pp. 324, 1503-5, 1927; Schofield, *Kuwait and Iraq*, p. 81.
13. Minute by P. M. Crosthwaite (Eastern Dept. of FO), 30 Nov. 1939, FO 371/23200, E7601/58/93; Baggallay to undersecretary of state for India, 16 Dec. 1939, R/15/1/541; Schofield, *Kuwait and Iraq*, p. 81.
14. Prior to Peel, 8 Feb. 1940, R/15/1/541; Schofield, *Kuwait and Iraq*, p. 82.
15. Sir Basil Newton (British ambassador in Baghdad) to Halifax, 16 Feb. 1940, R/15/1/541; GOI to SSI, 18 March 1940, L/P&S/12/2892, PZ 1624/40; Peel to undersecretary of state for foreign affairs, 19 April 1940, R/15/5/208; Schofield, *Kuwait and Iraq*, p. 82.
16. Prior to SSI, 21 March 1940, R/15/1/541.
17. Prior to SSI, 22 March 1940, L/P&S/12/2892, PZ 1715/40; Schofield, *Kuwait and Iraq*, p. 82.
18. Baggallay to undersecretary of state for India, 4 May 1940, R/15/5/208.
19. Newton to Halifax, 15 April 1940, FO 371/24545, E1758/309/91.
20. Baggallay to undersecretary of state for India, 5 May 1940, L/P&S/12/2884, PZ 2631/40.
21. See note 4.

22. Memorandum by Fone, 21 May 1938, R/15/1/541; note by E. B. Wakefield (Indian Civil Service), Nov. 1941, R/15/1/542; memorandum by the Research Dept. of FO, Jan. 1948, FO 371/68346, E2464/700/91; Finnie, *Shifting Lines*, pp. 62-69.

23. Memorandum by Fone, 21 May 1938, R/15/1/541; note by Wakefield, Nov. 1941, R/15/1/542; memorandum by the Research Dept. of FO, Jan. 1948, FO 371/68346, E2464/700/91; Finnie, *Shifting Lines*, pp. 73-84.

24. Peterson to Halifax, 19 April 1938, R/15/1/541; Albaharna, *Legal Status*, pp. 256-57; Finnie, *Shifting Lines*, pp. 126-27.
     One distinguished scholar also maintains that the Iraqi government's acceptance of the border in 1932 had no legal validity because it was not approved by Parliament and ratified by the king. Majid Khadduri, "Iraq's Claim to the Sovereignty of Kuwayt," *New York University Journal of International Law and Politics*, vol. 23 (1990), pp. 28-29.

25. H. A. Caccia (Eastern Dept. of FO) to Peel, 30 March 1942, R/15/1/543; minute by Crosthwaite, 29 April 1942, FO 371/31369, E2560/134/93; Baxter to Peel, 5 May 1942, L/P&S/12/2892, EXT 2359/42; Peel to Baxter, 16 June 1942, R/15/5/209.

26. Note by Wakefield, Nov. 1941, Lt.-Col. W. R. Hay (officiating political resident in the Persian Gulf) to SSI, 10 March 1942, R/15/1/542; Cornwallis to Eden, 14 March 1942, R/15/5/209; Caccia to Peel, 30 March 1942, R/15/1/543; Baxter to Peel, 5 May 1942, L/P&S/12/2892, EXT 2359/42; Peel to Baxter, 16 June 1942, R/15/5/209.

27. Hay to SSI, 10 March 1942, R/15/1/542; Caccia to Peel, 30 March 1942, R/15/1/543; Baxter to Peel, 5 May 1942, L/P&S/12/2892, EXT 2359/42; Peel to Baxter, 16 June 1942, R/15/5/209.

28. In 1915 Cox, in his capacity as chief political officer of the Mesopotamian Expeditionary Force and political resident in the Persian Gulf, negotiated the first British treaty with Ibn Saud. In this agreement too Cox inadvertently included an ambiguous phrase regarding Britain's responsibility to defend Ibn Saud against foreign powers without defining precisely which states or political entities would be considered foreign powers. In 1918-19, when Ibn Saud fought against King Husayn of the Hijaz, this oversight led to much controversy and recrimination. This question is discussed in Daniel Silverfarb, "The Anglo-Najd Treaty of 1915," *Middle Eastern Studies*, vol. 16 (1980), pp. 167-77.
     In 1922 Cox, in his capacity as British high commissioner for Iraq, was again careless while drafting a treaty with Ibn Saud. This agreement, known as the Uqair Protocol, stipulated that Iraq and Najd (as Ibn Saud's domains were then known) could not use the wells situated "in the vicinity of the border" for any military purpose. However, the inherently vague phrase "in the vicinity of the border" was not defined more exactly, and in the late 1920s this ambiguity was the source of considerable misunderstanding and bitterness between Ibn Saud and the British government. This question is discussed in Daniel Silverfarb, "Great Britain, Iraq, and Saudi Arabia: The Revolt of the Ikhwan, 1927-30," *International History Review*, vol. 4 (1982), pp. 222-48.

29. Baggallay to undersecretary of state for India, 5 May 1940, L/P&S/12/2884, PZ 2631/40.

30. Prior to SSI, 19 March 1940, FO 371/24545, E1326/309/91; Peel to undersecretary of state for foreign affairs, 24 March 1939, FO 371/23180, E2212/66/91; Peel to Prior, 15 May 1940, FO 371/24545, E1758/309/91; minute by E. W. R. Lumby (IO), 29 May 1942, L/P&S/12/2892, EXT 2359/42; Schofield, *Kuwait and Iraq*, pp. 84-85.

31. Major A. C. Galloway (political agent in Kuwait) to shaykh of Kuwait, 9 June 1940, shaykh of Kuwait to Galloway, 12 June 1940, L/P&S/12/2884, PZ 4538/4538/40; minute by Beckett, 23 March 1942, FO 371/31369, E1747/134/93; Caccia to Peel, 30 March 1942, R/15/1/543; Schofield, *Kuwait and Iraq*, p. 86.

32. Newton to Nuri al-Said (Iraqi foreign minister), 7 Oct. 1940, Newton to Halifax, 29 Nov. 1940, FO 371/24545, E2773/E2773/309/91; British embassy Baghdad to Iraqi Ministry of Foreign Affairs, 17 Feb. 1941, L/P&S/12/2884, EXT 1501/41; Newton to Eden, 29 March 1941, R/15/5/208; Schofield, *Kuwait and Iraq,* pp. 86-87.

33. Iraq's request is in Newton to FO, 26 April 1940, L/P&S/12/2892, PZ 2596/40. The views of the British military are in note by Commander A. J. Baker-Cresswell, 14 May 1940, note by Major W. S. Cox, 15 May 1940, C-in-C Middle East to WO, 17 May 1940, WO 201/1050; and WO to undersecretary of state for foreign affairs, 21 May 1940, FO 371/24559, E1883/630/93. The British government's refusal is in Newton to Nuri, 14 June 1940, FO 371/24559, E1883/630/93.

34. C-in-C Middle East to WO, 28 May 1941, FO 371/27106, E2687/2687/93; C-in-C India to WO, 17 June 1941, L/P&S/12/2892, EXT 4029/41; minutes of COS, 20 June 1941, CAB 79/12, COS(41)219; Schofield, *Kuwait and Iraq,* p. 89.

35. C-in-C East Indies to C-in-C India, 30 June 1941, L/P&S/12/2892, EXT 4029/41; WO to C-in-C India, 15 July 1941, FO 371/27106, E3826/2687/93; minutes of ME(O), 22 July 1941, L/P&S/12/2892, EXT 4343/41; GOI to SSI, 25 July 1941, R/15/5/208; Admiralty to C-in-C East Indies, 26 July 1941, minute by Lumby, 2 Aug. 1941, L/P&S/12/2892, EXT 4480/4397/41; IDC, 27 Aug. 1943, R/15/1/543.

36. FO to Baghdad, 24 July 1941, FO 371/27106, E3762/2687/93; SSI to Prior, 27 July 1941, R/15/5/208; Cornwallis to Eden, 31 July 1941, FO 371/27106, E4360/2687/93; minute by Lumby, 2 Aug. 1941, L/P&S/12/2892, EXT 4397/41; Prior to SSI, 3 Aug. 1941, R/15/5/185; SSI to Prior, 2 Sept. 1941, R/15/1/542; Baxter to Peel, 8 Oct. 1941, L/P&S/12/2892, EXT 6373/41; Schofield, *Kuwait and Iraq,* p. 89.

37. C-in-C India to WO, 18 Aug. 1941, L/P&S/12/2892, EXT 5043/41; Lt.-Col. F. H. Skinner (Hdq., Line of Communications Area Iraq) to Force Hdq., 27 Aug. 1941, FO 624/62; Cornwallis to Eden, 14 March 1942, R/15/5/209; Schofield, *Kuwait and Iraq,* p. 89.

38. Prior to SSI, 4 Oct. 1941, R/15/5/208; minute by Lumby, 16 Oct. 1941, L/P&S/12/2892, EXT 6373/41; Peel to Baxter, 20 Oct. 1941, FO 371/27106, E6847/2687/93; Schofield, *Kuwait and Iraq,* pp. 90-91.

39. Minutes by Crosthwaite, 4 March 1942 and 29 April 1942, FO 371/31369, E1388/ E2560/134/93; Caccia to Peel, 30 March 1942, R/15/1/543; Baxter to Peel, 5 May 1942, L/P&S/12/2892, EXT 2359/42; Schofield, *Kuwait and Iraq,* p. 91.

40. Minute by Crosthwaite, 5 Dec. 1942, FO 371/31369, E6989/134/93; minute by G. H. Baker (Eastern Dept. of FO), 20 May 1947, FO 371/61445, E993/993/91; Schofield, *Kuwait and Iraq,* p. 91.

41. Note by Lt.-Gen. E. P. Quinan (Commander, Tenth Army), 24 March 1942, L/P&S/12/2892, EXT 2259/42; Report by the War Cabinet's Principal Administrative Officers Committee, "Proposed Disposal of Um Qasr Installations," 29 March 1945, FO 371/52255, E4008/4008/91.

42. Minute by Peterson, 30 June 1943, FO 371/34999, E3969/124/93; Baxter to Colonel R. W. Spraggett (Admiralty), 9 July 1943, Baxter to secretary of the Admiralty, 14 Oct. 1943, L/P&S/12/2893, EXT 3716/5784/43.

43. WO to H. M. Eyres (Eastern Dept. of FO), 19 Sept. 1943, minute by Baxter, 1 Oct. 1943, undersecretary of state for air to undersecretary of state for foreign affairs, 18 Nov. 1943, FO 371/34999, E5638/E5638/E7172/124/93; Cornwallis to Sir Maurice Peterson (assistant undersecretary of state for foreign affairs), 19 March 1944, FO 371/40079, E2142/1134/93.

44. Smith to British embassy Baghdad, 13 Nov. 1944, L/P&S/12/2893, EXT 294/45.

45.   Cornwallis to Smith, 17 Nov. 1944, L/P&S/12/2893, EXT 294/45.
46.   Report by the War Cabinet's Principal Administrative Officers Committee, "Proposed Disposal of Um Qasr Installations," 29 March 1945, FO 371/52255, E4008/4008/91; Schofield, *Kuwait and Iraq,* p. 92.
47.   L. F. L. Pyman (Eastern Dept. of FO) to Captain G. D. Petherick (WO), 11 Jan. 1945, GOI to SSI, 23 Feb. 1945, L/P&S/12/2893, EXT 238/898/45; minutes of COS, 3 April 1945, CAB 79/31, COS(45)86; FO to Cornwallis, 15 April 1945, L/P&S/12/2893, EXT 1825/45.
48.   Schofield, *Kuwait and Iraq,* pp. 92-101.
      After the fall of the old regime, in the 1960s Iraq constructed its own port at Umm Qasr. Schofield, *Kuwait and Iraq,* pp. 90, 113.

NOTES TO CHAPTER 6

1.   The first section of this chapter on the wartime origins of Britain's postwar economic difficulties is based primarily on the statistical material that Britain presented to the United States in the autumn of 1945 during the course of financial negotiations in Washington. It was prepared by the Treasury, and is in Cmd. 6707. There is also good information on this subject in Alec Cairncross, *Years of Recovery: British Economic Policy 1945-51* (London, 1985), pp. 3-16; and L. S. Pressnell, *External Economic Policy since the War,* vol. 1: *The Post-War Financial Settlement* (London, 1987), pp. 1-15.
2.   *HC,* 21 May 1947, vol. 437, written answers, col. 262.
3.   Alan Bullock, *Ernest Bevin: Foreign Secretary 1945-1951* (New York, 1983), pp. 233, 240.
4.   Great Britain, Central Statistical Office, *Annual Abstract of Statistics: No. 84, 1935-1946* (London, 1948; reprint, Liechtenstein, 1970), p. 101.
5.   For good surveys of the Middle East during this period, see George Kirk, *Survey of International Affairs: The Middle East 1945-1950* (London, 1954); Howard M. Sachar, *Europe Leaves the Middle East, 1936-1954* (New York, 1972); and more recently William Roger Louis, *The British Empire in the Middle East 1945-1951: Arab Nationalism, the United States, and Postwar Imperialism* (Oxford, 1984).
6.   Thompson to Eden, 18 Aug. 1944 and 15 Sept. 1944, FO 921/300; Cornwallis to Eden, 9 Jan. 1945, FO 371/45302, E608/195/93; Thompson to FO, 26 July 1945, FO 371/45330, E5642/1393/93; Longrigg, *Iraq,* p. 313; Batatu, *Social Classes,* pp. 523-29.
7.   Minutes of COS, 20 May 1946, FO 371/52349, E4769/4768/65; R. G. Howe (assistant undersecretary of state for foreign affairs) to Stonehewer-Bird, 31 July 1946, FO 371/52417, E6294/521/93; Hdq. Middle East to Cabinet Offices, 2 Oct. 1946, FO 371/52350, E10519/4855/65; memorandum by Bevin, 3 March 1947, FO 371/61999, E1992/185/34; minute by Peter Garran (Eastern Dept. of FO), 13 Nov. 1947, FO 371/61597, E10892/3/93; Anita Inder Singh, "Post-Imperial British Attitudes to India: The Military Aspect, 1947-51," *The Round Table,* number 296 (1985), p. 362; Hugh Tinker, "The Contraction of Empire in Asia, 1945-48: The Military Dimension," *The Journal of Imperial and Commonwealth History,* vol. 16 (1988), p. 230.
8.   The campaign in Iraq during the First World War is discussed in Brigadier-General F. J. Moberly, *History of the Great War Based on Official Documents: The Campaign in Mesopotamia 1914-1918,* 4 vols. (London, 1923-27); and A. J. Barker, *The Neglected War: Mesopotamia 1914-1918* (London, 1967). The uprising of 1920 in Iraq is discussed in Lieutenant-General Sir Aylmer L. Haldane, *The Insurrection in Mesopotamia, 1920* (Edinburgh, 1922); and Longrigg, *Iraq,* pp. 113-26. The campaigns in Iraq and Iran during the Second World War are discussed in Playfair, *The Mediterranean and Middle East,*

pp. 177-97, 252-53; and Dharm Pal, *Official History of the Indian Armed Forces in the Second World War 1939-45: Campaign in Western Asia* (Calcutta, 1957).

9. Chancery Baghdad to FO, 29 July 1947, FO 371/61695, E7250/7250/93.

10. James S. Moose (U.S. chargé d'affaires in Baghdad) to secretary of state, 30 Sept. 1946 and 8 Oct. 1946, 890G.00/9-3046/10-846; George Wadsworth (U.S. ambassador in Baghdad) to secretary of state, 10 June 1947, 890G.00/6-1047; Busk to Michael Wright (assistant undersecretary of state for foreign affairs), 17 Sept. 1947, FO 371/61594, E8789/3/93.

11. Bullock, *Bevin,* pp. 113, 156, 241-42, 348-50; Louis, *British Empire,* pp. 6, 28, 46, 107-08; Raymond Smith and John Zametica, "The Cold Warrior: Clement Attlee Reconsidered, 1945-7," *International Affairs,* vol. 61 (1985), pp. 241-52. The quotation is in Bullock, p. 242.

12. Partha Sarathi Gupta, *Imperialism and the British Labour Movement: 1914-1964* (New York, 1975), pp. 287-88; Bullock, *Bevin,* pp. 156, 241, 354; Michael Asteris, "British Overseas Military Expenditure and the Balance of Payments," in Michael Bateman and Raymond Riley (eds.), *The Geography of Defence* (London, 1987), pp. 195-96. The quotation is in Asteris.

13. For Attlee's failure to press the issue, see Bullock, *Bevin,* pp. 244, 353-54, 842; and Louis, *British Empire,* p. 108.

14. Bullock, *Bevin,* pp. 113, 243, 350-51, 359, 839-40; Louis, *British Empire,* passim.

15. Howe to Bevin, 4 April 1946, FO 371/52318, E3476/291/65; memorandum by Garran, 6 Jan. 1947, FO 371/61874, E2932/951/31; Louis, *British Empire,* pp. 30-31.

16. Bullock, *Bevin,* pp. 34-35, 113, 243-44, 354, 470-71; Louis, *Middle East,* pp. 28, 55.

17. Memorandum by MFP, 3 Nov. 1945, FO 371/45270, E8775/571/65; MFP to FO, 19 March 1946, memoranda by MFP, 25 March 1946 and 17 Sept. 1946, FO 371/52343, E3407/E3373/E11103/2806/65.

18. The statistics in this paragraph are in note by MFP, Aug. 1946, memorandum by MFP, 17 Sept. 1946, FO 371/52343, E8603/E11103/2806/65; memorandum by the Middle East Secretariat of FO, 12 Dec. 1946, FO 371/61504, E344/87/65; brief by FO, no date but probably Oct. 1947, FO 371/61558, E9559/5764/65; and memorandum by MFP, 16 Dec. 1947, FO 371/61508, E12011/87/65. For Bevin's and the others' view on the need to remain in the Middle East to protect the oil facilities, see notes 14-17; and Phillip Darby, *British Defence Policy East of Suez: 1947-1968* (London, 1973), pp. 25-26.

19. HC, 16 May 1947, vol. 437, oral answers, cols. 1964-65.

20. See notes 14-16.

21. Ibid.

22. Ibid.

23. For Bevin's grand strategy in the Middle East, see Louis, *British Empire,* pp. vii, 3, 17-20, 46-47, 72, 628, 737; and for his failure, passim.

NOTES TO CHAPTER 7

1. Khadduri, *Independent Iraq,* pp. 252-53, 259; Batatu, *Social Classes,* p. 476.

2. Review by Thompson, no date, in Cornwallis to Eden, 8 Feb. 1944, FO 371/40041, E1143/37/93.

3. Cornwallis to Eden, 30 March 1945, FO 371/45302, E2431/195/93.

4. Thompson to Bevin, 28 Sept. 1945, FO 371/45281, E7496/6265/65.

5. Minute by Baxter, 7 March 1945, FO 371/45329, E1531/1190/93.

6. Minute by Hankey, 19 April 1945, FO 371/45302, E2431/195/93.

7. Report by the British embassy in Baghdad on the leading personalities in Iraq, 29 June

1940, FO 371/24562, E2329/2329/93; Sir Hugh Stonehewer-Bird (British ambassador in Baghdad) to Bevin, 31 Dec. 1945, FO 371/52401, E305/226/93; Khadduri, *Independent Iraq*, pp. 253-54, 259; Batatu, *Social Classes*, p. 530.

8. Stonehewer-Bird to Bevin, 30 April 1946, FO 371/52457, E4336/4070/93; Khadduri, *Independent Iraq*, p. 254; Batatu, *Social Classes*, pp. 530-31.

9. Stonehewer-Bird to Baxter, 25 April 1946, Stonehewer-Bird to Bevin, 30 April 1946, FO 371/52457, E4070/E4336/4070/93.

10. Stonehewer-Bird to Bevin, 17 April 1946, FO 371/52401, E3735/226/93; Khadduri, *Independent Iraq*, pp. 254, 259-60, 299; Batatu, *Social Classes*, pp. 299-300, 531; Phebe Marr, *The Modern History of Iraq* (Boulder, Colo., 1985), pp. 98-99.

11. Memorandum by Muhammad Hadid (vice president of the National Democratic party), 26 Aug. 1946, FO 624/94, part 4; Busk to Bevin, 19 Sept. 1946, minute by G. H. Baker (Eastern Dept. of FO), 26 Sept. 1946, FO 371/52402, E9585/E9585/226/93; Khadduri, *Independent Iraq*, pp. 259, 299-300; Batatu, *Social Classes*, pp. 305-10, 465; Marr, *Iraq*, pp. 98-99. The platform of the National Democratic party is in FO 624/95, part 3. There is an informative essay on Chadirchi in Khadduri, *Arab Contemporaries*, pp. 128-42.

12. James S. Moose (U.S. chargé d'affaires in Baghdad) to secretary of state, 29 Oct. 1946 (including the enclosure containing an informative interview with Aziz Sharif), 890G.00/10-2946; Khadduri, *Independent Iraq*, p. 300; Batatu, *Social Classes*, pp. 465, 479; Marr, *Iraq*, p. 99.

13. Khadduri, *Independent Iraq*, p. 360; Batatu, *Social Classes*, p. 531.

14. Khadduri, *Independent Iraq*, pp. 255-56, 260, 300; Batatu, *Social Classes*, pp. 350, 531.

15. Report by the British embassy in Baghdad on the leading personalities in Iraq, 29 June 1940, FO 371/24562, E2329/2329/93; C-in-C Middle East to WO, 5 June 1941, FO 371/27074, E2895/1/93; "The Report of the Iraqi Commission of Inquiry on the *Farhud*," 8 July 1941, in Norman A. Stillman, *The Jews of Arab Lands in Modern Times* (Philadelphia, 1991), pp. 405-17; Khadduri, *Independent Iraq*, p. 256; Batatu, *Social Classes*, pp. 350, 531.

16. Stonehewer-Bird to Bevin, 2 July 1946, FO 371/52401, E6456/226/93; Khadduri, *Independent Iraq*, pp. 256, 360; Batatu, *Social Classes*, pp. 531-32. The figure of 800 for the number of demonstrators is in Stonehewer-Bird. However, Batatu puts it at 3,000.

17. Memorandum by Hadid, 26 Aug. 1946, FO 624/95, part 4; Khadduri, *Independent Iraq*, pp. 256-57, 360-61; Batatu, *Social Classes*, pp. 532-33. The casualty figures are in Hadid. However, Batatu puts the number of fatalities at ten.

18. Stonehewer-Bird to FO, 4 July 1946, 5 July 1946, and 19 July 1946, FO 371/52459, E6246/E6336/E6919/5857/93.

19. Stonehewer-Bird to FO, 4 July 1946, FO to Baghdad, 12 July 1946, Douglas Busk (British chargé d'affaires in Baghdad) to Bevin, 13 Aug. 1946, FO 371/52459, E6246/E6246/E8267/5857/93; Busk to Bevin, 19 Sept. 1946, FO 371/52402, E9585/226/93.

20. Stonehewer-Bird to FO, 19 July 1946, FO 371/52459, E6919/5857/93; Busk to Bevin, 19 Sept. 1946, FO 371/52402, E9585/226/93.

21. Khadduri, *Independent Iraq*, p. 257; Batatu, *Social Classes*, p. 533. For the statement of the Iraqi Communist party on this question, see FO 624/100.

22. Stonehewer-Bird to FO, 16 Aug. 1946, Busk to Bevin, 16 Aug. 1946, FO 371/52468, E8113/E8334/8113/93; Khadduri, *Independent Iraq*, pp. 256, 300; Batatu, *Social Classes*, p. 532. The quotation is in Busk.

23. Busk to Bevin, 6 Sept. 1946, FO 371/52402, E9318/226/93.

24. Moose to secretary of state, 20 Aug. 1946 and 28 Aug. 1946, 890G.00/8-2046/8-2846; Busk to Bevin, 6 Sept. 1946, FO 371/52402, E9318/226/93; minute by Busk, 10 Oct.

1946, FO 624/95, part 5; Moose to secretary of state, 28 Oct. 1946, 890G.9111 RR/10-2846; Khadduri, *Independent Iraq*, pp. 24-25.

25. Busk to FO, 3 Oct. 1946, FO 371/52402, E9922/226/93.

26. Busk to FO, 3 Sept. 1946, FO 371/52402, E8794/226/93; minute by Perowne, 13 Nov. 1946, FO 624/95, part 5.

27. Busk to FO, 3 Sept. 1946, Busk to Bevin, 6 Sept. 1946, Busk to FO, 23 Sept. 1946, minute by Baker, 26 Sept. 1946, minute by Garran, 8 Oct. 1946, FO 371/52402, E8794/E9318/E9557/ E9585/E9922/226/93; Khadduri, *Independent Iraq*, p. 257; Batatu, *Social Classes*, p. 533.

28. Busk to FO, 5 Sept. 1946, FO to Baghdad, 11 Sept. 1946, minute by Baxter, 30 Sept. 1946, FO 371/52402, E8881/E8881/E9585/226/93; F. Brewis (British chargé d'affaires in Baghdad) to Bevin, 4 Oct. 1946, FO 371/52403, E10228/226/93.

29. Minute by Busk, 3 Sept. 1946, FO 624/95, part 4; minute by Howe, 24 Sept. 1946, FO 371/52459, E9719/5857/93; Busk to Bevin, 24 Sept. 1946, FO 371/52402, E9851/226/93. The quotation is in Busk of 24 Sept. 1946.

30. Busk to Bevin, 16 Aug. 1946, FO 371/52402, E8328/226/93.

31. Minute by Perowne, 4 Sept. 1946, FO 624/95, part 4.

32. Busk to Bevin, 16 Aug. 1946, FO 371/52402, E8328/226/93.

33. Memorandum by Hadid, 26 Aug. 1946, FO 624/95, part 4.

34. Busk to FO, 3 Oct. 1946, FO to Baghdad, 10 Oct. 1946, FO 371/52402, E9922/E9922/226/93; minute by Perowne, 10 Oct. 1946, FO 624/95, part 5; comment by Busk on minute by J. C. B. Richmond (oriental counsellor, British embassy Baghdad), 21 June 1947, FO 624/108, part 3; comment by Busk in Edmund J. Dorsz (U.S. chargé d'affaires in Baghdad) to secretary of state, 7 Feb. 1948, 890G.00/2-748.
     Britain's engineering of Arshad's dismissal suggests that, at least as far as Iraq was concerned, William Roger Louis is mistaken in his belief that Bevin did not intervene in the internal affairs of Middle Eastern countries to the extent of toppling governments. However, to be fair to Louis, in this particular case it is not clear that Bevin was aware of the activities of his officials. For Louis's contention, see *British Empire*, p. 3.

35. Stonehewer-Bird to Attlee, 26 Nov. 1946 and 10 Dec. 1946, FO 371/52405, E11846/E12399/ 226/93; Khadduri, *Independent Iraq*, pp. 257, 260; Batatu, *Social Classes*, p. 533.

36. Stonehewer-Bird to FO, 23 Dec. 1946, FO 371/52405, E12426/226/93; Stonehewer-Bird to Bevin, 2 April 1947, FO 371/61589, E3133/3/93; minute by Richmond, 7 June 1947, FO 624/108, part 3; lecture by Renton at Chatham House, 9 August 1948, Renton Papers; Sir Henry Mack (British ambassador in Baghdad) to Bevin, 17 Dec. 1948, FO 371/75128, E74/1016/93; Khadduri, *Independent Iraq*, p. 258.
     The illegal Communist party also called for a boycott of the elections. Their undated leaflet on this question is in Moose to secretary of state, 9 Jan. 1947, 890G.002/1-947.

37. Report by the British embassy in Baghdad on the leading personalities in Iraq, 29 June 1940, FO 371/24562, E2329/2329/93.

38. Sir Reader Bullard (British ambassador in Tehran) to FO, 19 May 1941, FO 371/27070, E2386/1/93; Cornwallis to Eden, 2 Aug. 1942, FO 371/31371, E4722/204/93; Henderson to secretary of state, 15 Sept. 1944, 890G.5043/9-1544; Busk to Bevin, 6 Sept. 1946, 19 Sept. 1946, and 24 Sept. 1946, FO 371/52402, E9318/E9585/ E9851/226/93; minutes by Garran and Baxter, 27 and 30 Sept. 1946, FO 371/52402, E9585/E9585/226/93; minute by Busk, 20 Dec. 1946, FO 624/95, part 5; Stonehewer-Bird to Bevin, 9 Jan. 1947, FO 371/61588, E845/3/93; Gerwin Gerke, "The Iraq

Development Board and British Policy, 1945-50," *Middle Eastern Studies,* vol. 27 (1991), p. 236.

39.   Busk to Bevin, 14 July 1947, FO 371/61592, E6723/3/93; Khadduri, *Independent Iraq,* pp. 261-62, 300, 361; Batatu, *Social Classes,* pp. 536-37, 540.

40.   Mack to Bevin, 17 Dec. 1948, FO 371/75128, E74/1016/93; Khadduri, *Independent Iraq,* pp. 273, 300; Batatu, *Social Classes,* p. 346.

41.   Supplementary report by Harry Fletcher (British information officer in Basra) on the living conditions of manual laborers in the Basra area, June 1948, in David H. McKillop (U.S. consul Basra) to secretary of state, 13 July 1948, 890G.504/7-1348.

42.   McKillop to secretary of state, 1 June 1948, 5 June 1948, 28 June 1948, Dorsz to secretary of state, 6 Dec. 1948, 890G.00/5-3148/6-448/6-2848/12-648; Mack to Bevin, 17 Dec. 1948, FO 371/75128, E74/1016/93; Khadduri, *Independent Iraq,* pp. 273, 300; Batatu, *Social Classes,* p. 346.
      The figure of 100 for the membership of the National Democratic party in December 1948 is in Mack. By comparison, Batatu (p. 465) maintains that in April 1947 the membership was nearly 7,000.
      After the end of martial law, in March 1950 the National Democrats resumed their political activity. Khadduri, *Independent Iraq,* p. 300.

43.   Memorandum by Garran, 26 July 1947, FO 371/61592, E7069/3/93; Busk to FO, 27 Aug. 1947, FO 371/61594, E7941/3/93; Busk to FO, 7 Nov. 1947, FO to Baghdad, 8 Nov. 1947, FO 371/61596, E10448/E10448/3/93.

44.   Mack to FO, 18 March 1948, FO 371/68381, E3643/68/65; Busk to Burrows, 5 April 1948, FO 371/68448, E4591/27/93; minute by Mack, 12 April 1948, FO 624/127; Mack to FO, 9 July 1948, FO 371/68450, E9452/27/93.

NOTES TO CHAPTER 8

1.   Report by Maj.-Gen. G. G. Waterhouse (head of the British military mission in Iraq), 31 Aug. 1940, FO 371/24551, E1235/15/93; report by Maj.-Gen. D. G. Bromilow (head of the British military mission in Iraq), 31 March 1944, Maj.-Gen. J. M. L. Renton (head of the British military mission in Iraq) to Tahsin Ali (Iraqi minister of defense), 8 July 1944, FO 371/40044, E2580/E4439/42/93.

2.   Reports by Lt.-Col. C. C. Aston (political adviser, central and southern Iraq), 8 Nov. 1941 and 14 Dec. 1941, FO 838/1; Cornwallis to Eden, 8 March 1942, FO 371/31371, E2596/204/93.

3.   Tarbush, *Role of the Military,* pp. 78-79.

4.   Comment by Muhammad al-Sadr (president of the Senate), in C. J. Edmonds (adviser to the Iraqi Ministry of Interior) to Cornwallis, 2 Sept. 1941. This document is printed in Elie Kedourie, "The Shiite Issue in Iraqi Politics, 1941," *Middle Eastern Studies,* vol. 24 (1988), p. 498. Sadr simply mentioned the thirty Shiites. For the total number of officers in the army at this time, see report by Bromilow, 31 Aug. 1942, FO 371/31366, E6144/101/93.

5.   Batatu, *Social Classes,* p. 423.

6.   Sir John Troutbeck to Sir Winston Churchill (prime minister), 23 May 1953, FO 371/104665, EQ1016/27. For more on Sunni Arab control of the army, also see Batatu, *Social Classes,* pp. 45, 765; and Eliezer Beeri, *Army Officers in Arab Politics and Society* (New York, 1970), p. 329.

7.   Report by Aston, 8 Nov. 1941, FO 838/1; Pool, "Politics of Patronage," p. 228.

8.   Batatu, *Social Classes,* p. 47.

9. FO to Baghdad, 5 June 1941, FO 371/27074, E2802/1/93; Cornwallis to FO, 8 June 1941, FO 371/27075, E2951/1/93; Cornwallis to Eden, 11 Nov. 1941, FO 371/27082, E8023/1/93; report by Aston, 14 Dec. 1941, FO 838/1; FO to Baghdad, 1 Nov. 1942, FO 371/31371, E6384/204/93.

    Before 1943 the number of ministers was not allowed to exceed nine. However, a minister could hold more than one portfolio. Khadduri, *Independent Iraq*, p. 202.

10. This question is discussed in chapter 1.

11. Bromilow to Hdq. Tenth Army, 4 March 1942, WO 201/1299; Cornwallis to Eden, 21 Feb. 1943, FO 371/35010, E1667/489/93; minute by Stewart Perowne (oriental counsellor, British embassy Baghdad), 24 Nov. 1943, FO 624/33/582; report by Renton, 31 March 1947, FO 371/61669, E3126/1244/93.

12. Reports by Bromilow, 28 Feb. 1942 and 31 Aug. 1942, FO 371/31366, E2238/E6144/101/93; report by Renton, 30 Sept. 1944, FO 371/40044, E6246/42/93; report by Renton, 31 March 1947, FO 371/61669, E3126/1244/93.

13. Report by Bromilow, 31 Aug. 1942, FO 371/31366, E6144/101/93; Lt.-Gen. H. Pownall (C-in-C PAIC) to secretary of state for war, 12 Oct. 1943, WO 32/10540; report by Renton, 30 Sept. 1944, FO 371/40044, E6246/42/93; report by Renton, 31 March 1945, FO 371/45342, E2435/2435/93.

    The figures for wages in the Iraqi army and the levies are in Renton's report of March 1945. The figure for the army applies to volunteers; the wages for conscripts were lower.

    In his report of September 1944 Renton says that he recently got the rations of the soldiers in the Iraqi army raised to the level of the levies.

14. Report by Bromilow, 31 March 1944, Renton to Tahsin Ali, 8 July 1944, FO 371/40044, E2580/E4439/42/93.

15. This question is discussed in chapter 1.

16. Sir Maurice Peterson (assistant undersecretary of state for foreign affairs) to Lt.-Gen. A. E. Nye (WO), 10 Nov. 1943, FO 371/34992, E6836/44/93.

17. Report by Bromilow, 30 Sept. 1943, FO 371/34989, E6659/21/93; report by Bromilow, 31 March 1944, report by Renton, 30 Sept. 1944, FO 371/40044, E2580/E6246/42/93; Renton to Iraqi minister of defense, 14 May 1945, FO 371/45342, E3661/2435/93.

18. J. V. W. Shaw (acting high commissioner for Transjordan) to Oliver F. G. Stanley (colonial secretary), 6 May 1944, FO 371/39988, E3083/41/65.

19. Reports by Bromilow, 31 May 1942 and 31 Aug. 1942, FO 371/31366, E3823/E6144/101/93; report by Renton, 30 Sept. 1944, FO 371/40044, E6246/42/93; C-in-C PAIC to WO, 10 Feb. 1945, FO 371/45298, E1095/182/93.

20. Report by the inspector-general of the Iraqi air force, 30 Nov. 1941, FO 371/31366, E1108/101/93; report by Bromilow, 30 Nov. 1942, FO 371/34989, E143/21/93; report by Wing-Commander M. H. Rhys (inspector-general of the Iraqi air force), 28 Feb. 1943, FO 371/35000, E2276/144/93; report by Rhys, 21 Dec. 1943, FO 371/40072, E854/653/93.

21. Cornwallis to FO, 12 Nov. 1941, FO 371/27120, E7491/7491/93.

22. Cornwallis to FO, 29 May 1942, FO 371/31351, E3354/2577/65.

23. This question is discussed in chapter 1.

24. Ibid.

25. Thompson to FO, 17 Aug. 1943, FO 371/35019, E5100/2351/93.

26. Report by Bromilow, 28 Feb. 1942, FO 371/31366, E2238/101/93.

27. For the armored cars, see Cornwallis to Eden, 2 Aug. 1942, FO 371/31371, E4722/204/93; report by Bromilow, 31 Aug. 1942, FO 371/31366, E6144/101/93; and

WO to FO, 9 Nov. 1942, FO 371/31338, E6582/49/65. For the tanks, see WO to Treasury, 6 Nov. 1942, Treasury to WO, 11 Nov. 1942, FO 371/31366, E6584/E6584/101/93; report by Renton, 30 Sept. 1944, FO 371/40044, E6246/42/93; B. T. White, *British Tanks and Fighting Vehicles 1914-1945* (London, 1970), pp. 18-19, 25, 54-59; and Ian Hogg, *Armour in Conflict* (London, 1980), pp. 85, 98, 102.

28. Cornwallis to FO, 29 Jan. 1942, FO to Treasury, 2 Feb. 1942, report by Bromilow, 31 Aug. 1942, FO 371/31366, E696/E696/E6144/101/93; report by Bromilow, 28 Feb. 1943, FO 371/34989, E2260/21/93.

29. Report by Bromilow, 28 Feb. 1942, FO 371/31366, E2238/101/93.

30. Report by Bromilow, 31 March 1944, FO 371/40044, E2580/42/93.

31. Cornwallis to FO, 11 Oct. 1943, FO 371/35019, E6106/2351/93.

32. Report by Bromilow, 28 Feb. 1942, FO 371/31366, E2238/101/93.

33. Report by Bromilow, 31 May 1942, FO 371/31366, E3823/101/93.

34. Report by Bromilow, 31 March 1944, FO 371/40044, E2580/42/93.

35. Cornwallis to FO, 10 Dec. 1943, FO 371/35013, E7769/489/93; Cornwallis to Eden, 13 Jan. 1944, FO 371/40041, E519/37/93.

36. Cornwallis to FO, 13 Dec. 1943, FO 371/35013, E7823/489/93; Cornwallis to FO, 31 Dec. 1943, FO 371/40038, E26/26/93.

37. Maj.-Gen. A. R. Selby (officiating C-in-C PAIC) to WO, 6 Jan. 1944, FO to Cornwallis, 15 Jan. 1944, WO to C-in-C PAIC, 26 Jan. 1944, FO 371/40044, E700/E171/E894/42/93; Cornwallis to FO, 27 Jan. 1944, FO 371/40072, E854/653/93.

38. Baxter to undersecretary of state for war, 23 Dec. 1943, FO 371/34976, E6532/2551/65; Cornwallis to FO, 1 Jan. 1944, Selby to WO, 6 Jan. 1944, FO to Cornwallis, 15 Jan. 1944, WO to C-in-C PAIC, 26 Jan. 1944, FO 371/40044, E171/E700/E171/E894/42/93; Cornwallis to FO, 27 Jan. 1944, FO 371/40072, E854/653/93; Cornwallis to Eden, 8 Feb. 1944, Cornwallis to Cadogan, 19 Feb. 1944, FO 371/40041, E1143/E1336/37/93.

39. Renton to Tahsin Ali, 8 July 1944, report by Renton, 30 Sept. 1944, FO 371/40044, E4439/E6246/42/93.

40. Cornwallis to Eden, 27 Sept. 1944, report by Renton, 30 Sept. 1944, FO 371/40044, E6246/E6246/42/93; report by Renton, 31 March 1945, FO 371/45342, E2435/2435/93; lecture by Renton at Chatham House, 9 August 1948, Renton Papers.
     Toward the end of 1945 Renton also secured a 25 percent pay increase for volunteers. Memorandum by Renton, no date but probably late 1945, FO 624/73.

41. Memorandum by Renton, 4 Aug. 1947, FO 371/61593, E7401/3/93.

42. Cornwallis to Eden, 27 Sept. 1944, FO 371/40044, E6246/42/93; Cornwallis to FO, 28 Sept. 1944, FO 371/40039, E6247/26/93; Cornwallis to Eden, 15 Jan. 1945, FO 371/45302, E627/195/93.

43. Cornwallis to Eden, 27 Sept. 1944, report by Renton, 30 Sept. 1944, FO 371/40044, E6246/E6246/42/93.

44. R. M. A. Hankey (Eastern Dept. of FO) to Col. H. C. Withers (WO), 30 Aug. 1944, Withers to Baxter, 3 Oct. 1944, FO 371/40044, E4489/E6068/42/93; Lt.-Gen. Sir Arthur Smith (C-in-C PAIC) to Cornwallis, 15 Oct. 1944, FO 624/66, part 8; Maj. Philip Antrobus (WO) to Baxter, 18 Dec. 1944, Hankey to Antrobus, 30 Dec. 1944, FO 371/40044, E7810/E7810/42/93; Cornwallis to FO, 16 Feb. 1945, FO 371/45298, E1180/182/53.

45. Hankey to Withers, 30 Aug. 1944, Withers to Baxter, 3 Oct. 1944, Hankey to Antrobus, 30 Dec. 1944, FO 371/40044, E4489/E6068/E7810/42/93; WO to C-in-C PAIC, 18 Feb. 1945, FO 371/45298, E1301/182/93.

46. COS to British Joint Staff Mission in Washington, 8 May 1945, FO 371/45342, E3069/2435/93; FO to Stonehewer-Bird, 7 July 1945, FO 371/45298, E4841/182/93; British Joint Staff Mission in Washington to COS, 4 Aug. 1945, FO 371/45342, E5835/2435/93.

47. WO to Treasury, 3 Dec. 1945, FO 371/45299, E9720/182/93; minute by J. Thyne Henderson (Eastern Dept. of FO), 2 July 1946, FO 371/52398, E6171/155/93; FO to Baghdad, 12 April 1947, FO 371/61589, E2885/3/93; minute by Pyman, 20 Aug. 1947, FO 371/61633, E7557/255/93; minute by Garran, 7 Oct. 1947, FO 371/61634, E8999/255/93.

48. Renton to Tahsin Ali, 8 July 1944, FO 371/40044, E4439/42/93; Renton to Holt, 19 Sept. 1944, FO 624/38/469; Withers to Baxter, 3 Oct. 1944, FO 371/40044, E6068/42/93; Lt.-Col. D. Kirkness (WO) to Henderson, 23 Aug. 1945, Thompson to FO, 4 Sept. 1945, Kirkness to Henderson, 12 Sept. 1945, FO 371/45299, E6313/E6533/E6892/182/93; White, *British Tanks*, pp. 19-20, 76-77; Hancock, *War Economy*, p. 362; Hogg, *Armour*, p. 95.

49. Report by Renton, 30 Sept. 1945, FO 371/45342, E7939/2435/93; W. M. Skilling (WO) to L. Petch (Treasury), 3 Dec. 1945, FO 371/45299, E9720/182/93; WO to C-in-C MELF, 7 Nov. 1946, Lt.-Col. J. Grose (WO) to Baxter, 17 Dec. 1946, FO 371/52399, E11051/E12309/155/93.

50. FO to Baghdad, 17 May 1947 and 19 May 1947, FO 371/61590, E4251/E4251/3/93; report by Renton, 31 March 1948, FO 371/68477, E4878/618/93; lecture by Renton at Chatham House, 9 August 1948, Renton Papers; White, *British Tanks*, pp. 67-68, 77-79; Hogg, *Armour*, pp. 109, 160.

51. Report by Renton, 31 March 1948, FO 371/68477, E4878/618/93; minute by Hankey, 22 April 1950, FO 371/81966, E1194/3; Walid Khalidi, *From Haven to Conquest: Readings in Zionism and the Palestine Problem until 1948* (Beirut, 1971), p. 869. By this time the nine cruiser tanks which the British had given Iraq in 1942 were no longer functional.

52. Actually there is some dispute about Israeli tank strength at the outset of the war in May 1948. Israeli and Zionist scholars generally insist that Israel did not have any tanks. However, a prominent Palestinian historian maintains that Israel had at least three tanks, and a British expert puts this figure at four. I believe that the Israeli and Zionist accounts are accurate because I have not seen any references to Israel using tanks before the ten days of fighting after the expiry of the first truce in July 1948. And, incidentally, I have not seen any references to Israel using tanks against Iraq at all, either during the initial four weeks of combat or during the ten days of fighting after the expiry of the first truce. The Israeli and Zionist scholars referred to are Moshe Pearlman, *The Army of Israel* (New York, 1950), pp. 125, 127; Jon and David Kimche, *Both Sides of the Hill: Britain and the Palestine War* (London, 1960), p. 162; Lieutenant-Colonel Netanel Lorch, *The Edge of the Sword: Israel's War of Independence 1947-1949* (New York, 1961), p. 134; and Chaim Herzog, *The Arab-Israeli Wars: War and Peace in the Middle East* (New York, 1982), p. 48. The Palestinian historian is Khalidi, *Haven*, p. 865; and the British expert is Edgar O'Ballance *The Arab-Israeli War 1948* (London, 1956), p. 74.

53. Report by Renton, 30 Sept. 1945, FO 371/45342, E7939/2435/93; report by Renton, 30 Sept. 1946, FO 371/52422, E10544/649/93.

54. WO to FO, 1 March 1947, FO 371/67029, R3520/34/19.

55. Sir Edmund L. Hall-Patch (deputy undersecretary of state for foreign affairs) to Maj.-Gen. F. E. W. Simpson (WO), 10 May 1947, FO 371/61590, E3695/3/93; Stonehewer-Bird to FO, 18 April 1947, FO 371/61589, E3302/3/93; Stonehewer-Bird to FO, 3 May 1947, FO 371/61590, E3695/3/93.

56. Stonehewer-Bird to FO, 11 May 1947, FO 371/61590, E3972/3/93; Simpson to Hall-
     Patch, 20 May 1947, FO 371/61591, E4409/3/93.
57. Busk to FO, 2 Sept. 1947, report by Renton, 30 Sept. 1947, FO 371/61670,
     E11722/E11722/1244/93; memorandum by COS, 16 Oct. 1947, DEFE 5/6, COS(47)219.
58. Michael Wright (assistant undersecretary of state for foreign affairs) to A. R. McBain
     (MOS), 30 July 1947, FO 371/61633, E6836/1255/93; memorandum by Renton, 4 Aug.
     1947, FO 371/61593, E7401/3/93; report by Renton, 31 March 1948, FO 371/68477,
     E4878/618/93; WO to FO, 20 May 1949, FO 371/75165, E6388/1191/93. The prohibi-
     tion on the export of military material to Iraq is discussed in chapter 13.
59. Sir Henry Mack (British ambassador in Baghdad) to FO, 8 March 1948, FO 371/68368,
     E3302/11/65.
60. Stonehewer-Bird to FO, 16 Jan. 1946, FO 371/52397, E1011/155/93; I. K. Petre (WO)
     to A. W. France (Treasury), 17 April 1946, FO 371/52398, E3614/155/93; report by
     Renton, 30 Sept. 1946, FO 371/52422, E10544/649/93; Maj. R. H. C. Bryers (WO) to
     M. T. Walker (Eastern Dept. of FO), 5 March 1948, FO 371/68412, E3491/1017/65; M.
     M. Postan, History of the Second World War, United Kingdom Civil Series: British War
     Production, rev. ed. (London, 1975), pp. 103, 176, 182.
61. Shabtai Teveth, "The Palestine Arab Refugee Problem and Its Origins," Middle Eastern
     Studies, vol. 26 (1990), pp. 245-47.
62. Lorch, Edge, p. 169; Khalidi, Haven, p. 868; Fauzi al-Qawuqji, "Memoirs, 1948, part 1,"
     Journal of Palestine Studies, vol. 1 (1972), p. 38; Hassan Mustapha, Mudhakkirat Mulhaq
     Askari fi Lundun Qabl Harb Filastin al-Awal wa fi Athnaha (Memoirs of the Military Attache
     in London before and during the First Palestinian War) (Baghdad, 1985), p. 187; Teveth,
     "Refugee Problem," pp. 245-47.
     The Iraqi, Syrian, and Lebanese artillery strength at the outset of the war in Palestine
     on 15 May 1948 is in Khalidi. Iraq's shortage of ammunition for the 25-pounders is in
     Mustapha. The Arab Liberation Army's artillery strength in the fighting before May 1948
     and at the outset of the war is in Qawuqji. (In his discussion of Arab artillery strength
     Khalidi ignores this force.) Israel's artillery strength in May and July 1948 is in Lorch and
     Teveth respectively.
     The importance of the Arab advantage in artillery in the fighting in Palestine is clearly
     seen in the memoirs of Fauzi al-Qawuqji, the commander of the Arab Liberation Army.
     In addition to the first part cited above, see the second part in Journal of Palestine Studies,
     vol. 2 (1972), pp. 3-33.
63. Thompson to FO, 17 July 1944, Baxter to undersecretary of state for air, 23 Sept. 1944,
     FO 371/40067, E4232/E5699/347/93; AM to FO, 29 Nov. 1944, FO 371/40072,
     E7398/653/93; AM to FO, 27 Sept. 1945, FO 371/45330, E7278/1393/93; Owen
     Thetford, Aircraft of the Royal Air Force since 1918, 7th ed. (London, 1979), pp. 53-58;
     Chaz Bowyer, The Encyclopedia of British Military Aircraft (London, 1982), p. 62.
64. Memorandum by Rhys, 21 Dec. 1943, memorandum by the AOC Iraq and Persia, 12
     Jan. 1943, Cornwallis to Eden, 27 Jan. 1944, FO 371/40072, E854/E854/E854/653/93;
     Chaplin to S. R. H. Glanville (AM), 23 Feb. 1944, WO to Chaplin, 12 March 1944,
     Glanville to R. G. Dundas (Eastern Dept. of FO), 4 April 1944, memorandum by Rhys,
     no date but probably early July 1944, FO 371/40072, E854/E1658/E2148/E4490/653/93;
     Thompson to FO, 26 July 1945, FO 371/45330, E5642/1393/93; Busk to FO, 14 May
     1947, Baxter to Group-Captain D. C. Stapleton (MOD), 16 May 1947, FO 371/61590,
     E4040/E4040/3/93.
65. Reports by Wing-Commander R. M. Bradley (inspector of the Iraqi air force), 31 March
     1945 and 30 Sept. 1945, FO 371/45330, E2744/E9531/1393/93.

66. Report by Bradley, 30 Sept. 1945, FO 371/45330, E9531/1393/93; report by Wing-Commander H. W. H. Fisher (inspector of the Iraqi air force), 31 March 1947, FO 371/61628, E3207/139/93; report by Fisher, 1 Oct. 1947, FO 371/61629, E11723/139/93.

67. For Iraqi air activity in the war in Palestine, including information on the use of the Ansons, see Sir Alec Kirkbride (British minister in Amman) to FO, 17 May 1948, FO 371/68372, E6393/11/65; Kirkbride to FO, 18 May 1948, FO 371/68373, E6494/11/65; Kirkbride to FO, 5 June 1948, FO 816/122; AM to FO, 16 July 1948, FO to AM, 30 July 1948, FO 371/68473, E9747/E9747/508/93; Kimche and Kimche, *Both Sides*, p. 152; and Khalidi, *Haven*, p. 868.

In his calculation of Arab air strength at the outset of the Arab-Israeli War on 15 May 1948, Khalidi lists the Iraqi Ansons as light transports and gives no indication that they had any other function. While the Ansons could be used for this purpose, we have observed that they were multipurpose aircraft that could also be used for ground attack. And as the archival references in this note make clear, during the war in Palestine the Iraqis did use them for ground attack.

In this connection it is also relevant to note that in 1944, when Iraq purchased the planes, the United States minister in Baghdad reported that they were "fitted out as bombers." Loy W. Henderson to secretary of state, 8 Sept. 1944, 890G.248/9-844.

68. Kimche and Kimche, *Both Sides*, pp. 162, 204; Lorch, *Edge*, pp. 134, 226-30; Khalidi, *Haven*, p. 866.

After an Egyptian air raid on its only air base on the morning of 15 May 1948, the first day of the Arab-Israeli War, Israel had only five operational aircraft, none of which were fighters or bombers. Colonel Eliezer Cohen, *Israel's Best Defense: The First Full Story of the Israeli Air Force* (New York, 1993), pp. 1-2, 25-26.

In his calculation of Israeli air strength at the outset of the Arab-Israeli War on 15 May 1948, Khalidi includes ten Messerschmitt fighter-bombers. While it is true that Israel owned the planes, his own footnote indicates that on 15 May they were still in Czechoslovakia and therefore obviously of no use to Israel. In fact, as Lorch points out (pp. 215, 230-31) it was not until 29 May that the Israelis assembled and used their first four Messerschmitts, losing two in an attack against the Egyptians.

Two weeks later, at the start of the first truce on 11 June, Israeli Messerschmitt strength consisted of one flyable aircraft and eight more planes in various states of assembly or repair. There were only four trained pilots for these aircraft. Ehud Yonay, *No Margin for Error: The Making of the Israeli Air Force* (New York, 1993), pp. 39-40.

69. Thompson to FO, 4 April 1945, AM to AOC Middle East, 16 May 1945, Stonehewer-Bird to FO, 22 July 1945, report by Bradley, 30 Sept. 1945, FO 371/45330, E2434/E3244/E5380/E9531/1393/93.

70. Sir Arthur Street (AM) to Sir Ronald Cambell (assistant undersecretary of state for foreign affairs), 27 Sept. 1945, Stonehewer-Bird to FO, 21 Oct. 1945, Howe to Street, 3 Nov. 1945, agenda for an IDC at the AM, 29 Nov. 1945, FO 371/45330, E7278/E8222/E8221/E9662/1393/93.

71. Howe to Street, 3 Nov. 1945, FO 371/45330, E8221/1393/93; Air Hdq. Iraq and Persia to Hdq. RAF Mediterranean and Middle East, 31 Dec. 1945, Hdq. RAF Mediterranean and Middle East to AM, 3 Jan. 1946, Stonehewer-Bird to FO, 4 Jan. 1946, FO to Baghdad, 16 Jan. 1946, FO 371/52388, E59/E59/E146/E364/54/93.

72. Meeting of the Dominions and Foreign Air Forces Committee, 2 Aug. 1946, FO 371/52388, E8243/54/93; Busk to Bevin, 13 Feb. 1947, report by Fisher, 31 March 1947, Baxter to Busk, 9 Aug. 1947, FO 371/61628, E1743/E3207/E4926/139/93.

73. *HC,* 5 May 1948, vol. 450, written answers, col. 140.
74. MOD to FO, 3 Dec. 1952, Admiralty to MOS, 5 Dec. 1952, FO 371/98757, EQ1193/56/57; Owen Thetford, *British Naval Aircraft since 1912,* 5th ed. (London, 1982), pp. 240-41; Bowyer, *Encyclopedia,* p. 176.
75. Report by Fisher, 31 March 1947, FO 371/61628, E3207/139/93; report by JPS, 11 Aug. 1947, DEFE 6/3, JP(47)108(Final); MOD to FO, 9 Feb. 1948, FO 371/68410, E1983/1017/65.
76. Report by Fisher, 31 March 1947, FO 371/61628, E3207/139/93.
77. Thompson to FO, 26 July 1945, FO 371/45330, E5642/1393/93; report by Renton, 30 Sept. 1945, Stonehewer-Bird to FO, 10 Oct. 1945, FO 371/45342, E7939/E7939/2435/93.
78. Report by Renton, 30 Sept. 1944, FO 371/40044, E6246/42/93.
79. These points come through in virtually all of Renton's reports. See, for example, 31 March 1945 and 30 Sept. 1945, FO 371/45342, E2435/E7939/2435/93; 31 March 1946 and 30 Sept. 1946, FO 371/52422, E4145/E10544/649/93; and 31 March 1947, FO 371/61669, E3126/1244/93. Also see Stonehewer-Bird to FO, 12 May 1945, 15 May 1945, 21 May 1945, and 12 July 1945, FO 371/45298, E3025/E3084/E3664/E5120/182/93.
80. The size of the British military mission varied over time. In September 1947, for example, it consisted of nineteen officers and twelve noncommissioned officers. The latter were RAF personnel charged with maintaining Iraqi aircraft and training Iraqi maintenance personnel. Memorandum by Major W. N. Seymour (WO), no date but submitted to FO on 19 Sept. 1947, FO 371/61670, E8813/1244/93; report by Fisher, 1 Oct. 1947, FO371/61629, E11723/139/93.
81. Report by Renton, 30 Sept. 1944, FO 371/40044, E6246/42/93; report by Renton, 31 March 1945, FO 371/45342, E2435/2435/93.
82. Report by Renton, 30 Sept. 1946, FO 371/52422, E10544/649/93.
83. *Liwa al-Istiqlal,* 4 Aug. 1946, FO 371/52422, E10544/649/93.
84. *Liwa al-Istiqlal,* 6 Jan. 1947, FO 371/61669, E3126/1244/93.
85. *Liwa al-Istiqlal,* 1 Sept. 1947, FO 371/61670, E11722/1244/93.
86. Report by Renton, 31 March 1948, FO 371/68477, E4878/618/93.
87. Memorandum by Renton, 31 Jan. 1948, FO 371/68476, E1858/618/93.
88. BMEO to FO, 2 Feb. 1948, Mack to FO, 10 Feb. 1948, FO to Baghdad, 16 March 1948, Mack to FO, 21 March 1948, FO 371/68476, E1815/E2034/E3249/E3731/618/93.
89. Mack to Bevin, 2 April 1948, FO 371/68476, E4652/618/93.

NOTES TO CHAPTER 9

1. The sterling area is discussed in David Wightman, "The Sterling Area," *Banca Nazionale del Lavoro,* vol. 4 (1951), pp. 61-69, 147-66; United States Economic Cooperation Administration Special Mission to the United Kingdom, *The Sterling Area: An American Analysis* (London, 1951); J. R. Sargent, "Britain and the Sterling Area," in G. D. N. Worswick and P. H. Ady (eds.), *The British Economy 1945-1950* (Oxford, 1952), pp. 531-49; A. R. Conan, *The Sterling Area* (London, 1952); Philip W. Bell, *The Sterling Area in the Postwar World: Internal Mechanism and Cohesion 1946-1952* (Oxford, 1956); Judd Polk, *Sterling: Its Meaning in World Finance* (New York, 1956); Elliot Zupnick, *Britain's Postwar Dollar Problem* (New York, 1957); and A. R. Conan, *The Rationale of the Sterling Area: Texts and Commentary* (London, 1961).
2. FO to Washington, 11 Sept. 1944, T 236/1177; memorandum by E. R. Lingeman (commercial counsellor, British embassy Baghdad), 23 Dec. 1944, in Cornwallis to Eden,

30 Dec. 1944, FO 624/39/572, part 2; D. Davidson (Treasury) to Winthrop Brown (U.S. embassy London), 20 Jan. 1945, FO 371/45290, E581/89/93.

3. FO to Washington, 11 Sept. 1944, T 236/1177; Cornwallis to FO, 26 Oct. 1944, FO 624/39/572, part 1; minute by W. S. Gilbert (Board of Trade), 13 Dec. 1944, memorandum by Lingeman, 23 Dec. 1944, in Cornwallis to Eden, 30 Dec. 1944, FO 624/39/572, part 2.

4. Gilbert to Jabr, 18 Dec. 1944, FO 371/45290, E368/89/93; memorandum by Lingeman, 23 Dec. 1944, in Cornwallis to Eden, 30 Dec. 1944, memorandum by C. E. Loombe (head of Iraq's currency control), no date, in Cornwallis to Eden, 30 Dec. 1944, FO 624/39/572, part 2; Cornwallis to Eden, 15 Jan. 1945, FO 371/45302, E627/195/93.

5. Memorandum by Lingeman, 23 Dec. 1944, in Cornwallis to Eden, 30 Dec. 1944, FO 624/39/572, part 2; memorandum by Treasury, no date, in FO to Cornwallis, 12 Feb. 1945, T 236/1177; Cornwallis to Eden, 21 March 1945, FO 371/45291, E2197/89/93; J. Pinsent (Treasury) to Baxter, 31 July 1945, FO 371/45293, E5718/89/93.

6. Memorandum by Lingeman, 23 Dec. 1944, in Cornwallis to Eden, 30 Dec. 1944, FO 624/39/572, part 2; Cornwallis to Eden, 15 Jan. 1945, FO 371/45302, E627/195/93; British embassy Baghdad to Iraqi minister of foreign affairs, 20 Feb. 1945, FO 371/45291, E1605/89/93.

7. Cornwallis to FO, 21 Dec. 1944, FO 624/39/572, part 2; acting secretary of state to U.S. legation Baghdad, 8 Feb. 1945, 890G.51/2-2844; Cornwallis to FO, 16 Feb. 1945, FO 371/45290, E1186/89/93; Cornwallis to Eden, 21 March 1945, FO 371/45291, E2197/89/93.

8. Gilbert to Jabr, 18 Dec. 1944, FO 371/45290, E368/89/93; Davidson to Lingeman, 22 Dec. 1944, memorandum by Lingeman, 23 Dec. 1944, in Cornwallis to Eden, 30 Dec. 1944, FO 624/39/572, part 2; Cornwallis to Eden, 15 Jan. 1945, FO 371/45302, E627/195/93; memorandum by Loombe, 19 Feb. 1945, FO 371/45291, E1579/89/93.

9. Cornwallis to Eden, 30 Dec. 1944 (including enclosed memorandum by Lingeman of 23 Dec. 1944), FO 624/39/572, part 2; memorandum by Loombe, 19 Feb. 1945, FO 371/45291, E1579/89/93.

10. This quotation is in Loy W. Henderson (U.S. minister in Baghdad) to secretary of state, 25 Jan. 1945, 890G.50/1-2545.

11. This quotation is in Cornwallis to Eden, 21 March 1945, FO 371/45291, E2197/89/93.

12. Cornwallis to Eden, 30 Dec. 1944 (including enclosed memorandum by Lingeman of 23 Dec. 1944), FO 624/39/572, part 2; memorandum by Treasury, no date, in FO to Cornwallis, 12 Feb. 1945, T 236/1177; Cornwallis to Eden, 19 March 1945, FO 371/45302, E2177/195/93.

13. Memorandum by Pelham, May 1945, FO 371/61648, E2466/453/93.

14. The text of this agreement is in Cmd. 6646.
Throughout the immediate postwar period the British government provided the IPC's dollar requirements directly to the company and did not charge any of them to Iraq's allocation. Busk to FO, 15 Sept. 1947, FO 371/61651, E8587/453/93.

15. Wightman, "Sterling Area," pp. 153, 159; Sargent, "Sterling Area," p. 538; Zupnick, *Dollar Problem,* p. 126.

16. Bell, *Sterling Area,* p. 57.
It should be noted that during this period almost none of Iraq's oil went to the United States. Indeed, according to the National Bank of Iraq, between 1948 and 1951 the cumulative total was only .7 percent. Iversen, *Monetary Policy,* p. 81.

17. Between 1946 and 1951 Malaya had a cumulative trade surplus with the United States and Canada of $1.5 billion, and the Gold Coast one of $347 million. Zupnick, *Dollar Problem,* p. 142.

18. Britain's use of the sterling area to exploit net dollar earning colonies like Malaya and the Gold Coast is discussed in Kenneth M. Wright, "Dollar Pooling in the Sterling Area, 1939-1952," *The American Economic Review*, vol. 44 (1954), pp. 561, 563, 569, 574; Partha Sarathi Gupta, "Imperialism and the Labour Government of 1945-51," in Jay Winter (ed.), *The Working Class in Modern British History: Essays in Honour of Henry Pelling* (Cambridge, 1983), pp. 110-11; D. K. Fieldhouse, "The Labour Governments and the Empire-Commonwealth, 1945-51," in Ritchie Ovendale (ed.), *The Foreign Policy of the British Labour Governments, 1945-1951* (Leicester, 1984), pp. 95-96; Scott Newton, "Britain, the Sterling Area and European Integration, 1945-50," *The Journal of Imperial and Commonwealth History*, vol. 13 (1985), p. 177; Allister E. Hinds, "Sterling and Imperial Policy, 1945-1951," *The Journal of Imperial and Commonwealth History*, vol. 15 (1987), pp. 162-63; Ronald Hyam, "Africa and the Labour Government, 1945-1951," *The Journal of Imperial and Commonwealth History*, vol. 16 (1988), pp. 148-49; Allister E. Hinds, "Imperial Policy and Colonial Sterling Balances 1943-56," *The Journal of Imperial and Commonwealth History*, vol. 19 (1991), pp. 36, 40-41; and Gerold Krozewski, "Sterling, the 'Minor' Territories, and the End of Formal Empire, 1939-1958," *Economic History Review*, vol. 46 (1993), pp. 245, 247-50, 259-60.

19. The extensions of this agreement are in Cmd. 6742, 6803, and 7110.

20. Statement by Salih Haidar (Iraqi Ministry of Finance) at a meeting of British and Iraqi officials in London, 27 June 1947, note by the Iraqi Ministry of Finance on Iraq's requirements from its sterling balances, no date but probably about 30 June 1947, T 236/1190.

21. Ibid.

22. Ibid.

23. Memorandum by Thompson, 29 Oct. 1945, FO 371/45254, E8476/175/65; Stonehewer-Bird to Bevin, 4 March 1946, FO 371/52423, E2469/652/93; Stonehewer-Bird to FO, 24 March 1946, FO 371/52367, E2630/9/93.

24. For the views of the Treasury on this question, see statement by Sir Wilfrid Eady (Treasury) to Iraqi minister of finance, 5 March 1947, T 236/1189; memoranda by Treasury, 24 March 1947, 19 May 1947, and no date but probably May 1947, T236/1274; and Treasury to FO, 7 Oct. 1947, FO 371/61558, E9559/5764/65.

    The Ministry of Supply and the Board of Trade supported the Treasury on this question. MOS to joint secretary of the ME(O), 19 March 1947, FO 371/61509, E2560/183/65; MOS to FO, 9 June 1947, FO 371/61511, E5023/183/65; BT to FO, 25 July 1947, FO 371/61500, E6731/44/65.

    Not surprisingly, the Foreign Office, which was the government department responsible for maintaining good relations with Iraq, was the one that was most eager to accommodate Iraq in the matter of supplies. Note by FO, 15 May 1947, FO 371/61499, E4195/44/65; comments by Bevin at a meeting of FO officials in London, 8 Oct. 1947, FO 371/61558, E9557/5764/65; Bevin to Hugh Dalton (chancellor of the exchequer), 15 Oct. 1947, FO 371/61595, E9513/3/93.

    Of course, the British pursued the same restrictive dollar and export policies toward their colonies, but this was no consolation to Iraq. Wright, "Dollar Pooling," p. 563; Fieldhouse, "Labour Governments," pp. 96-98; Hinds, "Colonial Sterling Balances," pp. 29-30, 33, 40-41; Krozewski, "'Minor' Territories," pp. 248, 259.

25. Statement by Eady to Iraqi minister of finance, 5 March 1947, T 236/1189.

26. The text of this agreement is in Cmd. 6968.

27. A record of the negotiations is in T 236/1189-90, and FO 371/61648-50.

28. Statement by Eady to Iraqi minister of finance, 5 March 1947, T 236/1189.

29. Statement by Cameron F. Cobbold (deputy governor of the Bank of England) at a meeting with Iraqi officials in Baghdad, 6 March 1947, T 236/1189; statement by Eady at a meeting of British and Iraqi officials in London, 20 June 1947, T 236/1190; FO to Baghdad, 3 July 1947, FO 371/61648, E5335/453/93; Nevile Butler (assistant undersecretary of state for foreign affairs) to Sir Orme Sargent (permanent undersecretary of state for foreign affairs), 8 July 1947, FO 371/61649, E6262/453/93.

30. Eady to Iraqi minister of finance, 5 March 1947, T 236/1189; FO to Baghdad, 3 July 1947 and 7 July 1947, FO 371/61648, E5335/E5335/453/93; FO to Baghdad, 26 July 1947 and 31 July 1947, FO 371/61650, E6708/E6708/453/93.

31. Statement by Ibrahim al-Kabir (director-general of the Iraqi Ministry of Finance) at a meeting of British and Iraqi officials in Baghdad, 6 March 1947, T 236/1189; FO to Baghdad, 3 July 1947, FO 371/61648, E5335/453/93. The newspaper article is in George Wadsworth (U.S. ambassador in Baghdad) to secretary of state, 5 March 1947, 890G.51/3-547.
Like Iraq, other holders of sterling balances, such as India, Egypt, and Iran, refused to write off any of them. B. R. Tomlinson, "Indo-British Relations in the Post-Colonial Era: The Sterling Balances Negotiations, 1947-49," *The Journal of Imperial and Commonwealth History*, vol. 13 (1985), pp. 147, 151; Pressnell, *External Economic Policy*, pp. 365-66; Frank Brenchley, *Britain and the Middle East: An Economic History 1945-87* (London, 1989), pp. 23-24.

32. Statement by Haidar at a meeting of British and Iraqi officials in London, 27 June 1947, T 236/1190; FO to Baghdad, 3 July 1947, FO 371/61648, E5335/453/93.

33. Statement by Ibrahim al-Kabir at a meeting of British and Iraqi officials in Baghdad, 6 March 1947, T 236/1189; statements by Ibrahim al-Kabir at meetings of British and Iraqi officials in London, 20 June 1947, 27 June 1947, and 1 July 1947, T 236/1190; statements by Fadhil al-Jamali (Iraqi minister for foreign affairs) at meetings of British and Iraqi officials in London, 18 June 1947 and 20 June 1947, T 236/1190; statement by Haidar at a meeting of British and Iraqi officials in London, 27 June 1947, T 236/1190.

34. Note by the Treasury on Iraq's statistical argument, no date but probably about 30 June 1947, statement by E. Rowe Dutton (Treasury) at a meeting of British and Iraqi officials in London, 2 July 1947, T 236/1190; FO to Baghdad, 3 July 1947, FO 371/61648, E5335/453/93; Abdul-Hassan Zalzalah, "Iraq in the Sterling Area 1932-1954: A Study in Economic-Political Relationships" (Ph.D. dissertation at Indiana University, 1957), p. 305. Like the British, the National Democratic party was critical of the Iraqi government's policy of permitting the importation of sizable quantities of luxury items. For example, in February 1947 *Sawt al-Ahali* maintained that "if non-essential consumer goods continue to arrive in the country at the present rate, it will not be long before our international credits are entirely wiped out." This article is in Wadsworth to secretary of state, 5 March 1947, 890G.51/3-547.

35. Butler to Bevin, 5 July 1947, Bevin to Dalton, 9 July 1947, FO 371/61649, E6032/E6145/453/93.

36. The text of this agreement is in Cmd. 7201.

37. Dalton to Zaid (Iraqi ambassador in London), 13 Aug. 1947, FO 371/61650, E7596/453/93.

38. Ibid.

39. *The Times*, 21 Aug. 1947, p. 8.

40. *The Financial Times*, 21 Aug. 1947, p. 4.

41. *The Economist*, 23 Aug. 1947, p. 337.

42. The first set of figures is in Scott Newton, "The Sterling Crisis of 1947 and the British Response to the Marshall Plan," *Economic History Review,* 2nd series, vol. 37 (1984), p. 397. The second set of figures is in FO to Baghdad, 18 Aug. 1947, FO 371/61651, E8332/453/93. The convertibility crisis of 1947 is discussed in Richard N. Gardner, *Sterling-Dollar Diplomacy in Current Perspective: The Origins and the Prospects of Our International Economic Order,* expanded ed. (New York, 1980), pp. 306-47; and Cairncross, *Years of Recovery,* pp. 121-64.

43. The exchange of letters with the United States on this question is in Cmd. 7210.

44. A record of these negotiations is in FO 371/61651-54.

45. Busk to FO, 15 Sept. 1947, FO 371/61651, E8587/453/93.

46. Pelham to FO, 6 Oct. 1947, FO 371/61652, E9288/453/93; note by Treasury, 12 Oct. 1947, CAB 134/47, BP(ON)(47)34. The figure of $4.1 billion is in Gardner, *Sterling-Dollar,* p. 308.

47. Pelham to FO, 6 Oct. 1947 and 7 Oct. 1947, FO 371/61652, E9288/E9290/453/93; note by BT, 20 Oct. 1947, CAB 134/47, BP(ON)(47)48; minutes of ONC, 23 Oct. 1947, CAB 134/46, BP(ON)(47)23.

48. The text of this agreement is in Cmd. 7269.

49. Note by Iliff on Iraq's dollar situation, 26 Aug. 1947, T 236/1195; Pelham to FO, 28 Sept. 1947, FO to Baghdad, 4 Oct. 1947, FO 371/61652, E8974/E8990/453/93; note by Treasury, 12 Oct. 1947, memorandum by FO, 21 Oct. 1947, CAB 134/47, BP(ON)(47)34, BP(ON)(47)50.

50. Bevin to Dalton, 15 Oct. 1947, FO 371/61595, E9513/3/93; memorandum by FO, 21 Oct. 1947, CAB 134/47, BP(ON)(47)50.

51. Bevin to Dalton, 15 Oct. 1947, FO 371/61595, E9513/3/93; memorandum by FO, 21 Oct. 1947, CAB 134/47, BP(ON)(47)50.

52. At this time Iraq's non-oil income was $9 million per year and its oil income was $8 million per year for a total of $17 million per year. However, in the financial agreement of November 1947 Britain promised to provide Iraq with $23 million on an annual basis. Memorandum by FO, 21 Oct. 1947, CAB 134/47, BP(ON)(47)50.
      Normally Iraq's earnings from the American companies share of the IPC's royalties and local expenditures were not included in calculations of Iraq's dollar earnings because the IPC had to spend large amounts of dollars to purchase materials in the United States for oilfield development and pipeline construction in Iraq. Thus if the American companies' share of the IPC's royalties and local expenditures was considered part of Iraq's dollar earnings, then logically the IPC's purchases in the United States should be considered part of Iraq's dollar expenditures. In October 1949 the British Treasury calculated that these two figures were roughly equal (note by Treasury, 13 Oct. 1949, CAB 134/567, ON(49)346). In any event, it is not clear that Iraq could have accessed any of these dollars if it left the sterling area because, in accordance with its interpretation of the terms of the concession, the IPC always paid Iraq in the sterling equivalent of gold.

53. Stonehewer-Bird to Bevin, 4 March 1946, FO 371/52423, E2469/652/93; Abdul Illah Hafidh (governor of the National Bank of Iraq) to the British Treasury, 30 May 1949, FO 371/75157, E6732/1113/93; Sassoon, *Economic Policy,* p. 207.

NOTES TO CHAPTER 10

1. Stonehewer-Bird to Eden, 7 May 1945, FO 371/45302, E3442/195/93; Stonehewer-Bird to FO, 18 July 1945, FO 371/45303, E5243/195/93; Stonehewer-Bird to FO, 15 April 1946 and 19 April 1946, FO 371/52401, E3618/E3559/226/93; Air Hdq. Iraq and Persia

to AM, 20 Nov. 1946, FO 371/52403, E11569/226/93; Stonehewer-Bird to Nevile Butler (assistant undersecretary of state for foreign affairs), 15 April 1947, FO 371/61589, E3447/3/93; Batatu, *Social Classes*, p. 546.

2. Report by JPS, 25 Oct. 1946, CAB 84/84, JP(46)178(Final); report by JPS, 17 Dec. 1946, CAB 84/85, JP(46)196(Final); report by JPS, 27 Dec. 1946, CAB 84/86, JP(46)232(Final); report by AM, 16 July 1947, FO 371/61592, E6407/3/93.

3. Louis, *British Empire*, p. 674.

4. Report by JPS, 25 Oct. 1946, CAB 84/84, JP(46)178(Final).

5. Ibid.; report by JPS, 27 Dec. 1946, CAB 84/86, JP(46)232(Final); report by AM, 16 July 1947, FO 371/61592, E6407/3/93.

6. Baxter to Group-Captain D. C. Stapleton (Cabinet Offices), 10 Dec. 1946, FO 371/52403, E11712/226/93; memorandum by Garran, 26 July 1947, minute by Wright, 30 July 1947, FO 371/61592, E7069/E7069/3/93; memorandum by Bevin, 3 Oct. 1947, FO 371/61594, E9265/3/93; Wright to Lt.-Gen. Sir Leslie Hollis (chief staff officer to the minister of defense), 7 Dec. 1947, FO 371/61600, E11979/3/93.

7. Stonehewer-Bird to Eden, 7 May 1945, Stonehewer-Bird to FO, 27 May 1945, FO 371/45302, E3442/E3437/195/93.

8. FO to Baghdad, 1 May 1946, Stonehewer-Bird to FO, 21 May 1946, FO 371/52401, E3559/E4799/226/93. The exchange of notes is in Cmd. 6918.

9. Stonehewer-Bird to Eden, 7 May 1945, minute by Baxter, 14 June 1945, FO 371/45302, E3442/E3442/195/93; John Balfour (British embassy Washington) to Baxter, 10 Dec. 1945, FO 371/45255, E9902/175/65; minute by Pyman, 9 March 1946, FO 371/52401, E1947/226/93.

10. Report by the British embassy in Baghdad on the leading personalities in Iraq, 29 June 1940, FO 371/24562, E2329/2329/93; report by Renton, 31 March 1948, FO 371/68477, E4878/618/93; Khadduri, *Independent Iraq*, pp. 261-62; Elie Kedourie, "The Iraqi Shiis and Their Fate," in Martin Kramer (ed.), *Shiism, Resistance, and Revolution* (Boulder, Colo., 1987), p. 153.

11. Minute by Butler, 21 April 1947, FO 371/61589, E3399/3/93; Hdq. MELF to MOD, 16 May 1947, Stonehewer-Bird to FO, 19 May 1947, FO 371/61590, E4274/E4252/3/93; report by the British military representatives on their talks with Iraqi leaders, 20 May 1947, Busk to Bevin, 23 May 1947, FO 371/61591, E5102/E4770/3/93; Baxter to Stapleton, 5 July 1947, FO 371/61526, E5890/754/65; Khadduri, *Independent Iraq*, pp. 262-63.

12. Hdq. MELF to MOD, 16 May 1947, FO 371/61590, E4274/3/93; report by the British military representatives on their talks with Iraqi leaders, 20 May 1947, FO 371/61591, E5102/3/93.

13. Report by AM, 16 July 1947, FO 371/61592, E6407/3/93; memorandum by COS, 15 Nov. 1947, DEFE 5/6, COS(47)219.

14. Report by the British military representatives on their talks with Iraqi leaders, 20 May 1947, FO 371/61591, E5102/3/93.

15. Ibid.; Busk to FO, 3 Nov. 1947, 3 Nov. 1947, and 6 Nov. 1947, FO 371/61596, E10295/E10297/E10432/3/93; minutes of COS, 7 Nov. 1947, DEFE 4/8, COS(47)137.

16. Busk to Bevin, 23 May 1947, FO 371/61591, E4770/3/93.

17. Report by AM, 16 July 1947, FO 371/61592, E6407/3/93; report by JPS, 17 Sept. 1947, DEFE 6/3, JP(47)126(Final); minutes of COS, 19 Sept. 1947, DEFE 4/7, COS(47)121.

18. Minutes by Garran, 1 Sept. 1947 and 4 Sept. 1947, FO 371/61594, E8230/E8408/3/93.

19. Minute by Garran, 16 Oct. 1947, Busk to FO, 3 Nov. 1947 and 7 Nov. 1947, FO 371/61596, E10298/E10297/E10453/3/93; Busk to FO, 26 Nov. 1947, FO 371/61597,

E11172/3/93; Busk to FO, 4 Dec. 1947, Busk to Bevin, 4 Dec. 1947, FO 371/61599, E11528/E11608/3/93.

20. Busk to FO, 29 Nov. 1947, FO 371/61598, E11286/3/93; Busk to FO, 4 Dec. 1947, FO 371/61599, E11528/3/93.

21. Busk to FO, 29 Nov. 1947, FO 371/61598, E11286/3/93; Bevin to Busk, 23 Dec. 1947, FO 371/61601, E12234/3/93.

22. Busk to FO, 24 Dec. 1947, FO 371/61601, E12235/3/93.

23. Meeting of the British and Iraqi delegations at FO, 7 Jan. 1948, FO 371/68442, E409/27/93.

24. Ibid.

25. Ibid.

26. Meeting of the British and Iraqi delegations at the FO, 9 Jan. 1948, FO 371/68442, E409/27/93.

27. Ibid.; Gregory Blaxland, *The Regiments Depart: A History of the British Army, 1945-1970* (London, 1971), p. 13.

28. The text of the treaty, without the accompanying unpublished letters, is in Cmd. 7309. The text of the treaty, with the accompanying unpublished letters, is in FO 371/68442, E651/27/93.

29. Marr (*Iraq*, pp. 102-3) maintains that the treaty gave Iraq control over the bases, provided for the removal of British military personnel from Iraq, and obliged Iraq to surrender the bases to Britain in time of war. None of these statements are true.

30. Memorandum by COS, 15 Nov. 1947, DEFE 5/6, COS(47)219; minute by Pyman, 27 Nov. 1947, FO 371/61597, E11172/3/93; FO to Baghdad, 1 Dec. 1947, FO 371/61598, E11312/3/93.

31. Note by Hector McNeil (parliamentary undersecretary of state for foreign affairs), 15 March 1948, FO 371/68447, E3627/27/93; Silverfarb, *Informal Empire,* p. 77.

32. Minute by the acting chief of the Air Staff, 2 Jan. 1948, Air 20/2534; brief by FO, 9 Jan. 1948, FO 371/68442, E457/27/93.

33. The Bevin-Sidky agreement is discussed in Louis, *British Empire,* pp. 244-53.

34. Jabr's desire for a triumph over the treaty to boost his prestige in Iraq is discussed in Busk to FO, 29 Nov. 1947, FO 371/61598, E11286/3/93; and Busk to Bevin, 4 Dec. 1947, FO 371/61599, E11608/3/93. The Anglo-Iraqi financial agrement of August 1947 and the suspension of the convertibility of sterling are discussed in chapter 9. The General Assembly resolution of November 1947 is discussed in chapter 12. The bread shortage in Iraq during this period is discussed in chapter 11.

35. Thompson to Bevin, 26 Sept. 1945, FO 371/45295, E7495/104/93; Stonehewer-Bird to Bevin, 4 March 1946, FO 371/52423, E2469/652/93; Stonehewer-Bird to Bevin, 21 March 1946, FO 371/52327, E2962/797/65; Busk to Wright, 17 Sept. 1947, FO 371/61594, E8789/3/93; Busk to Bevin, 4 Dec. 1947, FO 371/61599, E11608/3/93.

36. Note by McNeil, 15 March 1948, FO 371/68447, E3627/27/93.

37. Brig.-Gen. J. H. Dove (WO) to Pierson Dixon (Bevin's private secretary), 22 March 1947, FO 371/62000, E3977/185/34; Silverfarb, *Informal Empire,* pp. 47-55.

38. Minute by Pyman, 9 March 1946, FO 371/52401, E1947/226/93; memorandum by COS, 15 Nov. 1947, DEFE 5/6, COS(47)219.

39. Brief by FO, 9 Jan. 1948, meeting of the British and Iraqi delegations at the FO, 10 Jan. 1948, FO 371/68442, E457/E409/27/93.

40. Memorandum by COS, 15 Nov. 1947, DEFE 5/6, COS(47)219; Busk to FO, 24 Dec. 1947, FO 371/61601, E12235/3/93; Blaxland, *Regiments,* p. 219.

41. Stonehewer-Bird to Eden, 7 May 1945, Stonehewer-Bird to FO, 27 May 1945, FO 371/45302, E3442/E3437/195/93; Bevin to Stonehewer-Bird, 8 Feb. 1947, FO 371/61588, E1300/3/93; minute by Garran, 29 Oct. 1947, FO 371/61597, E10799/3/93.
42. Minute by Pyman, 9 March 1946, FO 371/52401, E1947/226/93; minute by Baxter, 20 March 1947, Butler to Stonehewer-Bird, 8 May 1947, FO 371/61588, E1300/E1300/3/93; Batatu, *Social Classes*, p. 270; Sassoon, *Economic Policy*, pp. 64-65.
43. Minute by Pyman, 9 March 1946, FO 371/52401, E1947/226/93; minute by Baker, 17 Feb. 1947, minute by W. E. Beckett (legal adviser at FO), 21 March 1947, Butler to Stonehewer-Bird, 8 May 1947, FO 371/61588, E1300/E1300/E1300/3/93; Busk to Butler, 24 May 1947, FO 371/61591, E4755/3/93.
44. Report by JPS, 11 Aug. 1947, DEFE 6/3, JP(47)108(Final); minutes of COS, 7 Nov. 1947, DEFE 4/8, COS(47)137; Sir Orme Sargent (permanent undersecretary of state for foreign affairs) to Sir Edward Bridges (Treasury), 14 Nov. 1947, FO 371/61597, E10892/3/93.
45. Meeting of the British and Iraqi delegations at the FO, 10 Jan. 1948, FO 371/68442, E409/27/93; memorandum by Renton, 31 Jan. 1948, FO 371/68476, E1858/618/93. Incidentally, the British were probably mistaken about the pro-British disposition of the Iraqi officers who had attended courses at British military academies. Indeed, of the fifteen members of the committee of Free Officers who led the revolt against the old regime in 1958, five including the chairman had studied in Britain. Batatu, *Social Classes*, pp. 778-81.
46. Meeting of the British and Iraqi delegations at the FO, 9 Jan. 1948, FO 371/68442, E409/27/93.

NOTES TO CHAPTER 11

1. Manifesto of the Istiqlal party, 18 Jan. 1948, FO 371/68448, E4898/27/93; press summary by the U.S. embassy in Baghdad, 26 Jan. 1948, 890G.9111 RR/1-2648; memorandum by the U.S. embassy in Baghdad on the press reaction to the treaty, 9 Feb. 1948, 741.90G/2-948.
2. Manifesto of the Istiqlal party, 18 Jan. 1948, FO 371/68448, E4898/27/93; G. C. Pelham (British chargé d'affaires in Baghdad) to FO, 22 Jan. 1948, FO 371/68444, E969/27/93; report by Renton, 31 March 1948, FO 371/68477, E4878/618/93; Mack to Bevin, 13 April 1948, FO 371/68448, E4898/27/93.
3. Minute by Burrows, 23 Jan. 1948, FO 371/68444, E1119/27/93.
4. Manifesto of the Istiqlal party, 18 Jan. 1948, FO 371/68448, E4898/27/93; Pelham to FO, 22 Jan. 1948, Busk to FO, 29 Jan. 1948, FO 371/68444, E969/E1369/27/93; Busk to FO, 4 Feb. 1948, FO 371/68445, E1708/27/93; Mack to Bevin, 13 April 1948, FO 371/68448, E4898/27/93.
5. Minute by Burrows, 23 Jan. 1948, FO 371/68444, E1119/27/93; note by McNeil, 15 March 1948, McNeil to A. T. Lennox-Boyd (member of Parliament) 18 March 1948, FO 371/68447, E3627/E3627/27/93.
6. Report by Renton, 31 March 1948, FO 371/68477, E4878/618/93; Mack to Bevin, 13 April 1948, FO 371/68448, E4898/27/93.
7. Burrows to Busk, 26 March 1948, FO 371/68447, E3886/27/93.
8. Manifesto of the Istiqlal party, 18 Jan. 1948, FO 371/68448, E4898/27/93; Pelham to FO, 22 Jan. 1948, minute by Burrows, 23 Jan. 1948, FO 371/68444, E969/E1119/27/93.
9. Manifesto of the Istiqlal party, 18 Jan. 1948, FO 371/68448, E4898/27/93.

10. Pelham to FO, 19 Jan. 1948, FO 371/68443, E805/27/93; Pelham to Attlee, 25 Jan. 1948, FO 371/68446, E2217/27/93; Busk to Borrows, 5 April 1948, FO 371/68448, E4591/27/93; memorandum by Walter W. Harris (U.S. embassy Baghdad) on the January riots, 7 April 1948, 890G.00/4-3048.

11. Pelham to FO, 22 Jan. 1948, FO 371/68444, E969/27/93; minute by J. C. B. Richmond (oriental counsellor, British embassy Baghdad), 22 Jan. 1948, Pelham to Attlee, 25 Jan. 1948, FO 371/68446, E2356/E2217/27/93; Khadduri, Independent Iraq, p. 264.
    In his memoirs Tawfiq al-Suwaydi, one of the negotiators of the Treaty of Portsmouth, maintains that Muhammad al-Sadr, a leading politician who succeeded Jabr as prime minister, had not even read the treaty. Tawfiq al-Suwaydi, Mudhakkirati: Nisf Qarn min Tarikh al-Iraq wa al-Qadiya al-Arabiyya (My Memoirs: Half a Century in the History of Iraq and the Arab Question) (Beirut, 1969), p. 480.

12. Busk to Bevin, 31 July 1947, FO 371/61592, E7156/3/93; Busk to Wright, 12 Aug. 1947, FO 624/109; Pelham to FO, 22 Jan. 1948, FO 371/68443, E949/27/93.

13. Busk to FO, 9 Sept. 1947, FO 371/61594, E8442/3/93; Busk to Bevin, 4 Dec. 1947, FO 371/61599, E11608/3/93; Pelham to FO, 22 Jan. 1948, FO 371/68443, E949/27/93; Mack to FO, 14 Feb. 1948, FO 371/68446, E2176/27/93; memorandum by Busk, 13 May 1948, FO 371/68386, E7383/103/65.

14. Wadsworth to secretary of state, 1 April 1947, 890G.002/4-147; Pelham to Attlee, 25 Jan. 1948, Busk to Bevin, 6 Feb. 1948, FO 371/68446, E2217/E2307/27/93; Abbas Kelidar, "The Shii Imami Community and Politics in the Arab East," Middle Eastern Studies, vol. 19 (1983), p. 15; Elie Kedourie, "Anti-Shiism in Iraq under the Monarchy," Middle Eastern Studies, vol. 24 (1988), pp. 249-53. The quotation is in Wadsworth.

15. Pelham to Attlee, 25 Jan. 1948, FO 371/68446, E2217/27/93; memorandum by Harris, 7 April 1948, 890G.00/4-3048.

16. Dorsz to secretary of state, 19 Aug. 1947, 890G.6131l/8-1947; memorandum by Pelham, 25 Nov. 1947, FO 371/61660, E11688/634/93; Dorsz to secretary of state, 28 Nov. 1947 and 29 Nov. 1947, 890G.61311/11-2847/11-2947; R. G. Dundas (Middle East Secretariat at FO) to A. E. T. Farquharson (MF), 20 Dec. 1947, FO 371/61660, E11688/634/93.

17. Minute by M. T. Walker (Eastern Dept. of FO), 27 Feb. 1948, FO 371/68446, E2693/27/93.

18. Pelham to FO, 23 Jan. 1948, FO 371/68444, E1043/27/93; Pelham to Attlee, 25 Jan. 1948, Busk to Bevin, 6 Feb. 1948, FO 371/68446, E2217/E2307/27/93; memorandum by Harris, 7 April 1948, 890G.00/4-3048.

19. Minute by Richmond, 22 Jan. 1948, FO 371/68446, E2356/27/93; minute by Burrows, 23 Jan. 1948, FO 371/68444, E1119/27/93; Pelham to Attlee, 25 Jan. 1948, Renton to WO, 5 Feb. 1948, FO 371/68446, E2217/E2693/27/93; memorandum by Harris, 7 April 1948, 890G.00/4-3048; Khadduri, Independent Iraq, pp. 264-65.

20. Minute by Busk, 23 Jan. 1948, FO 371/68444, E1122/27/93; Pelham to Attlee, 25 Jan. 1948, FO 371/68446, E2217/27/93; minute by Pyman, 29 Jan. 1948, FO 371/68444 E1352/27/93; Renton to WO, 5 Feb. 1948, Busk to Bevin, 6 Feb. 1948, FO 371/68446 E2693/E2307/27/93.

21. Renton to WO, 5 Feb. 1948, FO 371/68446, E2693/27/93.

22. Pelham to FO, 20 Jan. 1948, FO 371/68443, E861/27/93; memorandum by Harris, 7 April 1948, 890G.00/4-3048; Khadduri, Independent Iraq, pp. 360, 362; Batatu, Social Classes pp. 465, 478, 548-51.

23. Minute by K. C. Buss (Research Dept. of FO), 23 Feb. 1948, memorandum by the Eastern Dept. of FO, 7 April 1948, FO 371/68385, E4371/E4371/103/65; Humphrey

Trevelyan (British chargé d'affaires in Baghdad) to Burrows, 13 Sept. 1949, FO 371/75129, E11447/1018/93; Batatu, *Social Classes*, pp. 30, 345.

24. Pelham to Attlee, 25 Jan. 1948, FO 371/68446, E2217/27/93.
25. Busk to Bevin, 6 Feb. 1948, FO 371/68446, E2307/27/93; memorandum by the Eastern Dept. of FO, 7 April 1948, FO 371/68385, E4371/103/65; memorandum by Harris, 7 April 1948, 890G.00/4-3048; Khadduri, *Independent Iraq*, pp. 28, 47, 49, 129, 259, 288, 364; Batatu, *Social Classes*, pp. 476-77.
26. Busk to Wright, 17 Sept. 1947, FO 371/61594, E8789/3/93; Renton to WO, 5 Feb. 1948, minute by Walker, 27 Feb. 1948, FO 371/68446, E2693/E2693/27/93; Batatu, *Social Classes*, pp. 470-73.
     At their peak in 1943 the British military forces had employed nearly 70,000 Iraqis. By March 1946 this figure had declined to 30,000. The last British ground troops left Iraq in October 1947. For the 1943 figure, see Lt.-Gen. H. Pownall (C-in-C PAIC) to secretary of state for war, 12 Oct. 1943, WO 32/10540. For the 1946 figure, see Stonehewer-Bird to Bevin, 4 March 1946, FO 371/52423, E2469/652/93. For the withdrawal of British ground troops, see chapter 6.
27. Memorandum by G. C. Pelham (commercial counsellor, British embassy Baghdad), 25 Nov. 1947, FO 371/61660, E11688/634/93; Sir John Troutbeck (head of BMEO in Cairo) to Wright, 31 Dec. 1947, FO 371/68387, E436/120/65; Dorothea Seelye Franck and Peter G. Franck, "Economic Review: The Middle East Economy in 1948," *The Middle East Journal*, vol. 3 (1949), p. 202; Kathleen M. Langley, *The Industrialization of Iraq* (Cambridge, Mass., 1962), p. 199. The first set of figures is from the Iraqi Ministry of Economics, and is in Langley. The second set of figures is from the U.S. Dept. of Agriculture, and is in the Francks.
28. Memorandum by Pelham, 25 Nov. 1947, FO 371/61660, E11688/634/93; Dorsz to secretary of state, 29 Nov. 1947, 890G.6131I/11-2947; Busk to FO, 4 Feb. 1948, FO 371/68445, E1708/27/93; Renton to WO, 5 Feb. 1948, FO 371/68446, E2693/27/93; memorandum by Harris, 7 April 1948, 890G.00/4-3048; De Gaury, *Three Kings*, p. 149.
29. MF to FO, 21 Oct. 1947, FO 371/61698, E9916/8449/93; memorandum by Pelham, 25 Nov. 1947, FO 371/61660, E11688/634/93; review by Richmond, 6 Jan. 1948, FO 371/68443, E834/27/93; Wadsworth to secretary of state, 23 April 1948, 890G.6131/4-2348.
     In 1947 Iraq earned £6.1 million from barley exports. This amount was greater than the earnings from any other source. F. H. Gamble, *Iraq: Economic and Commercial Conditions in Iraq* (London, 1949), p. 18.
30. Report of the Iraq Currency Board for the year ending 31 March 1948, no date, in Edward S. Crocker (U.S. ambassador in Baghdad) to secretary of state, 18 May 1949, 890G.515/5-1849.
31. Pelham to FO, 19 Jan. 1948 and 20 Jan. 1948, FO 371/68443, E805/E861/27/93; Pelham to Attlee, 25 Jan. 1948, FO 371/68446, E2217/27/93; Khadduri, *Independent Iraq*, p. 260.
32. Busk to FO, 5 Dec. 1947, FO 371/61599, E11558/3/93; Dorsz to secretary of state, 18 Dec. 1947, 890G.9111 RR/12-1847; memorandum by Harris, 7 April 1948, 890G.00/4-3048.
33. Batatu, *Social Classes*, pp. 547-48.
34. Pelham to FO, 19 Jan. 1948, 20 Jan. 1948, and 21 Jan. 1948, FO 371/68443, E805/E861/E880/27/93; Pelham to Attlee, 25 Jan. 1948, FO 371/68446, E2217/27/93; calendar of events by the U.S. embassy in Baghdad, 9 Feb. 1948, 741.90G/2-948; Khadduri, *Independent Iraq*, pp. 267-69; Batatu, *Social Classes*, pp. 550-51.
35. Minute by Richmond, 22 Jan. 1948, FO 371/68446, E2356/27/93; Pelham to FO, 22 Jan. 1948 and 22. Jan. 1948, FO 371/68443, E932/E949/27/93; minute by Pelham, 23 Jan.

1948, Pelham to Attlee, 25 Jan. 1948, FO 371/68446, E2356/E2217/27/93; Batatu, *Social Classes*, p. 551.

36. Minute by Richmond, 22 Jan. 1948, minute by Pelham, 23 Jan. 1948, FO 371/68446, E2356/E2356/27/93.

37. Pelham to Attlee, 25 Jan. 1948, Renton to WO, 5 Feb. 1948, FO 371/68446, E2217/E2693/27/93; memorandum by the U.S. embassy in Baghdad on the press reaction to the treaty, 9 Feb. 1948, 741.90G/2-948; memorandum by the British embassy in Baghdad on the press reaction to the treaty, no date, FO 624/140; minute by Walker, 27 Feb. 1948, FO 371/68446, E2693/27/93.

38. Pelham to Attlee, 25 Jan. 1948, FO 371/68446, E2217/27/93; calendar of events by the U.S. embassy in Baghdad, 9 Feb. 1948, 741.90G/2-948; Batatu, *Social Classes*, pp. 552-54.

39. Minute by Busk, 23 Jan. 1948, Bevin to Busk, 26 Jan. 1948, FO 371/68444, E1122/E1163/27/93.

40. Minute by Busk, 23 Jan. 1948, FO 371/68444, E1122/27/93; FO to Baghdad, 24 Jan. 1948, FO 371/68443, E949/27/93; FO to Baghdad, 24 Jan. 1948, Bevin to Busk, 26 Jan. 1948, FO 371/68444, E1043/E1163/27/93.

41. Busk to FO, 27 Jan. 1948, FO 371/68444, E1231/27/93; Renton to WO, 5 Feb. 1948, FO 371/68446, E2693/27/93; calendar of events by the U.S. embassy in Baghdad, 9 Feb. 1948, 741.90G/2-948; memorandum by Harris, 7 April 1948, 890G.00/4-3048; Batatu, *Social Classes*, pp. 554-57. The government put the fatalities at twenty but Renton maintains that this figure was a serious underenumeration. The Liberal party newspaper put the fatalities at 105, and the U.S. embassy at about 125. Batatu estimates the combined dead and injured at 300-400.

42. Busk to FO, 27 Jan. 1948 and 28 Jan. 1948, FO 371/68444, E1231/E1252/27/93; calendar of events by the U.S. embassy in Baghdad, 9 Feb. 1948, 741.90G/2-948; Renton to Mack, 13 March 1948, FO 371/68477, E4878/618/93; Khadduri, *Independent Iraq*, p. 269.

43. Busk to FO, 27 Jan. 1948 and 28 Jan. 1948, FO 371/68444, E1231/E1252/27/93; minute by Busk, 14 Feb. 1948, FO 624/128, part 3.

44. Busk to FO, 27 Jan. 1948 and 28 Jan. 1948, FO 371/68444, E1231/E1252/27/93.

45. Busk to FO, 4 Feb. 1948, FO 371/68445, E1708/27/93; Renton to WO, 5 Feb. 1948, minute by Walker, 27 Feb. 1948, FO 371/68446, E2693/E2693/27/93; memorandum by the British embassy in Baghdad on the press reaction to the treaty, no date, FO 624/140.

46. David H. McKillop (U.S. consul in Basra) to secretary of state, 28 Jan. 1948 and 17 Feb. 1948, 890G.00/1-2848/2-1748.

47. Report by the British consul in Amara, 26 Jan. 1948, FO 838/7.

48. Memorandum by Harris, 7 April 1948, 890G.00/4-3048; Mack to FO, 13 April 1948, FO 371/68448, E4661/27/93; Batatu, *Social Classes*, p. 563.

49. Report by the British embassy in Baghdad on the leading personalities in Iraq, 29 June 1940, FO 371/24562, E2329/2329/93; Khadduri, *Independent Iraq*, p. 270.

50. Busk to FO, 29 Jan. 1948, FO 371/68444, E1296/27/93; Khadduri, *Independent Iraq*, p. 270.

51. Minute by Pyman, 29 Jan. 1948, Busk to FO, 29 Jan. 1948, FO to Baghdad, 3 Feb. 1948, FO 371/68444, E1352/E1369/E1369/27/93.

52. Busk to FO, 30 Jan. 1948, FO 371/68444, E1371/27/93; Busk to Bevin, 5 Feb. 1948, FO 371/68446, E2611/27/93; Mack to Bevin, 11 Feb. 1948, FO 371/68442, E651/27/93; Khadduri, *Independent Iraq*, p. 271. The quotation is in Mack.

53. Shakir, the first of the Portsmouth group to return to power, was reappointed to his former position as defense minister in October 1948. Continuing the rehabilitation of

the group, in January 1949 Nuri became prime minister, in March 1949 Jamali became foreign minister, and in February 1950 Tawfiq became prime minister and Jabr became minister of interior.

54. Report by JPS, 27 Dec. 1946, FO 371/52405, E12396/226/93; conversation between Bevin and Jamali in London, 11 July 1947, FO 371/61592, E6397/3/93; memorandum by the Eastern Dept. of FO, 7 April 1948, FO 371/68385, E4371/103/65.

55. For the views of Jamali, Jabr, and Nuri on the Soviet threat to Iraq, see conversation between Bevin and Jamali in London, 11 July 1947, FO 371/61592, E6397/3/93; BMEO to FO, 13 April 1948, FO 371/68448, E4871/27/93; and Mack to FO, 15 Jan. 1949, FO 371/75330, E717/1015/31. For the widespread support in Iraq for a policy of neutrality, see Busk to Burrows, 5 April 1948, FO 371/68448, E4591/27/93; memorandum by the Eastern Dept. of FO, 7 April 1948, FO 371/68385, E4371/103/65; Mack to Bevin, 13 April 1948, FO 371/68448, E4898/27/93; and memorandum by Busk, 13 May 1948, FO 371/68386, E7383/103/65.

56. Memorandum by the Eastern Dept. of FO, 7 April 1948, FO 371/68385, E4371/103/65.

57. According to a knowledgeable British journalist who was in Iraq a few weeks after the collapse of the Treaty of Portsmouth, "not even in Palestine have I met such universal and uninhibited anti-British sentiment. The whole country knew it and expressed it feelingly." Jon Kimche, "Iraq Breaks with Britain," *The Nineteenth Century and After,* vol. 143 (Jan.-June 1948), p. 301.

NOTES TO CHAPTER 12

1. The text of this resolution is in *FRUS 1948,* vol. 5, part 2, pp. 1709-30.

2. The civil war in Palestine is discussed in O'Ballance, *War,* pp. 31-67; Kimche and Kimche, *Both Sides,* pp. 73-141; Lorch, *Edge,* pp. 55-137; and more recently in Benny Morris, *The Birth of the Palestinian Refugee Problem, 1947-1949* (Cambridge, 1987), pp. 29-131.

3. Stonehewer-Bird to FO, 3 Aug. 1946, FO 371/52548, E7481/4/31; memorandum by G. J. Jenkins (British embassy Cairo), 30 Dec. 1947, FO 371/68365, E758/11/65; review by Richmond, 6 Jan. 1948, FO 371/68443, E834/27/93.

4. C. M. Pirie-Gordon (British chargé d'affaires in Amman) to FO, 13 Sept. 1947, British legation Beirut to FO, 19 Sept. 1947, FO 371/61529, E8505/E8745/754/65; BMEO to FO, 10 Dec. 1947, FO 371/61580, E11726/11280/65; note by I. N. Clayton (BMEO) on the proceedings of the Arab premiers in Cairo 8-17 Dec. 1947, no date, comments by Jabr in a meeting with Rice (British embassy Baghdad), 3 Jan. 1948, FO 371/68364, E31/E392/11/65; Walid Khalidi, "The Arab Perspective," in William Roger Louis and Robert W. Stookey (eds.), *The End of the Palestine Mandate* (Austin, Tex., 1986), pp. 116-24; Michael Eppel, "The Iraqi Domestic Scene and Its Bearing on the Question of Palestine, 1947," *Asian and African Studies,* vol. 24 (1990), pp. 51, 63-68. The quotation is from a meeting with Clayton in Cairo on 9 Dec. 1947, and is in BMEO to FO, 10 Dec. 1947.

5. Busk to FO, 2 Dec. 1947, FO 371/61598, E11451/3/93; Busk to FO, 9 Dec. 1947 and 11 Dec. 1947, FO 371/61600, E11732/E11778/3/93; Busk to FO, 14 Dec. 1947, FO 371/61583, E12199/11607/65; Eppel, "Domestic Scene," p. 64.

6. C. P. Bradburne (British vice-consul in Kirkuk) to R. A. Beaumont (British consul in Mosul), 12 Feb. 1948, Bradburne to British embassy Baghdad, 19 Nov. 1948, FO 624/138. For more on Kurdish indifference to the plight of the Palestinian Arabs, see report by Bradburne, 7 July 1947, FO 624/117; Bradburne to Richmond, 10 Sept. 1947, FO 624/124, part 4; political summary by Bradburne, Jan. 1948, FO 624/138; and Longrigg, *Iraq,* pp. 352-53.

7.   Busk to FO, 23 Oct. 1947, FO 371/61595, E9935/3/93. The Anglo-Iraqi financial agree-
     ment of 13 August 1947 and the suspension of the convertibility of sterling one week
     later are discussed in chapter 9.
8.   Busk to Bevin, 31 July 1947, FO 371/61592, E7156/3/93; Eppel, "Domestic Scene," p. 66.
     The negotiations for the Treaty of Portsmouth are discussed in chapter 10.
9.   The bread shortage in Iraq during this period is discussed in chapter 11.
10. Minute by Butler, 21 April 1947, FO 371/61589, E3399/3/93; Eppel, "Domestic Scene,"
     pp. 51-52, 63-65, 72.
11. Sir Alec Kirkbride (British minister in Amman) to FO, 15 Nov. 1947, FO 371/61888,
     E10740/951/31; FO to Baghdad, 2 Dec. 1947, Busk to FO, 4 Dec. 1947, Kirkbride to
     Burrows, 8 Dec. 1947, FO 371/61580, E11477/E11444/E12009/11280/65; Busk to FO,
     12 Dec. 1947, FO 371/61600, E11819/3/93; minute by Burrows, 23 Dec. 1947, FO
     371/61893, E12286/951/31.
     In 1946, when Transjordan became independent from Britain, it changed its name to
     Jordan or, officially, "The Hashemite Kingdom of the Jordan." However, for reasons that
     are not clear, for the next few years the new title was not widely used outside of Jordan.
     For example, as we shall observe in the following chapter, the United Nations Security
     Council used the old name in its arms embargo resolution of 29 May 1948. In June 1949
     the Jordanian government protested at the continued use of the former title. FRUS 1949,
     vol. 6, p. 1080. Except in quotations, I have used the new name for the entire period
     after it was adopted.
12. Kirkbride to FO, 15 Nov. 1947, FO 371/61888, E10740/951/31; Kirkbride to FO, 29
     Nov. 1947, 4 Dec. 1947, and 6 Dec. 1947, FO 371/61580, E11280/ E11489/
     E11533/11280/65; Mary C. Wilson, King Abdullah, Britain and the Making of Jordan
     (Cambridge, 1987), p. 166; Ilan Pappe, Britain and the Arab-Israeli Conflict, 1948-51 (New
     York, 1988), pp. 9-10; Avi Shlaim, Collusion across the Jordan: King Abdullah, the Zionist
     Movement, and the Partition of Palestine (Oxford, 1988), pp. 110-16; Bruce Maddy-
     Weitzman, The Crystallization of the Arab State System, 1945-1954 (Syracuse, 1993), pp.
     51, 57.
13. Pelham to FO, 16 Jan. 1948 and 22 Jan. 1948, Busk to FO, 27 Jan. 1948, FO 371/68365,
     E726/E1062/E1255/11/65; minute by Harold Beeley (Eastern Dept. of FO), 2 Feb. 1948,
     FO 371/68366, E1702/11/65.
14. British embassy Baghdad to Iraqi Ministry of Foreign Affairs, 31 Jan. 1948, FO 371/68367,
     E1195/11/65; British embassy Baghdad to Iraqi Ministry of Foreign Affairs, 13 Feb.
     1948, FO 371/68368, E2726/11/65; Iraqi Ministry of Foreign Affairs to British embassy
     Baghdad, 28 Feb. 1948, FO 371/68369, E3616/11/65; Mack to Bevin, 4 Jan. 1949, FO
     371/75125, E773/1011/93.
15. Sir Ronald Campbell (British ambassador in Cairo) to FO, 12 Feb. 1948, FO 371/68367,
     E2120/11/65.
16. Ibid.; minute by Burrows, 21 Feb. 1948, FO 371/68367, E2120/11/65; FO to Baghdad,
     27 Feb. 1948, FO 371/68368, E2564/11/65.
17. See note 2.
18. Mack to FO, 24 April 1948, FO 371/68471B, E5142/262/93; Kirkbride to FO, 25 April
     1948, FO 371/68370, E5159/11/65; Mack to FO, 28 April 1948, FO 371/68448,
     E5426/27/93; Mack to FO, 29 April 1948, FO 371/68371, E5476/11/65; Barry Rubin, The
     Arab States and the Palestine Conflict (Syracuse, 1981), pp. 191-99; Fred J. Khouri, The
     Arab-Israeli Dilemma, 3rd ed. (Syracuse, 1985), p. 69; Khalidi, "Arab Perspective," p. 132;
     Maddy-Weitzman, Crystallization, p. 64.

19. Pappe, *Conflict*, pp. 17-20; Shlaim, *Collusion*, pp. 202-4; Benny Morris, *1948 and After: Israel and the Palestinians* (Oxford, 1990), p. 11.
20. Mack to FO, 1 March 1948, FO 371/68368, E2947/11/65; Mack to FO, 9 May 1948, FO 371/68550, E6026/4/31; Mack to FO, 16 May 1948, FO 371/68372, E6337/11/65; Lorch, *Edge*, pp. 167-69; Shlaim, *Collusion*, pp. 199-202; Maddy-Weitzman, *Crystallization*, p. 57.
21. Mack to FO, 8 March 1948, FO 371/68368, E3302/11/65; Kirkbride to FO, 25 April 1948, FO 371/68370, E5159/11/65; S. Pinkney Tuck (U.S. ambassador in Cairo) to secretary of state, 14 May 1948, *FRUS 1948*, vol. 5, part 2, p. 991; minute by Burrows, 4 Jan. 1949, minute by Walker, 7 Jan. 1949, FO 371/75164, E520/E520/1191/93; report by Brig.-Gen. J. H. R. Orlebar (British military attaché in Baghdad), 27 Feb. 1950, FO 371/82450, EQ1201/1; Humphrey Trevelyan (British chargé d'affaires in Baghdad) to K. C. Younger (minister of state at FO), 21 July 1950, FO 371/82490, EQ1641/7; Lt.-Gen. Sir John Bagot Glubb, *A Soldier with the Arabs* (London, 1957), p. 94; Kimche and Kimche, *Both Sides*, p. 162; Salih Saib al-Juburi, *Mihnat Filastin wa Asrarha al-Siyasiya wa al-Askariya* (*The Palestinian Misfortune and Its Political and Military Secrets*) (Beirut, 1970), pp. 139-41; Khalidi, *Haven*, p. 867; Shlaim, *Collusion*, p. 240; Maddy-Weitzman, *Crystallization*, p. 66.

There is some dispute over the size of the initial Iraqi contribution to the Arab side in the war in Palestine. Both Glubb, the commander of the Arab Legion, and the Kimche brothers, semi-official Israeli historians, put the figure at 3,000. Relying on Iraqi sources, Khalidi maintains that the number was 4,000. However, Saib, the chief of the Iraqi General Staff, puts the total at 6,300. Also suggesting a higher figure, on 11 May 1948, four days before the commencement of hostilities, a British intelligence report given to the United States military attaché in Cairo (reported by Tuck) estimated that there were 5,000 Iraqi troops in Jordan. It is difficult to judge the accuracy of these claims, and so I have compromised on a figure of 4,500.

The figure of 45,000 for the Iraqi armed forces is in Orlebar. The figure of 6,000 for the mobile police is in Trevelyan. The figure of 20,000 for Iraq's ultimate troop strength in Palestine is in Burrows and Walker.

22. Lorch, *Edge*, pp. 167-68.
23. Kimche and Kimche, *Both Sides*, pp. 160-62. According to a contemporaneous diary entry by Israeli Prime Minister David Ben-Gurion, at the outset of the war on 15 May 1948 the Israelis had 30,000 troops but only 12,000 of them were armed. This diary entry is cited in Simha Flapan, *The Birth of Israel: Myths and Realities* (New York, 1987), p. 193.
24. In the nearly six months of fighting before the beginning of the inter-state war on 15 May 1948, the Jewish community in Palestine, which only numbered about 650,000, suffered 1,345 military fatalities. This figure, of course, excludes civilian fatalities and all of the wounded. Flapan, *Birth*, p. 198.
25. Wasson to secretary of state, 14 May 1948, 890G.248/5-1448; Kirkbride to FO, 17 May 1948, FO 371/68372, E6393/11/65; Kirkbride to FO, 18 May 1948, FO 371/68373, E6494/11/65; Kirkbride to FO, 5 June 1948, FO 816/122; AM to FO, 16 July 1948, FO to AM, 30 July 1948, FO 371/68473, E9747/E9747/508/93; Kimche and Kimche, *Both Sides*, p. 152; Khalidi, *Haven*, p. 868. Also see the explanation in chapter 8, note 67.
26. Kimche and Kimche, *Both Sides*, pp. 162, 204; Lorch, *Edge*, pp. 134, 226-30; Khalidi, *Haven*, p. 866. Also see the explanation in chapter 8, note 68.
27. Khalidi, *Haven*, pp. 868-69.
28. Lorch, *Edge*, pp. 134, 153, 169. Also see the discussion of this question in chapter 8.
29. O'Ballance, *War*, pp. 115-19; Lorch, *Edge*, pp. 167-76.

30. The supply of arms is discussed in the following chapter.
31. BMEO to FO, 25 May 1948, FO 371/68373, E7048/11/65.
32. Busk to FO, 2 Dec. 1947, minute by Walker, 9 Dec. 1947, FO 371/61598, E11451/
E11451/3/93; Mack to FO, 13 July 1948, FO 371/68450, E9504/27/93; Wright to Mack,
23 July 1948, chancery Baghdad to FO, 28 July 1948, FO 371/68451, E10026/ E10369/27/93.
33. The text of this resolution is in *FRUS 1948*, vol. 5, part 2, pp. 1077-78.
34. Mack to FO, 29 May 1948, FO 371/68557, E7160/4/31; Mack to FO, 31 May 1948, FO
371/68558, E7213/4/31.
35. Pappe, *Conflict*, p. 36.
36. Note by J. E. Cable (Eastern Dept. of FO), 29 June 1948, FO 371/68450, E9046/27/93;
Mack to Bevin, 4 Jan. 1949, FO 371/75125, E773/1011/93; Khadduri, *Independent Iraq*,
p. 272.
37. Mack to Wright, 12 July 1948, FO 371/68450, E9780/27/93.
38. Mack to FO, 4 Nov. 1948, FO 371/68453, E14249/27/93.
39. SWB, Middle East, 12 Aug. 1948, p. 55.
40. Mack to Bevin, 6 Dec. 1948, FO 371/68453, E15849/27/93.
41. The text of Bernadotte's proposal of June 1948 is in *FRUS 1948*, vol. 5, part 2, pp. 1152-
54.
42. Mack to Wright, 15 June 1948, FO 371/68567, E8761/4/31; FO to Amman, 6 July 1948,
Mack to FO, 7 July 1948 and 7 July 1948, FO 371/68375, E9168/E9170/E9171/11/65;
Cambell to FO, 7 July 1948, FO 371/68569, E9164/4/31.
43. Kirkbride to FO, 7 July 1948 and 8 July 1948, FO 371/68375, E9169/E9250/11/65;
Wilson, *Abdullah*, pp. 174-76.
44. Minute by Richmond, 28 June 1948, FO 624/126, part 12; Meyer (U.S. chargé d'affaires
in Baghdad) to secretary of state, 6 July 1948, 890G.00/7-648; Cambell to FO, 7 July
1948 and 8 July 1948, FO 371/68375, E9186/E9215/11/65; Kirk, *Survey*, pp. 279-80;
Khouri, *Dilemma*, pp. 75-79.
45. Lorch, *Edge*, pp. 166, 198, 246, 251-52. The quotation is on p. 251.
46. Ibid., pp. 250-58, 324-28.
47. Kimche and Kimche, *Both Sides*, p. 220.
48. The truce formally expired on 9 July, but on the Egyptian front fighting recommenced
one day early. Lorch, *Edge*, p. 300.
49. Chancery Baghdad to chancery Amman, 6 Oct. 1948, FO 816/130; Glubb, *Soldier*,
pp. 157-66; Lorch, *Edge*, pp. 279-87; Morris, *Birth*, pp. 203-11.
50. Lorch, *Edge*, pp. 269-70, 301.
51. The text of this resolution is in *FRUS 1948*, vol. 5, part 2, pp. 1224-25.
52. Mack to FO, 21 July 1948 and 21 July 1948, FO 371/68575, E9867/E9896/4/31; Mack
to FO, 21 July 1948, FO 371/68450, E9945/27/93; Richmond to FO, 24 July 1948, FO
371/68451, E10024/27/93; Mack to Bevin, 6 Dec. 1948, FO 371/68453, E15849/27/93;
Shlaim, *Collusion*, p. 266; Maddy-Weitzman, *Crystallization*, p. 78.
53. The text of Bernadotte's proposal of September 1948 is in *FRUS 1948*, vol. 5, part 2,
pp. 1401-6.
54. FO to Amman, 28 Sept. 1948, FO 371/68641, E12502/375/31; memorandum by Wright,
11 Oct. 1948, FO 371/68379, E13309/32/65; Pappe, *Conflict*, pp. 45-48.
55. Khouri, *Dilemma*, p. 83; Pappe, *Conflict*, pp. 82-84; Shlaim, *Collusion*, pp. 296-303.
56. FO to Baghdad, 28 Sept. 1948, FO 371/68641, E12502/375/31; Chapman-Andrews
(British chargé d'affaires in Cairo) to FO, 2 Oct. 1948, FO 371/68642, E12792/375/31.
57. Chapman-Andrews to FO, 2 Oct. 1948 and 6 Oct. 1948, FO 371/68642,
E12792/13042/375/31; Mack to FO, 13 Oct. 1948, FO 371/68643, E13348/375/31;

Mack to Bevin, 4 Jan. 1949, FO 371/75125, E773/1011/93; Sassoon, *Economic Policy*, pp. 98-99.

58. Kirkbride to FO, 19 Oct. 1948, FO 816/131; Mack to FO, 22 Oct. 1948, FO 371/68689, E13669/11366/31; Kirkbride to FO, 2 Nov. 1948, FO 371/68690, E14112/11366/31; Kirkbride to FO, 13 Nov. 1948, FO 816/133; Mack to FO, 30 Dec. 1948, FO 371/68692, E16455/11366/31; Lorch, *Edge*, pp. 335-68, 383-436.
59. Khadduri, *Independent Iraq*, p. 273.
60. Kirkbride to British high commissioner for Transjordan, 28 Nov. 1944, FO 371/39991, E7855/41/65.
61. Kirkbride to FO, 4 June 1948, FO 816/122.
62. Mack to Wright, 21 July 1948, FO 371/68576, E10107/4/31.
63. Dorsz to secretary of state, 29 Nov. 1948, 890G.9111 RR/11-2948.
64. Mack to FO, 15 Jan. 1949 and 17 Jan. 1949, FO 371/75330, E717/E813/1015/31; BMEO to FO, 10 March 1949, FO 371/75332, E3335/1015/31.
65. Mack to FO, 11 Feb. 1949, FO 371/75331, E2039/1015/31; Iraqi Ministry of Foreign Affairs to British embassy Baghdad, 8 March 1949, FO 371/75165, E3656/1191/93; Kirk, *Survey*, p. 297; Shlaim, *Collusion*, p. 404.
66. Mack to FO, 13 April 1949, FO 371/75387, E4751/1095/31; Iraqi Ministry of Foreign Affairs to British embassy Baghdad, 21 April 1949, FO 371/75165, E5588/1191/93.
67. Iraq never released its casualty figures for the war in Palestine. Arif al-Arif, a Palestinian historian, maintains that total Arab fatalities in the war were 17,000 of which 13,000 were Palestinian. Israeli scholars consider both figures too high. Teveth, "Refugee Problem," p. 223.
68. Mack to FO, 27 April 1948 and 28 April 1948, FO 371/68448, E5362/E5426/27/93; Iraqi Ministry of Foreign Affairs to British embassy Baghdad, 16 May 1948, FO 371/68374, E7809/11/65; chancery Baghdad to FO, 17 Sept. 1948, FO 371/68452, E12555/27/93; Mack to Bevin, 6 Dec. 1948, FO 371/68453, E15849/27/93.
69. Comment by Salih Jabr in an interview with Rice in Baghdad, 3 Jan. 1948, British embassy Washington to DOS, 5 Jan. 1948, FO 371/68364, E392/E525/11/65.
70. Chancery Baghdad to FO, 17 Sept. 1948, FO 371/68452, E12555/27/93; Mack to Bevin, 6 Dec. 1948, FO 371/68453, E15849/27/93; BMEO to FO, 10 March 1949, FO 371/75332, E3335/1015/31.
71. Richmond to Walker, 24 Aug. 1948, FO 371/68451, E11431/27/93; Mack to Bevin, 5 Nov. 1948, FO 371/68453, E14852/27/93; Mack to FO, 10 Dec. 1948, FO 624/126, file 22.
72. Chancery Baghdad to chancery Amman, 6 Oct. 1948, FO 816/130.
73. Bevin to Mack, 29 Sept. 1948, FO 371/68452, E12768/27/93.
74. FO to Cairo, 25 Aug. 1948, FO 371/68583, E11295/4/31; chancery Baghdad to chancery Amman, 6 Oct. 1948, FO 816/130; Joseph Jermiah Zasloff, *Great Britain and Palestine: A Study of the Problem before the United Nations* (Munich, 1952), pp. 133-38; Kirk, *Survey*, pp. 272-75.
75. The oil pipeline to Haifa is discussed in chapter 16.

NOTES TO CHAPTER 13

1. Silverfarb, *Informal Empire*, p. 77.
2. Iraq's contemplated military intervention in Palestine is discussed in chapter 12.
3. The Treaty of Portsmouth is discussed in chapters 10 and 11.
4. Bevin to Albert Alexander (minister of defense), 23 July 1947, FO 371/61592, E6594/3/93; memorandum by Bevin, 17 Sept. 1947, CAB 131/4, DO(47)69; minutes of

Defence Committee, 24 Sept. 1947, CAB 131/5, DO(47)21; minute by Garran, 7 Oct. 1947, FO 371/61634, E8999/255/93; minute by Burrows, 10 Dec. 1947, FO 371/61571, E11857/9590/65; minute of a meeting of ministers at No. 10 Downing St., 9 Jan. 1948, FO 371/68443, E691/27/93.

5. Loy W. Henderson (director of the Office of Near Eastern and African Affairs) to George C. Marshall (secretary of state), 10 Nov. 1947, Robert A. Lovett (acting secretary of state) to Marshall, 6 Dec. 1947, *FRUS 1947*, vol. 5, pp. 1249, 1300; Shlomo Slonim, "The 1948 American Embargo on Arms to Palestine," *Palestine Science Quarterly*, vol. 94 (1979), pp. 497-98.

6. Meeting in Washington of DOS officials and representatives from the Jewish Agency, 8 Dec. 1947, *FRUS 1947*, vol. 5, p. 1303; Marshall to U.S. embassy London, 26 Jan. 1948, *FRUS 1948*, vol. 5, part 2, pp. 562-63; Lord Inverchapel (British ambassador in Washington) to FO, 26 Jan. 1948, FO 371/68410, E1105/1017/65; Slonim, "American Embargo", pp. 499-501.

7. Marshall to U.S. embassy London, 26 Jan. 1948, *FRUS 1948*, vol. 5, part 2, pp. 562-63; Inverchapel to FO, 26 Jan. 1948, FO 371/68410, E1105/1017/65; Slonim, "American Embargo", pp. 501-2.

8. FO to Washington, 29 Jan. 1948, FO 371/68410, E1229/1017/65.

9. Inverchapel to FO, 29 Jan. 1948, FO to Washington, 30 Jan. 1948, FO 371/68648, E1348/E1348/1078/31.

10. *HC*, 4 Feb. 1948, vol. 446, oral answers, col. 1805; *HC*, 18 Feb. 1948, vol. 447, written answers, col. 223.

11. FO to Baghdad, 19 Feb. 1948, FO 371/68476, E2034/618/93; meeting of the Joint War Production Staff, 26 May 1948, DEFE 7/833.

12. FO to Baghdad, 24 Feb. 1948, FO 371/68411, E2278/1017/65; MOS to FO, 5 April 1950, FO 371/87957, E1192/61. The Sea Fury aircraft is discussed in chapter 8.

13. Major R. H. C. Bryers (WO) to Walker, 5 March 1948, FO 371/68412, E3491/1017/65. The 25-pounder field gun is discussed in chapter 8.

14. Major I. H. Battye (WO) to Beeley, 2 April 1948, FO 371/68412, E4326/1017/65.

15. Major J. R. I. Doyle (WO) to Walker, 14 May 1948, FO 371/68470, E6438/184/93.

16. Walker to Squadron-Leader C. F. M. Mervyn-Jones (AM), 19 March 1948, Air Vice-Marshal R. M. Foster (AM) to Burrows, 22 April 1948, Burrows to Foster, 11 May 1948, FO 371/68473, E3288/E5238/E5238/508/93; Thetford, *Royal Air Force*, pp. 183-84.

17. The text of this resolution is in *FRUS 1948*, vol. 5, part 2, pp. 827-28.

18. Slonim, "American Embargo," pp. 507-11.

19. The Arab intervention in Palestine is discussed in chapter 12.

20. Memorandum by Burrows, 20 May 1948, FO 371/68413, E7794/1017/65.

21. Mack to FO, 19 May 1948, FO 371/68412, E6515/1017/65; memorandum by Burrows, 20 May 1948, FO 371/68413, E7794/1017/65; FO to Baghdad, 10 June 1948, FO 371/68412, E7210/1017/65.

22. The text of this resolution is in *FRUS 1948*, vol. 5, part 2, pp. 1077-78.

23. Leland M. Goodrich and Edvard Hambro, *Charter of the United Nations: Commentary and Documents*, 2nd ed. (London, 1949), pp. 208-9.

24. Ibid., pp. 517-19.

25. WO to C-in-C MELF, 31 May 1948, FO 371/68413, E7602/1017/65; FO to British embassy Baghdad, 10 June 1948, FO 371/68412, E7210/1017/65; Bevin to Dr. S. Segal (member of Parliament), 19 June 1948, FO 371/68563, E7746/4/31; Kirk, *Survey*, p. 276. The State Department quotation is from the footnote of Lovett to Warren R. Austin

(U.S. representative at the UN), 1 June 1948, *FRUS 1948*, vol. 5, part 2, pp. 1086-87. The Bernadotte quotation is from a note that he sent to the Arab states and Israel on 7 June 1948, and is in *FRUS 1948*, vol. 5, part 2, p. 1102.

26. WO to FO, 30 June 1948, Iraqi embassy London to FO, 30 July 1948, FO 371/68413, E9016/E9016/1017/65.

27. FO to Busk, 9 Aug. 1947, FO 371/61628, E4926/139/93; MOD to FO, 9 Feb. 1948, FO 371/68410, E1983/1017/65; FO to Baghdad, 10 June 1948, FO 371/68412, E7210/1017/65; FO to AM, 30 July 1948, FO 371/68473, E9747/508/93; note by the vice chief of the Air Staff, 7 Oct. 1948, FO 371/68419, E14450/1017/65.

28. Mack to FO, 18 June 1948, FO 371/68470, E8294/184/93; Mack to FO, 7 July 1948, FO 371/68375, E9171/11/65.

29. Alexander to Bevin, 11 June 1948, FO 371/68413, E8059/1017/65.

30. Bevin to Alexander, 19 June 1948, FO 371/68413, E8059/1017/65; FO to Baghdad, 29 June 1948, FO to Amman, 29 June 1948, FO 371/68470, E8294/E8294/184/93.

31. The text of this resolution is in *FRUS 1948*, vol. 5, part 2, pp. 1224-25.

32. Richmond to FO, 4 Sept. 1948, FO 371/68376, E11622/11/65; Mack to FO, 29 Sept. 1948, FO 371/68452, E12808/27/93; Mack to FO, 25 Oct. 1948, FO 371/68474, E13753/508/93; Iraqi Ministry of Foreign Affairs to British embassy Baghdad, 6 Oct. 1948, FO 371/68453, E13626/27/93; Mack to FO, 3 Jan. 1949, FO 371/75164, E68/1191/93.

33. Cambell to FO, 30 July 1948, FO 371/68414, E10224/1017/65; Mack to FO, 1 April 1949, FO 371/75165, E4792/1191/93.

Still, Iraq did not have entirely clean hands when it came to obeying the United Nations. As we observed in the previous chapter, during the cease-fire between 11 June and 9 July 1948, when the Security Council had prohibited all countries from introducing troops and military equipment into Palestine, Iraq increased its troop strength to a total of about 10,000 men and brought into Palestine eleven large truck convoys full of arms and ammunition. And after the second truce entered into effect on 18 July 1948 Iraq violated it by continuing to send troops into Palestine. As a result of these reinforcements, by January 1949 the Iraqi expeditionary force numbered about 20,000 men.

34. Iraqi embassy London to FO, 30 July 1948, FO 371/68471A, E10537/184/93; Richmond to FO, 31 July 1948, FO 371/68414, E10342/1017/65; Richmond to Burrows, 17 Aug. 1948, FO 371/68451, E11180/27/93; Iraqi Ministry of Foreign Affairs to British embassy Baghdad, 6 Oct. 1948, FO 371/68453, E13626/27/93; Mack to FO, 10 Nov. 1948, FO 371/68421, E15722/1017/65; Ali Jawdat al-Ayyubi (Iraqi foreign minister) to Mack, 8 Dec. 1948, FO 371/68471A, E16072/184/93.

35. Richmond to Burrows, 5 Aug. 1948, FO 371/68471A, E10592/184/93.

36. Mack to Bevin, 15 Oct. 1948, FO 371/68453, E13626/27/93; minute by Walker, 26 Oct. 1948, FO 371/68419, E14450/1017/65; AM to FO, 22 Dec. 1948, FO 371/68478, E16332/618/93.

Lorch (*Edge*, p. 226) maintains that during the war Britain regularly supplied the Iraqi air force with spare parts and ammunition in contravention of the United Nations arms embargo. This statement is not true.

37. Richmond to FO, 31 July 1948, FO 371/68414, E10342/1017/65; Richmond to Burrows, 5 Aug. 1948, FO 371/68471A, E10592/184/93; Mack to FO, 29 Sept. 1948, FO 371/68452, E12808/27/93; Mack to Bevin, 15 Oct. 1948, FO 371/68453, E13626/27/93; Mack to FO, 10 Nov. 1948, FO 371/68421, E15722/1017/65; Mack to FO, 7 Jan. 1949, FO 371/75167, E374/1194/93.

38. Mack to Wright, 17 July 1948, Richmond to Burrows, 5 Aug. 1948, Mack to FO, 11 Dec. 1948, Mack to Bevin, 13 Dec. 1948, FO 371/68471A, E10095/E10592/E15835/E16072/184/93.

39. Note by Burrows, 5 Aug. 1948, FO 371/68379, E10548/32/65; minute by Burrows, 21 Oct. 1948, Sargent to Sir Harold Parker (MOD), 25 Oct. 1948, FO 371/68471A, E13953/E13561/184/93; minute by Walker, 26 Oct. 1948, Bevin to Alexander, 5 Nov. 1948, FO 371/68419, E14450/E14450/1017/65; Wright to Lt.-Gen. Sir Leslie Hollis (MOD), 12 Jan. 1949, FO 371/75164, E520/1191/93.

40. Foster to Burrows, 30 Aug. 1948, FO 371/68471A, E11496/184/93; note by the vice chief of the Air Staff, 7 Oct. 1948, Hollis to Alexander, 14 Oct. 1948, Alexander to Bevin, 22 Oct. 1948, FO 371/68419, E14450/E14450/E14450/1017/65; Foster to Wright, 22 Dec. 1948, FO 371/68478, E16332/618/93.

41. Minute by Walker, 26 Oct. 1948, FO 371/68419, E14450/1017/65.

42. Bevin to Alexander, 5 Nov. 1948, FO 371/68419, E14450/1017/65.

43. AM to FO, 17 Jan. 1949, FO 371/75099, E1325/1192/65.

44. FO to British embassy Baghdad, 11 Jan. 1949, FO 371/75164, E520/1191/93; Hdq. RAF Mediterranean and Middle East to AM, 18 Jan. 1949, FO 371/75099, E1325/1192/65; FO to British embassy Baghdad, 2 Feb. 1949, FO 371/75164, E587/1191/93.

45. Burrows to Richmond, 12 Nov. 1948, chancery Baghdad to FO, 30 Nov. 1948, FO 371/68471A, E11496/E15674/184/93.

46. FO to Baghdad, 2 Feb. 1949, Trevelyan to FO, 4 Feb. 1949, FO 371/75164, E587/E1711/1191/93.

47. IDC, 15 Jan. 1949, FO 371/75099, E1025/1192/65; Bevin to Mack, 31 Jan. 1949, FO 371/75164, E1580/1191/93; Mack to FO, 13 April 1949, FO 371/75387, E4751/1095/31; Mack to FO, 27 April 1949 and 16 May 1949, FO 371/75165, E5347/E6222/1191/93; Kirk, Survey, p. 294.

48. Minute by Frank Roberts (Bevin's principal private secretary), 12 Jan. 1949, FO 371/75099, E886/1192/65; minute by Roberts, 11 Feb. 1949, minute by Wright, 3 March 1949, Alexander to Bevin, 16 March 1949, Sir William Strang (permanent undersecretary of state for foreign affairs) to Bevin, 1 April 1949, Bevin to Strang, 5 April 1949, FO 371/75100, E2763/E3041/E4334/E4342/E4470/1192/65.

49. FO to Washington, 25 April 1949, FO 371/75165, E5347/1191/93; Franks to FO, 29 April 1949, FO 371/75101, E5456/1192/65.

50. Franks to FO, 29 April 1949, FO 371/75101, E5456/1192/65.

51. Bevin to FO, 26 May 1949, FO 371/75101, E6540/1192/65.

52. Cadogan to FO, 28 May 1949, FO 371/75101, E6643/1192/65.

53. Bevin to FO, 1 June 1949, FO 371/75102, E7271/1192/65.

54. FO to AM, 9 June 1949, FO 371/75102, E7015/1192/65.

55. The text of this resolution is in FRUS 1949, vol. 6, pp. 1302-3.

56. FO to Baghdad, 23 Aug. 1949, FO 371/75165, E10349/1191/93.

NOTES TO CHAPTER 14

1. The figure of ID 1.5 million per year for Iraq's military commitment in Palestine is from Iraqi Minister of Finance Ali Mumtaz, and is in Mack to FO, 4 Oct. 1948, FO 371/68466, E12903/112/93.
   According to the National Bank of Iraq, Iraq's total expenditure (including ordinary expenditure and expenditure from the separate capital works budget) for the financial year which began on 1 April 1948 was ID 29.6 million. Iversen, Monetary Policy, p. 57.

For Iraq the cost of Palestine actually began before the war when it contributed to an Arab League fund to support Palestinian military activity against the Jews. Busk to Bevin, 26 Nov. 1947, FO 371/61653, E11754/453/93; Rubin, *Arab States*, pp. 169-70; Sassoon, *Economic Policy*, p. 97.

2. The figure of £1 million per year for Iraq's loss from the closure of the 12-inch pipeline to Haifa is from Mumtaz, and is in Iraq Command Intelligence Report, 27 Sept. 1948, FO 371/68465, E12581/112/93. The Haifa pipeline is discussed in more detail in chapter 16.

3. The figure of £3 million per year for Iraq's potential earnings from both pipelines to Haifa is from the IPC, and is in meeting of FO, MFP, IPC, and AIOC officials at the FO, 1 March 1949, FO 371/75114, E2980/1531/65.
    According to the National Bank of Iraq, Iraq's total revenue (including ordinary revenue and revenue from the separate capital works budget) for the financial year which began on 1 April 1948 was ID 25.6 million. Iversen, *Monetary Policy*, p. 57.

4. Mack to FO, 20 Sept. 1948, FO 371/68465, E12270/112/93; Humphrey Trevelyan (British chargé d'affaires in Baghdad), to B. A. B. Burrows (head of the Eastern Dept. of FO), 14 July 1949, FO 371/75157, E9234/1113/93; meeting of FO, MFP, Treasury, and Bank of England officials with Nuri al-Said (Iraqi prime minister) in London, 8 Aug. 1949, FO 371/75158, E9766/1113/93; Mack to Bevin, 23 March 1950, FO 371/82422, EQ1103/1. The Jewish question in Iraq during this period is discussed in Nissim Rejwan, *The Jews of Iraq: 3,000 Years of History and Culture* (Boulder, Colo., 1985), pp. 217-48; Abbas Shiblak, *The Lure of Zion: The Case of the Iraqi Jews* (London, 1986), pp. 58-129; Elie Kedourie, "The Break Between Muslims and Jews in Iraq," in Mark R. Cohen and Abraham L. Udovitch (eds.), *Jews Among Arabs: Contacts and Boundaries* (Princeton, N.J., 1989), pp. 21-63; and Norman A. Stillman, *The Jews of Arab Lands in Modern Times* (Philadelphia, 1991), pp. 116-20, 151-52, 158-64.

5. The figures for British military expenditure are from the National Bank of Iraq, and are in memorandum by Judd Polk (U.S. Treasury representative in the Middle East) on Iraq's financial position, 6 July 1949, in Edward S. Crocker (U.S. ambassador in Baghdad) to secretary of state, 25 July 1949, 890G.51/7-2549.

6. Memorandum by G. C. Pelham (commercial counsellor, British embassy Baghdad), 25 Nov. 1947, FO 371/61660, E11688/634/93; Sir John Troutbeck (head of BMEO in Cairo) to Wright, 31 Dec. 1947, FO 371/68387, E436/120/65; minute by Pelham, 7 Aug. 1948, FO 624/141, vol. 2; Franck and Franck, "Economic Review," p. 202; Langley, *Industrialization*, p. 199. The first set of figures is from the Iraqi Ministry of Economics, and is in Langley. The second set of figures is from the U.S. Dept. of Agriculture, and is in the Francks. The third set of figures is from Mumtaz, and is in minute by Pelham.

7. Mack to FO, 10 Nov. 1948, FO 371/68467, E14510/112/93; minute by Chadwick, 14 Jan. 1949, FO 371/75156, E1250/1113/93. The figures for government officials, police officers, and salaries are in Mack. The figure of ID 29.6 million for Iraq's total expenditure is in note 1.

8. Memorandum by Burrows, 27 April 1948, FO 371/68461, E6109/112/93; L. Waight (British Treasury representative in the Middle East) to Burrows, 11 Sept. 1948, FO 371/68466, E13017/112/93; minute by Chadwick, 14 Jan. 1949, FO 371/75156, E1250/1113/93.

9. Dorsz to secretary of state, 21 Dec. 1948, 890G.51/12-2048.

10. Trevelyan to Burrows, 14 July 1949, FO 371/75157, E9234/1113/93.

11. Burrows to Trevelyan, 12 Aug. 1949, FO 371/75158, E9766/1113/93.

12. Memorandum by Burrows, 27 April 1948, FO 371/68461, E6109/112/93; Crawford (BMEO) to R. G. Dundas (Middle East Secretariat of FO), 19 May 1948, FO 371/68409B, E6898/966/65; Waight to Burrows, 11 Sept. 1948, FO 371/68466, E13017/112/93; Sassoon, *Economic Policy*, pp. 84, 97.
13. Mack to FO, 14 April 1948, FO 371/68448, E4688/27/93; memorandum by Burrows, 27 April 1948, FO 371/68461, E6109/112/93; minute by Walker, 26 Aug. 1948, FO 371/68466, E13016/112/93; meeting of various British officials and Nuri al-Said (Iraqi prime minister) in London, 8 Aug. 1949, FO 371/75158, E9766/1113/93.
14. Mack to FO, 8 April 1948, 13 April 1948, and 14 April 1948, FO 371/68448, E4500/E4661/E4688/27/93.
15. Mack to FO, 14 April 1948, FO 371/68448, E4688/27/93; memorandum by Walker, 23 April 1948, Mack to FO, 13 May 1948, FO 371/68461, E6109/E6256/112/93; Mack to FO, 14 May 1948, FO 371/68462, E6275/112/93.
16. Wright to Baghdad, 10 May 1948, FO 371/68449, E5648/27/93. For more on the unwillingness of the Foreign Office to assist the Sadr government, see memorandum by Burrows, 27 April 1948, minute by Walker, 6 May 1948, and FO to Baghdad, 10 May 1948, FO 371/68461, E6109/E6109/E6109/112/93.
17. Both of these remarks were made at an IDC at the FO, 14 May 1948, FO 371/68462, E6663/112/93.
18. Memorandum by Burrows, 27 April 1948, FO 371/68461, E6109/112/93; Norman Young (Treasury) to Walker, 21 May 1948, FO 371/68462, E6663/112/93; Treasury to FO, 27 July 1948, FO 371/68379, E7795/32/65.
19. Meeting of FO, IPC, and AIOC officials at the FO, 18 May 1948, FO 371/68462, E6664/112/93; report by JPS, 12 Sept. 1950, DEFE 6/14, JP(50)98(Final).
20. Meeting of FO, IPC, and AIOC officials at the FO, 18 May 1948, FO 371/68462, E6664/112/93; FO to Baghdad, 20 May 1948, FO 371/68461, E6256/112/93.
21. Mack to FO, 20 Sept. 1948 and 2 Oct. 1948, FO 371/68465, E12270/E12810/112/93; Mack to FO, 4 Oct. 1948, FO 371/68466, E12912/112/93.
22. Iraq Command Intelligence Report, 27 Sept. 1948, FO 371/68465, E12581/112/93; Mumtaz to Muzahim, 26 Oct. 1948, T 236/2107; chancery Baghdad to FO, 11 April 1949, FO 371/75157, E4930/1113/93; Sassoon, *Economic Policy*, p. 200.
23. Richmond to FO, 4 Aug. 1948 and 5 Aug. 1948, minute by Walker, 17 Aug. 1948, FO 371/68464, E10384/E10434/E10764/112/93.
24. Richmond to FO, 5 Aug. 1948, FO 371/68464, E10434/112/93.
25. Mack to FO, 20 Sept. 1948 and 25 Sept. 1948, FO 371/68465, E12270/E12514/112/93.
26. Minute by Dundas, 12 Aug. 1948, minute by Walker, 17 Aug. 1948, FO 371/68464, E10775/E10764/112/93; minute by Pyman, 25 Sept. 1948, Sargent to Sir Edward Bridges (Treasury), 27 Sept. 1948, FO 371/68465, E12683/E12683/112/93.
27. Bridges to Sargent, 1 Oct. 1948, FO 371/68466, E12839/112/93.
28. Meeting of FO, MFP, IPC, and AIOC officials at the FO, 1 Oct. 1948, FO 371/68466, E12847/112/93.
29. Ibid.; meeting of FO, MFP, IPC, and AIOC officials at the FO, 5 Oct. 1948, FO 371/68466, E13064/112/93.
30. Meeting of FO and Treasury officials at the FO, 6 Oct. 1948, FO to Baghdad, 6 Oct. 1948 and 8 Oct. 1948, FO 371/68466, E13038/E12978/E13046/112/93; Mack to Wright, 19 Nov. 1948, FO 371/68467, E15160/112/93; minute by Walker, 29 Nov. 1948, FO 371/68439, E15408/14608/65.
    Even without the encouragement of the Foreign Office, between April and August 1948 the Iraqi government had withdrawn £2 million from the board to pay for current

expenses. However, these withdrawals had not reduced the note cover to below 100 percent. Minute by Walker, 26 Aug. 1948, Waight to Burrows, 11 Sept. 1948, FO 371/68466, E13016/E13017/112/93.

In February 1949 the total present market value of the sterling assets held by the board was about £1 million below the total amount of dinars in circulation. C. E. Loombe (Bank of England) to M. Loughnane (Treasury), 23 Feb. 1949, FO 371/75156, E2581/1113/93.

On 1 July 1949 the functions of the Iraq Currency Board were transferred to the newly created National Bank of Iraq. The funds of the board were deposited in the Bank of England. Crocker to secretary of state, 24 April 1949, 890G.00/4-1149; Sassoon, *Economic Policy,* p. 106.

31. Mack to FO, 4 Nov. 1948, FO 371/68453, E14249/27/93; Mack to FO, 10 Nov. 1948, FO 371/68467, E14510/112/93.

32. Khadduri, *Independent Iraq,* p. 273.

33. Trevelyan to Burrows, 10 Jan. 1949, Mack to FO, 18 Jan. 1949, FO 371/75156, E853/E819/1113/93.

34. Mack to FO, 10 March 1949, FO 371/75157, E3313/1113/93; Mack to Bevin, 17 May 1949, FO 371/75129, E6601/1018/93; Burrows to Trevelyan, 12 Aug. 1949, FO 371/75158, E9766/1113/93.

35. Trevelyan to Burrows, 14 July 1949, minute by Chadwick, 19 July 1949, FO 371/75157, E9234/E8688/1113/93; meeting of FO, MFP, Treasury, and Bank of England officials with Nuri al-Said in London, 8 Aug. 1949, brief by Chadwick, 18 Aug. 1949, FO 371/75158, E9766/E10245/1113/93.

36. The Haifa pipeline is discussed in chapter 16.

37. Mack to FO, 11 Jan. 1949, FO to Baghdad, 20 Jan. 1949, Trevelyan to Burrows, 26 Jan. 1949, FO 371/75156, E570/E819/E1831/1113/93.

38. Meeting of FO, MFP, Treasury, IPC, and AIOC officials at the FO, 25 Jan. 1949, FO 371/75156, E1349/1113/93; IPC headquarters in Tripoli to IPC headquarters in London, 6 March 1949, FO 371/75157, E3144/1113/93.

39. Joint note by FO and Treasury, 29 Jan. 1949, Walker to Treasury, 17 Feb. 1949, Mack to Walker, 17 Feb. 1949, FO 371/75156, E1459/E2306/E2508/1113/93; note by FO, 24 May 1949, T. L. Rowan (Treasury) to Sir Stafford Cripps (chancellor of the exchequer), 31 May 1949, CAB 134/565, ON(49)183, ON(49)196; minutes of ONC, 31 May 1949, CAB 134/562, ON(49)46.

40. Barings to Abdul Illah Hafidh (governor of the National Bank of Iraq), 14 June 1949, FO 371/75158, E9372/1113/93.

41. Trevelyan to Burrows, 22 July 1949, FO 371/75157, E9320/1113/93; minute by Chadwick, 23 July 1949, FO 371/75158, E9354/1113/93.

42. Minutes by Chadwick, 23 July 1949 and 23 July 1949, FO 371/75158, E9354/ E9372/ 1113/93.

43. FO to British embassy Baghdad, 5 Nov. 1949 and 19 Nov. 1949, FO 371/75159, E12942/E14026/1113/93.

44. Mack to FO, 21 Nov. 1949, meeting of FO officials and representatives of the National Bank of Iraq at the FO, 22 Nov. 1949, FO 371/75159, E14031/E14251/1113/93.

45. Minute by Treasury, 24 Nov. 1949, FO to British embassy Baghdad, 25 Nov. 1949, FO 371/75159, E14252/E14254/1113/93.

46. The text of the loan agreement is in FO 371/75159, E14559/1113/93.

47. Mack to FO, 14 Oct. 1948, Troutbeck to Bevin, 7 Dec. 1948, FO 371/68467, E13625/E15800/112/93.

48. In 1947 the wheat harvest was 235,000 tons, while in 1950 it was 520,000 tons. Showing similar improvement, between 1947 and 1950 the barley harvest increased from 500,000 tons to 851,000 tons. These figures are from the Iraqi Ministry of Economics, and are in Langley, *Industrialization*, p. 199.

49. This loan, in July 1950, was for $12.8 million. Sassoon, *Economic Policy*, p. 95.

50. The oil pipeline to Tripoli is discussed in chapter 16.

51. I am treating this question in a forthcoming article in *Middle Eastern Studies*.

52. Charles Issawi and Mohammed Yeganeh, *The Economics of Middle Eastern Oil* (New York, 1962), pp. 194-95.

53. I am treating this question in a forthcoming article in *Middle Eastern Studies*.

54. Issawi and Yeganeh, *Economics*, pp. 194-95.

NOTES TO CHAPTER 15

1. Khadduri, *Independent Iraq*, p. 46; Kedourie, *Chatham House*, pp. 213-15, 258, 271-72; Ahmed M. Gomaa, *The Foundation of the League of Arab States: Wartime Diplomacy and Inter-Arab Politics 1941 to 1945* (London, 1977), p. 66; Yehoshua Porath, *In Search of Arab Unity: 1930-1945* (London, 1986), p. 269.

2. Cornwallis to Eden, 31 Oct. 1944, FO 371/40042, E7011/37/93; Porath, *Arab Unity*, pp. 1-3, 7-8, 312.

3. Cornwallis to Peterson, 11 Jan. 1944, FO 371/39987, E521/41/65; report by CICI, 23 Oct. 1944, FO 624/66, part 8; Porath, *Arab Unity*, pp. 2-3, 269.

4. Gomaa, *Foundation*, passim; Porath, *Arab Unity*, passim.

5. Sir Ronald Cambell (British ambassador in Cairo) to FO, 27 March 1949, FO 371/75058, E4138/1028/65; Sir Henry Mack (British ambassador in Baghdad) to FO, 1 April 1949, FO 371/75550, E4273/10393/89; Mack to Bevin, 11 June 1949, FO 371/75551, E7730/10393/89; Majid Khadduri, "The Scheme of Fertile Crescent Unity: A Study in Inter-Arab Relations," in Richard N. Frye (ed.), *The Near East and the Great Powers* (Cambridge, Mass., 1951), p. 156; Patrick Seale, *The Struggle for Syria: A Study of Post-War Arab Politics 1945-1958* (London, 1965; reprint, New Haven, Conn., 1987), p. 46.

6. Seale, *Struggle*, pp. 8-9, 78, 80, 82; Kedourie, *Chatham House*, p. 272.

7. Humphrey Trevelyan (British chargé d'affaires in Baghdad) to Bevin, 22 Aug. 1949, FO 371/75129, E10547/1018/93; Porath, *Arab Unity*, pp. 39-57, 216-23, 312.

8. Jamali's interview with the Egyptian newspaper is in chancery Cairo to FO, 14 July 1949, FO 371/75551, E8978/10393/89. For Jamali's views on the question of union with Syria, also see Cambell to FO, 27 March 1949, FO 371/75058, E4138/1028/65; and minute by British embassy Baghdad, 7 April 1949, FO 624/150, part 11. For Jamali as part of the Iraqi establishment, see Kedourie, "Iraqi Shiis," p. 153.

9. Chancery Baghdad to FO, 15 Oct. 1949, FO 371/75554, E12743/10393/89; Dorsz to secretary of state, 17 Oct. 1949, 890G.9111 RR/10-1749.

10. This quotation is in Dorsz to secretary of state, 8 Oct. 1949, 890G.9111 RR/10-849.

11. This quotation is in Dorsz to secretary of state, 17 Oct. 1949, 890G.911 RR/10-1749.

12. This quotation is in Abubaker M. Saad, "Iraq and Arab Politics: The Nuri as-Said Era, 1941-1958" (Ph.D. dissertation at the University of Washington, 1987), p. 150.

13. Chancery Baghdad to FO, 5 July 1949, FO 371/75060, E8438/10210/65; Mack to FO, 6 Oct. 1949, FO 371/75553, E12019/10393/89; Seale, *Struggle*, pp. 52, 81.

14. Seale, *Struggle*, pp. 15, 24-36, 45.

15. Ibid., pp. 33, 37-45, 48, 58-63.

16. Mack to FO, 15 April 1949, FO 371/75550, E4828/10393/89; Khadduri, "Fertile Crescent," pp. 156-57; Seale, *Struggle,* pp. 47, 50.

17. Mack to Bevin, 11 June 1949, FO 371/75551, E7730/10393/89; Khadduri, "Fertile Crescent," pp. 157-58; Seale, *Struggle,* pp. 49-61.

18. Mack to FO, 9 April 1949 and 9 April 1949, FO 371/75550, E4605/E4606/10393/89; Mack to FO, 12 June 1949, FO 371/75551, E7212/10393/89.

19. Mack to FO, 9 April 1949, 18 April 1949, and 26 May 1949, FO 371/75550, E4605/E4889/E6617/10393/89; Mack to FO, 12 June 1949, FO 371/75551, E7212/10393/89. The quotation is in Mack of 18 April 1949.

20. Mack to FO, 9 April 1949, 9 April 1949, 18 April 1949, 14 May 1949, 26 May 1949, and 1 June 1949, FO 371/75550, E4605/E4606/E4889/E6144/E6617/E6830/10393/89.

21. Sir Oliver Harvey (British ambassador in Paris) to FO, 12 April 1949, FO 371/75077, E4737/1072/65; report by the Permanent Undersecretary's Committee, 30 April 1949, FO 371/75067, E13989/1052/65; Harvey to FO, 18 June 1949, FO 371/75551, E7431/10393/89; report by Sir William Strang (permanent undersecretary of state for foreign affairs), 4 July 1949, FO 371/75067, E8752/1052/65; Seale, *Struggle,* pp. 52-54.

22. All of these quotations are in Seale, *Struggle,* pp. 52-53.

23. Mack to FO, 14 Nov. 1949, FO 371/75555, E13775/10393/89; Harvey to FO, 15 Nov. 1949, FO 371/75079, E13899/1074/65.

24. Troutbeck to Wright, 3 March 1949, FO 371/75064, E3158/1052/65.

25. Report by Strang, 4 July 1949, FO 371/75067, E8752/10393/1052/65.

26. Minute by Burrows, 13 Oct. 1949, FO 371/75554, E12799/10393/89.

27. FO to Baghdad, 28 May 1949, FO 371/75550, E6617/10393/89; R. D. Scott-Fox (British minister in Jidda) to FO, 17 June 1949, FO 371/75551, E7418/10393/89; Troutbeck to FO, 20 June 1949, FO 371/75059, E7539/1028/65; Sir Oliver Franks (British ambassador in Washington) to FO, 2 Nov. 1949, FO 371/75183, E13276/1571/93.

28. Mack to FO, 27 April 1949, FO 371/75134, E5348/1024/93; P. M. Broadmead (British minister in Damascus) to FO, 5 Oct. 1949, Sir Alec Kirkbride (British minister in Amman) to FO, 5 Oct. 1949, 7 Oct. 1949, and 11 Oct. 1949, FO 371/75553, E12053/E12066/E12201/E12316/10393/89.

29. FO to Baghdad, 28 May 1949, FO 371/75550, E6617/10393/89; Sir Knox Helm (British minister in Tel Aviv) to FO, 18 Oct. 1949, FO 371/75554, E12601/10393/89.

30. Douglas Little, "Cold War and Covert Action: The United States and Syria, 1945-1958," *The Middle East Journal,* vol. 44 (1990), p. 57.

31. FO to Baghdad, 16 June 1949, FO 371/75551, E7212/10393/89; report by Strang, 4 July 1949, FO 371/75067, E8752/1052/65; M. C. G. Man (British chargé d'affaires in Damascus) to FO, 19 July 1949, FO 371/75551, E8853/10393/89; meeting in London of FO officials with British representatives in the Middle East, 21 July 1949, FO 371/75072, E9043/1058/65; Pappe, *Conflict,* p. 133.

32. Broadmead to FO, 10 June 1949, FO 371/75550, E7165/10393/89; FO to Council of Ministers, 18 June 1949, FO 371/75551, E7392/10393/89.

33. Troutbeck to FO, 30 May 1949, FO 371/75550, E6770/10393/89; FO to Baghdad, 16 June 1949, FO 371/75551, E7212/10393/89.

34. Minute by Lance Thirkell (Eastern Dept. of FO), 19 April 1949, FO 371/75077, E5503/1072/65; Mack to FO, 14 May 1949, FO 371/75550, E6144/10393/89; brief by George Clutton (head of the African Dept. of FO), 24 Aug. 1949, FO 371/75063, E10409/1051/65.

35. Mack to FO, 18 June 1949, FO 371/75551, E7433/10393/89; Seale, *Struggle,* pp. 73-74; Louis, *British Empire,* p. 625; Maddy-Weitzman, *Crystallization,* pp. 114-15.

36. Seale, *Struggle*, pp. 29-30, 46-47, 76-77.
37. Man to FO, 28 Aug. 1949, FO 371/75551, E10496/10393/89; Man's conversation with Nazim Qudsi (Syrian minister of foreign affairs), 28 Aug. 1949, Man to FO, 25 Sept. 1949, Broadmead to FO, 30 Sept. 1949 and 3 Oct. 1949, FO 371/75552, E10713/ E11670/ E11929/E12008/10393/89.
38. Minute by Chadwick, 25 Aug. 1949, FO 371/75552, E11098/10393/89; Trevelyan to FO, 29 Aug. 1949, FO 371/75551, E10601/10393/89; Dorsz to secretary of State, 7 Nov. 1949, 890G.00/11-749; Khadduri, *Independent Iraq*, p. 274; Seale, *Struggle*, pp. 83-84, 89; Maddy-Weitzman, *Crystallization*, p. 123. The quotation is in Dorsz.
39. Minute by Chadwick, 25 Aug. 1949, Broadmead to FO, 30 Sept. 1949, FO 371/75552, E11098/E11929/10393/89; Seale, *Struggle*, pp. 79-81; Maddy-Weitzman, *Crystallization*, p. 119.
40. Minutes of COS, 19 Sept. 1949, DEFE 4/24, COS(49)138; FO to Baghdad, 28 Sept. 1949, Trevelyan to FO, 30 Sept. 1949, FO 371/75552, E11670/E11888/10393/89; Maddy-Weitzman, *Crystallization*, p. 126.
41. Broadmead to FO, 5 Oct. 1949, FO 371/75553, E12089/10393/89; Maddy-Weitzman, *Crystallization*, p. 119.
42. FO to Washington, 28 Sept. 1949, FO 371/75552, E11670/10393/89; minutes by Burrows, 8 Oct. 1949 and 13 Oct. 1949, FO 371/75554, E12754/E12799/10393/89; FO to Baghdad, 17 Oct. 1949, FO 371/75553, E12531/10393/89; Maddy-Weitzman, *Crystallization*, p. 119.
43. Trevelyan to FO, 17 Sept. 1949, Broadmead to FO, 30 Sept. 1949, FO 371/75552, E11330/E11929/10393/89; Broadmead to FO, 7 Oct. 1949 and 10 Oct. 1949, FO 371/75553, E12139/E12311/10393/89; Broadmead to FO, 14 Oct. 1949, FO 371/75554, E12568/10393/89; Khadduri, "Fertile Crescent," pp. 165-66; Seale, *Struggle*, pp. 79, 81, 90-91; Maddy-Weitzman, *Crystallization*, pp. 122-23.
44. Trevelyan to FO, 17 Sept. 1949, Man to Burrows, 26 Sept. 1949, FO 371/75552, E11330/E11978/10393/89. The quotation is in Trevelyan.
    In contrast to the view presented in this paragraph, Michael Eppel maintains that in the autumn of 1949 Nuri considered Iraqi-Syrian federation under Hashemite rule to be "a dangerous illusion." However, Eppel does not provide a footnote or any other evidence to support his contention. "Iraqi Politics and Regional Policies, 1945-49," *Middle Eastern Studies*, vol. 28 (1992), p. 117.
    Certainly the British ambassador in Baghdad did not view the situation as Eppel does. On the contrary, in reference to this period he wrote that "Nuri Pasha was itching to use it [the Iraqi army] in Syria, and I believe that our constant pressure on him and on the Regent was the main factor in preventing him from indulging in this adventure." Mack to Bevin, 24 Jan. 1951, FO 371/91633, EQ1017/1.
    In his recently published book on inter-Arab relations, Maddy-Weitzman also maintains that Nuri's interest in union with Syria was genuine. *Crystallization*, pp. 116-17.
45. Trevelyan to FO, 17 Sept. 1949, FO to Baghdad, 19 Sept. 1949, FO 371/75552, E11330/E11330/10393/89; minute by Burrows, 13 Oct. 1949, FO 371/75554, E12799/10393/89; FO to Baghdad, 17 Oct. 1949, FO 371/75553, E12531/10393/89; Maddy-Weitzman, *Crystallization*, p. 126.

NOTES TO CHAPTER 16

1. Longrigg, *Oil*, pp. 43-47, 66-83; Shwadran, *Oil*, pp. 195-252.
2. Longrigg, *Oil*, pp. 76-77; Shwadran, *Oil*, pp. 240-42.

3. For the production totals, see Longrigg, *Oil,* p. 478. For Iraqi concern about the slow rate of development and belief that the IPC was deliberately holding down production in Iraq, see V. S. Butler (MFP) to J. Skliros (IPC), 5 Jan. 1949, FO 371/75115, E1211/1533/65; minute by Chadwick, 30 March 1949, FO 371/75178, E4534/1533/93; meeting between Bevin and Nuri at FO, 19 Aug. 1949, FO 371/75136, E10221/1026/93; and minute by Burrows, 27 Aug. 1949, FO 371/75179, E10746/1533/93. For Iraqi belief that the British government had considerable influence over the IPC, see FO to Baghdad, 8 Oct. 1948, FO 371/68466, E13046/112/93; Mack to FO, 29 Nov. 1949, FO 371/75179, E14379/1533/93; Mack to Wright, 14 April 1950, FO 371/82465, EQ1531/56; and Mack to Bevin, 18 May 1950, FO 371/82466, EQ1531/18.

    Incidentally, some British officials shared the Iraqi belief that the IPC was deliberately holding down production in Iraq. See, for example, Burrows to Butler 19 Nov. 1949, FO 371/75408, E13697/1531/31; and note by E. W. Noonan (petroleum attaché at BMEO), no date, in Mack to Bevin, 24 May 1950, FO 371/82466, EQ1531/75.

4. Silverfarb, *Informal Empire,* pp. 97-105.
5. Longrigg, *Oil,* p. 121; Silverfarb, *Informal Empire,* p. 99.
6. Longrigg, *Oil,* pp. 179-80; Shwadran, *Oil,* p. 242.
7. James S. Moose (U.S. chargé d'affaires in Baghdad) to George C. Marshall (secretary of state), 13 Jan. 1947, *FRUS 1947,* vol. 5, p. 633; Longrigg, *Oil,* pp. 179-80; Edith and E. F. Penrose, *Iraq: International Relations and National Development* (London, 1978), p. 147.
8. Longrigg, *Oil,* pp. 206-8.
9. Memorandum by Gordon Mattison (chief of the DOS's Division of Near Eastern Affairs), 12 July 1949, *FRUS 1949,* vol. 6, p. 137; Longrigg, *Oil,* p. 180; Shwadran, *Oil,* p. 242.
10. Meeting of FO, MFP, IPC, and AIOC officials at FO, 1 March 1949, FO 371/75114, E2980/1531/65.
11. Memorandum by Mattison, 12 July 1949, *FRUS 1949,* vol. 6, p. 137; meeting in London of FO, MFP, and Treasury officials with British representatives in the Middle East, 22 July 1949, FO 371/75072, E9044/1058/65.
12. The DOS's calculation is in report by the Policy Planning Staff, 19 Jan. 1948, *FRUS 1948,* vol. 5, part 2, p. 550. For more on the shortage of oil during this period, see Robert A. Lovett (acting secretary of state) to W. Averell Harriman (secretary of commerce), 8 Sept. 1947, *FRUS 1947,* vol. 5, p. 666; BMEO to Beirut, 23 Oct. 1947, FO 371/61508, E10075/87/65; meeting of British and Iraqi officials at FO, 16 Jan. 1948, FO 371/68445, E1619/27/93; and Loy W. Henderson (director of the Office of Near Eastern and African Affairs) to Marshall, 10 Feb. 1948, *FRUS 1948,* vol. 5, part 1, p. 6.
13. BMEO to Beirut, 23 Oct. 1947, FO 371/61508, E10075/87/65; meeting of British and Iraqi officials at FO, 16 Jan. 1948, FO 371/68445, E1619/27/93; *The Economist,* 26 July 1947, pp. 160-61. The 59 percent figure is in *The Economist.*
14. BMEO to Beirut, 23 Oct. 1947, FO 371/61508, E10075/87/65; minute by Burrows, 10 Feb. 1948, FO 371/68479, E2553/620/93; meeting of FO, MFP, IPC, and AIOC officials at FO, 1 March 1949, FO 371/75114, E2980/1531/65; note by Burrows, 29 Sept. 1949, FO 371/75407, E12029/1531/31.
15. Memorandum by MFP, August 1947, FO 371/61508, E12011/87/65; *The Petroleum Times,* "Review of Middle East Oil," June 1948, pp. 84-85.
16. *HC,* 31 Oct. 1949, vol. 469, written answers, col. 2.
17. *HC,* 21 Nov. 1949, vol. 470, written answers, cols. 9-10. For more on the importance to Britain of purchasing oil in sterling rather than dollars, see meeting of British and Iraqi

officials at FO, 16 Jan. 1948, FO 371/68445, E1619/27/93; minute by E. A. Berthoud (assistant undersecretary supervising the Economic Relations Dept. of FO), 20 July 1948, FO 371/68407, E10169/371/65; and meeting in London of FO, MFP, and Treasury officials with British representatives in the Middle East, 22 July 1949, FO 371/75072, E9044/1058/65.

18. Meeting of Wright and DOS officials in Washington, 17 Nov. 1949, FO 371/75409, E14785/1531/31; meeting of FO officials, 13 June 1950, FO 371/82467, EQ1531/100. The $50 million figure applies to the period after the devaluation of sterling in September 1949. For the period before that date we should reduce it by 30 percent, which was the amount of the devaluation.

19. Meeting of FO officials, 13 June 1950, FO 371/82467, EQ1531/100.

20. The figure of £1.6 million is from the AIOC, and is in meeting of FO, MFP, and AIOC officials at FO, 9 Aug. 1949, FO 371/75404, E9551/1531/31. For more information on Israeli losses from the closure of the pipeline and refinery, see meeting of FO, MFP, IPC, and AIOC officials at FO, 30 Nov. 1948, FO 371/68439, E15443/14608/65; FO to Baghdad, 3 Jan. 1950, FO 371/75179, E15417/1533/93; and meeting of FO officials, 13 June 1950, FO 371/82467, EQ1531/100.
Before the refinery was closed about 2,000 local people worked there. *The Economist,* 30 April 1949, p. 787.

21. Meeting of Bevin and Nuri at FO, 19 Aug. 1949, FO 371/75136, E10221/1026/93.

22. FO to Baghdad, 6 Oct. 1948 and 8 Oct. 1948, FO 371/68466, E12978/E13046/112/93; FO to Baghdad, 10 Nov. 1948, FO 371/68453, E14294/27/93; minute by J. G. S. Beith (Eastern Dept. of FO), 3 Jan. 1949, FO 371/75114, E233/1531/65.

23. Lewis W. Douglas (U.S. ambassador in London) to Marshall, 18 June 1948, Marshall to U.S. embassy London, 29 June 1948, Douglas to Marshall, 27 Aug. 1948, Stanton Griffis (U.S. ambassador in Cairo) to Marshall, 15 Sept. 1948, *FRUS 1948,* vol. 5, part 2, pp. 1123, 1157, 1356, 1399.

24. The text of the Bernadotte Plan of September 1948 is in *FRUS 1948,* vol. 5, part 2, pp. 1401-6.

25. Mack to Burrows, 2 March 1949, FO 371/75178, E3235/1533/93.

26. Meeting of FO, MFP, IPC, and AIOC officials at FO, 30 Nov. 1948, FO 371/68439, E15443/14608/65; brief by Walker, 10 Jan. 1949, FO 371/75051, E937/1023/65.

27. Meeting of FO, MFP, IPC, and AIOC officials at FO, 4 Jan. 1949, FO 371/75114, E233/1531/65.

28. Note by Mack, 19 Jan. 1949, FO 371/75330, E1111/1015/31; Mack to Burrows, 2 March 1949, FO 371/75178, E3235/1533/93.

29. Meeting of FO, MFP, IPC, and AIOC officials at FO, 30 Nov. 1948, FO 371/68439, E15443/14608/65; meetings of FO, MFP, IPC, and AIOC officials at FO, 4 Jan. 1949 and 1 March 1949, FO 371/75114, E233/E2980/1531/65.

30. Minute by Chadwick, 30 March 1949, FO 371/75178, E4534/1533/93; memorandum by Mattison, 12 July 1949, *FRUS 1949,* vol. 6, p. 138.

31. Meeting of FO, MFP, Treasury, IPC, and AIOC officials at FO, 25 Jan. 1949, FO 371/75156, E1349/1113/93; Mack to Burrows, 2 March 1949, FO 371/75178, E3235/1533/93; minute by Chadwick, 20 July 1949, FO 371/75404, E9515/1531/31; Chadwick to Trevelyan, 11 Aug. 1949, FO 371/75158, E9354/1113/93; meeting of FO, MFP, IPC, and AIOC officials at FO, 6 Sept. 1949, FO 371/75114, E10948/1531/65; W. L. F. Nuttall (MFP) to Furlonge, 7 Jan. 1950, FO 371/82464, EQ1531/2.

32. Minute by Chadwick, 18 May 1949, FO 371/75178, E5537/1533/93.

33. This quotation is in Trevelyan to Burrows, 22 July 1949, FO 371/75404, E9291/1531/31.
34. Trevelyan to FO, 29 Aug. 1949, FO 371/75405, E10498/1531/31. For more on the strength of public opinion in Iraq on this question, see chancery Baghdad to FO, 17 Sept. 1948, FO 371/68452, E12555/27/93; Mack to FO, 7 Oct. 1948, FO 371/68466, E13046/112/93; Trevelyan to Burrows, 9 Aug. 1949, FO 371/75404, E10034/1531/31; and chancery Baghdad to FO, 17 Jan. 1950, FO 371/82464, EQ1531/9.
35. Meeting of FO, MFP, IPC, and AIOC officials at FO, 1 March 1949, FO 371/75114, E2980/1531/65.
36. Meeting in London of FO, MFP, and Treasury officials with British representatives in the Middle East, 22 July 1949, FO 371/75072, E9044/1058/65; meeting of FO, MFP, AIOC, and Shell officials at FO, 12 Jan. 1950, minute by A. M. Williams (Eastern Dept. of FO), 23 Feb. 1950, FO 371/82464, EQ1531/7/19; minute by Wright, 25 July 1950, FO 371/82468, EQ1531/136.
37. Longrigg, *Oil*, p. 180; Shwadran, *Oil*, p. 242.
38. Meeting of FO, MFP, AIOC, and Shell officials at FO, 31 Aug. 1949, FO 371/75179, E10747/1533/93.
39. Minute by G. W. Furlonge (Eastern Dept. of FO), 16 Dec. 1949, FO 371/75409, E15117/1531/31; secretary of state to U.S. embassy Baghdad, 30 Dec. 1949, *FRUS 1949*, vol. 6, p. 164, n. 6.
40. Minute by Furlonge, 15 June 1950, FO 371/82468, EQ1531/124; FO to Tel Aviv, 28 June 1950, FO 371/82467, EQ1531/112.
    Two months after the decision was made to resume operations, in August 1950 the refinery was actually opened. Minute by D. N. Brinson (Economic Relations Dept. of FO), 6 Nov. 1950, FO 371/82610, ER1532/43.
41. Meeting of FO, MFP, IPC, and AIOC officials at FO, 1 March 1949, FO 371/75114, E2980/1531/65; Mack to Burrows, 10 March 1949, FO 371/75178, E3550/1533/93.
42. Meeting of FO, MFP, Treasury, AIOC, and Shell officials at FO, 10 Nov. 1949, FO 371/75408, E13714/1531/31; MFP to FO, 21 Nov. 1949, meeting of FO, MFP, Treasury, AIOC, and Shell officials at FO, 5 Dec. 1949, FO 371/75179, E14084/E14665/1533/93. In Kuwait the AIOC and the American-owned Gulf Oil Corporation shared the concession. However, in 1947 Shell acquired the right to purchase a varying but very large amount of Gulf's production. Wayne A. Leeman, *The Price of Middle East Oil: An Essay in Political Economy* (Ithaca, N.Y., 1962), p. 161; Longrigg, *Oil*, pp. 220-21.
43. Wright to Butler, 21 Feb. 1949, FO 371/75403, E2117/1531/31; meeting of FO, MFP, Treasury, AIOC, and Shell officials at FO, 10 Nov. 1949, FO 371/75408, E13714/1531/31; minute by Williams, 15 Nov. 1949, note by Nuttall, 17 Nov. 1949, FO 371/75409, E13971/E13972/1531/31; L. G. Holliday (commercial counsellor, British embassy Paris) to FO, 24 Jan. 1950, FO 371/82464, EQ1531/11; French embassy Washington to DOS, 26 April 1951, 887.2553/4-2651; Horst Mendershausen, "Dollar Shortage and Oil Surplus in 1949-1950," *Essays in International Finance*, no. 11 (1950), p. 3; Edith Penrose, *The Large International Firm in Developing Countries: The International Petroleum Industry* (London, 1968), p. 158; Irvine H. Anderson, *ARAMCO, the United States, and Saudi Arabia: A Study of the Dynamics of Foreign Oil Policy 1933-1950* (Princeton, N.J., 1981), pp. 158-59.
44. Minute by Williams, 15 Nov. 1949, meeting of FO, MFP, and IPC officials at FO, 18 Nov. 1949, FO 371/75409, E13971/E13973/1531/31; meeting of FO, MFP, Treasury, AIOC, and Shell officials at FO, 5 Dec. 1949, meeting of FO, MFP, and IPC officials at FO, 13 Dec. 1949, FO 371/75179, E14665/E14844/1533/93; meeting of DOS, SONJ, and

Socony-Vacuum officials at DOS, 16 Dec. 1949, 890G.6363/12-1649; Longrigg, *Oil*, p. 181; Penrose and Penrose, *Iraq*, p. 148; Anderson, *ARAMCO*, pp. 156, 175-78, 199.

45. Longrigg, *Oil*, pp. 181, 186-88; Shwadran, *Oil*, p. 242.
46. Longrigg, *Oil*, p. 478.
47. Ibid.

NOTES TO CONCLUSION

1. In August 1950 there were 1,513 men in the levies. Of this number 23 were British, 873 Assyrians, 419 Arabs, 197 Kurds, and 1 Yazidi. Trevelyan to FO, 2 Oct. 1950, FO 371/82500, EQ1823/4.
2. In April 1949 there were two British officers as instructors in the Iraqi Staff College, and six British officers and noncommissioned officers as instructors in the Iraqi air force. Chancery Baghdad to FO, 29 April 1949, FO 371/75068, E6110/1053/65.
3. Iraq during this period would appear to support Ronald Robinson's and John Gallagher's contention that local collaborators were a vital ingredient in upholding European influence and rule in Africa and Asia. See, for example, Robinson, "Non-European Foundations of European Imperialism: Sketch for a Theory of Collaboration," in Roger Owen and Bob Sutcliffe (eds.), *Studies in the Theory of Imperialism* (London, 1972), pp. 117-42; and Gallagher, "The Decline, Revival and Fall of the British Empire," in Gallagher, *The Decline, Revival and Fall of the British Empire: The Ford Lectures and Other Essays* (Cambridge, 1982), pp. 73-153.
4. In the spring of 1949 the king went to Harrow. Prior to that he had had a British tutor, and even earlier he had had a British governess. Stonehewer-Bird to Bevin, 4 March 1946, FO 371/52423, E2469/652/93; Longrigg, *Iraq*, p. 364; De Gaury, *Three Kings*, pp. 166-67. In 1943, when the king was nine, a British official observed that he spoke English better than Arabic. Perowne to Baxter, 31 Aug. 1943, FO 371/34990, E5262/44/93.
5. Chancery Baghdad to FO, 29 April 1949, FO 371/75068, E6110/1053/65.
6. Cornwallis to Eden, 15 Jan. 1945, FO 371/45302, E627/195/93; Thompson to Bevin, 26 Sept. 1945, FO 371/45295, E7495/104/93; Stonehewer-Bird to Bevin, 4 March 1946, FO 371/52423, E2469/652/93; Busk to Bevin, 4 Dec. 1947, FO 371/61599, E11608/3/93; Mack to Bevin, 5 Nov. 1948, FO 371/68453, E14852/27/93.
7. Cornwallis to Eden, 15 Jan. 1945, FO 371/45302, E627/195/93; Thompson to Bevin, 26 Sept. 1945, FO 371/45295, E7495/104/93; Stonehewer-Bird to Bevin, 21 March 1946, FO 371/52327, E2962/797/65; Busk to Wright, 17 Sept. 1947, FO 371/61594, E8789/3/93; Burrows to Mack, 5 Oct. 1948, FO 371/68466, E13094/112/93.
8. Jabr's statement is in meeting of British and Iraqi officials at FO, 16 Jan. 1948, FO 371/68445, E1619/27/93; and Muzahim's pledge is in Richmond to Burrows, 5 Aug. 1948, FO 371/68465, E10868/112/93.
9. Memorandum by DOS, no date but probably Sept. 1947, *FRUS 1947*, vol. 5, p. 514; Dorsz to secretary of state, 13 Sept. 1949, 890G.24 FLC/9-1349; meeting in Washington of DOS officials and representatives from the Iraqi embassy, 11 Jan. 1950, *FRUS 1950*, vol. 5, p. 637; policy statement by DOS, 9 Nov. 1950, *FRUS 1950*, vol. 5, pp. 652, 654; Frederick W. Axelgard, "U.S. Policy toward Iraq, 1946-1958" (Ph.D. dissertation at the Fletcher School of Law and Diplomacy, Tufts University, 1988), pp. 36-38, 62-67. The statistics in this paragraph are in "Facts and Figures: United States Aid to the Middle East 1940-1951," *Middle Eastern Affairs*, vol. 4 (1953), p. 59.
10. Busk to Bevin, 31 July 1947, FO 371/61592, E7156/3/93; Busk to Wright, 17 Sept. 1947, FO 371/61594, E8789/3/93; *The Economist*, 31 Jan. 1948, p. 172.

In 1943 there were about 170 Egyptian teachers employed in Iraq. I do not have figures for the later period. T. M. Wilson (U.S. minister in Baghdad) to secretary of state, 4 Sept. 1943, 890G.42/57.

11. Richmond to Walker, 24 Aug. 1948, G. C. Littler (acting consul-general Basra) to the chargé d'affaires, British embassy Baghdad, 26 Aug. 1948, FO 371/68451, E11431/E11645/27/93; Batatu, *Social Classes*, pp. 765-66; Shlaim, *Collusion*, p. 405.

12. Pool, "Politics of Patronage," pp. 235, 252.

13. Marr, *Iraq*, p. 138.

14. Pool, "Politics of Patronage," pp. 238-42.

15. Batatu, *Social Classes*, pp. 35, 473; Penrose and Penrose, *Iraq*, pp. 164-65.

16. Cornwallis to FO, 4 March 1945, FO 371/45329, E1531/1190/93.

17. In 1958 the number of troops who revolted against the government was only 3,000, two-thirds of whom did not have any ammunition and the remainder of whom had only a few rounds each. Opposing them were 2,000 soldiers of the palace guard, but the regent apparently ordered them not to resist. He also did not make any effort to rally other troops around the country or the police force within Baghdad. Batatu, *Social Classes*, pp. 801, 805.

18. For Britain's inability to provide many of the experts that Iraq wanted to employ, see Cornwallis to Eden, 15 Jan. 1945, FO 371/45302, E627/195/93; minute by Garran, 18 Feb. 1947, FO 371/61588, E1300/3/93; chancery Baghdad to FO, 29 April 1949, FO 371/75068, E6110/1053/65; and Mack to FO, 29 Dec. 1949, FO 371/75140, E15398/10345/93.

19. Longrigg, *Oil*, p. 478.

20. Ibid.

21. Zuhayr Mikdashi, *A Financial Analysis of Middle Eastern Oil Concessions: 1901-65* (New York, 1966), pp. 159, 248.

22. In the immediate postwar period British and American military leaders generally concluded that in the event of war they would not be able to prevent the Soviet Union from overrunning Iraq, although they believed that the bases could still be useful for conducting delaying actions. Elizabeth Monroe, "Mr. Bevin's 'Arab Policy,'" *St. Antony's Papers*, no. 11 (1961), p. 19; Elizabeth Monroe, *Britain's Moment in the Middle East 1914-1956* (London, 1963), p. 160; David R. Devereaux, *The Formulation of British Defense Policy towards the Middle East, 1948-56* (New York, 1990), pp. 3, 19-23; John Kent, "The Egyptian Base and the Defence of the Middle East, 1945-54," *The Journal of Imperial and Commonwealth History*, vol. 21 (1993), pp. 49, 63.

23. Chancery Baghdad to FO, 26 Jan. 1950, FO 371/82452, EQ1227/1.

24. FO to Washington, 16 Oct. 1953, DEFE 7/152; Darby, *Defence Policy*, p. 35.

BIBLIOGRAPHY

In a study involving postwar Britain and the Middle East the amount of archival and published material is very large. I have therefore restricted this list to files and works actually cited in the notes.

ARCHIVAL SOURCES
Public Record Office

AIR MINISTRY

AIR 8	Papers of the chief of the Air Staff.
AIR 20	Unregistered papers of the Air Ministry.
AIR 23	Papers of overseas commands.
AIR 24	Operations record books.

CABINET OFFICE

CAB 69	Minutes and memoranda of the Defence Committee before 1 January 1946.
CAB 79	Minutes of the Chiefs of Staff before 1 January 1947.
CAB 80	Memoranda of the Chiefs of Staff before 1 January 1947.
CAB 84	Reports of the Joint Planning Staff before 1 January 1947.
CAB 131	Minutes and memoranda of the Defence Committee after 1 January 1946.
CAB 134	Minutes and memoranda of various cabinet committees after 1 January 1945.

FOREIGN OFFICE

FO 371	General correspondence of the Foreign Office.
FO 624	British embassy in Baghdad.
FO 816	British legation in Amman.
FO 838	British consulate in Amara.
FO 921	Minister of State's Office in Cairo.

MINISTRY OF DEFENCE

DEFE 4	Minutes of the Chiefs of Staff after 1 January 1947.
DEFE 5	Memoranda of the Chiefs of Staff after 1 January 1947.
DEFE 6	Reports of the Joint Planning Staff after 1 January 1947.
DEFE 7	Registered papers, general series.

TREASURY

T 236	Overseas Finance Division.

WAR OFFICE

WO 32	Registered papers, general series.
WO 106	Directorate of Military Operations and Intelligence.
WO 201	Middle East Forces.

India Office Library and Records

L/P&S/12	Correspondence of the India Office's Political and Secret Department.
L/P&S/18	Memoranda of the India Office's Political and Secret Department.
R/15/1	Bushire political residency.
R/15/2	Bahrain political agency.
R/15/5	Kuwait political agency.

Middle East Centre, St. Antony's College, Oxford

C. J. Edmonds Papers.

J. M. L. Renton Papers.

British Broadcasting Corporation

Summary of World Broadcasts.

National Archives, Washington

RG 59   Records of the Department of State.
Decimal files on Iraq.

PUBLISHED SOURCES

Documents

BRITISH

Annual Abstract of Statistics: No. 84, 1935-1946. London, 1948.
   Reprint. Liechtenstein, 1970.

Cmd. 6646. *Agreement between His Majesty's Government in the United Kingdom and the Iraqi Government Concerning Iraqi Foreign Exchange Requirements for 1945, Baghdad, 28th May, 1945.* London, 1945.

Cmd. 6707. *Statistical Material Presented during the Washington Negotiations.* London, 1945.

Cmd. 6742. *Correspondence between His Majesty's Government in the United Kingdom and the Iraqi Government Concerning the Prolongation of Existing Arrangement Regarding Iraqi Foreign Exchange Requirements, Baghdad, 17th January, 1946.* London, 1946.

Cmd. 6803. *Correspondence between His Majesty's Government in the United Kingdom and the Iraqi Government Concerning the Prolongation of Existing Arrangements Regarding Iraqi Foreign Exchange Requirements, Baghdad, 8th April, 1946.* London, 1946.

Cmd. 6918. *Exchange of Notes between His Majesty's Government in the United Kingdom and the Government of Iraq Respecting the Status of the Iraqi Diplomatic Mission in London and the Precedence of His Majesty's Ambassador at Baghdad, Baghdad, 2nd August, 1946.* London, 1946.

Cmd. 6968. *Financial Agreement between His Majesty's Government in the United Kingdom and the Government of the United States, Washington, 6th December, 1945.* London, 1946.

Cmd. 7110. *Exchange of Notes between His Majesty's Government in the United Kingdom and the Government of Iraq Concerning the Prolongation of Existing Arrangements Regarding Iraqi Foreign Exchange Requirements, Baghdad, 10th/22nd February, 1947.* London, 1947.

Cmd. 7201. *Financial Agreement between the Government of the United Kingdom and the Government of Iraq, London, 13th August, 1947.* London, 1947.

Cmd. 7210. *Exchange of Letters between His Majesty's Government and the United States Government dated 20th August, 1947.* London, 1947.

Cmd. 7269. *Financial Agreement between the Government of the United Kingdom and the Government of Iraq Supplementary to the Agreement of 13th August, 1947, Baghdad, 17th November, 1947.* London, 1947.
Cmd. 7309. *Treaty of Alliance between His Majesty in Respect of the United Kingdom of Great Britain and Northern Ireland and His Majesty the King of Iraq, Portsmouth, 15th January, 1948.* London, 1948.
Parliamentary Debates, House of Commons.

UNITED STATES

Foreign Relations of the United States 1947, vol. 5: *The Near East and Africa.* Washington, 1971.
Foreign Relations of the United States 1948, vol. 5, part 1: *The Near East, South Asia, and Africa.* Washington, 1975.
Foreign Relations of the United States 1948, vol. 5, part 2: *The Near East, South Asia, and Africa.* Washington, 1976.
Foreign Relations of the United States 1949, vol. 6: *The Near East, South Asia, and Africa.* Washington, 1977.
Foreign Relations of the United States 1950, vol. 5: *The Near East, South Asia, and Africa.* Washington, 1978.

OTHER

Hurewitz, J. C. (ed.). *The Middle East and North Africa in World Politics: A Documentary Record,* 2nd ed., vol. 1: *European Expansion, 1535-1914.* New Haven, Conn., 1975.
————. (ed.). *The Middle East and North Africa in World Politics: A Documentary Record,* 2nd ed., vol. 2: *British-French Supremacy, 1914-1945.* New Haven, Conn., 1979.

Books

Albaharna, Husain M. *The Legal Status of the Arabian Gulf States: A Study of Their Treaty Relations and Their International Problems.* Manchester, 1968.
Anderson, Irvine H. *ARAMCO, the United States, and Saudi Arabia: A Study of the Dynamics of Foreign Oil Policy 1933-1950.* Princeton, N.J., 1981.
Antonius, George. *The Arab Awakening: The Story of the Arab National Movement.* London, 1938.
Arfa, Hassan. *The Kurds: An Historical and Political Study.* London, 1966.
Barker, A. J. *The Neglected War: Mesopotamia 1914-1918.* London, 1967.
Batatu, Hanna. *The Old Social Classes and the Revolutionary Movements of Iraq: A Study of Iraq's Old Landed and Commercial Classes and of Its Communists, Bathists, and Free Officers.* Princeton, N.J., 1978.
Beeri, Eliezer. *Army Officers in Arab Politics and Society.* New York, 1970.
Bell, Philip W. *The Sterling Area in the Postwar World: Internal Mechanism and Cohesion 1946-1952.* Oxford, 1956.
Birdwood, Lord. *Nuri as-Said: A Study in Arab Leadership.* London, 1959.
Blaxland, Gregory. *The Regiments Depart: A History of the British Army, 1945-1970.* London, 1971.
Bowyer, Chaz. *The Encyclopedia of British Military Aircraft.* London, 1982.
Brenchley, Frank. *Britain and the Middle East: An Economic History 1945-87.* London, 1989.
Bullock, Alan. *Ernest Bevin: Foreign Secretary 1945-1951.* New York, 1983.
Busch, Briton Cooper. *Britain and the Persian Gulf, 1894-1914.* Berkeley, Calif., 1967.
Cairncross, Alec. *Years of Recovery: British Economic Policy 1945-51.* London, 1985.
Cohen, Colonel Eliezer. *Israel's Best Defense: The First Full Story of the Israeli Air Force.* New York, 1993.

Conan, A. R. *The Sterling Area.* London, 1952.
———. *The Rationale of the Sterling Area: Texts and Commentary.* London, 1961.
Crystal, Jill. *Oil and Politics in the Gulf: Rulers and Merchants in Kuwait and Qatar.* Cambridge, 1990.
Darby, Phillip. *British Defence Policy East of Suez: 1947-1968.* London, 1973.
De Gaury, Gerald. *Three Kings in Baghdad: 1921-1958.* London, 1961.
Devereux, David R. *The Formulation of British Defense Policy towards the Middle East, 1948-56.* New York, 1990.
Eagleton, Jr., William. *The Kurdish Republic of 1946.* London, 1963.
Finnie, David H. *Shifting Lines in the Sand: Kuwait's Elusive Frontier with Iraq.* Cambridge, Mass., 1992.
Flapan, Simha. *The Birth of Israel: Myths and Realities.* New York, 1987.
Gamble, F. H. *Iraq: Economic and Commercial Conditions in Iraq.* London, 1949.
Gardner, Richard N. *Sterling-Dollar Diplomacy in Current Perspective: The Origins and the Prospects of Our International Economic Order.* Expanded ed. New York, 1980.
Glubb, Lieutenant-General Sir John Bagot. *A Soldier with the Arabs.* London, 1957.
Gomaa, Ahmed M. *The Foundation of the League of Arab States: Wartime Diplomacy and Inter-Arab Politics 1941 to 1945.* London, 1977.
Goodrich, Leland M. and Edvard Hambro. *Charter of the United Nations: Commentary and Documents.* 2nd ed. London, 1949.
Great Britain, Admiralty, Naval Intelligence Division. *Iraq and the Persian Gulf.* London, 1944.
Gupta, Partha Sarathi. *Imperialism and the British Labour Movement: 1914-1964.* New York, 1975.
Haldane, Lieutenant-General Sir Aylmer L. *The Insurrection in Mesopotamia, 1920.* Edinburgh, 1922.
Hancock, W. K. and M. M. Gowing. *History of the Second World War, United Kingdom Civil Series: British War Economy.* Rev. ed. London, 1975.
Herzog, Chaim. *The Arab-Israeli Wars: War and Peace in the Middle East.* New York, 1982.
Hogg, Ian. *Armour in Conflict.* London, 1980.
Issawi, Charles and Mohammed Yeganeh. *The Economics of Middle Eastern Oil.* New York, 1962.
Iversen, Carl. *A Report on Monetary Policy in Iraq.* Copenhagen, 1954.
Izady, Mehrdad R. *The Kurds: A Concise Handbook.* Washington, 1992.
Al-Juburi, Salih Saib. *Mihnat Filastin wa Asrarha al-Siyasiya wa al-Askariya (The Palestinian Misfortune and Its Political and Military Secrets).* Beirut, 1970.
Kedourie, Elie. *The Chatham House Version and Other Middle-Eastern Studies.* New York, 1970.
Khadduri, Majid. *Independent Iraq 1932-1958: A Study in Iraqi Politics.* 2nd ed. London, 1960.
———. *Arab Contemporaries: The Role of Personalities in Politics.* Baltimore, 1973.
Khalidi, Walid. *From Haven to Conquest: Readings in Zionism and the Palestine Problem until 1948.* Beirut, 1971.
Khouri, Fred J. *The Arab-Israeli Dilemma.* 3rd ed. Syracuse, 1985.
Kimche, Jon and David. *Both Sides of the Hill: Britain and the Palestine War.* London, 1960.
Kirk, George. *Survey of International Affairs: The Middle East 1945-1950.* London, 1954.
Langley, Kathleen M. *The Industrialization of Iraq.* Cambridge, Mass., 1962.
Leeman, Wayne A. *The Price of Middle East Oil: An Essay in Political Economy.* Ithaca, N.Y., 1962.
Lloyd, E. M. H. *Food and Inflation in the Middle East: 1940-45.* Stanford, Calif., 1956.
Longrigg, Stephen H. *Iraq, 1900 to 1950: A Political, Social, and Economic History.* London, 1953.
———. *Oil in the Middle East: Its Discovery and Development.* 3rd ed. London, 1968.
Lorch, Lieutenant-Colonel Netanel. *The Edge of the Sword: Israel's War of Independence 1947-1949.* New York, 1961.
Lorimer, J. G. *Gazetteer of the Persian Gulf, Oman, and Central Arabia,* vol. 2: *Geographical and Statistical.* Calcutta, 1908. Reprint. Farnborough, 1970.
Louis, William Roger. *The British Empire in the Middle East 1945-1951: Arab Nationalism, the United States, and Postwar Imperialism.* Oxford, 1984.

Maddy-Weitzman, Bruce. *The Crystallization of the Arab State System, 1945-1954.* Syracuse, 1993.

Marr, Phebe. *The Modern History of Iraq.* Boulder, Colo., 1985.

Mikdashi, Zuhayr. *A Financial Analysis of Middle Eastern Oil Concessions: 1901-65.* New York, 1966.

Moberly, Brigadier-General F. J. *History of the Great War Based on Official Documents: The Campaign in Mesopotamia 1914-1918.* 4 vols. London, 1923-27.

Monroe, Elizabeth. *Britain's Moment in the Middle East 1914-1956.* London, 1963.

Morris, Benny. *The Birth of the Palestinian Refugee Problem, 1947-1949.* Cambridge, 1987.

————. *1948 and After: Israel and the Palestinians.* Oxford, 1990.

Motter, T. H. Vail. *United States Army in World War II, The Middle East Theater: The Persian Corridor and Aid to Russia.* Washington, 1952.

Mustapha, Hassan. *Mudhakkirat Mulhaq Askari fi Lundun Qabl Harb Filastin al-Awal wa fi Athnaha (Memoirs of the Military Attache in London before and during the First Palestinian War).* Baghdad, 1985.

Nakash, Yitzhak. *The Shiis of Iraq.* Princeton, N.J., 1994.

O'Ballance, Edgar. *The Arab-Israeli War 1948.* London, 1956.

Pal, Dharm. *Official History of the Indian Armed Forces in the Second World War 1939-45: Campaign in Western Asia.* Calcutta, 1957.

Pappe, Ilan. *Britain and the Arab-Israeli Conflict, 1948-51.* New York, 1988.

Pearlman, Moshe. *The Army of Israel.* New York, 1950.

Penrose, Edith. *The Large International Firm in Developing Countries: The International Petroleum Industry.* London, 1968.

Penrose, Edith and E. F. *Iraq: International Relations and National Development.* London, 1978.

Playfair, Major-General I. S. O. *History of the Second World War, United Kingdom Military Series: The Mediterranean and Middle East,* vol. 2: *The Germans Come to the Help of Their Ally (1941).* London, 1956.

Polk, Judd. *Sterling: Its Meaning in World Finance.* New York, 1956.

Porath, Yehoshua. *In Search of Arab Unity: 1930-1945.* London, 1986.

Postan, M. M. *History of the Second World War, United Kingdom Civil Series: British War Production.* Rev. ed. London, 1975.

Pressnell, L. S. *External Economic Policy since the War,* vol. 1: *The Post-War Financial Settlement.* London, 1987.

Prest, A. R. *War Economies of Primary Producing Countries.* Cambridge, 1948.

Rejwan, Nissim. *The Jews of Iraq: 3,000 Years of History and Culture.* Boulder, Colo., 1985.

Rubin, Barry. *The Arab States and the Palestine Conflict.* Syracuse, 1981.

Sachar, Howard M. *Europe Leaves the Middle East, 1936-1954.* New York, 1972.

Sassoon, Joseph. *Economic Policy in Iraq: 1932-1950.* London, 1987.

Schofield, Richard. *Kuwait and Iraq: Historical Claims and Territorial Disputes.* London, 1991.

Seale, Patrick. *The Struggle for Syria: A Study of Post-War Arab Politics 1945-1958.* London, 1965. Reprint. New Haven, Conn., 1987.

Shiblak, Abbas. *The Lure of Zion: The Case of the Iraqi Jews.* London, 1986.

Shlaim, Avi. *Collusion across the Jordan: King Abdullah, the Zionist Movement, and the Partition of Palestine.* Oxford, 1988.

Shwadran, Benjamin. *The Middle East, Oil and the Great Powers.* 3rd ed. New York, 1973.

Silverfarb, Daniel. *Britain's Informal Empire in the Middle East: A Case Study of Iraq, 1929-1941.* New York, 1986.

Stillman, Norman A. *The Jews of Arab Lands in Modern Times.* Philadelphia, 1991.

Al-Suwaydi, Tawfiq. *Mudhakkirati: Nisf Qarn min Tarikh al-Iraq wa al-Qadiya al-Arabiyya (My Memoirs: Half a Century in the History of Iraq and the Arab Question).* Beirut, 1969.

Tarbush, Mohammad A. *The Role of the Military in Politics: A Case Study of Iraq to 1941*. London, 1982.

Thetford, Owen. *Aircraft of the Royal Air Force since 1918*. 7th ed. London, 1979.

———. *British Naval Aircraft since 1912*. 5th ed. London, 1982.

United States Economic Cooperation Administration Special Mission to the United Kingdom. *The Sterling Area: An American Analysis*. London, 1951.

Al-Uzri, Abd al-Karim. *Tarikh fi Dhikrayat al-Iraq 1930-1958 (Iraqi Memoirs 1930-1958)*. Beirut, 1982.

Van Bruinessen, Martin. *Agha, Shaikh and State: On the Social and Political Organization of Kurdistan*. Utrecht, 1978.

White, B. T. *British Tanks and Fighting Vehicles 1914-1945*. London, 1970.

Wilkinson, John C. *Arabia's Frontiers: The Story of Britain's Boundary Drawing in the Desert*. London, 1991.

Wilson, Mary C. *King Abdullah, Britain and the Making of Jordan*. Cambridge, 1987.

Yonay, Ehud. *No Margin for Error: The Making of the Israeli Air Force*. New York, 1993.

Zasloff, Joseph Jermiah. *Great Britain and Palestine: A Study of the Problem before the United Nations*. Munich, 1952.

Zupnick, Elliot. *Britain's Postwar Dollar Problem*. New York, 1957.

Articles

Adams, Doris G. "Current Population Trends in Iraq." *Middle East Journal*, vol. 10 (1956).

Asteris, Michael. "British Overseas Military Expenditure and the Balance of Payments." In Bateman, Michael, and Raymond Riley (eds.). *The Geography of Defence*. London, 1987.

Eppel, Michael. "The Iraqi Domestic Scene and Its Bearing on the Question of Palestine, 1947." *Asian and African Studies*, vol. 24 (1990).

———. "Iraqi Politics and Regional Policies, 1945-49." *Middle Eastern Studies*, vol. 28 (1992).

"Facts and Figures: United States Aid to the Middle East 1940-1951." *Middle Eastern Affairs*, vol. 4 (1953).

Fieldhouse, D. K. "The Labour Governments and the Empire-Commonwealth, 1945-51." In Ovendale, Ritchie (ed.). *The Foreign Policy of the British Labour Governments, 1945-1951*. Leicester, 1984.

Franck, Dorothea Seelye and Peter G. "Economic Review: The Middle East Economy in 1948." *The Middle East Journal*, vol. 3 (1949).

Gallagher, John. "The Decline, Revival and Fall of the British Empire." In Gallagher, John. *The Decline, Revival and Fall of the British Empire: The Ford Lectures and Other Essays*. Cambridge, 1982.

Gerke, Gerwin. "The Iraq Development Board and British Policy, 1945-1950." *Middle Eastern Studies*, vol. 27 (1991).

Gupta, Partha Sarathi. "Imperialism and the Labour Government of 1945-51." In Winter, Jay (ed.). *The Working Class in Modern British History: Essays in Honour of Henry Pelling*. Cambridge, 1983.

Hinds, Allister E. "Sterling and Imperial Policy, 1945-1951." *The Journal of Imperial and Commonwealth History*, vol. 15 (1987).

———. "Imperial Policy and Colonial Sterling Balances 1943-56." *The Journal of Imperial and Commonwealth History*, vol. 19 (1991).

Hyam, Ronald. "Africa and the Labour Government, 1945-1951." *The Journal of Imperial and Commonwealth History*, vol. 16 (1988).

Kedourie, Elie. "The Iraqi Shiis and Their Fate." In Kramer, Martin (ed.). *Shiism, Resistance, and Revolution.* Boulder, Colo., 1987.
———. "Anti-Shiism in Iraq under the Monarchy." *Middle Eastern Studies,* vol. 24 (1988).
———. "The Shiite Issue in Iraqi Politics, 1941." *Middle Eastern Studies,* vol. 24 (1988).
———. "The Break between Muslims and Jews in Iraq." In Cohen, Mark R. and Abraham L. Udovitch (eds.). *Jews among Arabs: Contacts and Boundaries.* Princeton, N.J., 1989.
Kelidar, Abbas. "The Shii Imami Community and Politics in the Arab East." *Middle Eastern Studies,* vol. 19 (1983).
Kent, John. "The Egyptian Base and the Defence of the Middle East, 1945-54." *The Journal of Imperial and Commonwealth History,* vol. 21 (1993).
Khadduri, Majid. "The Scheme of Fertile Crescent Unity: A Study in Inter-Arab Relations." In Frye, Richard N. (ed.). *The Near East and the Great Powers.* Cambridge, Mass., 1951.
———. "Iraq's Claim to the Sovereignty of Kuwait." *New York University Journal of International Law and Politics,* vol. 23 (1990).
Khalidi, Walid. "The Arab Perspective." In Louis, William Roger and Robert W. Stookey (eds.). *The End of the Palestine Mandate.* Austin, Tex., 1986.
Kimche, Jon. "Iraq Breaks with Britain." *The Nineteenth Century and After,* vol. 143 (1948).
Krozewski, Gerold. "Sterling, the 'Minor' Territories, and the End of Formal Empire, 1939-1958." *Economic History Review,* vol. 46 (1993).
Little, Douglas. "Cold War and Covert Action: The United States and Syria, 1945-1958." *Middle East Journal,* vol. 44 (1990).
Mendershausen, Horst. "Dollar Shortage and Oil Surplus in 1949-1950." *Essays in International Finance,* no. 11 (1950).
Monroe, Elizabeth. "Mr. Bevin's 'Arab Policy.'" *St. Antony's Papers,* no. 11 (1961).
Newton, Scott. "The Sterling Crisis of 1947 and the British Response to the Marshall Plan." *Economic History Review,* 2nd series, vol. 37 (1984).
———. "Britain, the Sterling Area and European Integration, 1945-50." *The Journal of Imperial and Commonwealth History,* vol. 13 (1985).
Al-Qawuqji, Fauzi. "Memoirs, 1948." Parts 1 and 2. *Journal of Palestine Studies,* vol. 1 (1972) and vol. 2 (1972).
Robinson, Ronald. "Non-European Foundations of European Imperialism: Sketch for a Theory of Collaboration." In Owen, Roger and Bob Sutcliffe (eds.). *Studies in the Theory of Imperialism.* London, 1972.
Roosevelt, Jr., Archie. "The Kurdish Republic of Mahabad." *The Middle East Journal,* vol. 1 (1947).
Salih, Kamal Osman. "The 1938 Kuwait Legislative Council." *Middle Eastern Studies,* vol. 28 (1992).
Sargent, J. R. "Britain and the Sterling Area." In Worswick, G. D. N. and P. H. Ady (eds.). *The British Economy 1945-1950.* Oxford, 1952.
Schatkowski Schilcher, L. "The Famine of 1915-1918 in Greater Syria." In Spagnolo, John P. (ed.). *Problems of the Modern Middle East in Historical Perspective: Essays in Honour of Albert Hourani.* Reading, 1992.
Shannon, H. A. "The Sterling Balances of the Sterling Area 1939-49." *The Economic Journal,* vol. 60 (1950).
Silverfarb, Daniel. "The Anglo-Najd Treaty of 1915." *Middle Eastern Studies,* vol. 16 (1980).
———. "The British Government and the Question of Umm Qasr 1938-1945." *Asian and African Studies,* vol. 16 (1982).
———. "Great Britain, Iraq, and Saudi Arabia: The Revolt of the Ikhwan, 1927-30." *International History Review,* vol. 4 (1982).

————. "Britain, the United States, and the Security of the Saudi Arabian Oilfields in 1942." *The Historical Journal*, vol. 26 (1983).

Singh, Anita Inder. "Post-Imperial British Attitudes to India: The Military Aspect, 1947-51." *The Round Table*, number 296 (1985).

Slonim, Shlomo. "The 1948 America Embargo on Arms to Palestine." *Political Science Quarterly*, vol. 94 (1979).

Smith, Raymond and John Zametica. "The Cold Warrior: Clement Attlee Reconsidered, 1945-7." *International Affairs*, vol. 61 (1985).

Teveth, Shabtai. "The Palestine Arab Refugee Problem and Its Origins." *Middle Eastern Studies*, vol. 26 (1990).

Tinker, Hugh. "The Contraction of Empire in Asia, 1945-48: The Military Dimension." *The Journal of Imperial and Commonwealth History*, vol. 16 (1988).

Tomlinson, B. R. "Indo-British Relations in the Post-Colonial Era: The Sterling Balances Negotiations, 1947-49." *The Journal of Imperial and Commonwealth History*, vol. 13 (1985).

Wightman, David. "The Sterling Area." *Banca Nazionale del Lavoro*, vol. 4 (1951).

Wright, Kenneth M. "Dollar Pooling in the Sterling Area, 1939-1952." *The American Economic Review*, vol. 44 (1954).

Magazines and Newspapers

The Economist
The Financial Times
The Petroleum Times
The Times

DOCTORAL DISSERTATIONS

Axelgard, Frederick W. "US Policy toward Iraq, 1946-1958." Fletcher School of Law and Diplomacy, Tufts University, 1988.

Jwaideh, Wadie. "The Kurdish Nationalist Movement: Its Origins and Development." Syracuse University, 1960.

Pool, David. "The Politics of Patronage: Elites and Social Structure in Iraq." Princeton University, 1972.

Saad, Abubaker M. "Iraq and Arab Politics: The Nuri as-Said Era, 1941-1958." University of Washington, 1987.

Zalzalah, Abdul-Hassan. "Iraq in the Sterling Area 1932-1954: A Study in Economic-Political Relationships." Indiana University, 1957.

INDEX